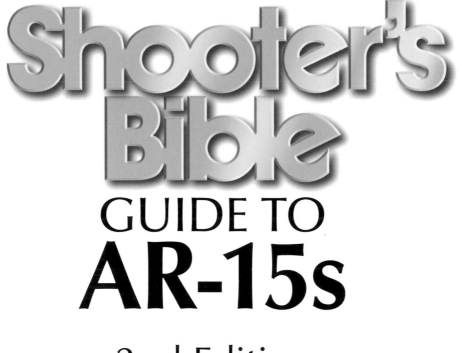

Shooter's Bible

GUIDE TO
AR-15s

2nd Edition

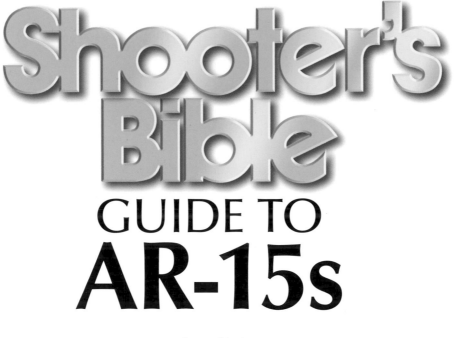

Shooter's Bible
GUIDE TO
AR-15s

2nd Edition

A COMPREHENSIVE GUIDE TO MODERN
SPORTING RIFLES AND THEIR VARIANTS

DOUG HOWLETT
AND
ROBB MANNING

FOREWORD BY TIGER MCKEE

SKYHORSE PUBLISHING

Skyhorse Publishing books may be purchased in bulk at special discounts for sales promotion, corporate gifts, fund-raising, or educational purposes. Special editions can also be created to specifications. For details, contact the Special Sales Department, Skyhorse Publishing, 307 West 36th Street, 11th Floor, New York, NY 10018 or info@skyhorsepublishing.com.

Skyhorse® and Skyhorse Publishing® are registered trademarks of Skyhorse Publishing, Inc.®, a Delaware corporation.

Visit our website at www.skyhorsepublishing.com.

10 9 8 7 6 5 4 3

Library of Congress Cataloging-in-Publication Data is available on file.

Cover design by Brian Peterson

Print ISBN: 978-1-5107-1-097-9
Ebook ISBN: 978-1-5107-1-098-6

Printed in China

CONTENTS

FOREWORD BY TIGER MCKEE

*I*t wasn't that many years ago that when someone showed up at the shootin' range with an AR, everyone there would gather around and look upon it with wonder and fascination. Today, it's hard to find someone who considers themselves an avid shooter who doesn't own an AR, or more likely even, several of them. The "black rifle" has replaced the M1 carbine as "America's sweetheart." Accompanying this rise in popularity is an abundance of parts and accessories that are available to customize the platform. Today you can build an AR to suit any purpose or taste.

Whether you're interested in competition, hunting or personal defense, the AR can do the job. The key as an owner of one (or many) is to understand why the rifle came about—its purpose and design—how it functions, and the many ways to modify the weapon to suit your individual needs.

I was introduced to the AR rifle at an early age. My dad was in the Special Forces; at one time he commanded the 20th Group. It was here I got my introduction the tactical rifles, specifically AR-style rifles. Dad would take me to the armory and pass me off on troops who taught me how to field strip, clean and assemble the AR-type rifle. I read and studied military field and technical manuals on the rifle. The AR was completely different from all the other rifles I grew up shooting; I was in love. In 1980 I bought an original AR-15, which had a 20-inch thin barrel and triangular handguards. Next came a Colt AR-15 A2 H-Bar, which was capable of shooting 1-inch groups at 100 yards. I was hooked. Things would never be the same.

It wasn't long before I bought a lower receiver and parts kit, took my military manuals and put together my own 16-inch CAR. I shot the rifles a lot for fun back then, ultimately using them in competition. I thought I knew a lot about them. Then I made the trip to Thunder Ranch in Texas for an Urban Rifle class. Attending that first class with instructor Clint Smith changed my life. On the drive back to Alabama, I told my training partner, Ed Aldrich, "Someday, I'm gonna be teaching there." I worked hard, practiced a lot and eventually got hired on.

At this point in time Thunder Ranch was *the* place to go if you wanted to learn about ARs. Every agency, department and serious civilian shooter in America and beyond came to Thunder Ranch to get schooled up on shooting the rifles. All different type of ARs, including carbines and accessories—the good, the bad, the ugly and all in between—showed up at Thunder Ranch to be tested. Even the military sent their first SPRs—the "Special Operations Forces Precision Rifle," which became the Mk12—there for formal testing in 2000. And there I was, lucky enough to be right in the middle of it all. This was an incredible experience, and definitely influenced the techniques I still teach today at my own firearms academy in Alabama.

In those early days there was a lot of trial and error to discovering how a piece of gear worked and what applications it was best suited for. Today, we have more schools, websites, videos and books like this to educate and inform us on the AR, its history and most importantly, its applications.

Once you understand the modular system of the AR, it's an easy step to equipping or setting one up for what you need. After getting it all together, it's time to train and practice, learning how to take advantage of all this firearm has to offer. This book will help guide you through the process of understanding the AR, putting together your "baby" and learning how to use it safely and efficiently.

Tiger McKee
Shootrite Firearms Academy
February 2016

INTRODUCTION

AR-15s—The Most Popular Firearms Today

A lot has happened in the tactical rifle world since the first edition of this book in 2011. Just a few years prior, Barack Obama was elected president, the first Democrat to hold the high office in 8 years. To make matters worse, at the time Democrats enjoyed majority status in the House of Representatives as well, a mix that generally results in attempts to restrict gunowners' rights. And since the Clinton Assualt Weapons Ban from 1994 to 2004 had placed tactical rifles such as the AR-15 squarely in anti-gunners' sights, there was every reason to believe attempts to restrict the guns were on the horizon. The rush to buy was on.

As one gun dealer I interviewed at the time put it, as soon as election returns began to suggest Obama's victory, "customers began flooding into the store." And for pretty much the next couple of years, sales overall soared. Never mind that the administration's and Congress's attention became focused on passing the dubiously named Affordable Care Act and no serious anti-gun threats materialized. Where buying and selling are concerned, perception often drives

more decisions than reality. At the height of this first Obama-era sales craze, it was nothing for companies to be backordered on every AR rifle they made for as much as a year.

Some companies like Del-Ton simply didn't even bother to introduce a new model one year as most companies typically do. The reason? They were still playing catch up with all of the orders they had amassed in the crush. Friends I hadn't heard from in years, many of them not even prior gun owners, began calling me to see if I had any inside connections so they could buy a gun. I didn't. I was like everybody else out there. I had to wait my turn for guns to become available. A number of gun writers even were faced with the odd situation of not being able to get guns to test for articles, because each one was spoken for as soon as it came off the production line.

Virtually every AR manufacturer was in the same boat, They simply couldn't keep up with demand, a phenomenon that stretched into the ammunition world as well. To solve the problem and make the most of the opportunity, those companies with the capital and ability worked to ramp up production, meaning investment in expanding production capability and hiring more people at a time when virtually every other

⌄ AR-15s are no longer merely functional; they are also works of high-performing art, as these Colt Competition Rifles attest.

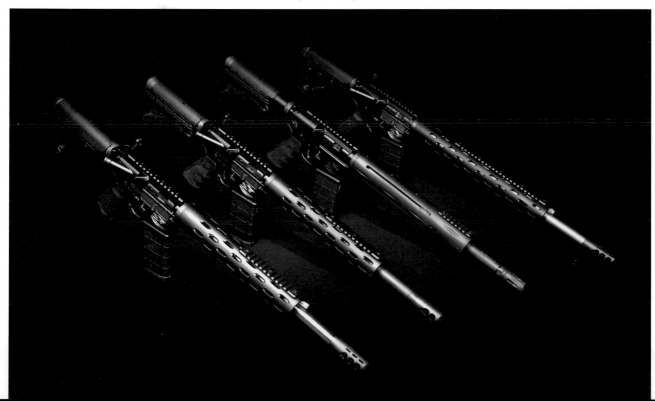

industry in the country was mired in recession. But ramping up production took time, so the racks at gun shops remained empty and if a shop was lucky enough to get a few guns in for sale, they often went instantly and for two to three times what they had sold for prior to November 2008.

Because no records are kept of exactly how many guns are sold in the United States, the next best way of guesstimating the number of guns that trade hands each month and year, at least through licensed gun dealers is to take a look at the FBI's NICS National Instant Criminal Background Check System) numbers. In the month President Obama was elected, even though he had yet to take office, overall background numbers increased by 346,356, from 1,183,279 in October to 1,529,635. The following month was nearly the same. For 2009, the President's first year in office, total background checks grew by more than 1.5 million. To be fair, an overall upward sales trend, using NICS statistics as a basis, technically began in 2006, about

the time of the first whispers of potential candidates to succeed then president George W. Bush. That year saw background checks jump to 10 million, a roughly 1.1 million increase over the average number from 2000 to 2005, which hovered in the 8 million to 8.9 million range. Bear in mind, not all of these were AR rifles, as these numbers account for background checks on all gun sales and transfers of which handguns still remain the top sellers, even despite the tactical rifle's rise in popularity. But make no mistake, where long guns are concerned, tactical rifle sales, specifically ARs, are the number-one seller driving the market.

Since that time, sales have continued to steadily climb, even soar at time, bumped by fears of more restrictive legislation due to political and societal events. The tragic mass shooting at Sandy Hook Elementary School in Connecticut in 2012, President Obama's re-election that same year, and to a lesser extent, Obama's executive orders on guns in 2015 all drove sales upward, though how much the latter will

⌄ Attend any gun or shooting industry trade show and the biggest crowds will be found around modern firearms and their accessories.

impact sales for the long term remains to be seen as it just occurred a few weeks prior to this writing.

In late 2014 and early 2015, some manufacturers, who had ramped up extensively to meet the AR sales demand, were bemoaning the leveling off of and even in some situations, perceived drop in AR sales. Sales did level off to more realistic demand expectations, bringing the prices of the average gun back to more reasonable levels, many now available for at or just under $1,000. But overall sales are still at all-time historical highs with total background checks in the slow year of 2014 still at 20.9 million, a mere drop of less than 125,000 from the previous year which at the time, set an all-time high in checks at 21 million. But even as gun dealers and manufacturers were bemoaning a slow down in early 2015, that year ultimately set a new record in NICS entries with 23.1 million background checks performed.

It is believed that much of that increase was in part due to the strong demand for handguns for concealed carry, so some AR makers may not have enjoyed as big a bump percentage-wise as they would've liked as interest likely remained modestly steady in tactical rifles but exploded for handguns, particularly following the terrorist attack/shooting in San Bernadino, Calif., in December 2015. That month alone saw total background checks soar to 3.3 million, a 1.1 million increase over the previous month alone.

Another gauge of how popular AR rifles and the tactical models overall continue to be is to look at the number of firearms manufactured each year. According to the Bureau of Alcohol, Tobacco, Firearms and Explosives (formerly known as the ATF or BATF, but now technically the BATFE) annual statistical report, "Firearms Commerce in the United States, 2015," we can see that at least up until 2013, the last year numbers are available, the overall manufacture of rifles has soared:

Year	Rifles (Manufactured)	Total Firearms (Manufactured)
2007	1.6 million	3.9 million
2008	1.7 million	4.5 million
2009	2.2 million	5.5 million
2010	1.8 million	5.5 million
2011	2.3 million	6.5 million
2012	3.1 million	8.6 million
2013	4 million	10.8 million

Several inferences can be drawn from these numbers. Certainly the overall number of rifles has grown precipitously, but not as much as the overall number of firearms meaning clearly, the handgun market still remains king in popularity among new gun buyers, whether it be a first-time purchaser or a long-time gunowner adding to his collection. Public safety fears as a result of highly publicized violent crimes, particularly mass shootings, and laws making it easier for law-abiding citizens to secure concealed carry permits are combining to drive that market.

But talk to anyone who manufactures both traditional rifles and tactical rifles, and they will tell you, tactical guns, specifically AR-style rifles, continue to drive the majority of long gun sales and a good portion of overall firearms sales right behind handguns. Thus, it is a fair assumption to say that the majority of the 229 percent increase in overall rifles being manufactured between 2007 and 2013 were indeed tactical rifles, and the majority of those, ARs. Just to keep it all in perspective, that 229 percent increase in rifles compares to a 318 percent increase over the same time frame in total handguns made. Either way you look at it, the gun industry continues to be robust, a key component of which is AR-style rifles and their related accessories.

TIMES THEY ARE A CHANGIN'

This is a huge jump from 1994, when the firearms were vilified by the Clinton Administration and front and center of the then President's Assault Weapons Ban, which had just gone into effect. (Should another Clinton be elected to the White House, she has already promised to make gun control a key goal.) At the time, anti-gunners and sympathetic politicians twisted fact and fueled emotion enough to convince much of the non-shooting public that modern tactical rifles, such as ARs, were weapons with fully automatic firing capabilities that were used in a large number of violent crimes in the United States. They claimed the "AR" in AR-15

stood for "automatic rifle" or "assault rifle," without ever digging deep enough to merely realize it stood for ArmaLite, the company responsible for first designing the rifle. Never mind that full-auto firearms had been severely restricted from public availability since the 1930s, and that tactical rifles being used in the commission of crimes was extremely rare—and still is despite a very small handful (yet no less tragic) of highly publicized mass shootings. A mere 2 percent of murders in the United States in 2014, according to FBI statistics, involved the use of a rifle, and that is all types of rifles, not just tactical-style ones. For the anti-gun crowd, now those are real inconvenient truths.

My how times have changed since the sunsetting of the Clinton Assault Weapons Ban in 2004. As noted, AR-platform rifles continue to ride a wave of popularity and interest not enjoyed by any type of firearm in our lifetime short of semi-auto handguns. Indeed, in 2010, the NRA reported that since 1986, more than 2.5 million of the guns had been sold in the United States. That number has probably almost doubled

⌄ While the AR was originally designed for the 5.56mm cartridge, it now comes in a variety of calibers including the affordable .22.

INTRODUCTION

⋀ Predator hunters were among some of the first civilian groups to fully embrace the AR's performance and versatility.

⋀ ARs come in countless variations and are one of the most common types of guns found on gun ranges today.

since then. Also, in 2010, a survey conducted on behalf of the National Shooting Sports Foundation (NSSF) revealed that in 2009, more than 8.9 million recreational and competitive shooters reported shooting ARs in the previous 12-month period. That means of 34.4 million formal and informal sport and target shooters, approximately 26 percent shot ARs.

That is more than shot trap (7.6 million), skeet (7 million) and even the very popular sporting clays, which enjoyed the participation of an estimated 8.4 million shooters that same year. And what about those hunters, who in the 1990s, weren't very familiar with ARs? Even they have become more commonplace in hunt camps across the country thanks in large part to the growing ranks of predator and varmint hunters, and the availability of more deer-sized calibers now offered in the AR-platform.

So why the big change in attitude surrounding modern tactical rifles? Steve Sanetti, president of the NSSF, points to a number of key reasons.

"9/11 certainly had something to do with it for one," says Sanetti. "That is when we noticed a sea change in the public's attitude toward firearms in general. There became a lot more interest in the practical firearms people would need to make themselves feel more secure in their homes and on the street."

As law enforcement beefed up tactical units and armor to appropriately address future domestic threats, and the military deployments to Afghanistan and Iraq became commonplace, ARs in particular became much more visible. Mirroring what was occurring in society, the guns also became more visible in the movies, again raising the awareness of ARs among the public consciousness.

"What the military and law enforcement uses, tends to be what people want to own," says Sanetti. "They see what they regard as the authorities, or the professionals, using, and they rightfully feel like it must be the best, so they want to own the same thing. With the police and military using them, ARs have become synonymous with effectiveness and reliability."

The AR's inherent utility, accuracy and ability to be modified to suit an individual shooter's preferences remain key selling points. In fact, on those grounds alone, ARs virtually sell themselves—particularly as more sportsmen become educated on their attributes and get a chance to shoot them firsthand.

"Across many product lines today, not just firearms, there is a trend among manufacturers to create products that, as delivered, have broad appeal, but can also be customized to fit the individual owner's wants and needs. The AR fits extremely well into that model," says Sanetti.

1. History of the AR

For all of its popularity among the military, law enforcement and civilian shooters today, the AR-15 almost never happened. Or at the very least, its development was almost grounded before it really got the chance to fly. Dissatisfied with the overall performance of the M14 rifle that was in service at the time, the Army in the 1950s sought the assistance of commercial gun manufacturers in developing a .22-caliber firearm capable of replacing it in combat.

As the military had crossed the bridge from a post-World War II era, the focus of many of the branches was on devising tactics, equipment and machinery capable of countering the nuclear capabilities of our new age Cold War enemies. Partially responsible for this task within the U.S. Army was the Operations Research Office, created after World War II. However, the ORO increasingly found itself attempting to solve non-nuclear related challenges prompted by our country's engagement in North Korea. One such concern, recounted in the late Edward C. Ezell's book, *The Great Rifle Controversy*, one of the most detailed and comprehensive examinations of military small arms development in the United States between the close of World War II and the early 1980s, was that "ORO investigators discovered that very little was known about the nature of inflicting wounds on the human body in combat."

As a result, the Infantry Division of ORO began to study the issue by analyzing more than 3 million casualties from World Wars I and II, as well as those that had occurred in Korea up to that point. For the first time, an analysis suggested that more soldiers were killed by randomly dispersed fire than carefully aimed shots, suggesting that a light-recoiling rifle that could rapidly launch multiple projectiles in a controlled, yet simultaneously spread pattern, could ultimately be more effective on the battlefield.

Following several years of studying the idea, the Continental Army Command (CONARC) decided to seek the development of a 5.56mm rifle. They reached out to both Winchester, owned by Olin, which now only manufactures the ammunition under that brand, and the ArmaLite Division of Fairchild Engine & Airplane Corp., which today is simply known as ArmaLite Inc. (But ironically no longer owns the trademark for the actual AR-15 name. More on that in a moment.)

ArmaLite's New Concept Rifle

According to a history of ArmaLite, Inc., recognizing that there had been little done in the way of advancing fundamental small arms design and function in the past 50 years, Fairchild executives president Richard S. Boutelle, a gun enthusiast, and Paul S. Cleveland, corporate secretary, wanted to focus on developing fine sporting arms for the commercial market with the hope that their work would catch the eyes of military leaders and provoke some interest. However, shortly after establishing the ArmaLite Division, the company was

⌃ Today's M4, an AR variant, is the top choice among many of our nation's military. Photo Credit: DoD Photos

invited by the U.S. Air Force to submit a rifle design that would replace the branch's survival rifle. Within a matter of weeks, ArmaLite submitted a rifle dubbed the AR-5 to the Air Force for evaluation. The rifle was built around the .22 Hornet. The Air Force adopted the rifle, which was officially designated the MA-1 Survival Rifle. This success forced the company to rethink its original decision to pursue the commercial market and instead, they changed course and focused exclusively on developing arms for the military.

From there, three people involved with ArmaLite came together to alter the course of modern firearms as we know them. According to ArmaLite, it was the idea of George Sullivan, a chief patent counsel for Lockheed Aircraft Corporation, to use the "latest technical advances in plastics and alloys" to build firearms that were lighter and more functional than then-available models. In fact, Sullivan, a tinkerer himself, had begun work on some of his ideas in his garage following World War II. Charles Dorchester directed and coordinated all of ArmaLite Division's development programs and would later go on to run the entire company. But perhaps most recognizable of the three whom would go on to change history and the one historical scholars credit for the birth of the AR platform was Eugene Stoner. Stoner, who had served as a Marine during the war and was considered an ordnance expert, was made chief engineer of the ArmaLite Division in 1954. He had been working on developing small arms independently since the war as well. It is Stoner's patents that "form the basis of much of ArmaLite's work," according to the company's historical records.

In 1955, the Army was looking to update or replace the service rifle of the time, the M1 Garand, and were considering two versions: Springfield Armory's T-44, merely an updated version of the Garand, and the T-48, a version of the 7.62x51mm FN FAL, which was developed and manufactured by Fabrique Nationale de Herstal, known today primarily as FN Herstal. The FAL would ultimately go on to be adopted by as the primary service rifle used by many NATO coun-

tries including Belgium, Great Britain, Canada and Australia.

To compete with these firearms, Stoner took a totally new approach in firearms design of the day and created the AR-10. The first version of the AR-10 was made with aircraft grade aluminum receivers, keeping the weight down considerably from what it looked like it might weigh. In fact, empty, the rifle weighed less than 7 pounds. The receivers could be made from such lightweight material because the bolt locked into a steel extension that attached to the barrel, not directly in the receiver itself. Stocks, pistol grips and fore-ends were all plastic compared to the wood-grain furniture more common to guns of the day. Unfortunately, despite capturing the attention of more than a few military leaders intrigued by the firearm's unique design, the ArmaLite Division had gotten involved too late to adequately compete. An article that first appeared in the May 1962 issue of *American Rifleman* magazine noted that the initial AR-10 had also fallen prey to flaws with its original composite steel-aluminum barrel and a complicated flash suppressor.

According to Ezell, however, of those leaders intrigued by the AR-10's design included CONARC's commander, Gen. Willard G. Wyman. In 1957, Wyman personally asked Stoner to design a 5.56mm rifle for the Army similar to the AR-10. That scaled-down rifle would go on to become the AR-15.

The first AR-15s had steel barrels and an Army-developed BAR-type flash suppressor. And while Stoner's design has been called genius by many, the real genius may have been found in the engineer's ability to borrow features from a number of popular and proven European gun designs and combine them

⌄ In the form of the M16, the AR made its way into the hands of our military by 1963. Photo Credit: DoD Photos

⌃ Eugene Stoner, creator of the AR design.

in a single platform. The now-ubiquitous hinge design of the AR, not unlike that of a break-open shotgun, was similar to a design used in the Czech ZH or ZB 29 rifle and adopted in the FN. The rear sight was built into the rear of the carrying handle like the British EM 2, the hinged cover on the ejection port resembled that of the German Sturmgewehr 44, the locking system was similar to the one used in the Johns Semiautomatic Rifle from the 1940s and the straight stock, designed to better accommodate recoil and manage multiple shots, was similar to a number of auto and semi-auto rifle designs getting some play at the time, including as Ezell pointed out, the Harvey T25.

Stoner's gas operating system, which employed, and still does on direct impingement ARs, a tube beneath the front sight and directed gas back to the bolt in order to cycle rounds during firing, had been used in the both Swedish M42 Ljungman and the French MAS 1949.

"Stoner's achievement in the AR-15 was the combination of all of these ideas into an attractive package," wrote Ezell. Of course, once designed, the rifle still had to win favor with the military, a battle that almost ended the AR-15's prominent role in history right there.

To begin, ArmaLite was so small, it didn't have a full research facility or the staff to completely develop a fully tested prototype. Instead, they had to rely on military testers, many whom had their own prejudices against this new weapon and did it few favors to discover if it could actually serve soldiers well. There were some key leaders in the Army who simply didn't like the fact that the new gun hadn't been developed within the branch's own usual channels. Others simply didn't like the new configuration of the gun, much as some traditional-minded hunters view the firearm even today. Rain tests conducted on a test sample of the rifles originally suggested that shooting the guns with water in the barrels could result in burst barrels—something that was believed at the time to be "characteristic of high-velocity rifles having a bore diameter of less than .25 caliber," according to Ezell. ArmaLite strengthened the barrels in response, but still concerns over the hazard persisted. Arctic tests conducted on the rifles to determine how they would perform in freezing weather also proved disappointing to testers, though the Winchester .224 rifle still being considered

at the time also failed in this respect. In the end, the test board reviewing the new rifles suggested that a ".223 (5.56mm) round was not a suitable replacement for the 7.62 NATO round" and that development of a heavier .258 caliber (6.35mm) cartridge be pursued (Ezell). In light of the recommendations, Army Chief of Staff Gen. Maxwell Taylor ruled the branch would continue procuring the heavier and already NATO approved 7.62 M14 rifles.

SECOND CHANCE

After all of the expense in developing the AR-15, it was a tough financial blow to a small company like Fairchild, which, struggling to make ends meet, had actually already begun to search for a company to which to license the production of both the AR-15 and the AR-10. The company had invested in the AR-15 project alone $1.45 million, an amount that by today's corporate standards would be fairly cheap but for any small company, then or now, could be a backbreaker. Fairchild decided to recoup some of the costs of the protracted project by selling the manufacturing and marketing rights to what was then called Colt's Patent Firearms Manufacturing Company, but is better known today simply as Colt's Manufacturing, LLC, or merely Colt. The company bought the rights to both firearms (a version of the AR-10 had already been sold to the Dutch and was being marketed in Southeast Asia where conflicts were erupting in what was then a little-known country called Vietnam) for $75,000 cash payment and a guarantee of a 4 ½ percent royalty on all future sales.

In *The Black Rifle: M16 Retrospective* by R. Blake Stevens and Edward C. Ezell, the authors note that at the time, Colt was also suffering financially as a result of dried up military and civilian markets following WWII. The company also hadn't retooled its manufacturing facilities in nearly a century. The Maryland-based firm of Cooper-MacDonald, which through one of its principles, Robert W. "Bobby" MacDonald already promoted the Dutch AR in Southeast Asia, worked with both ArmaLite and Colt and had been the connection that brought the sale of the ARs together. Interestingly, Cooper-MacDonald made more off the sale of the guns to Colt than

The first true military version of the AR-15, the M16, got its first full trial during the Vietnam War. Photo Credit: DoD Photos

Fairchild, netting $250,000 and a 1 percent royalty on all future guns sold.

MacDonald, who had extensive contacts in Southeast Asia and saw the AR-15 as an ideal gun for the "smaller statured" fighters of the region, immediately began marketing the gun in that part of the world and, under orders from Colt, to the U.S. military once again. They wanted to see the AR-15 given another chance.

Initially Army representatives refused. But Colt had better luck when they decided to bypass the branch and seek other military buyers. Ultimately, Air Force Vice Chief of Staff Gen. Curtis LeMay, who witnessed a demonstration of the guns, suggested that the Air Force test the AR-15 as a replacement for the M2 carbines used by its sentries. The tests proved positive and the Air Force placed an initial order for 8,500 rifles (Ezell). Sometimes it just takes that one lucky break to get the door to open wider than your foot and allow you to walk on through.

Studies by the Defense Department, who agreed to give the gun another look, also proved favorable, causing questions to be asked all the way up the chain of command as to why the disparity between the Army's original findings and the reports coming out about the gun then. Indeed, both Secretary of Defense Robert McNamara and even then President John F. Kennedy had questions. Ultimately, the Army was forced to reevaluate the rifle the result being in 1963 that the decision was made to end procurement of the M14. At the same time, McNamara ordered the purchase of 85,000 AR-15s for the Army and 19,000 for the Air Force, who was already using some of the guns, to begin the following year (Ezell).

The purchase was initially intended to be a one-time deal—enough to fill the gap until another weapons testing program was complete and a new firearm developed, but history proves that did not become the case. To meet demand for the growing conflict in Vietnam, the Army ordered more of the rifles and reclassified it as the M16.

NOT DONE YET

Once the AR-15/M16 made its way to soldiers' hands and was finally being tested on the battlefield, problems began to arise. While the overall opinion was that most soldiers liked the overall design and concept of the rifle, its immediate popularity was hindered by a few problems operators encountered in the field—mainly the gun malfunctioning during combat. Reviews revealed several causes for this including ammunition that didn't function properly in the rifle because of its high-residue powder. The Army had insisted on a faster-burning ball-type powder for use in the field instead of the cleaner burning powder Stoner had used in developing the rifle because they wanted

HISTORY OF THE AR

History of the AR • **17**

⌃ While the design of the M16 was generally well received by Vietnam-era soldiers, the model was not without its problems, primarily malfunctions when dirty.

to generate higher muzzle velocities. The Army also failed to secure chrome-lined barrels and chambers in the rifles, which resisted heat and fouling better as well as corrosion and pitting. Perhaps most egregiously ignored was the lack of proper cleaning supplies and quite simply a failure to properly train troops with the new rifle and enforce its frequent cleaning.

In fact, according to former long-distance AR competition shooter John Murphy, who has shot ARs extensively and studied their history, the original M16 was originally billed as a gun that didn't require much care or cleaning.

"The chamber on the .223 was not chrome plated. It got so hot that cases were sticking and with all of the gunk and powder, the gun would jam up," says Murphy. "The gun was marketed as one that didn't need cleaning, which was bunk. You have to always clean a gun." The cleaning of magazines was also found to be crucial as they would fill with grime and quit feeding rounds into the chamber during firing. Indeed when asked about how often he cleaned his M4, the military's modern, shorter version of the original M16 design, one recently retired Navy SEAL who has seen action in both Afghanistan and Iraq, said simply "every chance you get. Your life depends on it."

As more troops began carrying the new rifle into Vietnam, training and cleaning procedures—for both the rifle and its magazine—improved and with it, fewer reports of malfunctioning guns. In fact, the lack of proper cleaning seemed to fix much of what the initial concerns about the M16 were. Improvements in the propellant used in the military-issued ammunition also reduced reports of problems with the guns.

Over the years, the gun design has undergone a number of improvements and variations as requested by various branches of the military—and even by some civilian engineers and shooters—including the addition of: a forward assist, to aid in locking the bolt forward in rare instances when it fails to do so; flat-top receivers; heavier barrels; adjustable windage rear sights; selector switch functions that reduced full-auto firing to the firing of three-round bursts; a gas piston operating system as an option to the direct impingement design; and other minor tweaks including adjustments in stock length, thickness of barrels and stock design and functionality. Where the military design has wandered, the civilian market has followed.

One of the most notable changes in the rifle over time occurred with its rifling. Original models often had a 1-in-14-inch (1:14) or 1-in-12-inch (1:12) twist for use with the lighter 55-grain bullets used for combat at the time. This worked great for shooting targets under 300 yards and indeed, most combat engagement occurred at 100 yards or less, most often due to terrain features and limitations more so than an inability of the shooter. However, for long range shooting—ranges of out to 600 yards as was required in high-power competition matches or sniping—the gun was inadequate.

⌃ Today, popularity of the AR among hunters is one of the driving forces behind the platform's high sales numbers.

To improve the M16's early performance, rifling in the barrel was changed to a 1:7 twist in order to better accommodate 62-grain bullets. »

The 1:12 twist was unable to stabilize longer, heavier bullets needed for long distance shooting.

In "The Making of a Match Rifle," originally published in the July 1999 issue of *American Rifleman* by former Shooting Editor Glenn M. Gilbert, the author recounts how improvements in this area evolved following the adoption by NATO of a standard 5.56mm round loaded with a heavier 62-grain bullet, and which was fired from a barrel with a 1:9 twist. That bullet was designed by FN. In response, "the Army quickly developed a copy of the 62-grain FN bullet and standardized it as the M855 in 1981."

The rifling in the barrel of M16 was soon tightened to a 1:7 twist in order to accommodate the heavier bullet as well as tracers that were planned for the newly rifled firearms. Over time, the twist rate and development of longer bullets in the 77-grain and 80-grain arena solved the long range dilemma and produced a rifle that both military sharpshooters and civilian competitors could come to rely on. And indeed, once those problems were solved, the AR became a preferred gun of many competitors such as John Murphy.

"The Marines were the first ones to successfully carry the ARs to Camp Perry in 1994, and they cleaned everyone's clock with the new twist rates and the longer bullets," says Murphy.

Gilbert sums the AR's evolution up in his article by writing, "The AR-15 has come a long way. Long derided as a plastic toy, it is now the benchmark in accuracy among semi-auto rifles." It is this mix of both short-range application and long-range accuracy, combined with the multiple levels of personalization and functionality that have many experts predicting that the heyday of the AR is indeed here.

This sentiment, in fact, is continuing forward along dual paths. While there are a number of competing—and darn good—tactical rifle platforms available (the FN SCAR, HK416 and SIG 556xi are just a few that come immediately to mind), the U.S. Army, after a multi-year effort to find a suitable replacement for the M4 recently decided to scrap the search and commit to converting the M4 to M4A1s. The M4, successor variant of the M16, with a shorter barrel, flat top, collapsible stock and less weight, has been in use since 1994. While it has received periodic upgrades over the years, the transition to the M4A1, with a heavier barrel, full-auto firing capability and ambidextrous controls, is underway and should be complete by 2020 according to reports by the *Army Times*. From a military perspective at least, this move cements the continuation of the AR's place as the weapon of choice for many of our nation's servicemen and women on the battlefield.

Despite criticisms of the platform's ability to perform without malfunctioning in sandy or dirty environments, an *Army Times* article cites testing data that showed "today's M4 and M4A1 indicate a 98.3 percent probability of completing a mission with a basic ammunition load (209 rounds) without failure." To those supporters cheering on a new small-arms alternative to the AR, the Army scrapped the effort to find a replacement after determining that all of the potential replacements didn't provide sufficient improvements over current performance levels . . . particularly not enough to justify the additional cost it would take to swap out the entire branch's shoulder-fired weapons.

On the civilian front, increasing acceptance by competitive shooters, driven in large part by 3Gun competitors, and certainly hunters, who continue to embrace the platform, are driving high-end performance features on some models and more hunt-friendly features and broader caliber offerings on others. This latter development has been one of the most visible in recent years as manufacturers seek to keep rifles moving off shelves even as buying patterns settle into more stable, yet realistic numbers following the boom years of 2008–09 and 2012–13. But more on that later in the book.

2. Breaking Down the AR

*C*leaning and caring for the AR rifle is one of the easiest aspects of owning them. To the uninitiated, the hard lines, levers and industrial look of these firearms might seem intimidating, but the reality, as anyone who has spent 10 minutes with one will realize, is that the gun's design boasts an amazing simplicity in both its operation and its disassembly and assembly. So much so that one message board poster once responded to another that "if you can operate a can opener, you can pretty much take down an AR-15." One poster even shared a video on YouTube of an eleven-year-old girl breaking one down and putting it back together as a prime example of its simplicity in design. Despite this, there are still a number of users who puzzle over the best way to care for their AR.

THE BASICS

No doubt plenty of AR users have this information down, but it would be remiss to ignore the basic steps to breaking down the AR in a book such as this. Here is a quick overview of the design and function of the typical AR-15. Please note that with so many manufacturers developing customized models to fit a growing audience, many of today's guns will have additional or different features, but the basic operation and design will be the same. If not, then it isn't an AR.

1. Buttstock—Can be either collapsible (shown) or fixed. Fixed models typically have storage space in rear of stock for storing cleaning kit or adding extra weight for competitive shooters. Buttstock houses the buffer tube, which returns the carrier bolt assembly forward during shot cycling.

2. Charging Handle—Used to open or release bolt for loading. Charging handle can have a standard latch, midsize latch or an oversize latch (located on left side) for easier catch, particularly when used with large bell optics.

3. Rear Sight—Can be flip down or fixed model. Many variations available. Works great as a back-up should mounted optics fail or become destroyed.

4. Upper Receiver—Houses bolt carrier assembly and provides attachment for barrel. Flat-top design with a single rail for the mounting of optics, but can also include a carrying handle, though these are seldom actually used for carrying the rifle.

5. Hand Guard Slip Ring and Delta Ring—Holds front handguard (fore-end) in place and is also where rear of barrel screws into the upper receiver.

6. Fore-end—Can consist of plastic handguards (pictured) or guards with either integral or installed rails for the attachment of lights, lasers or other accessories. On free-float barrels, fore-end would be open instead of attaching behind the gas block, which captures and directs gasses rearward through gas tube, which runs beneath fore-end and slams bolt rearward upon firing in order to cycle rounds.

7. Front Sight Post—Can be fixed or flip-down so as not to interfere with sighting with attached optics. And of course, some full-rail flat-top models forgo any sights at all, providing the gunowner with unfettered freedom to select their preferred sighting system(s).

8. Barrel—Most today have a 1:9 or 1:7 twist (if chambered for .223) and are threaded at both ends to screw into the barrel extension and pinned in place in the upper receiver to accept a muzzlebrake, flash hider or suppressor.

9. Muzzlebrake/Flash Hider—Attaches to end of the barrel. Muzzlebrakes help reduce muzzle flip and manage recoil (and also increases muzzle blast), while flash hiders or flash suppressors reduce flash signature of shot. Sound suppressors can also be installed and reduce the amount of sound typically produced by firing a shot.

10. Ejection Port and Ejection Port Cover—Allows for ejection of spent ammunition and visual inspection of whether the firearm is loaded or not. Ejection Port Cover is a spring-loaded cover that when closed is designed to reduce the amount of dirt and grime able to enter ejection port. Upon closing bolt or firing, the cover opens automatically.

11. Magazine Release Button—Allows magazine to be dropped free from the bottom of the lower receiver.

12. Magazine—Stores ammunition and supplies it to firearm during firing. Can be made from aluminum or polymer and are typically designed to hold 5, 10, 20 or 30 rounds. Forty-, 60- and even 100-round stack and drum mags are available.

13. Lower Receiver—Houses trigger assembly, magazine and pistol grip. Buffer tube attaches to the lower and the magazine latch and bolt-stop are also on the side. This is the one part of the gun that has the serial number and must be purchased through an FFL-licensed dealer.

14. Pistol Grip—Provides a fourth point of contact with rifle for improved firing control.

15. Forward Assist—Absent on original AR-15 and M16 design, was added later to help move bolt forward when normal charging failed to lock rifle into battery. The forward assist ratchets against grooves in the bolt and moves it forward into a locked position. When forward assist was added, blast deflector was also added.

16. Safety Selector—Rotates 90-degrees so operator can put on "safe" mode or release safety for firing. Full-auto capable guns also rotate 180 degrees in order to select "full auto" mode.

17. Trigger—Like on any gun, is control used to fire rounds.

18. Bolt Catch—Locks bolt open and releases it shut and into battery upon depressing. Is actuated by an empty magazine for faster reloads.

FIELD STRIPPING

When it was originally designed, the AR was errantly billed as a rifle that didn't require much cleaning in order to maintain a high level of performance. American soldiers in Vietnam quickly learned that was not the case, the lesson costing some soldiers their lives. All firearms require cleaning and it is important that every owner—even if they don't plan on swapping out the various parts of the AR themselves—at least be able to properly break it down and maintain. To properly field strip your AR, follow these steps.

Clearing the Rifle

1. As with any firearm, safety is always paramount when working on or handling a gun in your home, on the range, or in the field, and the first rule at all times before taking a gun apart is to inspect that it is unloaded. The first thing you will need to do is turn the selector switch to safe and remove the magazine. Note that if the rifle has been fired, you can't put it on safety with a standard AR trigger.

2. If the rifle won't go to safe, lock the bolt to the rear by pulling the charging handle back and depressing the bolt catch. Then return the charging handle to the locked position and look into the chamber to visually confirm that the rifle is empty.

3. Turn the selector switch on safety and release the bolt.

Disassembly

1. First slide the takedown pin out near the rear of the lower receiver until it is sticking all the way out of the right side of the receiver.
2. Rotate the upper receiver forward so the bolt carrier group is accessible.

3. Squeeze the carrier latch on the charging handle and pull the charging handle straight to the rear of the receiver until it is almost fully extended. Then slide the bolt carrier group free from the upper receiver. The charging handle will then slip right out as well.

4. Slide the hinge pin at the front of the lower receiver out in the same fashion as you did the rear pin. Then lift the upper receiver and barrel free of the lower receiver and set it aside.

5. To disassemble the bolt, first extract the firing pin retaining pin.

6. Then withdraw the firing pin through the rear of the carrier assembly.

7. Rotate the carrier key (also known as a bolt cam pin) on the top of the bolt carrier assembly 90 degrees and lift it out. This releases the bolt so you can withdraw it from the front of the carrier. Note that in the bolt, there are small gas rings that should be changed out between every 2,000 or 3,000 rounds to 10,000 rounds depending on the frequency and type of shooting you are doing.

8. At the front of the bolt, there is an extractor and ejector in the bolt. Both are held in place by small springs and a rubber bumper inside the spring that works like a shock absorber. This is a fairly recent upgrade to the bolt design and may not appear in earlier manuals. Remove the extractor pin pushing it with the tip of the firing pin. Be careful not to damage the tip of the firing pin. Some cleaning manuals recommend removing the extractor for cleaning as well, but if you are not careful, it is easy to let these springs get away from you and lose them. Be careful not to damage the tip of your firing pin.

9. Lift the extractor and spring from the bolt. As noted, be extremely careful to keep the spring and extractor together.

10. Lastly, remove the buffer tube and spring. Push the tube back and depress the small detent that holds the buffer tube and spring in place. Allow the tube and spring to gently slide out. Separate the buffer and the spring for cleaning.

Cleaning Your Rifle

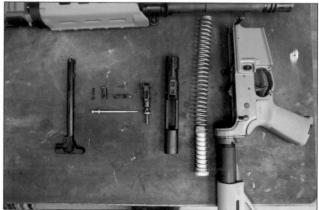

1. Blow out the buffer tube and wipe the buffer spring with a brush and mild solvent. Then wipe dry. Run a pipe cleaner through the drain hole in the rear of the buttstock in order to keep it clear.

2. A cleaning solvent and a toothbrush are all you need to wipe all of the working parts down including the bolt carrier group and all of its related parts. Be sure to brush down the dirt and grime from the trigger mechanism and the entire lower receiver. Brush down the inside of the upper receiver cleaning the chamber and barrel extension and run a bore snake or solvent soaked brush through the barrel a couple of times from the breech, so that you don't risk damage to the crown. Follow the brush with several dry patches.

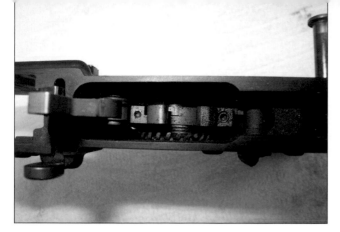

3. Inspect all working parts, particularly the carrier key, firing pin, firing pin retaining pin, extractor and extractor spring for pits, cracks or any other damage that could affect the operation of your rifle and if any problems are observed, replace the parts of concern.

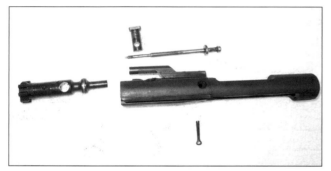

4. Very lightly lubricate the bolt and carrier. That's all the lubrication you need. Said one armorer, "Some guys just wash their parts down in oil and then when they go to the range and shoot, we call them coon eyes, because when the remove their shooting glasses they have raccoon eyes from where their guns have shot off all the oil vapor from where they oiled it down too much." Don't be that guy!

Reassembly

You are basically going to simply reverse the steps you took to disassemble the rifle.
1. First, slide the spring and buffer back into the tube locking it securely behind the detent.

2. If you removed the extractor and extractor spring, insert them back into the bolt, securing them in place with the extractor pin.
3. Slide the bolt back into the front of the carrier by lining the extractor up on the right side.

4. Push the carrier key back into the hole at the top of the bolt carrier assembly and rotate it 90 degrees back into place. If it isn't rotated the right way, you will not be able to see daylight through the hole where the firing pin will slide. You must be able to see daylight through the hole, remove the carrier key and reinstall it until you have the holes properly aligned.

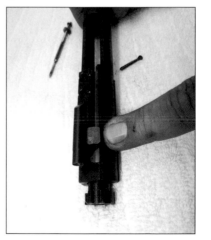

5. Slide the firing pin back into the rear of the bolt carrier assembly and secure it with the firing pin retaining pin. Note that the pin will not poke through the bolt until it is fully locked back into place on the carrier assembly.

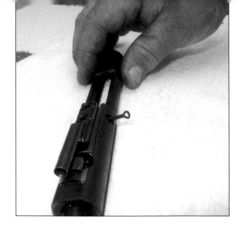

6. Slide the charging handle into the rear of the receiver sliding it near the top groove where you will feel it drop in after a couple of inches.

7. Before sliding the charging handle all of the way in, take the bolt carrier group ensuring that bolt is in fully forward position and insert the key into the charging handle. Then slide it into the rear of the upper receiver with the gas tube in the groove along the bottom of the charging handle, continue to slide both of them forward until they lock into place.

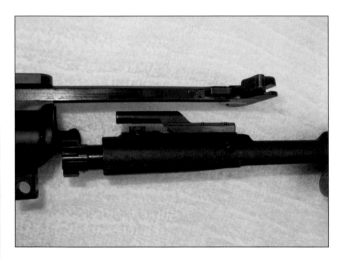

8. Hook the upper receiver into the lower receiver where the hinge pin aligns with the appropriate holes in the upper and push the hinge pin into place until it locks. Swing the upper and lower receivers closed and then slide the takedown pin back into place.

Mag Maintenance

When gun jams or other firing problems occur, it is as often a cause of a malfunctioning magazine as it is shoddy ammo or actual problems with the firearms. Like your rifle, magazines need to be maintained and cleaned for optimal performance and life. Make it a habit whenever field stripping and cleaning your rifle, to also clean whatever magazines you've been shooting with as well. Or as former Naval armorer and current gunsmith at Chesapeake Gun and Pawn in Chesapeake, Virginia, explains, magazines are cheap enough and easy enough to get, so buy a collection of them and swap them out as you shoot, simply discarding any that don't deliver 100 percent performance. But for those gunowners who like to make their gear last, here's how to maintain that mag.

1. Check that the magazine is empty.

2. Turn the magazine over and using a small punch, depress the catch through the small hole in the magazine floor plate and slide it back to release the plate.

3. Carefully slide the floor plate free of the magazine while keeping the magazine spring retained. Then, gently allow the spring to uncoil and remove it from the magazine.

4. Pull the follower from the magazine as well.

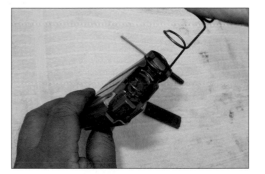

5. Now that the magazine is disassembled, you can scrub it down with the same brush and solvent you used for cleaning your rifle, but the easiest way to clean magazines is to simply place them in the dishwasher. Regardless of whether they are made from aluminum or polymer, just place the floor plate, follower and spring in the silver wear holders in the dishwasher and the magazine box in the top rack. Put the washer on the pots and pans cycle so they get hot and dry and let it go. Before putting the magazine back together, spray the spring down with a silicone-based spray so it is not collecting dirt and grease. Note: Inspect all of the parts for cracks, nicks or other damage that could affect their performance and if you note any problems that could hamper the magazine's fluid operation, throw it away and

get a new one. (See Chapter 6: Outfitting Your Rig on the section about "Magazines.")

Magazine Reassembly

To reassemble the magazine, simply slide the follower in the bottom of the box first, followed by the spring and the floor plate. Slide it forward until it snaps into the locked position and then check to make sure the floor plate stiffly depresses and springs back into place as it should.

Direct Impingement and Gas Piston

When Stoner created the AR-15, he designed it so that when a shot was fired, the gases traveling down the barrel would escape through a small hole in the barrel beneath the front site and then travel rearward through a gas tube, back to the receiver and slam the bolt rearward, ejecting the spent shell and allowing a new cartridge to feed from the magazine below. This direct impingement system wasn't really anything new. As noted in Chapter 2, it had been used in the both Swedish M42 Ljungman and the French MAS 1949, but it did work very well and continues to do so even today.

However, an increasing number of ARs today are using what is called a gas piston system. Like direct impingement, it is still gas operated, however, rather than gases blowing all the way through a tube to the bolt, where the tube would normally run, the gas hits a piston and pushes the piston rearward to create the cycling action. The gas piston uses a shorter tube than a direct impingement model with the advantages that you don't get the blowback or any of the gas or fouling blowing back into the action. In theory, and no doubt many will argue in practice, this allows the gun to remain cleaner longer, reducing the chances of a jam due to a gummed up action. Because the gas doesn't have to travel as far to generate the required action, a piston rifle can even shoot a little faster.

That being said, however, a direct impingement AR should shoot slightly more accurately because you don't have the extra parts slamming together like you do in a piston gun. Because there are more parts, a piston gun also tends to be more expensive, has more parts that can break, wear or corrode and can even slightly add a little more overall weight to the gun. Of course, we're talking ounces on the latter.

Barring performance concerns, one gunsmith I spoke with said most casual and even serious shooters are better off sticking with direct impingement rifles. Why?

"They are proven, they are more accurate when shooting at distance and for the amount of shooting most guys are going to do (even competitive shooters), they are never going to need to worry about fouling the gun so much that it's going to quit working on them," he says.

Of course, now to muddy the works, while gas piston guns to this point have worked on a short stroke system, along comes a company out of Idaho called Primary Weapons Systems (PWS) that has created a long-stroke piston gun that reduces the amount of moving parts hitting together with each shot.

"Our push-rod long-stroke piston is the only one on the market," says Dan Hawkins, marketing director at PWS. "It is based on the system used in the AK-47 platform and brings the reliability of the AK to the AR platform." He explains their guns provide shooters with the benefits of a piston system—less cleaning, more reliability—with the smooth cycling of a direct impingement. This is because their long stroke piston is connected to the operating rod, with is connected directly to the bolt carrier group. As one unit, there are no parts needing to slam into another in order to operate the rifle. He points out that the long stroke design also eliminates carrier tilt, an event that occurs with short stroke pistons because they strike the bolt in an off-center axis, actually driving the carrier down as it drives it backwards and ultimately potentially affecting accuracy.

"It's the difference between pushing a person across a room and having to punch them all the way across a room. Naturally, pushing the person is going to be a less violent and much more practical way to achieve that," Hawkins says.

Clearing a Jam

From time to time, particularly during high volume and rapid-fire shooting, you will likely encounter a jam with your AR and will need to safely clear it. Military references suggest the shooter first engage in a S.P.O.R.T.S. sequence immediately upon a experiencing a malfunction. S.P.O.R.T.S. is:

Slap the bottom of the magazine to make sure it is fully seated

Pull the charging handle all the way to the rear

Observe for the ejection of a live round or spent cartridge

Release the charging handle

Tap the forward assist to ensure the bolt is fully locked

Squeeze the trigger downrange in an attempt to fire.

If that doesn't clear the jam, then the shooter should take the steps to mortar the rifle.

Mortar Method of Clearing a Jam

1. Remove the magazine from the rifle and, if possible, put the gun on safety.
2. Remember to treat the gun as loaded, always keeping it pointed in a safe direction. Find a solid,

⩘ The first step when clearing a jam is to remove the magazine and, if possible, put the gun on safety.

yet nonabrasive surface such as a lawn or grass. If using a hard floor or cement pad, place a towel or piece of carpet where you will mortar the rifle in order to protect the buttstock. If your AR has a collapsible stock, slide it all the way in.

3. With the rifle pointing up, grasp the fore-end of the rifle in one hand and the charging handle in the other. From about 6 to 8 inches from the surface, strike the rifle butt on the ground, using the momentum to drive the charging handle to where it is fully extended.

4. Inspect the chamber to ensure that the round ejected. If it doesn't come all of the way out, release the charging handle without riding it and try it again. If the cartridge is partially extended from the chamber, spray lubricant such as WD-40 down the barrel and give it a minute or two to work in.

5. Repeat the mortar procedure until the round is expelled.

6. In the event mortaring fails to remove a round or stuck casing, you will have to push it back out with a cleaning rod from the muzzle end of the gun. In the event of a ruptured casing, AR owners should carry a Ruptured Case Extractor (RUP), also called a Broken Shell Extractor, which, in the event of a ruptured case stuck in the chamber, attaches to the bolt face and when the bolt is closed, slides through the case. It is shaped like a mushroom on the end, so when you draw the bolt back open the RUP catches and pulls on the front of the case, drawing it from the chamber.

7. Once the casing is removed, inspect the chamber and upon observing that it is clear, clean the gun down if you are able, reinsert the magazine, release the bolt and fire.

According to the *M16/M4 Handbook* by Mike Pannone, the only time a S.P.O.R.T.S. sequence should not be initiated is when the shooter observes a "stove-pipe" malfunction—one in which the brass from an expended round is sticking out of the ejection port at a 90-degree angle. Attempting to charge the rifle with a stove-pipe will be futile, so the shooter should simply pull the brass free of the ejection port or rotate the gun so the ejection port is facing down and slightly retract the charging handle until the cartridge falls free. At that point, you are clear to reload and fire.

3. New Rifles

556 Tactical LLC: Stryke-15

Aero Precision: M4E1 16-in. 5.56

Aero Precision: M4E1 16-in. .223 Wylde

556 TACTICAL LLC

STRYKE-15

Action: semi-auto
Stock: B5 Systems Bravo
Barrel: 16-in. M4 profile, 1:9 or 1:7 (barrel options can be changed)
Sights: Optics ready
Weight: N/A
Caliber: 5.56 NATO
Magazine: Two 30-round (where allowed by law)
Features: 556 Tactical Evo Rail System in choice of 7-in., 9-in., 10-in., 11-in., 12.37-in., or 15-in. Rail System or the new 556 Tactical SKR Rail System in 12.1-in. or 15-in., 556 Tactical forged matched upper/lower receivers hard anodize finish type III, 556 Tactical Stryker Series compensator or StrykeHyde Flash Hider, B5 Systems Grip, NoMar Sling Plate. Includes black tactical, Cerakote options available.
MSRP: **$1,295**

ACCURATE ARMORY

AAR-10

Action: semi-auto
Stock: N/A
Barrel: 1:11 twist, 416R stainless steel

Sights: Flip-up rear sight (not included on upper)
Weight: N/A
Caliber: .308
Magazine: One 20-round
Features: Barrels are custom machined from match-grade 416R stainless steel featuring Caudle 3 land polygonal rifling. Shot peened and MP tested bolt,TiN or nickel-boron, carrier with properly staked carrier key,TiN or nickel-boron, Lantac Flash Suppressor, or silencer mount of choice, 5/8 x 24 threads. Extended feed ramps, MP HP tested with certification, in house Cerakote finish of choice, mid-length gas system, forged flat-top upper receiver, patent-pending CMR rail system is a lightweight, rugged, one piece, free float hand guard that, when installed, gives the upper a continuous twelve o'clock rail.
MSRP: . . . . **Starts at $2,995 without optics, scope or mounts**

AERO PRECISION

M4E1 16-IN. 5.56

Action: semi-auto
Stock: Magpul STR

Barrel: 16-in. Mid 5.56, 4150 CMV, QPQ Finish, 1:7 twist
Sights: Not included
Weight: 6.5–7 lb.
Caliber: 5.56 NATO
Magazine: None
Features: 7075-T6 forged aluminum upper and lower, matte black hard coat anodized mil-spec 8625 type III class II finish, properly staked M16 phosphate BCG, mil-spec buffer kit, A2 flash hider, Magpul MOE grip. *Available in 12-in. and 15-in. KeyMod, Quad Rail, and M-LOK free float handguard configurations.
MSRP: . . . . **Starting at $974**

M4E1 16-IN. .223 WYLDE

Action: semi-auto
Stock: Magpul STR
Barrel: 16-in. Mid .223 Wylde, 416 stainless steel, bead blasted finish, 1:8 twist
Sights: Not included
Weight: 6.5–7 lb.
Caliber: .223 Wylde
Magazine: Not included
Features: 7075-T6 forged aluminum upper and lower, matte black hard coat anodized mil-spec 8625 type III class II finish, properly staked M16 phosphate BCG, mil-spec buffer kit, A2 flash hider, Magpul MOE grip. *Available in 12-in. and 15-in. KeyMod, Quad Rail, and M-LOK free float handguard configurations.
MSRP: . . . . **Starting at $999**

Anderson Manufacturing: AM15-M4 Tiger

BCI Defense, LLC: SQS15 Professional Series Model

ALEX PRO FIREARMS

22-250

Action: semi-auto
Stock: Magpul Moe Rifle
Barrel: 24-in. stainless steel Nitride finish, 1:14 twist rifle-length gas system
Sights: None
Weight: N/A
Caliber: 22 250 Rem.
Magazine: One 8-round APF (patent pending)
Features: NiB BCG, 15.5-in. T-mod free-float rail.
MSRP: .... **Black $1,874 or FDE $1,974**

AMERICAN SPIRIT ARMS

ASA- 308-SPR SCR

Action: semi-auto
Stock: 6-position mil-spec dia. receiver extension. Vltor Emod collapsible butt stock
Barrel: 18-in. mid-length gas heavy barrel, 416R stainless steel match, 1:10 RH twist, threaded 5/8x24
Sights: Optional flip up sights
Weight: 8.8 lb. unloaded
Overall Length: 37.5–41-in.
Caliber: 7.62x51 (.308)
Magazine: 10, 20, 25 round
Features: 7075 side charging receiver with mil-spec 1913 rail, 7075 lower receiver, Samson EVO 12-in. rail, ASA 4 lb. single-stage trigger, lifetime warranty, accuracy guarantee ½ to 1 MOA.
MSRP: **$2,799**

ANDERSON MANUFACTURING

AM15-M4 TIGER

Action: semi-auto
Stock: Magpul
Barrel: 16-inch M4 counter 4140, 1:8 twist
Sights: None, optics ready
Weight: 6.3 lb. without magazine
Caliber: .223/5.56 NATO
Magazine: One 30-round
Features: Forged 7075-T6 receiver, tiger-striped upper, Anderson's EXT free float forearm, Anderson Knight Stalker flash hider, low-profile gas block, match-grade trigger and hammer, standard charging handle, ambidextrous sling mounts.
MSRP: .... **N/A**

BARNES PRECISION MACHINE, INC.

LR10 20-IN. AND CQB10 16-IN.

Action: semi-auto
Stock: Magpul PRS /MOE Rifle on LR10, or Magpul MOE carbine on CQB10
Barrel: 1:10 twist 20-in., 16-in. stainless steel Nitro Met processed, with M118 LR chamber, 20-in. full-length gas system, 16-in. mid-length gas system
Sights: Magpul MBUS
Weight: LR10 9.7 lb., CQB10 8.9 lb.
Caliber: .308/7.62
Magazine: Magpul 20-round included—works with Magpul/Lancer/KAC SR25

Features: Mil-spec type III hard coat anodized upper and lower receivers, machined from 7075 billet aluminum; Geissele or HiperFire trigger group; Barnes Precision Machine PSFFRS (Picatinny Spec free-float rail system) with proprietary long barrel nut design, for unmatched rigidity of free-float rail system—with four hardened steel sling swivel inserts, bipod mount, Magpul 5/9 slot rail sections, used by top military, law enforcement, 3 Gun competitors worldwide; nickel-boron processed bolt carrier group; "Heavy Metal" buffer system for the ultimate in recoil reduction, enhanced reliability; BPMA2 flash hider/breeching tip, available with Miculek-style muzzlebrake for the ultimate in reduction of muzzle flip/recoil. Users manual, warranty. Shipped in a Patriot Cases hard case.
MSRP: **CQB10 16-in. $2,550 LR10 20-in. $2,700**

BCI DEFENSE, LLC

SQS15 PROFESSIONAL SERIES MODEL

Action: semi-auto
Stock: Enhanced 6-position stock with quick disconnect socket
Barrel: Slim profile 16-In. Ultralight Nitride Barrel with low profile gas block
Sights: Optional
Weight: 5.91 lb.
Caliber: 5.56mm, .223 Rem. operation
Magazine: One 30-round

BCI Defense, LLC: SQS15 Sentry Model

Black Dawn Armory: BDR-10 (243-22W)

Black Dawn Armory: BDR- 50 (16LMR)

Features: Upper, lower, 15-in. BCID rail, flash hider; enhanced winter trigger guard; BCID "PTC" (Positive Thumb Curve) ambi safety selector; enhanced charging handle and receiver extension (buffer tube) by BCI Defense; machined seamless from 7075-T6 aluminum; type III class II anodizing or Cerakote. Upper receiver enhancements include M4 feed ramps and Dry Teflon lubricant; Azimuth Enhanced Nitride bolt carrier group, ALG Defense Trigger (ACT Trigger), and Upgraded ERGO Grip. Each rifle ships with cable lock, 30-round magazine and lifetime guarantee card. Available in multiple Cerakote colors.
MSRP: **$1,149**

SQS15 SENTRY MODEL

Action: semi-auto
Stock: 6-position stock with quick disconnect socket
Barrel: SOCOM profile 16-in. Nitride barrel w/ Picatinny rail gas block
Sights: Optional
Weight: 6.34 lb.
Caliber: 5.56mm, .223 Rem. operation
Magazine: One 30-round
Features: Upper, lower, winter trigger guard; charging handle and receiver extension (buffer tube) by BCI Defense; machined seamless from 7075-T6 aluminum; type III class II anodizing; upper receiver

enhancements include M4 feed ramps and dry teflon lubricant; Azimuth mil-spec Nitride bolt carrier group, ALG Defense trigger (QMS trigger), and free float quad rail. Each rifle ships with cable lock, 30-round magazine, and lifetime warranty card.
MSRP: **$895**

BLACK DAWN ARMORY

BDR-10 (308-16XKR)

Action: semi-auto
Stock: Mapgul MOE collapsible
Barrel: 16-in., 4150 Nitride medium profile, 1:10 twist
Sights: None (A4 flat top for optics)
Weight: 8.6 lb.
Caliber: .308 Win.
Magazine: One 20-round
Features: Mil-spec type III hard coat anodized upper and lower; forged 7075-T6 aluminum, 12-in. free float KeyMod rail; nickel-boron BCG, ALG QMS trigger; billet CH with badger latch; adjustable gas block; hard case and ACC; lifetime warranty.
MSRP: **$1,799**

BDR-10 (18ZKL)

Action: semi-auto
Stock: Magpul MOE rifle
Barrel: 18-in., 4150 Nitride medium profile, 1:10
Sights: None (A4 flat top for optics)
Weight: 9.5 lb.

Caliber: .308 Win.
Magazine: One 20-round
Features: Mil-spec type III hard coat anodized upper & lower, forged 7075-T6 aluminum, 15-in. free float KeyMod rail, nickel-boron BCG, ALG QMS trigger, billet CH with badger latch, adjustable gas block, hard case + ACC, lifetime warranty.
MSRP: **$1,999**

BDR-10 (243-22W)

Action: semi-auto
Stock: Magpul MOE rifle
Barrel: 22-in., stainless medium, profile 1:8
Sights: None (A4 flat top for optics)
Weight: 10.6 lb.
Caliber: .243 Win.
Magazine: One 20-round
Features: Mil-spec-type III hard coat anodized upper & lower, forged 7075-T6 aluminum, 15-in. free-float KeyMod rail, nickel-boron bolt carrier group, QMS trigger, billet charging handle with Badger latch, adjustable gas block, hard case, lifetime warranty.
MSRP: **$1,999**

BDR-50 (16LMR)

Action: semi-auto
Stock: Magpul MOE collapsible
Barrel: 16-in. stainless barrel, 1:12
Sights: None (A4 flat top for optics)
Weight: 9.6 lb.
Caliber: 12.7x42

Black Dawn Armory: BDP-300 (8SFC)

Christensen Arms: CA-15 C-2

Christensen Arms: CA-15 VTac 3G

CMMG: MK47 Mutant AKM

Magazine: One 30-round
Features: Mil-spec-type III hard coat anodized upper & lower, forged 7075-T6 aluminum, 12-in. free-float MMR rail, QMS trigger, hard case, lifetime warranty.
MSRP: **$1,519**

BDP-300 (8SFC)

Action: semi-auto
Stock: None
Barrel: 8-in.
Sights: None (A4 flat top for optics)
Weight: 6.5 lb.
Caliber: 300 BLK
Magazine: One 30-round
Features: Mil-spec type III hard coat anodized upper & lower, forged 7075-T6 aluminum, Odin Works pistol buffer tube, ion bond bolt carrier group, ALG QMS trigger, 7-in. free-float rail, lifetime warranty.
MSRP: **$1,199**

CHRISTENSEN ARMS

CA-15 C-2

Action: semi-auto, direct impingement
Stock: Magpul CTR

Barrel: 416R stainless steel, button-rifled, match-grade, fluted light target; 16-in., 18-in., 20-in., and 24-in. length
Sights: N/A
Weight: 5.7 lb.
Caliber: .204 Ruger, .223 Wylde, 300 BLK
Magazine: Magpul 30-round
Features: Guaranteed SUB MOA accuracy; billet machined upper and lower; carbon fiber handguard—in either KeyMod or M-LOK configuration, match trigger, stainless steel flash suppressor.
MSRP: **$2,000**

CA-15 VTAC 3G

Action: semi-auto, direct impingement
Stock: BCM Gunfighter
Barrel: 416R stainless steel, button-rifled, match-grade, fluted light target contour OR carbon fiber-wrapped target contour; 16-in.; 1:8 twist rate
Sights: N/A
Weight: 5.6 lb.
Caliber: .223 Wylde
Magazine: Magpul 30-round
Features: guaranteed SUB MOA

accuracy; billet machined upper and lower; carbon fiber handguard—in either KeyMod or M-LOK configuration, low-mass bolt carrier; adjustable gas block; stainless steel or titanium side baffle muzzle brake.
MSRP: . . . . **$2,700–$2,900**

CMMG

MK47 MUTANT T

Action: semi-auto
Stock: A4 6 position collapsible stock
Barrel: 16.1-in. medium taper profile
Sights: N/A
Weight: 7 lb.
Caliber: 7.62x39mm
Magazine: Magpul PMAG 30 AK/AKM MOE
Features: The Mk47 MUTANT utilizes a unique bolt carrier group derived from the massive AR-10 group, which aside from being shortened to a length of 8 inches, retains all of the material on the bolt face for added durability and strength.
MSRP: **$1,499**

CMMG: MK47 Mutant AKM 2

MK47 MUTANT AKM

Action: semi-auto
Stock: Magpul CTR
Barrel: 16.1-in. medium taper profile
Sights: N/A
Weight: 7 lb.
Caliber: 7.62x39mm
Magazine: Magpul PMAG 30 AK/AKM MOE
Features: The Mk47 MUTANT utilizes a unique bolt carrier group derived from the massive AR-10 group, which aside from being shortened to a length of eight inches, retains all of the material on the bolt face for added durability and strength.
MSRP: **$1,649**

MK47 MUTANT AKM 2

Action: semi-auto
Stock: Magpul CTR
Barrel: 16.1-in. medium taper profile
Sights: N/A
Weight: 7 lb.
Caliber: 7.62x39mm
Magazine: Magpul PMAG 30 AK/AKM MOE
Features: The Mk47 Mutant features a Geissele SSA two-stage trigger and utilizes a unique bolt carrier group derived from the massive AR10 group, which aside from being shortened to a length of eight inches, retains all of the material on the bolt face for added durability and strength.
MSRP: **$1,849**

COLT

EXPANSE M4

Action: semi-auto, direct gas system
Stock: Matte black, six-position adjustable stock
Barrel: 16.1-in, 6-groove, 1:7 RH twist, non-chrome lined barrel
Sights: Adjustable post front sight, no rear sight
Weight: 6.44 lb.
Caliber: 5.56
Magazine: 30 round
Features: N/A
MSRP: **$699**

DANIEL DEFENSE

DD5V1

Action: Mid-length direct impingement
Stock: Daniel Defense buttstock and pistol grip with Soft Touch overmolding
Barrel: Cold hammer forged, chromoly vanadium steel, 16-in. S2W profile, mid-length gas system, chrome lined, mil-spec heavy phosphate coated, MP tested, with 4-bolt connection system
Sights: None
Weight: 8.3 lb.
Caliber: 7.62mm NATO
Magazine: 20 round (SR-25)
Handguard: DD5 handguard with KeyMod attachment on sides/bottom and continuous Picatinny rail on top.
Features: Lower receiver with ambidextrous controls, Geissele SSA two-stage trigger, integral oversized trigger guard, enhanced magazine well, rear receiver QD swivel attachment point, optimized upper receiver with indexing marks and extended feed ramps, improved bolt carrier group with properly staked gas key and low friction coating, pinned low-profile gas block, Daniel Defense Superior Suppression Device Ext, custom Daniel Defense full-latch impact plastic case, lifetime satisfaction guarantee, made in the United States.
MSRP: **$2,899**

M4 CARBINE, V7 & V7LW

Action: Mid-length direct impingement
Stock: Daniel Defense buttstock and pistol grip with Soft Touch overmolding
Barrel: Cold hammer forged, chromoly vanadium steel, 16-in. government profile or lightweight profile, mid-length gas system, chrome lined, mil-spec heavy phosphate coated, MP tested
Sights: None
Weight: 6.20 lb. & 6.05 lb. (LW)
Caliber: 5.56mm NATO
Magazine: 30 round
Handguard: MFR XS 15.0 handguard with M-LOK attachment on sides/bottom and continuous Picatinny rail on top.
Features: Mil-spec lower receiver with enhanced magazine well, rear receiver QD swivel attachment point, mil-spec upper receiver with indexing marks and M4 feed ramps, mil-spec MP-tested bolt carrier group with properly staked gas key, pinned low-profile gas block, Daniel Defense Flash Suppressor, custom Daniel Defense full-latch impact plastic case, lifetime satisfaction guarantee, made in the United States.
MSRP: **$1,599**

DPMS: GII AP4

M4 CARBINE, V4S

Action: Carbine length direct impingement
Stock: Daniel Defense buttstock and pistol grip with Soft Touch overmolding
Barrel: Cold hammer forged, chrome-moly vanadium steel, 11.5-in. government profile, carbine-length gas system, chrome lined, mil-spec heavy phosphate coated, MP tested
Sights: None
Weight: 5.85 lb.
Caliber: 5.56mm NATO
Magazine: 30 round
Handguard: DDM4 Rail 10.0 handguard with 1913 Picatinny rail attachment and QD attachment points front and back on both sides.
Features: Mil-spec lower receiver with enhanced magazine well, rear receiver QD swivel attachment point, mil-spec upper receiver with indexing marks and M4 feed ramps, mil-spec MP-tested bolt carrier group with properly staked gas key, pinned low-profile gas block, Daniel Defense Flash Suppressor, custom Daniel Defense full-latch impact plastic case, lifetime satisfaction guarantee, made in the United States.
MSRP: **$1,689**

M4 CARBINE, 300S

Action: Pistol-length direct impingement
Stock: Daniel Defense buttstock and pistol grip with Soft Touch overmolding
Barrel: Cold hammer forged, chromoly vanadium steel, 10.3-in. S2W profile, pistol-length gas system, salt bath Nitride treated, MP tested
Sights: None
Weight: 5.77 lb.
Caliber: 300 BLK
Magazine: 30 round
Handguard: DDM4 Rail 9.0 handguard with 1913 Picatinny rail attachment and QD attachment points front and back on both sides.
Features: Mil-spec lower receiver with enhanced magazine well, rear receiver QD swivel attachment point, mil-spec upper receiver with indexing marks and M4 feed ramps, mil-spec MP-tested bolt carrier group with properly staked gas key, pinned low-profile gas block, Daniel Defense Flash Suppressor, custom Daniel Defense full-latch impact plastic case, lifetime satisfaction guarantee, made in the United States.
MSRP: **$1,749**

M4 CARBINE, V11 & V11LW

Action: Mid-length direct impingement
Stock: Daniel Defense Buttstock and pistol grip with Soft Touch Overmolding
Barrel: Cold hammer forged, chromoly vanadium steel, 16-in. government profile or lightweight profile, mid-length gas system, chrome lined, mil-spec heavy phosphate coated, MP tested
Sights: None
Weight: 6.28 lb. and 6.15 lb. (LW)
Caliber: 5.56mm NATO
Magazine: 30 round
Handguard: SLiM rail 15.0 handguard with KeyMod attachment on sides, bottom, and continuous Picatinny rail on top.
Features: Mil-spec lower receiver with enhanced magazine well, rear receiver QD swivel attachment point, mil-spec upper receiver with indexing marks and M4 feed ramps, mil-spec MP-tested bolt carrier group with properly staked gas key, pinned low-profile gas block, Daniel Defense Flash Suppressor, custom Daniel Defense full-latch impact plastic case, lifetime satisfaction guarantee, made in the United States.
MSRP: **$1,599**

M4 CARBINE, V11SLW

Action: Mid-length direct impingement
Stock: Daniel Defense buttstock and pistol grip with Soft Touch overmolding
Barrel: Cold hammer forged, chromoly vanadium steel, 14.5-in. lightweight profile, mid-length gas system, chrome lined, mil-spec heavy phosphate coated, MP tested
Sights: None
Weight: 6.09 lb.
Caliber: 5.56mm NATO
Magazine: 30 round
Handguard: SLiM rail 12.0 handguard with KeyMod attachment on sides, bottom, and continuous Picatinny rail on top.
Features: Mil-spec lower receiver with enhanced magazine well, rear receiver QD swivel attachment point, mil-spec upper receiver with indexing marks and M4 feed ramps, mil-spec MP-tested bolt carrier group with properly staked gas key, pinned low-profile gas block, pinned and welded Daniel Defense Flash Suppressor, custom Daniel Defense full-latch impact plastic case, lifetime satisfaction guarantee, made in the United States.
MSRP: **$1,669**

DPMS

GII AP4

Action: semi-auto
Stock: M4 6-position collapsible, Glacier Guard handguard, A2 pistol grip
Barrel: 16-in lightweight 4150 chromelined, 1:10 twist, cancellation brake flash hider
Sights: F-marked front sight base, Magpul BUIS
Weight: 7.25 lb.

DPMS: GII Recon

DPMS: GII MOE

DPMS: GII SASS

DPMS: GII Hunter

Caliber: .308/7.62 NATO
Magazine: N/A
Features: Forged 7075-T6 Lvl 3 anodized, Teflon-coated lower and upper.
MSRP: **$1,399**

GII RECON

Action: semi-auto
Stock: Magpul MOE 6-position collapsible, DPMS 4 Rail free float tube, Magpul MOE pistol grip
Barrel: 16-in 416 stainless, bead blasted mid-length, 1:10 twist, Advanced Armament 51T Blackout Silencer adapter
Sights: Magpul front and rear BUIS
Weight: 8.5 lb.
Caliber: .308/7.62 NATO
Magazine: N/A
Features: Forged 7075-T6 Lvl 3 anodized, Teflon-coated lower and upper.
MSRP: **$1,659**

GII MOE

Action: semi-auto
Stock: Magpul MOE carbine stock, MOE carbine-length AR-15/M16 handguard, Magpul MOE pistol grip
Barrel: 16-in lightweight, 4150 chromelined, 1:10 twist, cancellation brake flash hider
Sights: F marked front sight base, Magpul BUIS
Weight: 7.25 lb.
Caliber: .308/7.62 NATO
Magazine: N/A
Features: Forged 7075-T6 Lvl 3 anodized, Teflon-coated lower and upper.
MSRP: **$1,499**

GII SASS

Action: semi-auto
Stock: Magpul PRS rifle stock, DPMS 4 Rail free float tube, Panther Tactical pistol grip

Barrel: 18-in 416 stainless, Teflon-coated, fluted bull barrel, mid-length, 1:10 twist, Panther flash hider
Sights: Magpul front and rear BUIS
Weight: 10.5 lb.
Caliber: .308/7.62 NATO
Magazine: N/A
Features: Forged 7075-T6 Lvl 3 anodized, Teflon-coated lower and upper.
MSRP: **$2,279**

GII HUNTER

Action: semi-auto
Stock: Magpul MOE stock, DPMS carbon-fiber free-float tube, Hogue pistol grip
Barrel: 20-in 416 stainless, Teflon-coated, 1:10 twist
Sights: None
Weight: 7.76 lb.
Caliber: .308/7.62 NATO
Magazine: N/A
Features: Forged 7075-T6 Lvl 3 anodized, Teflon-coated lower and upper.
MSRP: **$1,599**

DPMS: GII Bull

FN 15 Tactical 300 BLK

Heckler & Koch: MR762A1 II

GII BULL

Action: semi-auto
Stock: DPMS carbon-fiber free-float tube, A2 pistol grip
Barrel: 24-in 416 stainless bull, 1:10 twist
Sights: None
Weight: 10 lb.
Caliber: .308/7.62 NATO
Magazine: N/A
Features: Forged 7075-T6 Lvl 3 anodized, Teflon-coated lower and upper.
MSRP: **$1,299**

GII COMPACT HUNTER

Action: semi-auto
Stock: B5 Sopmod stock, carbon-fiber free-float tube, Hogue pistol grip
Barrel: 16-in mid-length 416 stainless, Teflon-coated, 1:10 twist
Sights: None
Weight: 6.9 lb.
Caliber: .308/7.62 NATO
Magazine: N/A
Features: Forged 7075-T6 Lvl 3 anodized, Teflon-coated lower and upper, DPMS two-stage trigger.
MSRP: **$1,599**

FN

FN 15 COMPETITION

Action: semi-auto
Stock: Magpul MOE SL buttsock, Magpul MOE grip, Mega Arms rail system with M-LOK

Barrel: 18-in. match-grade cold hammer-forged chrome-lined, 1:8 RH twist, SureFire ProComp 556 muzzle break
Sights: Magpul MBUS sights
Weight: 8.1 lb.
Caliber: 5.56
Magazine: 30-round Magpul PMAG
Features: Hard anodized aluminum billet upper and lower from 7075-T651 aluminum, anodized blue, ambidextrous bolt catch release, nickel-boron carrier bolt assembly, Timney competiton trigger.
MSRP: **$2,249**

FN 15 TACTICAL 300 BLK

Action: semi-auto
Stock: Magpul MOE SL buttsock, Magpul MOE grip, Midwest Industries LWM 12-in. handguard with M-LOK
Barrel: 18-in. match-grade cold hammer-forged chrome-lined, 1.7 RH twist, SureFire ProComp 556 muzzle break
Sights: Magpul MBUS sights
Weight: 6.6 lb.
Caliber: 300 BLK
Magazine: 30-round Magpul PMAG
Features: hard anodized aluminum billet upper and lower from 7075-T651 aluminum, anodized blue, ambidextrous bolt catch release, nickel-boron carrier bolt assembly, Timney competiton trigger.
MSRP: **$1,479**

HECKLER & KOCH

MR762A1 II

Action: semi-auto gas operated
Stock: Adjustable buttstock 5 positions, 80mm of travel with movable cheek rest
Barrel: 16.5 in.
Sights: No mechanical sights, Leupold 3-9VX-R Patrol 3-9x40mm
Weight: 10.58 lb
Caliber: 7.62mm
Magazine: 10- to 20-round capacity
Features: Rifle with empty magazine, mounted scope, and bipod 13.3 lb.
MSRP: **$3,999**

HM DEFENSE

HM15F-556

Action: semi-auto
Stock: Magpul MOE
Barrel: 16 in. chromoly spiral fluted Triple Honed HBAR, 1:8 twist
Sights: None
Weight: 6 lb. 9 oz
Caliber: 5.56 Nato/.223
Magazine: Magpul PMAG
Features: Full billet upper and lower black colored type III hard anodized, 14-in. length black colored Picatinny rail, CNC machined V1-556 black flash hider, MOE Magpul black grip, HM QD end plate, CNC machined steel gas block, carbine gas system.
MSRP: . . . . **N/A**

Iron Ridge Arms: IRA-X -THOR

Iron Ridge Arms: IRA-X -THOR-S

Kavod Custom: VPS-15 9mm Suppressed SBR

IRON RIDGE ARMS

IRA-X -THOR/ THOR-S

Action: semi-auto
Stock: Magpul PRS. type/ or customer choice
Barrel: Bartlein barrels/ Obermeyer/ Chandlin barrel options per customer specs/14.5-in. ATF SOT class III item, 16-in., 18-in., 20-in., 22-in., 24-in., 26-in.
Sights: Magpul iron sights or customer choice
Weight: 8.5–13 lb.
Caliber: .308
Magazine: 5, 10, 15, 20, 25 round
Features: Mil-spec ano type III/ Iron Armor ceramic coating, oversized HD upper and lower construction, SureFire Muzzle break rifle cut barrels, Iron Ridge Gen II custom manufactured triggers.
MSRP: **$4,200**

JARD

J17

Action: semi-auto

Stock: AR style
Barrel: 20 in.
Sights: None
Weight: 8 lb.
Caliber: .17 WSM/.17 HMR
Magazine: 10 round, 20 round optional
Features: N/A
MSRP: . . . . **$1,191–$1,392**

J23

Action: semi-auto
Stock: None
Barrel: 7 inch
Sights: None
Weight: 4 lb.
Caliber: .223 Wylde
Magazine: AR style
Features: AR style pistol.
MSRP: **$1,009**

J24

Action: semi-auto
Stock: AR style
Barrel: 22-in. varmint weight, fluted
Sights: None
Weight: 7 lb.
Caliber: .223 Wylde, .204 Ruger

Magazine: AR style
Features: Large diameter barrel thread
MSRP: **$1,181**

KAVOD CUSTOM

VPS-15 9MM SUPPRESSED SBR

Action: semi-auto
Stock: Magpul stealth gray MOE mil-spec
Barrel: 8.5-in. Nitride coated 1:10 twist threaded ½x36
Sights: None
Weight: 6 lb. with suppressor
Caliber: 9mm
Magazine: Two 32-round
Features: Free-floating 13-in. aluminum handguard with continuous top rail and three rail stubs. Magpul stealth gray trigger guard, MOE stock, and MOE+ rubber coated grip. 8.5-in. barrel with removable Gemtech Tundra suppressor. Includes conversion parts to mount the suppressor on a barrel threaded ½x28 for use on a pistol. Requires two NFA tax stamps (SBR and Suppressor).
MSRP: **$1,750**

KNIGHTS ARMAMENT

SR-15 CQB MOD 2 M-LOK

Action: semi-auto
Stock: URX4 M-LOK handguard, 6-position stock
Barrel: 11.5-in. hammer-forged chrome-lined barrel, 1:7 twist, 3-prong flash hider
Sights: Flip-up sights
Weight: 6.1 lb.
Caliber: 5.56
Magazine: N/A
Features: Two-stage match trigger, ambidextrous controls.
MSRP: . . . . **N/A**

SR-15 E3 CARBINE MOD 2 M-LOK

Action: semi-auto
Stock: URX4 M-LOK handguard, 6-position stock
Barrel: 14.5-in. hammer-forged chrome-lined barrel, 1:7 twist, 3-prong flash hider
Sights: Flip-up sights
Weight: 6.4 lb.
Caliber: 5.56
Magazine: N/A
Features: Two-stage match trigger, ambidextrous controls.
MSRP: . . . . **N/A**

SR-15 E3 MOD 2 M-LOK

Action: semi-auto
Stock: URX4 M-LOK handguard, 6-position stock
Barrel: 16-in. hammer-forged chrome-lined barrel, 1:7 twist, 3-prong flash hider
Sights: Flip-up sights
Weight: 6.55 lb.
Caliber: 5.56
Magazine: N/A
Features: Two-stage match trigger, ambidextrous controls.
MSRP: . . . . **N/A**

SR-15 E3 LPR MOD 2 M-LOK

Action: semi-auto
Stock: URX4 M-LOK handguard, 6-position stock

Barrel: 18-in. stainless steel barrel, 1:7 twist, 3-prong flash hider
Sights: Flip-up sights
Weight: 7.4 lb.
Caliber: 5.56
Magazine: N/A
Features: Two-stage match trigger, ambidextrous controls.
MSRP: . . . . **N/A**

SR-25 E2 ACC M-LOK

Action: semi-auto
Stock: 6-position stock
Barrel: 16-in. 5R cut, chrome-lined barrel, 1:10 twist, 7.62 QDC flash suppressor
Sights: Flip-up sights
Weight: 8.4 lb.
Caliber: 7.62 NATO/.308
Magazine: N/A
Features: Two-stage match trigger, ambidextrous controls.
MSRP: . . . . **N/A**

SR-25 E2 APC M-LOK

Action: semi-auto
Stock: 6-position stock
Barrel: 16-in. 5R cut, chrome-lined barrel, 1:10 twist, 7.62 QDC flash suppressor
Sights: Flip-up sights
Weight: 9 lb.
Caliber: 7.62 NATO/.308
Magazine: N/A
Features: Two-stage match trigger, ambidextrous controls.
MSRP: . . . . **N/A**

SR-25 E2 APR M-LOK

Action: semi-auto
Stock: 6-position stock
Barrel: 20-in. 5R cut, chrome-lined barrel, 1:10 twist, 7.62 QDC flash suppressor
Sights: Flip-up sights
Weight: 10.5 lb.
Caliber: 7.62 NATO/.308
Magazine: N/A
Features: Two-stage match trigger, ambidextrous controls.
MSRP: . . . . **N/A**

SR-30 M-LOK

Action: semi-auto
Stock: 6-position stock
Barrel: 9.5-in. chrome-lined barrel, 1:7 twist, QDC flash suppressor
Sights: Flip-up sights
Weight: 6.2 lb.
Caliber: 300 BLK
Magazine: N/A
Features: Two-stage match trigger, ambidextrous controls.
MSRP: . . . . **N/A**

LEWIS MACHINE & TOOL

CQB16-MARS

Action: semi-auto
Stock: LMT SOPMOD buttstock
Barrel: 16-in. chrome-lined 1:7 twist
Sights: LMT tactical adjustable rear and tactical front
Weight: 7.3 lb.
Caliber: 5.56
Magazine: Standard AR-15 type
Features: Monolithic upper featuring ambi charging handle with tactical latch assembly, ambi selector, ambi mag release, ambi bolt catch/release, available with winter trigger guard, QD end plate and flared mag well.
MSRP: **$2,347**

MRP16-MARS

Action: semi-auto
Stock: LMT SOPMOD buttstock
Barrel: 16-in. chrome-lined 1:7 twist
Sights: LMT tactical adjustable rear and tactical front
Weight: 7.9 lb.
Caliber: 5.56
Magazine: Standard AR-15 type
Features: Rifle length monolithic upper featuring ambi charging handle with tactical latch assembly, ambi selector, ambi mag release, ambi bolt catch/release available with winter trigger guard, QD end plate, and flared mag well.
MSRP: **$2,633**

Lewis Machine & Tool: LM8MRP-MARS

Lewis Machine & Tool: LM8PDW

Lewis Machine & Tool: LM8MRP-SC

LM8MRP-MARS

Action: semi-auto
Stock: LMT SOPMOD buttstock
Barrel: 16-in. chrome lined 1:7 twist
Sights: LMT tactical adjustable rear and tactical front
Weight: 7 lb.
Caliber: 5.56
Magazine: Standard AR-15 type
Features: Slick monolithic upper featuring ambi charging handle with tactical latch assembly, ambi selector, ambi mag release, ambi bolt catch/release, available with winter trigger guard, QD end plate, and flared mag well.
MSRP: $2,574

LM8PDW

Action: semi-auto
Stock: Modified LMT SOPMOD buttstock
Barrel: 10.5-in. chrome-lined 1:7 twist
Sights: LMT flip-up sights
Weight: 7 lb.
Caliber: 5.56 or 300 BLK
Magazine: Standard AR-15 type
Features: Modified, shortened LMT SOPMOD stock, extension tube,

redesigned buffer, and buffer spring with a drop-in weight for the bolt carrier, overall length reduced to 24.5-in.
MSRP: $2,691

LM8MRP-SC (SLK8)

Action: semi-auto
Stock: LMT SOPMOD buttstock
Barrel: 16-in. blackened stainless steel 1:7 twist, 5R cut
Sights: N/A
Weight: 7.3 lb.
Caliber: 5.56
Magazine: 30 round
Features: Long, slick monolithic upper receiver, tactical charging handle, two-stage match trigger, ambi selector.
MSRP: $2,525
California Legal: $2,545

LM8MWS

Action: semi-auto
Stock: LMT SOPMOD buttstock
Barrel: 16-in. chrome lined 1:10 twist
Sights: LMT tactical adjustable rear and tactical front
Weight: 10.03 lb.
Caliber: .308
Magazine: 20 round

Features: Slick monolithic upper receiver, tactical charging handle, two-stage trigger, ambi selector and ambi mag release.
MSRP: $3,306
California Legal: $3,356

LM8MWS-F

Action: semi-auto
Stock: LMT SOPMOD buttstock
Barrel: 16-in. blackened stainless steel 1:11 twist
Sights: LMT tactical adjustable rear and tactical front
Weight: 10.03 lb.
Caliber: .308
Magazine: 20 round
Features: Slick monolithic upper receiver, tactical charging handle, two-stage trigger, ambi selector and ambi mag release.
MSRP: $3,306
California Legal: $3,356

LM8MWS-LT

Action: semi-auto
Stock: LMT SOPMOD buttstock
Barrel: Lightweight 16-in. chrome-lined 1:10 twist

Sights: LMT tactical adjustable rear and tactical front
Weight: 9.37 lb.
Caliber: .308
Magazine: 20 round
Features: Slick monolithic upper receiver, tactical charging handle, two-stage trigger, ambi selector, and ambi mag release.
MSRP: **$3,356**
California Legal: **$3,406**

LWRC DI 5.56

Action: semi-auto, direct impingement
Stock: LWRCI adjustable compact stock, modular one-piece free-float rail, angled ergonomic foregrip w/ QD sling point, rail panels and hand stop, Magpul MOE grip
Barrel: 16.1-in, 1:7 RH, A2 birdcage flash hider
Sights: N/A
Weight: 6.6 lb.
Caliber: 5.56
Magazine: N/A
Features: LWRCI proprietary DI bolt carrier group; fully ambidextrous lower controls, mag release, bolt catch/release; enhanced fire control group.
MSRP: . . . . **N/A**

IC A5 INDIVIDUAL CARBINE

Action: LWRCI patented short stroke gas piston, semi-auto
Stock: LWRCI adjustable compact stock
Barrel: 10.5-in., 14.7-in., 16.1-in. LWRCI NiCorr treated cold hammer forged spiral fluted barrel, 1:7 RH rifling
Sights: LWRCI Skirmish BUIS
Weight: 7 lb.
Caliber: 5.56 NATO
Magazine: 10- or 30-round Magpul PMAG
Features: Monoforge upper receiver with integrated rail base, 12-in. user configurable rail system, scalloped cut rail for easy access to two-position adjustable gas block to switch between suppressed and unsuppressed shooting, full length top Picatinny rail accommodates both day and night optics, LWRCI Enhanced Fire Control

Group, dual control fully ambidextrous lower receiver includes bolt catch and release, magazine release, and fire control access from both sides of the rifle, LWRCI ambidextrous charging handle, nickel-boron coated bolt carrier for unparalled wear resistance, corrosion resistance and permanent lubricity, Magpul MOE+ grip, integrated quick detach LWRCI ambidextrous sling mount, available in anodized black and FDE/ OD green and patriot brown LWRCI Cerakote finish options.
MSRP: $2,599 black, $2,749 FDE/OD green/patriot brown Cerakote

IC PSD PERSONAL SECURITY DETAIL INDIVIDUAL CARBINE

Action: LWRCI patented short stroke gas-piston, semi-auto
Stock: LWRCI adjustable compact stock
Barrel: 8.5-in. LWRCI NiCorr treated cold hammer forged spiral fluted barrel, 1:7 RH rifling
Sights: LWRCI Skirmish BUIS
Weight: 5.9 lb.
Caliber: 5.56 NATO
Magazine: 10- or 30-round Magpul PMAG
Features: Monoforge upper receiver with LWRCI 7-in. rail system, LWRCI Enhanced Fire Control Group, dual control fully ambidextrous lower receiver includes bolt catch and release, magazine release and fire control access from both sides of the rifle, LWRCI ambidextrous charging handle, nickel-boron coated bolt carrier for unparalled wear resistance, corrosion resistance and permanent lubricity, Magpul MOE+ grip, integrated quick detach LWRCI ambidextrous sling mount, available in anodized black and FDE/ OD green and patriot brown LWRCI Cerakote finish options.
MSRP: $2,349 black, $2,499 FDE/OD green/patriot brown Cerakote

IC PSD PISTOL

Action: LWRCI patented short stroke gas-piston, semi-auto

Stock: LWRCI adjustable compact stock
Barrel: 8.5-in. LWRCI NiCorr treated cold hammer forged spiral fluted barrel, 1:7 RH rifling
Sights: LWRCI Skirmish BUIS
Weight: 5.9 lb.
Caliber: 5.56 NATO
Magazine: 10- or 30-round Magpul PMAG
Features: Monoforge upper receiver with LWRCI 7-in. rail system, LWRCI Enhanced Fire Control Group, dual control fully ambidextrous lower receiver includes bolt catch and release, magazine release and fire control access from both sides of the rifle, LWRCI ambidextrous charging handle PSD pistol buffer tube recoil system delivers IC performance on a pistol platform, nickel-boron coated bolt carrier for unparalled wear resistance, corrosion resistance and permanent lubricity, Magpul MOE+ grip, integrated quick detach LWRCI ambidextrous sling mount, available in anodized black and FDE/ OD green and patriot brown LWRCI Cerakote finish options.
MSRP: $2,229 black, $2,379 FDE/OD green/patriot brown Cerakote

IC PDW PERSONAL DEFENSE WEAPON INDIVIDUAL CARBINE

Action: LWRCI patented short stroke gas-piston, semi-auto
Stock: LWRCI PDW quick deploy 2-position
Barrel: 8.5-in. LWRCI NiCorr treated cold hammer forged spiral fluted barrel, 1:7 RH rifling
Sights: LWRCI Skirmish BUIS
Weight: 5.9 lb.
Caliber: 5.56 NATO
Magazine: 10- or 30-round Magpul PMAG
Features: Monoforge upper receiver with modular 7 rail system, NiCorr treated barrel with LWRCI compact high efficiency flash hider, LWRCI Enhanced Fire Control Group, dual control fully ambidextrous lower receiver includes bolt catch and release, magazine release and fire control access from both sides of the

rifle, LWRCI ambidextrous charging handle, nickel-boron coated bolt carrier for unparalled wear resistance, corrosion resistance and permanent lubricity, Magpul K grip, integrated quick detach LWRCI ambidextrous sling mount, LWRCI modular railskins with integrated hand stop, available in anodized black and FDE/OD green and patriot brown LWRCI Cerakote finish options.

MSRP: $2,499 black, $2,649 FDE/OD green/patriot brown Cerakote

SIX 8 A5

Action: LWRCI patented short stroke gas-piston, semi-auto
Stock: LWRCI adjustable compact stock with integral sling attachment point
Barrel: 12.7-in., 14.7-in., 16.1-in. LWRCI NiCorr treated cold hammer forged spiral fluted barrel
Sights: LWRCI Skirmish BUIS
Weight: 7.3 (16.1-in.)
Caliber: 6.8 SPC
Magazine: Proprietary Magpul high reliability magazine with high visibility follower
Features: Proprietary upper and lower receiver optimized for the 6.8 SPC cartridge, monoforge upper receiver with integrated rail base, 12-in. user configurable rail system, scalloped cut rail for easy access to two-position adjustable gas block to switch between suppressed and unsuppressed shooting, full length top Picatinny rail accommodates both day and night optics, enlarged ejection port allows unhindered ejection of 6.8 casings, advanced combat bolt in 6.8 features a fully supported bolt face, dual extractor springs and claw extractor provides 20 percent more purchase on the case rim, LWRCI Enhanced Fire Control Group, LWRCI ambidextrous charging handle, Magpul MOE+ grip, available in anodized black and FDE/ OD green and patriot brown LWRCI Cerakote finish options.

MSRP: $2,599 black, $2,749 FDE/OD green/patriot brown Cerakote

R.E.P.R.—RAPID ENGAGEMENT PRECISION RIFLE—20-IN SPIRAL

Action: LWRCI patented short stroke gas-piston semi-auto
Stock: Magpul PRS precision rifle stock
Barrel: 20-in. LWRCI NiCorr treated cold hammer forged spiral fluted barrel, 1:10 RH rifling
Sights: LWRCI Skirmish BUIS
Weight: 11.25 lb.
Caliber: 7.62 NATO
Magazine: 10- to 20-round Magpul PMAG
Features: 12.5-in. modular rail system, removable top-rail with 100 percent return to zero=no tool installation, upper and lower receivers machined from billet aluminum, two-position adjustable gas block for easy switch from normal to suppressed shooting, side-mounted, non reciprocating charging handle, Geissele SSA two-stage trigger, nickel-boron coated bolt carrier for unparalled wear resistance, corrosion resistance and permanent lubricity, Magpul MOE+ grip, LWRCI A2 birdcage flash hider, available in anodized black and FDE/ OD green and patriot brown LWRCI Cerakote finish options.

MSRP: $3,950 black, $4,100 FDE/OD green/patriot brown Cerakote

MGI

MGI'S SURVIVAL PACKAGE

Action: semi-auto, gas impingement
Stock: 6-position telescoping buttstock with MGI logo
Barrel: 16-in. M4 profile with A2 flash suppressor
Sights: Optics ready
Weight: 28 lb.
Caliber: 5.56, 300 BLK, 9mm SMG, 7.76x39
Magazine: 30 round
Features: N/A
MSRP: $3,299

MOSSBERG

MMR HUNTER (.308 WIN.)

Action: semi-auto
Stock: A2-style buttstock, slender checkered free floating fore-end tube
Barrel: Free floating 20-in. 1:10 twist barrel
Sights: None
Weight: N/A
Caliber: .308 Win. (7.62mm NATO)
Magazine: 5 round
Features: Single-stage trigger, Picatinny rail flat-top upper for optics, shell deflector ramp behind ejection port, available in three versions: black, Mossy Oak Treestand camo, or camo stock, fore-end and grip.
MSRP: . . . . $1,360–$1,448

OLYMPIC ARMS

MPR308-15

Action: semi-auto
Stock: A2 trapdoor
Barrel: 24-in. 1:10 416 stainless steel, National Match Button rifled barrel
Sights: Picatinny flat top, with Picatinny gas block, optics ready.
Weight: 9.9 lb.
Length: 42.75-in.
Caliber: 7.62x51 NATO, .308 Win.
Alternate caliber uppers
available in: 7mm-08
.300 Win. Short Mag
.260 Rem.
.243 Win.
Magazine: Billet aluminum—10 rounds
Features: Billet upper and lower receivers, .96-in. diameter bull barrel, rifle-length predator-style aluminum free-floating handguard, quick detachable from pivot pin assembly for switching between 5.56 and .308 uppers, threaded muzzles available, capable of accepting Olympic Arms .308-style AR uppers in a variety of calibers—plus any standard AR-15 upper of any caliber.
MSRP: $1,689

Olympic Arms: MPR308-15

Olympic Arms: MPR308-15M

Olympic Arms: MPR308-15C

MPR308-15M

Action: semi-auto
Stock: 6-position collapsible M4 style (commercial dimension)
Barrel: 18-in. 1:10 416 stainless steel, National Match button rifled barrel
Sights: Picatinny flat top, with low profile gas block, optics ready.
Weight: 8.9 lb.
Length: 34.75-in.
Caliber: 7.62x51 NATO, .308 Win.
Alt. caliber uppers available in: 7mm-08
.300 Win. Short Mag
.260 Rem.
.243 Win.
Magazine: Billet aluminum, 10 rounds
Features: Billet upper and lower receivers, .96-in. diameter bull barrel, thread muzzle (5/8x24) with thread protector, mid-length predator-style aluminum free-floating handguard, low-profile gas block under handguard, quick detachable from pivot pin assembly for switching between .308 and 5.56 uppers, threaded muzzles available, capable of accepting Olympic Arms .308-style AR uppers in a variety of calibers—PLUS any standard AR-15 upper of any caliber.
MSRP: $1,559

MPR308-15C

Action: semi-auto
Stock: 6-position collapsible M4 style (commercial dimension)

Barrel: 16-in. 1:10 416 stainless steel, National Match button rifled barrel
Sights: Picatinny flat top, with Picatinny gas block., optics ready.
Weight: 7.4 lb.
Length: 32.75-in.
Caliber: 7.62x51 NATO, .308 Win.
Alt. caliber uppers available in: 7mm-08
.300 Win. Short Mag
.260 Rem.
.243 Win.
Magazine: Billet aluminum—10 rounds
Features: Billet upper and lower receivers, .960-in. diameter bull barrel, thread muzzle (5/8x24) with thread protector, carbine-length predator-style aluminum free-floating handguard, low-profile gas block under handguard, quick detachable from pivot pin assembly for switching between .308 and 5.56 uppers, capable of accepting Olympic Arms .308-style AR uppers in a variety of calibers—PLUS any standard AR-15 upper of any caliber.
MSRP: $1,268

PEC ARMORY

556 AR-15 RIFLE

Action: semi-auto
Stock: Magpul ACS buttstock
Barrel: 16-in. M4 profile barrel, standard 1:9 twist (other twist rates available upon request)
Sights: Front and rear Magpul BUIS sights
Weight: N/A
Caliber: 5.56 NATO
Magazine: Two 30-round
Features: 7075 billet upper and lower receiver, PEC Armory proprietary 12.5-in. rail, PEC Armory micro slicked bolt carrier, standard mil-spec trigger group, available in FDE, coyote tan, OD green, graphite black, and burnt bronze.
MSRP: . . . . N/A

300 AAC BLACKOUT AR-15 RIFLE

Action: semi-auto
Stock: Magpul ACS buttstock
Barrel: 16-in. M4 profile barrel, standard 1:8 twist (other twist rates available upon request)
Sights: front and rear Magpul BUIS sights

Weight: N/A
Caliber: 300 BLK
Magazine: Two 30-round
Features: 7075 billet upper and lower receiver, PEC Armory proprietary 12.5-in. rail, PEC Armory micro slicked bolt carrier, standard mil-spec trigger group, avail in burnt bronze, graphite black, OD green, tungsten grey, coyote tan, and FDE.
MSRP: . . . . N/A

PRECISION REFLEX INC. (PRI)

MARK 12 MOD O GEN II, 07-556G2RB-SPR-17

Action: semi-auto
Stock: B5 6-position butt stock with a PRi rifle-length carbon fiber forearm.
Barrel: 18-in. Douglas stainless steel barrel with a 1:7 twist
Sights: PRi flip up front sight gas block and PRi flip up rear sight
Weight: N/A
Caliber: 5.56 NATO chamber
Magazine: 10-round PRi steel
Features: MOA accuracy, mil-spec type III hard coat anodized upper & lower, A4M4 feed ramp, forged rigid 7075 aluminum, rifle-length carbon fiber forearm with heat shield, full-length top rail and AE brake and color, operator's manual and warranty card, hard case.
MSRP: $1,975

PRIMARY WEAPONS SYSTEMS

DI-14LE RIFLE

Action: semi-auto
Stock: Standard M4 furniture
Barrel: 14.5-in.
Sights: Magpul MOE
Weight: 6 lb. 7 oz.
Caliber: .223 Wylde
Magazine: Magpul
Features: With the modern Musket rifle arriving in the PWS lineup, LE departments jumped at the chance to provide officers the expert

craftsmanship and innovative upgrades PWS is known for at an affordable cost. PWS offers an officer purchase program for approved Law Enforcement personnel and departments. Utilizing only the highest quality barrel blanks, PWS DI barrels are turned in house then Isonite QPQ treated for hardness and corrosion resistance.
MSRP: $1,399

DI-16LE RIFLE

Action: semi-auto
Stock: Standard M4 furniture
Barrel: 16-in.
Sights: Magpul MOE
Weight: 6 lb. 12 oz.
Caliber: .223 Wylde
Magazine: Magpul
Features: With the success of the MK1 and MK2 rifle series and a DI accessory line designed to reliably enhance any AR platform, PWS' next logical step was to supply customers with the best DI AR-15 rifle available. The shortest Modern Musket Rifle, the DI-14 has a permanently pinned muzzle device in accordance with NFA regulations. The DI-14 retains lethal capability out to 500 meters with varying types of ammunition. Utilizing only the highest quality barrel blanks, PWS DI barrels are turned in house then Isonite QPQ treated for hardness and corrosion resistance.
MSRP: $1,399

MK212SD RIFLE

Action: semi-auto
Stock: Magpul MOE stock and grip
Barrel: 12.75-in.
Sights: Magpul MBUS
Weight: 8 lb. 7.5 oz.
Caliber: .308 Match
Magazine: Magpul
Features: The PWS long-stroke piston system combines the agility of the AR-15 with the reliability of the AK-47 into a sleek and efficient design. A floating piston head, detachable for charging handle replacement, is attached directly to the operating rod, which in turn is securely attached to the carrier. With only one moving assembly, the PWS

long-stock system offers a lighter recoil impulse, while at the same time proving increased longevity and durability. A dedicated suppressed weapon system, the MK212SD is configured for the lightest recoil possible in a suppressed semi-auto .308 weapon platform, and requires the use of a suppressor to operate. Utilizing only the highest quality barrel blanks, PWS barrels are turned in house then Isonite QPQ treated for hardness and corrosion resistance.
MSRP: $2,299

MK212SD-PISTOL

Action: semi-auto
Stock: Magpul grip
Barrel: 12.75-in.
Sights: Magpul MBUS
Weight: 8 lb. 10.5 oz.
Caliber: .308 Match
Magazine: Magpul
Features: The PWS long-stroke piston system combines the agility of the AR-15 with the reliability of the AK-47 into a sleek and efficient design. A floating piston head, detachable for charging handle replacement, is attached directly to the operating rod, which in turn is securely attached to the carrier. With only one moving assembly, the PWS long-stock system offers a lighter recoil impulse, while at the same time proving increased longevity and durability. A dedicated suppressed weapon system, the MK212SD is configured for the lightest recoil possible in a suppressed semi-auto .308 weapon platform, and requires the use of a suppressor to operate. Utilizing only the highest quality barrel blanks, PWS barrels are turned in house then Isonite QPQ treated for hardness and corrosion resistance.
MSRP: $2,299

QUALITY ARMS

M4 BASIC

Action: semi-auto
Stock: M4, 6-position collapsible stock

Barrel: 16-in. barrel with a 1:9 twist
Sights: A2 forged front sight, removable carry handle/rear sight
Weight: N/A
Caliber: 5.56
Magazine: 30-round Magpul
Features: Quality Arms forged mil-spec lower receiver, standard M3/M4 forged mil-spec upper receiver, A3/A4 forged flat top upper standard A2 grip, upgrade to Magpul furnature for an additional $100, black soft tactical case, Quality Arms USB flash drive with warranty and instructional information.
MSRP: **$775**

QUENTIN DEFENSE QUENTIN DEFENSE 18-IN. ELITE COMPETITION RIFLE

Action: semi-auto
Stock: Magpul MOE stock
Barrel: Quentin Defense 18-in. 1:8 5.56mm match barrel, 4150 chromoly with Nitride finish.
Sights: None, optics ready
Weight: N/A
Caliber: 5.56
Magazine: N/A
Features: Billet upper and lower receiver set, ambi bolt release, Quentin Defense drop in single-stage trigger, X-Tech adjustable grip, M16 bolt carrier group, Quentin Defense 15-in. M-LOK free-float handguard, billet 4140 chromoly lo-pro gas block with Nitride finish, Q-Comp 556 tunable muzzle device, mil-spec receiver extension.
MSRP: **$1,600**

R GUNS

PISTOL A3 11.5

Action: semi-auto
Stock: SIG Brace
Barrel: 11.5-in. 1:9 twist 5.56×45mm NATO pistol
Sights: Flip up rear sight, A-frame front sight
Weight: N/A
Caliber: 5.56
Magazine: 30 round

Features: Magpul MOE hand guard, MOE Vortex flash suppressor carry case.
MSRP: **$950**

RANGER PROOF

RANGER PROOF CARBINE

Action: semi-auto
Stock: B5 Systems Bravo stock
Barrel: 16-in. 416R match-grade barrel with mid-length gas system, low-profile gas block, 1:8 twist, .223 Wylde chamber, medium contour, (1 MOA capability), 5.56×45 NATO 1:7 twist, mid-length gas system also available
Sights: This rifle is "optics ready" and ships in a hard, padded carry/display case; runs just as well with a red dot, HWS, or a magnified optic.
Weight: 12 lb.
Caliber: .223 Wylde or 5.56 x 45
Magazine: 30 round
Features: RPC2 billet lower, Primary Weapon Systems buffer tube, Primary Weapon Systems buffer (H2), Ranger Proof Enhanced BCG, 15.5-in. KeyMod rail, Griffin Armament M4SD flash comp muzzle device or PWS FSC556 comes standard (based on availablility). LANTAC Dragon is available as an upgrade: short throw ambi safety selector, B5 Systems Bravo stock, ERGO pistol grip, CMC 3.5 lb. flat bow trigger with enhanced pins (not C-Clips), XMR (Extended Magazine Release) from Odin Works and the reversible hand stop from Zero Bravo. Rifle is shipped completely assembled, tested and tuned if required. Rifle will ship in a hard, padded carry case.
MSRP: **$2,129**

RP ENTRY LEVEL CARBINE (ELC)

Action: semi-auto
Stock: B5 Systems SOPMOD Bravo
Barrel: 416 stainless steel barrel, button rifled and ISONITE QPQ coated,16-in. 1:8 twist, mid-length gas system, 5.56 chamber, (or you can

choose to spec a 14.5-in. barrel with a pinned, welded muzzle device)
Sights: None, optics ready
Weight: 14 lb.
Caliber: 5.56
Magazine: 30 round
Features: Standard cut, M16 style "full auto" (heavy) carrier, with the same manufacturing specs as the top of the line Ranger Proof enhanced bolt carrier. This ELC carrier is black Nitride coated (ISONITE QPQ) and features the exact same bolt as the RPC BCG. The only difference is the profile. It is a standard mil-spec pattern BCG.

The ELC will also have the same free floating KeyMod rail that the RPC uses, only the ELC will have a 12.5-in. rail instead of the 15.5-in. rail that the RPC has. Upper and lower Receivers are 7075-T6 forged units, mil-spec trigger guard, BCM large latch "GunFighter" charging handle, all upper, lower components for the base ELC are mil-spec, CMC 3.5 lb. flat bow trigger, six position mil-spec buffer tube, with staked castle nut, QD end plate, rear selector detent, spring held in place by a 4-40 set screw.
MSRP: **$1,529**

REBEL ARMS CORP

RBR-15 MOD II S

Action: semi-auto
Stock: Mission First Tactical BATTLELINK Minimalist Stock
Barrel: Rebel Arms 14.5-in. 5.56 NATO 4150 CMV Nitride medium contour 1:7 barrel
Sights: N/A
Weight: 6.6 lb.
Caliber: 5.56x45 NATO
Magazine: Hexmag
Features: Hiperfire Hipertouch 24C, Enhanced Nitride BCG & buffer, mid-length gas system, Griffin Armament M4SD muzzle brake, free floating Rebel Arms 13.5-in. Solo KeyMod handguard, Mission First Tactical ENGAGE pistol grip, Griffin Armament SN-ACH (Suppressor

Rebel Arms Corp: RBR-15 Mod II S

Normalized ambi configurable handle), Griffin Armament AMBI safety selector.

MSRP: . . . . **$1,615–$2,350**

RED X ARMS

7.5 RXA15 NATO MOE PISTOL

Action: semi-auto
Stock: SIG Brace, free-floating carbine length RXA quad rail handguard, made from 6000 series aluminum and black hard coat anodized, Magpul MOE grip
Barrel: 7.5-in. 416 stainless steel barrel chambered in 5.56 NATO, 1:9 twist, button rifled, piston gas system, M4 feedramps, ½x28 threads with stainless steel A2 compensator
Sights: None, optics ready
Weight: N/A
Caliber: 5.66
Magazine: One 30-round PMAG black
Features: 7075-T6 forged aluminum flattop upper receiver with M4 feedramps, black hard coat anodized and T-marked, 750 low-profile gas block. made from 6000 series aluminum and black hard coat anodized, M16 bolt carrier group, chrome-lined gas key properly staked with Grade 8 fasteners, cam pin, firing pin, and firing pin retaining pin, standard mil-spec 7075-T6 aluminum charging handle, 7075-T6 forged aluminum receiver, black hard coat anodized mil-spec lower parts kit,

Magpul MOE trigger guard, available in black and FDE.
MSRP: **$999**

RENO GUNS & RANGE (AKA BATTLE BORN GUNS) BATTLE BORN CUSTOM FLAT TOP UPPER

Action: semi-auto
Stock: N/A
Barrel: 7.5-in., 8-in., 10.5-in., 11.5-in., 16-in., 18-in.
Sights: N/A
Weight: N/A
Caliber: 5.56mm, 300 BLK, 9mm
Magazine: N/A
Features: N/A
MSRP: . . . . **$700–$1,000**

REVOLUTION ARMS

REV ARMS RAL—5.56 NATO S.E.L. 16-IN.

Action: semi-auto
Stock: N/A
Barrel: N/A
Sights: N/A
Weight: N/A
Caliber: 5.56
Magazine: N/A
Features: REV RAL, M-LOK handguard, Single Edge Land rifling, guaranteed sub MOA using match-grade ammo, 1:7 twist, proprietary target crown 4150 CMV, black Nitride .750 steel gas block, black Nitride mid-length gas impingement system

A2 flash hider, forged, mil-spec upper receiver, hand trued receiver face, dust cover and forward assist, slick side upper available upon request, mil-spec charging handle, hand fitted black nitride BCG.
MSRP: **$695**

ROCK RIVER ARMS

RRA LAR-15 IRS SERIES

Action: semi-auto
Stock: RRA Operator CAR stock/ Hogue rubber grip
Barrel: 16-in. Fluted chromoly
Sights: integral folding sights
Weight: 7.6 lb.
Caliber: 5.56mm
Magazine: One
Features: Two-stage trigger, new RRA Helical brake.
MSRP: **$1,540**

RRA LAR-15 LIGHTWEIGHT CAR

Action: semi-auto
Stock: RRA 6-position tactical CAR stock
Barrel: 16-in. chromoly lightweight
Sights: Rail
Weight: 5.6 lb.
Caliber: 5.56mm
Magazine: One
Features: Hogue rubber grip.
MSRP: **$1,325**

NEW RIFLES

RRA LAR-15 LIGHTWEIGHT MOUNTAIN RIFLE

Action: semi-auto
Stock: RRA 6-position tactical CAR stock
Barrel: 16-in. chromoly lightweight
Sights: Rail
Weight: 6.2 lb.
Caliber: 5.56mm
Magazine: One
Features: RRA two-stage trigger/RRA winter trigger guard, Hogue rubber pistol grip.
MSRP: $1,150

RRA LAR-15 LIGHTWEIGHT XL

Action: semi-auto
Stock: RRA 6-position tactical CAR stock
Barrel: 16-in. chromoly lightweight
Sights: Rail (STD model), integrated folding sights (XL model)
Weight: 6.1 lb.
Caliber: 5.56mm
Magazine: One
Features: Hogue rubber grip, RRA carbon fiber free float XL length handguard.
MSRP: $1,400

RRA LAR-15 NSP CAR

Action: semi-auto
Stock: RRA NSP CAR stock/NSP overmolded pistol grip
Barrel: 16-in. fluted R-4 profile chromoly
Sights: RRA NSP flip front and rear sights
Weight: 7 lb.
Caliber: 5.56mm
Magazine: One
Features: Two-stage trigger.
MSRP: $1,120

RRA LAR-15 PDW A4 SBR

Action: semi-auto
Stock: NEAG CCS Compact Carbine Stock
Barrel: 10.5-in. chrome-lined chromoly
Sights: Rail
Weight: 7.2 lb.
Caliber: 5.56mm

Magazine: One
Features: STC-1 rail handguard with integral folding vertical grip, Hogue rubber pistol grip.
MSRP: $1,625

RRA LAR-15 TEXAS RIFLE

Action: semi-auto
Stock: RRA Operator A2 stock
Barrel: 16-in. fluted stainless steel, black Cerakoted
Sights: Rail
Weight: 7.6 lb.
Caliber: .223 Wylde Chamber for 5.56mm and .223 Cal
Magazine: One
Features: Two-stage trigger, Hogue rubber pistol grip.
MSRP: $1,700

RRA LAR-47 COYOTE CARBINE

Action: semi-auto
Stock: RRA NSP 6-position CAR Stock
Barrel: 16-in. chrome lined HBAR
Sights: Rail
Weight: 7.8 lb.
Caliber: 7.62x39mm
Magazine: One
Features: Hogue rubber grip.
MSRP: $1,740

RRA LAR-47 X-SERIES

Action: semi-auto
Stock: RRA Operator A2 or RRA Operator CAR black or tan
Barrel: 18-in. fluted bead blasted stainless steel bull barrel or RRA TRO-XL Extended length free-float rail
Sights: Rail
Weight: 8.2 lb.
Caliber: 7.62x39mm
Magazine: One
Features: Hogue grip—black or tan.
MSRP: Black with RRA Beast muzzle brake: $1,600
Tan with RRA Hunter muzzle brake: $1,650

RRA LAR-300 X-SERIES

Action: semi-auto
Stock: RRA Operator A2 or RRA Operator CAR- black or tan

Barrel: 18-in. fluted bead blasted stainless steel barrel
Sights: Rail
Weight: 7.9 lb.
Caliber: 300 BLK
Magazine: One
Features: Hogue grip or RRA two-stage trigger and winter trigger guard black or tan.
MSRP: . . . . black with RRA Beast muzzle brake: $1,585; tan with RRA Hunter muzzle brake: $1,635

SEEKINS PRECISION

SP10 .308

Action: semi-auto
Stock: Magpul STR
Barrel: 18-in. stainless steel 416R match-grade barrel
Sights: None
Weight: 8.90 lb.
Caliber: .308
Magazine: 20 round
Features: Mil-spec type III hard coat anodized 7075-T6 billet completely ambidextrous lower and upper with integrated rail mounts, 15-in. SP3R handguard, M4 feed ramp, CMC 3.5 lb. trigger, adjustable gas block, BCM Mod 3 charging handle, ATC muzzle break, ERGO Deluxe Grip, proprietary buffer system.
MSRP: $2,489

SIG SAUER

SIG MCX

Action: semi-auto
Stock: Side folding skeletonized aluminum, accepts all AR stocks
Barrel: Carbine, 16-in.; SBR, 9-in.
Sights: Flip up iron sights
Weight: 6 lb. (carbine)
Caliber: 300 BLK; 5.56mm
Magazine: 30 round
Features: Modular configuration, multi-caliber, first rifle designed to be short, silenced and 300 BLK.
MSRP: $1,866

Sharps Rifle Company: AR-15

Smith & Wesson: M&P 15-22 Sport

SHARPS RIFLE COMPANY

AR-15

Action: semi-auto
Stock:
Barrel: M4, 16-in., 18-in., and 20-in. (24-in. available by special order), type 216 R, high pressure grade stainless steel, 1:10 twist, Caudle 3 land polygonal rifling, in HBAR and LT contours in stainless steel or black oxide
Sights: None
Weight: 7 lb.
Caliber: .25-45 Sharps
Magazine: 20 round
Features: M4 feed ramp, Relia-bolt and Balanced Bolt carrier group of S7 tool steel coated with NP3 or NP3 Plus, Diamondhead floating handguard, 5/8x24 muzzle thread, thread protector, SRC rifle case.
MSRP: $1,399

SMITH & WESSON

M&P 15-22 SPORT

Action: semi-auto
Stock: 6-position CAR stock, polymer, 10-in M&P Slim handguard with Magpul M-LOK

Barrel: 16.5-in.
Sights: Folding front and rear MBUS
Weight: 5 lb.
Caliber: .22 LR
Magazine: 25 round
Features: Easy to mount M-LOK accessories, 2-in. M-LOK rail panel, shell deflector, charging handle, additional variants with performance features, various camo options and New Jersey, Massachusetts, Connecticut, Maryland, and 10-round compliant models available.
MSRP: **$449 ($449–$709 for variants)**

TACTICAL FIREARMS SOLUTIONS, LLC

TFS "GENESIS" IN 300 BLACKOUT AND .458 SOCOM, AND THE "REVELATION" .308 AR-10 TFS "GENESIS"

Action: semi-auto
Stock: Collapsible Mission First "Minimalist" stock
Barrel: 16-in., 5.56 NATO, 1:7 twist, mid-length gas system, chrome lined 16-in., .223 Wylde, 1:8 twist, mid-length gas system, chrome lined
Sights: N/A (available upon request)

Show: Knights Armament Micro flip sights
Weight: Sub-7 lb.
Caliber: 5.56 NATO, 300 BLK, .458 SOCOM
Magazine: 30-round Magpul PMAG
Features: Nickel-boron plating on all aluminum parts, NiB battleworn finish, NiB full auto bolt carrier, Elf match trigger (optional upgrade), Enhanced Parts Kit, Magpul K+ grip, lightweight slim M-LOK 15-in. rail, TFS custom "leveler" muzzle brake, 7075 billet aluminum receiver set.
MSRP: **$1,800–$2,200 depending on configuration**

TRITON MFG

TR15

Action: semi-auto
Stock: Magpul MOE
Barrel: 16-in. chromoly vanadium 4150 barrel, chambered in 5.56 NATO, with a 1:7 twist, finished off with a Triton 15-in. TSR or KeyMod free-float rail, low-profile gas block and an A2 flash hider.
Sights: None, optics ready
Weight: N/A
Caliber: 5.56
Magazine: One 30-round

Yankee Hill Machine: Model-57 Specter XL

Features: Machined from 7075-T6 aircraft grade billet aluminum, matte black hard coat anodized per mil 8625 type III class II, precision broached magazine well with beveled feed lips, machined and engraved to be compatible with 45- and 60-degree short throw fire control selectors such as the BAD_ASS ST 45 lever, caliber marking of "multi" so it can be used with many different caliber uppers, compatible with all standard AR-15 components and magazines and most aftermarket parts. Take down pin spring and detent hole is threaded for a 4-40 set screw for easy capturing (hardware included), Triton MFG Premium BGC, Triton MFG charging handle, ambidextrous trigger finger rests with grooves (above and below mag release/ mag catch) compatible with Norgon and other aftermarket ambidextrous mag releases, threaded bolt catch pin, integrated large opening "winter" trigger guard, manufactured to mil-spec.
MSRP: . . . . N/A

WILSON COMBAT

.308 PROJECT

Action: semi-auto
Stock: Wilson/Rogers Super Stoc
Barrel: 14.7-in., 16-in., 18-in., 20-in.
Sights: N/A
Weight: 7–9 lb.
Caliber: .308
Magazine: 12, 20, 30 round
Features: Billet upper and Lowe recievers, lo-profile gas system, accu-tac flash hider.
MSRP: . . . . N/A

URBAN SUPER SNIPER

Action: semi-auto
Stock: Wilson/Rogers Super Stoc
Barrel: 18-in.
Sights: N/A
Weight: 7 lb. 5 oz.
Caliber: .223 Wylde
Magazine: 10, 20, 30 round
Features: The Urban Super Sniper has 18-in. long, 1:8 twist, medium heavy-weight, fluted, stainless steel premium match-grade barrel—optimized for accuracy with a .223 Wylde chamber and precision target crown.
MSRP: . . . . N/A

YANKEE HILL MACHINE

MODEL-57 SPECTER

Action: semi-auto
Stock: Magpul CTR 6-position stock
Barrel: 16-in. Exclusive Model 57 fluting, threaded
Sights: YHM Q.D.S. Sight System Hooded YHM-5040-H
Weight: 7.2 lb.
Caliber: 5.56mm, 6.8 SPC II, 300 BLK
Magazine: Two 30-round PMAGs (windowless black)
Features: YHM Slant Series mid-length handguard, KeyMod mounting system at 3, 6, and 9 o'clock positions, billet upper and lower receiver, YHM Slant compensator/muzzle break, two-stage trigger, Q.D.S hooded sights, tactical charging handle, YHM patented E-Z pull pins takedown pins, Magpul pistol grip, Magpul stock, two 30-round PMAG, two rubber handguard covers.
MSRP: . . . . $2,195–$2,265

MODEL-57 SPECTER XL

Action: semi-auto
Stock: Magpul CTR 6-position stock
Barrel: 16-in. exclusive Model 57 fluting, threaded
Sights: YHM Q.D.S. sight system hooded YHM-5040-H
Weight: 7.2 lb.
Caliber: 5.56mm, 6.8 SPC II, 300 BLK
Magazine: Two 30-round PMAG (windowless black)
Features: YHM Slant Series rifle-length handguard, KeyMod mounting system at 3, 6, and 9 o'clock positions, billet upper and lower receiver, YHM slant compensator/muzzle break, two-stage trigger, Q.D.S hooded sights, tactical charging handle, YHM patented E-Z pull pins takedown pins, Magpul pistol grip, Magpul stock, two 30-round PMAGs, two rubber handguard covers.
MSRP: . . . . $2,295–$2,365

YHM-8020
YHM-15 PISTOL 9MM

Action: semi-auto gas blow back
Stock: N/A (pistol buffer tube)
Barrel: 5.5-in. threaded barrel
Sights: None
Weight: 5.04 lb.
Caliber: 9mm
Magazine: One 32-round Metalform
Features: Light, ergonomic, octagonal KeyMod mini-length handguard with KeyMod mounting options on seven sides and Picatinny rail that bridges the gap along the top. All mil-spec internal parts, mil-spec forged 7075-T6 aluminum YHM lower receiver and flat-top upper receiver, T-marked upper receiver, mil-spec bolt carrier assembly, forward assist, YHM Phantom 5c2 flash hider/compensator, YHM patented E-Z pull takedown pins.
MSRP: $1,557

Yankee Hill Machine: YHM-8020

YHM-8010
YHM-15 PISTOL 5.56MM

Action: semi-auto, direct impingement
Stock: N/A (pistol buffer tube)
Barrel: 10.5-in. threaded barrel
Sights: None
Weight: 5.4 lb.
Caliber: 5.56mm
Magazine: One 30-round
Features: Light, ergonomic, octagonal KeyMod mid-length handguard with KeyMod mounting options on seven sides and Picatinny rail that bridges the gap along the top. All mil-spec internal parts, mil-spec forged 7075-T6 aluminum YHM lower receiver and flat-top upper receiver, T-marked upper receiver, mil-spec bolt carrier assembly, forward assist, YHM Phantom 5c2 flash hider/compensator, YHM patented E-Z pull takedown pins.
MSRP: $1,205

YHM-8540
S.L.K. SPECTER CARBINE

Action: semi-auto, direct impingement
Stock: 6-position collapsible stock
Barrel: 16-in. threaded and fluted barrel
Sights: YHM Q.D.S. quick deploy flip sights YHM-5040
Weight: 6.3 lb.
Caliber: 5.56mm, 6.8 SPC II, 300 BLK
Magazine: One 30-round
Features: Light, ergonomic, slim KeyMod mid-length handguard with KeyMod mounting options on three sides and continuous Picatinny rail along the top. All mil-spec internal parts, mil-spec forged 7075-T6 aluminum YHM lower receiver and flat-top upper receiver, T-marked upper receiver, mil-spec bolt carrier assembly, forward assist, YHM Phantom 5c2 flash hider/compensator.
MSRP: . . . . $1,700–$1,781

YHM-8550
S.L.K. SPECTER XL

Action: semi-auto, direct impingement
Stock: 6-position collapsible stock
Barrel: 16-in. threaded and fluted barrel
Sights: YHM Q.D.S. quick deploy flip sights YHM-5040
Weight: 6.3 lb.
Caliber: 5.56mm, 6.8 SPC II, 300 BLK
Magazine: One 30-round
Features: Light, ergonomic, slim KeyMod rifle-length handguard with KeyMod mounting options on three sides and continuous Picatinny rail along the top. All mil-spec internal parts, mil-spec forged 7075-T6 aluminum YHM lower receiver and flat-top upper receiver, T-marked upper receiver, mil-spec bolt carrier assembly, forward assist, YHM Phantom 5c2 flash hider/compensator.
MSRP: . . . . $1,725–$1,806

KR7 SERIES
ENTRY LEVEL CARBINE

Action: semi-auto
Stock: 6-position collapsible stock
Barrel: 16-in. threaded barrel with low profile gas block
Sights: None
Weight: 6.3 lb.
Caliber: 5.56mm, 6.8 SPC II, 300 BLK
Magazine: One 30-round
Features: Light, ergonomic, octagonal KeyMod mid-length handguard with KeyMod mounting options on seven sides and Picatinny rail that bridges the gap along the top. All mil-spec internal parts, mil-spec forged 7075-T6 aluminum YHM lower receiver and flat-top upper receiver, T-marked upper receiver, mil-spec bolt carrier assembly, forward assist, YHM Phantom 5c2 flash hider/compensator, YHM KR7 mid-length handguard.
MSRP: . . . . $1,284–$1,338

SOC-8510-OD

Action: semi-auto, direct impingement
Stock: 6-position collapsible stock
Barrel: 16-in. threaded and fluted barrel
Sights: YHM Q.D.S. quick deploy flip sights YHM-5040
Weight: 6.9 lb.
Caliber: 5.56mm
Magazine: One 30-round Gen2 black windowless PMAG
Features: Light, ergonomic, slim mid-length handguard with custom mounting options and Picatinny rail along the top. YHM-7284 patented E-Z pull takedown pins. ERGO 6-position stock, ERGO ambidextrous pistol grip. All mil-spec internal parts, mil-spec forged 7075-T6 aluminum YHM lower receiver and flat-top upper receiver, T-marked upper receiver, mil-spec bolt carrier assembly, forward assist, YHM Phantom 5c2 flash hider/compensator Cerakoted in olive drab with tan furniture.
MSRP: $1,950

YHM-175-DE
DESERT ENFORCER

Action: semi-auto, direct impingement
Stock: 6-position collapsible stock
Barrel: 16-in. threaded and fluted barrel
Sights: YHM Q.D.S. quick deploy flip sights YHM-5040
Weight: 6.9 lb.
Caliber: 5.56mm
Magazine: One 30-round Gen2 black windowless PMAG
Features: Light, ergonomic, slim mid-length handguard with custom mounting options and Picatinny rail along the top. YHM-7284 Patented E-Z Pull Takedown pins. Magpul collapsible 6-position stock, Magpul MOE pistol grip. All mil-spec internal parts, mil-spec forged 7075-T6 aluminum YHM lower receiver and flat-top upper receiver, T-marked upper receiver, mil-spec bolt carrier assembly, forward assist, YHM Annihilator YHM-27-ZH flash hider Cerakoted in flat dark earth.
MSRP: $2,050

4. AR Rifle Models

Following is undoubtedly the most comprehensive listing of current AR-style rifle models available in print or on the web, though it is by no means exhaustive. The knowledgeable reader will no doubt find a favorite small manufacturer or favorite model of gun not listed here. Some companies simply have so many guns, it was impractical to list them all. Others were, for inexplicable reasons other than they were too busy, unable to respond to the authors' requests for information and photography, didn't have adequate information available on their websites (some had no websites) or they themselves didn't even have detailed information on their firearm models available. And admittedly, with so many small gunmakers coming into the fold—and just as quickly falling back out of it, capturing every manufacturer is a target even a custom-built AR couldn't hit.

Speaking of custom builders, many, if they did not make predetermined firearm packages, were not included, but are listed in appendices of this book. Likewise, even AR manufacturers whose firearms are not listed in this chapter are at least listed in an appendix at the back of this book. Please check out GuidetoARs.com frequently for updates on gun listings that were missed in this book, previews of new ARs and accessories coming to the market, tips on getting better performance out of your rifle and for detailed reviews on new AR models coming to a store shelf near you. Also, if you are an AR manufacturer and were not listed, please make us aware of your company and its offerings. Contact us through GuidetoARs.com where we will be happy to include your gun models or accessories and will know how to reach you more directly when working on the next edition of *The Shooter's Bible Guide to AR-15s*.

2VETS ARMS
2VA BRAVO

Action: semi-auto
Stock: B5 Systems
Barrel: 16-in. 4140 CMOV barrel, 1:7
Sights: A2 front sight base
Weight: N/A
Caliber: .556
Magazine: N/A
Features: Arms 7075-T6 billet side charged upper receiver.
MSRP: **$1,300**

2VA SOPMOD

Action: semi-auto
Stock: B5 Systems
Barrel: 16-in. 416R stainless steel barrel, 1:7 RH twist
Sights: N/A
Weight: N/A
Caliber: 5.56
Magazine: N/A
Features: 7075-T6 billet side charged upper receiver, 7075-T6 billet lower receiver, ALG Defense GI fire controls, carbine gas system, 10-in. quad rail.
MSRP: **$1,499**

2VA NATO GENESIS SERIES

Action: semi-auto
Stock: B5 Systems
Barrel: 13.7-in. barrel, B.E. Meyers 249 flash hider
Sights: N/A
Weight: N/A
Caliber: .556
Magazine: N/A
Features: 2VA 7075 billet A4 upper, 2VA 7075 billet lower, ambi charging handle, M-LOK rail.
MSRP: **$1,575**

2VA .308 SPECIAL PURPOSE RIFLE

Action: semi-auto
Stock: B5 Systems Bravo
Barrel: 18-in., 1:10 RH twist, full fluted 416R stainless match-grade barrel w/ black Nitride finish
Sights: N/A
Weight: 7 lb. 13 oz.
Caliber: .308
Magazine: N/A
Features: 7075-T6 matched set billet receivers, ambidextrous side charging system, ambidextrous safety selector,

two-stage trigger from Geissele Automatics (G2S-E), B5 Systems Bravo collapsible buttstock, 14-in. P3R lightweight free-float rail, 18-in. full fluted 416R stainless match-grade barrel with black Nitride finish.
MSRP: **$1,875**

2VA ALPHA

Action: semi-auto
Stock: B5 SOPMOD Alpha stock, BCM Gunfighter grip
Barrel: 16-in. 416R stainless steel match barrel with full flutes
Sights: N/A
Weight: N/A
Caliber: 5.56
Magazine: N/A
Features: Arms 7075-T6 billet side charged upper receiver, 7075 forged lower receiver, mid-length gas system, Geissele SSA fire controls, KNS anti-rotation pins, Battle Arms Development ambi selector, Phase 5 enhanced side charged compatible BAD lever, 13-in. KeyMod compatible free-float rail.
MSRP: **$1,875**

Accurate Armory: Classic Carbine

Accurate Armory: LE Carbine

Accurate Armory: LE Middy

ACCURATE ARMORY

CLASSIC CARBINE

Action: semi-auto
Stock: M4 stock
Barrel: 4150 chromoly match-grade 16-in. barrel
Sights: N/A
Weight: N/A
Caliber: 5.56mm NATO
Magazine: N/A
Features: Standard carbine-length gas system, M4 feed ramp barrel extension, M4 feed ramp flat top receiver, anodized ramps, T-marked upper receivers, enhanced flared mag well, tight controlled match fit between upper and lower receivers, manganese phosphate barrel finish on entire barrel, M4 profile barrels, HPT (High Pressure Test, per mil-spec) barrels, MPI (Magnetic Particle Inspected, per mil-spec) barrels, bolt machined from mil-spec carpenter No. 158 steel, 100 percent HPT bolt (High Pressure Tested/Proof), 100 percent MPI bolt (Magnetic

Particle Inspected), shot peened bolt, chrome lined carrier (M16 AUTO), chrome lined gas key, gas key staked per mil-spec, black extractor insert, receivers machined from aluminum forgings 7075-T6, receivers hard coat anodize per MIL-A-8625f, type III, class II, mil-spec 7075-T6 receiver extension, staked M4 lock.
MSRP: . . . . **N/A**

LE CARBINE

Action: semi-auto
Stock: Standard M4-type handguards
Barrel: 16-in. cold hammer forged, 1:9 twist, A2 flash suppressor
Sights: Fixed front sight base, F-marked
Weight: N/A
Caliber: 5.56
Magazine: One 30-round
Features: Barrel made of mil-spec M249 machine gun barrel steel, with heavy M249 chrome lining (approximately two times as thick as an M4 or M16), same weight as M4

barrel, 1 lb. 9 oz., but improved contour for maximum rigidity, M-203 notch, extended feed ramps, MP HP tested with certification, mil-spec Phosphate finish, carbine-length gas system, flat-top upper receiver, shot peened and MP tested bolt, auto carrier with properly staked carrier key, ½x28 threads.
MSRP: . . . . **N/A**

LE MIDDY

Action: semi-auto
Stock: Standard M4 type handguards
Barrel: 16-in. cold hammer forged, 1:9, or 1:7 twist
Sights: Fixed front sight base, F-marked
Weight: N/A
Caliber: 5.56
Magazine: One 30-round
Features: Barrel made of mil-spec M-249 machine gun barrel steel, with heavy M-249 chrome lining (approximately two times as thick as an M4 or M16), mid-length gas system, extended feed ramps, MP HP tested with certification, mil-spec Phosphate finish, flat-top upper receiver, shot peened and MP tested bolt, auto carrier with properly staked carrier key, A2 flash suppressor, ½x28 threads.
MSRP: . . . . **N/A**

SBR

Action: semi-auto
Stock: Standard M4 type handguards
Barrel: 7.5 to 14.5 cold hammer forged, 1:9 or 1:7 twist, A2 flash suppressor
Sights: Fixed front sight base, F-marked
Weight: N/A
Caliber: 5.56
Magazine: One 30-round
Features: Barrel made of mil-spec M-249 machine gun barrel steel, with heavy M-249 chrome lining (approximately 2 times as thick as an M4 or M16), carbine-length gas system, extended feed ramps, MP HP tested with certification, mil-spec phosphate finish, flat-top upper receiver, shot peened and MP tested bolt, auto carrier with properly staked carrier key, ½x28 threads.
MSRP: . . . . N/A

AR PISTOL

Action: semi-auto
Stock: N/A
Barrel: 7.5 to 8.5 Cold Hammer Forged, 1:9 twist, A2 Flash Suppressor (Optional PWS Flash Hider)
Sights: N/A
Weight: N/A
Caliber: 5.56mm or 300 BLK
Magazine: One 20-round
Features: Barrel made of mil-spec M249 machine gun barrel steel, with heavy M249 chrome lining (appx. two times as thick as an M4 or M16), pistol-length gas system, extended feed ramps, MP HP tested with certification, mil-spec Phosphate finish, flat-top upper receiver, Samson Evo handguards, Thordsen Cheek Riser, shot peened and MP tested bolt, auto carrier with properly staked carrier key, ½x28 threads (5.56), 5/8x24 threads (300 BLK).
MSRP: $1,345 and up depending on features

ADAMS ARMS

14.5-IN. MID TACTICAL EVO RIFLE

Action: semi-auto
Stock: Enhanced 6-position buttstock
Barrel: 14.5-in. government contour 4150 CM melonited barrel 1:7 twist
Sights: None
Weight: 6.9 lb.
Caliber: .223/5.56x45mm NATO
Magazine: 30-round GI Aluminum
Features: Mid, short stroke piston operated. mil-spec forged 7075-T6 lower receiver, type III class II hard coat anodized finish, beveled magwell, machined chevrons in front strap, mil-spec forged 7075-T6 M4 upper receiver, type III class II hard coat anodized finish, M4 feed ramps, 1913 Picatinny rail flat top with dry lube internal finish and laser engraved T markings, pinned manimal flash hider, Samson Evolution free float lightweight modular rail system, ERGO Grip, mil-spec trigger, ½x28 muzzle thread.
MSRP: $1,378.22

12.5-IN. XLP EVO UPGRADED PISTOL 300 BLK

Action: semi-auto
Stock: None
Barrel: 12.5-in. medium contour 4150 CM Melonited barrel 1:9 twist
Sights: None
Weight: 5.95 lb.
Caliber: 300 BLK
Magazine: 30-round GI Aluminum
Features: Short stroke piston operated, mil-spec forged 7075-T6 lower receiver, type III class II hard coat anodized finish, beveled magwell, machined chevrons in front strap, mil-spec forged 7075-T6 M4 upper receiver, type III class II hard coat anodized finish, M4 feed ramps, 1913 Picatinny rail flat top with dry lube internal finish and laser engraved T-markings, pistol buffer tube without adjustable positions, VDI .30 Cal Jet Comp, Samson 12-in. Evolution free float lightweight modular rail system,

XLP low profile gas block (five settings: 100 percent, 75 percent, 50 percent, 25 percent, off), upgraded JP fire control group, Magpul MOE grip. muzzle thread pattern: 5/8x24.
MSRP: $1,605

16-IN. CARBINE BASE RIFLE

Action: semi-auto
Stock: Mil-spec 6-position retractable stock
Barrel: 16-in. M4 profile 4150 CM Melonited barrel 1:7 twist
Sights: None
Weight: 6.21 lb.
Caliber: .223/5.56x45mm NATO
Magazine: 30-round GI aluminum magazine
Features: Carbine, short stroke piston operated, mil-spec forged 7075-T6 lower receiver, type III class II hard coat anodized finish, beveled magwell, machined chevrons in front strap, mil-spec forged 7075-T6 M4 upper receiver, type III class II hard coat anodized finish, M4 feed ramps, 1913 Picatinny rail flat top with dry lube internal finish and laser engraved T-markings, A2 flash hider, muzzle thread pattern: ½x28, M4 style Thermoset molded polymer hand guards with lower heat shield, standard A2 grip, mil-spec trigger.
MSRP: $994

SMALL FRAME .308 — ALPHA-S RIFLE

Action: semi-auto
Stock: Adjustable
Barrel: Voodoo Innovations Melonited barrels, 18-in., 1:10 twist
Sights: Optional
Weight: 8.85 lb.
Caliber: .308 Win.
Magazine: 20 round
Features: An upgraded version of the small frame short-stroke piston AR-style rifle, this model includes the XLP low profile block, Samson 15-in. Evolution rail, Magpul K2 Grip, AR Gold Trigger, and a Luth-AR buttstock. Over 50 percent of the rifle is reciprocal to standard AR-15 parts and accessories, making this a compact, reliable, and lightweight package with

added rail space and options, VDI Jet compensator.

MSRP: **$2,265**

16-IN. MID BASE RIFLE

Action: semi-auto
Stock: mil-spec 6-position retractable stock
Barrel: 16-in. government contour 4150 CM Melonited barrel 1:7 twist
Sights: None
Weight: 6.415 lb.
Caliber: .223/5.56x45mm NATO
Magazine: 30-round GI aluminum
Features: Mid, short stroke piston operated, mil-spec forged 7075-T6 lower receiver, type III class II hard coat anodized finish, beveled magwell, machined chevrons in front strap, mil-spec forged 7075-T6 M4 upper receiver, type III class II hard coat anodized finish, M4 feed ramps, 1913 Picatinny rail flat top with dry lube internal finish and laser engraved T-markings, A2 flash hider, muzzle thread pattern: 1/2x28, two-piece polymer mid-length, standard A2 grip, mil-spec trigger.

MSRP: **$1,016**

16-IN. MID TACTICAL EVO RIFLE

Action: semi-auto
Stock: Enhanced 6-position buttstock
Barrel: 16-in. government contour 4150 CM Melonited barrel, 1:7 twist
Sights: N/A
Weight: 7.097 lb.
Caliber: .223/5.56x45mm NATO
Magazine: 30-round GI aluminum
Features: Mid, short stroke piston operated, mil-spec forged 7075-T6 lower receiver, type III class II hard coat anodized finish, beveled magwell, machined chevrons in front strap, mil-spec forged 7075-T6 M4 upper receiver, type III class II hard coat anodized finish, M4 feed ramps, 1913 Picatinny rail flat top with dry lube internal finish and laser engraved T-markings, A2 flash hider, Samson free float lightweight modular rail system.

MSRP: **$1,349**

7.5-IN. TACTICAL EVO BASE PISTOL

Action: semi-auto
Stock: Samson free-float lightweight modular rail system
Barrel: 7.5-in. government contour, 4150 CM Melonited barrel, 1:7 twist, A2 flash hider
Sights: N/A
Weight: N/A
Caliber: .223/5.56x45mm NATO
Magazine: 30-round GI aluminum
Features: pistol, short stroke piston operated, mil-spec forged 7075-T6 lower receiver, type III class II hard coat anodized finish, beveled magwell, machined chevrons in front strap, mil-spec forged 7075-T6 M4 upper receiver, type III class II hard coat anodized finish, M4 feed ramps, 1913 Picatinny rail flat top with dry lube internal finish and laser engraved T-markings, pistol buffer tube without adjustable positions, standard adjustable gas block (three settings—standard fire, suppressed fire, off).

MSRP: **$1,098**

16.5-IN. C.O.R. ULTRA LITE RIFLE

Action: semi-auto
Stock: N/A
Barrel: 16.5-in. ultralite contour 4150 CM Melonited barrel, 1:7 twist
Sights: N/A
Weight: 7.13 lb.
Caliber: .223/5.56x45mm NATO
Magazine: 30-round GI aluminum magazine
Features: Mil-spec forged 7075-T6 lower receiver, type III class II hard coat anodized finish, beveled magwell, machined chevrons in front strap, mil-spec forged 7075-T6 M4 upper receiver, type III class II hard coat anodized finish, M4 feed ramps, 1913 Picatinny rail flat top with dry lube internal finish and laser engraved T-markings, Magpul MOE rifle stock, Hiperfire HIPERTOUCH 24 competition fire control, low mass bolt carrier, Magpul K2 grip, VDI Jet compensation, Samson free float lightweight modular rail system,

hand stop, 2-in. rails, and QD mount.

MSRP: **$1,799**

16-IN. MID TACTICAL EVO RIFLE—XLP

Action: semi-auto
Stock: SOPMOD style collapsible stock
Barrel: 16-in. government contour 4150 CM Melonited barrel, 1:7 twist
Sights: N/A
Weight: 7.097 lb.
Caliber: .223/5.56x45mm NATO
Magazine: 30-round GI aluminum
Features: Mil-spec forged 7075-T6 lower receiver, type III class II hard coat anodized finish, beveled magwell, machined chevrons in front strap, mil-spec forged 7075-T6 M4 upper receiver, type III class II hard coat anodized finish, M4 feed ramps, 1913 Picatinny rail flat top with dry lube internal finish and laser engraved T-markings, A2 flash hider, Samson free float lightweight modular rail system, XLP multi-adjustable low profile gas block.

MSRP: **$1,389**

SMALL FRAME .308— PATROL ENHANCED

Action: semi-auto
Stock: Collapsible
Barrel: Voodoo Innovations Melonited barrels, 16-in., 1:10 twist
Sights: Optional
Weight: 7.80 lb.
Caliber: .308 Win.
Magazine: 20 round
Features: An upgraded version of the BASE small frame short-stroke piston AR-style rifle, this model includes the Magpul MOE Handguard, Magpul K2 Grip, and an enhanced SOPMOD-style buttstock. Over 50 percent of the rifle is reciprocal to standard AR-15 parts and accessories, making this a compact, reliable, and lightweight package.

MSRP: **$1,489**

16-IN. MID TACTICAL EVO RIFLE—XLP

Action: semi-auto

Stock: SOPMOD style collapsible stock
Barrel: 16-in. government contour 4150 CM Melonited barrel 1:7 twist
Sights: N/A
Weight: 7.097 lb.
Caliber: 223/5.56x45mm NATO
Magazine: 30-round GI aluminum
Features: Mil-spec forged 7075-T6 lower receiver, type III class II hard coat anodized finish, beveled magwell, machined chevrons in front strap, mil-spec forged 7075-T6 M4 upper receiver, type III class II hard coat anodized finish, M4 feed ramps, 1913 Picatinny rail flat top with dry lube internal finish and laser engraved T-markings, A2 flash hider, Samson free float lightweight modular rail system, XLP aulti-adjustable low profile gas block.
MSRP: **$1,389**

14.5-IN. MID TACTICAL EVO RIFLE—XLP

Action: semi-auto
Stock: Enhanced 6-position buttstock
Barrel: 14.5-in. government contour 4150 CM Melonited barrel, 1:7 twist
Sights: None
Weight: 6.889 lb.
Caliber: .223/5.56x45mm NATO
Magazine: 30-round GI aluminum
Features: Mid, short stroke piston operated, mil-spec forged 7075-T6 lower receiver, type III class II hard coat anodized finish, beveled magwell, machined chevrons in front strap, mil-spec forged 7075-T6 M4 upper receiver, type III class II hard coat anodized finish, M4 feed ramps, 1913 Picatinny rail flat top with dry lube internal finish and laser engraved T-markings, pinned manimal flash hider, Samson free-float lightweight modular rail system, muzzle thread pattern: 1/2x28, ERGO Grip, XLP multi-adjustable low-profile gas block.
MSRP: **$1,418**

16.5-IN. ULTRA LITE ADVANCED DISSIPATOR RIFLE

Action: semi-auto
Stock: Magpul MOE
Barrel: VDI 16.5-in. ultralite contour

4150 CM Melonited barrel, 1:7 twist
Sights: N/A
Weight: N/A
Caliber: .223/5.56x45mm NATO
Magazine: 30-round Magpul PMAG
Features: Rifle, short stroke piston operated, mil-spec forged 7075-T6 lower receiver, type III class II hard coat anodized finish, beveled magwell, machined chevrons in front strap, mil-spec forged 7075-T6 M4 upper receiver, type III class II hard coat anodized finish, M4 feed ramps, 1913 Picatinny rail flat top with dry lube internal finish and laser engraved T-markings, low mass bolt carrier, Magpul MOE Grip, Magpul MOE hand guard and trigger guard.
MSRP: **$1,326**

14.5-IN. TACTICAL EVO RIFLE 300 BLK

Action: semi-auto
Stock: Magpul MOE 6-position stock
Barrel: 14.5-in. medium contour 4150 CM Melonited barrel, 1:12 twist
Sights: None
Weight: 7.23 lb.
Caliber: 300 BLK
Magazine: 30-round Magpul PMAG
Features: Short stroke piston operated, mil-spec forged 7075-T6 lower receiver, type III class II hard coat anodized finish, beveled magwell, machined chevrons in front strap, mil-spec forged 7075-T6 M4 upper receiver, type III class II hard coat anodized finish, M4 feed ramps, 1913 Picatinny rail flat top with dry lube internal finish and laser engraved T-markings, Magpul MOE grip, Magpul MOE hand guard and trigger guard, VDI Jet Comp, VDI LifeCoat firing pin, Samson 12.37-in. Evolution free float lightweight modular rail system.
MSRP: **$1,476**

11.5-IN. TACTICAL EVO UPGRADED PISTOL

Action: semi-auto
Stock: None
Barrel: 11.5-in. government contour 4150 CM Melonited barrel, 1:7 twist
Sights: Samson fixed front & rear

Weight: 6 lb.
Caliber: .223/5.56x45mm NATO
Magazine: 30-round GI aluminum
Features: Carbine, short stroke piston operated, mil-spec forged 7075-T6 lower receiver, type III class II hard coat anodized finish, beveled magwell, machined chevrons in front strap, mil-spec forged 7075-T6 M4 upper receiver, type III class II hard coat anodized finish, M4 feed ramps, 1913 Picatinny rail flat top with dry lube internal finish and laser engraved T-markings, pistol buffer tube without adjustable positions, A2 flash hider, Samson free float lightweight modular rail system, standard adjustable gas block (three settings—standard fire, suppressed fire, off), upgraded JP fire control group, ERGO Grip, muzzle thread pattern: 1/2x28.
MSRP: **$1,099**

7.5-IN. TACTICAL EVO UPGRADED PISTOL

Action: semi-auto
Stock: None
Barrel: 7.5-in. government contour 4150 CM Melonited barrel, 1:7 twist
Sights: Samson fixed front & rear
Weight: 5.75 lb.
Caliber: .223/5.56x45mm NATO
Magazine: 30-round GI aluminum
Features: Pistol, short stroke piston operated, mil-spec forged 7075-T6 lower receiver, type III class II hard coat anodized finish, beveled magwell, machined chevrons in front strap, mil-spec forged 7075-T6 M4 upper receiver, type III class II hard coat anodized finish, M4 feed ramps, 1913 Picatinny rail flat top with dry lube internal finish and laser engraved T-markings, pistol buffer tube without adjustable positions, A2 Flash Hider, Samson 4-in. Extended Evolution rail, standard adjustable gas block (three settings—standard fire, suppressed fire, off), upgraded JP fire control group, ERGO grip, muzzle thread pattern: 1/2x28.
MSRP: **$1,099**

Adcor: Elite

Adcor: Elite GI

ADCOR

ELITE

Action: semi-auto
Stock: Custom rifle stock
Barrel: 1:7 twist chrome-lined barrel 10.5-in., 14.5-in., 16-in., 18-in., 20-in.
Sights: Optics ready
Weight: 6.45–7.8 lb. (depending on barrel length)
Caliber: 5.56
Magazine: N/A
Features: Gas piston system with multi-position regulator, custom ergonomic rifle grip with aggressive texturing, two-piece keyed quad rail system, tool-less field strip design, manufactured from billet 7075-T6 aircraft quality aluminum, machined by state-of-the-art CNC equipment at Adcor Defense.
MSRP: . . . . **N/A**

ELITE GI

Action: semi-auto
Stock: Custom rifle stock
Barrel: 1:7 twist, chrome-lined barrel; 16-in., 18-in.
Sights: N/A
Weight: N/A
Caliber: N/A

Magazine: N/A
Features: Gas impingement rifle from Adcor Defense with enhanced features, multi-position gas regulator with removable gas tube, custom ergonomic rifle grip with aggressive texturing. KeyMod, highly rigid rail system (7075-T6) mounts seamlessly to upper receiver, upper and lower rails separate with the push of a button (no special tools needed), manufactured from billet 7075-T6 aircraft quality aluminum, machined by state-of-the-art CNC equipment at Adcor Defense.
MSRP: . . . . **N/A**

ALEXANDER ARMS

6.5 GRENDEL ENTRY

Action: semi-auto
Stock: Free-float composite handguard
Barrel: 19.5-in. stainless steel, free-float
Sights: None
Weight: N/A
Caliber: 6.5 Grendel
Magazine: N/A
Features: Flat-top receiver, Shilen barrel option available, standard trigger, various upgraded adjustable stock options.
MSRP: **$1,469**

6.5 GRENDEL HUNTER

Action: semi-auto
Stock: Full-length military handguard
Barrel: 19.5-in. match-grade stainless-steel, 1:9
Sights: None
Weight: N/A
Caliber: 6.5 Grendel
Magazine: N/A
Features: Flat-top receiver, Shilen barrel option available, standard trigger, various upgraded adjustable stock options, Picatinny rail front gas block, black furniture is standard but coyote brown furniture can be ordered at no extra cost.
MSRP: **$1,370**

6.5 GRENDEL GDMR (GRENDEL DESIGNATED MARKSMAN RIFLE)

Action: semi-auto
Stock: Olive drab furniture includes Magpul PRS stock with ERGO Grip and rail covers
Barrel: Precision-cut rifled barrel, 16-in. barrel is 1:8 twist, 20-in. and 24-in. lengths are 1:8, free floated
Sights: 30mm SPR scope mount, troy BUIS set
Weight: N/A

Caliber: 6.5 Grendel
Magazine: N/A
Features: Mk3 monolithic upper, precision tactical trigger, LaRuc QD bipod mount.
MSRP: $3,650

6.5 GRENDEL OVERWATCH

Action: semi-auto
Stock: Free-float composite handguard
Barrel: Match-grade stainless steel barrel, 1:9 twist
Sights: None
Weight: N/A
Caliber: 6.5 Grendel
Magazine: One 10-round
Features: Flat-top upper receiver, low-profile gas block, standard configuration is in black.
MSRP: $1,499

.50 BEOWULF ENTRY

Action: semi-auto
Stock: Basic full-length handguard
Barrel: 16.5-in. chromemoly barrel with 1:20 twist
Sights: None
Weight: N/A
Caliber: .50 Beowulf
Magazine: 7 round
Features: Standard Picatinny rail gas block, rifle is standard in black but is available in coyote brown furniture for no additional charge.
MSRP: $1,250

.50 BEOWULF PRECISION

Action: semi-auto
Stock: Composite free-float handguard
Barrel: 16.5-in. chromoly barrel
Sights: None
Weight: N/A
Caliber: .50 Beowulf
Magazine: 7 round
Features: Flat-top receiver, low-profile gas block, ships in soft carry bag, standard configuration is in black but is also available in outfitter tuff pattern.
MSRP: $1,350

.50 BEOWULF ADVANCED WEAPON SYSTEM

Action: semi-auto

Stock: Midwest Industries four rail handguard, fixed
Barrel: 16-in. barrel
Sights: None
Weight: N/A
Caliber: .50 Beowulf
Magazine: 7 round
Features: Picatinny rail receiver, comes with soft carry bag.
MSRP: $1,450

.50 BEOWULF OVERMATCH PLUS

Action: semi-auto
Stock: Fixed
Barrel: 16.5-in. chromoly barrel
Sights: Detachable front sight and rear carry handle
Weight: N/A
Caliber: .50 Beowulf
Magazine: 7 round
Features: Flat-top receiver, Picatinny rail gas block, ships with soft carry bag.
MSRP: $1,450

17 HMR

Action: semi-auto
Stock: Standard handguard is our G10 composite, non-vented, mid-length free-float tube, collapsible buttstock
Barrel: 18-in. stainless, button-rifled 1:10 twist barrel with straight flutes, muzzle threaded ½x28 RH for standard .223/5.56 muzzle devices, six vent A1 flash hider included
Sights: None
Weight: N/A
Caliber: .17 HMR
Magazine: Two 10-round
Features: Upper includes the lower conversion parts kit.
MSRP: $1,175

ALEX PRO FIREARMS

ECONO CARBINE RI-013

Action: semi-auto
Stock: Mil-spec 6-position
Barrel: 16-in. .223 Wylde 1:9 twist carbine gas system 4140 chromoly steel
Sights: Vortex strikefire II
Weight: N/A

Caliber: .223 Wylde
Magazine: One 30-round PMAG
Features: Phosphate M16 BCG, Magpul MOE M-LOK handguard.
MSRP: $800

ECONO 300 BLK RI-013BO

Action: semi-auto
Stock: 6-position mil-spec
Barrel: 16-in. 300 BLK 1:8 twist carbine gas system 4140 chromoly steel fluted
Sights: Vortex strikefire II
Weight: N/A
Caliber: 300 BLK
Magazine: One 30-round PMAG
Features: phosphate M16 BCG, Magpul MOE M-LOK handguard.
MSRP: $900

CARBINE RI-001

Action: semi-auto
Stock: 6-position mil-spec
Barrel: 16-in. 5.56 NATO 1:7 twist mid-length gas system 4140 chromoly steel
Sights: N/A
Weight: N/A
Caliber: 5.56 NATO
Magazine: One 30-round PMAG
Features: NiB M16 BCG 12.5-in. APF T-mod free-float rail, Magpul enhanced trigger guard.
MSRP: $999

300 BLK CARBINE RI-011

Action: semi-auto
Stock: 6-position mil-spec
Barrel: 16-in. 300 BLK 1:8 twist carbine gas system 4140 chromoly steel fluted
Sights: N/A
Weight: N/A
Caliber: 300 BLK
Magazine: One 30-round PMAG
Features: NiB M16 BCG 12.5-in. APF T-mod free-float rail, Magpul enhanced trigger guard.
MSRP: $999

MATCH CARBINE RI-006

Action: semi-auto
Stock: Magpul CTR mil-spec
Barrel: 16-in. stainless steel 1:8 twist

mid-length gas system
Sights: N/A
Weight: N/A
Caliber: .223 Wylde
Magazine: One 30-round PMAG
Features: NiB M16 BCG, 15.5-in. T-mod free-float rail, CMC 3.5 lb flat blade trigger, APF enhanced trigger guard, Butcher-16 muzzle brake.
MSRP: $1,200

TACTICAL VARMINT RI-009

Action: semi-auto
Stock: Magpul ACS mil-spec
Barrel: 18-in. stainless steel .223 Wylde 1:8 twist rifle-length gas system
Sights: N/A
Weight: N/A
Caliber: .223 Wylde
Magazine: One 30-round PMAG
Features: NiB M16 BCG, 15.5-in. APF T-mod free-float rail, stark SE-1 grip.
MSRP: $1,230

3-GUN RI-005

Action: semi-auto
Stock: Magpul UBR
Barrel: 18-in. stainless steel .223 Wylde 1:8 twist rifle-length gas system
Sights: N/A
Weight: N/A
Caliber: .223 Wylde
Magazine: One 40-round PMAG
Features: NiB M16 BCG, 15.5-in. APF T-mod free-float rail APF Butcher muzzle brake, CMC 3.5 lb. flatblade trigger, APF enhanced trigger guard.
MSRP: $1,350

VARMINT RI-004/RI-004 BW

Action: semi-auto
Stock: Magpul MOE rifle
Barrel: 20-in. stainless steel .223 Wylde 1:8 twist rifle-length gas system fluted
Sights: N/A
Weight: N/A
Caliber: .223 Wylde
Magazine: One 30-round PMAG
Features: NiB M16 BCG, APF 15.5-in. T-mod free-float rail, available in Backlands west or Winter Mothwing camouflage hydro dip, Stark SE-1 grip.
MSRP: $1,500

204 RI-023

Action: semi-auto
Stock: Magpul MOE rifle
Barrel: 24-in. stainless steel 1:12 twist .936 diameter heavy barrel fluted
Sights: N/A
Weight: N/A
Caliber: 204 Ruger
Magazine: One 30-round PMAG
Features: NiB M16 BCG 14-in. APF modular quad rail, Magpul Moe grip, APF enhanced trigger guard.
MSRP: $1,200

TARGET RI-010

Action: semi-auto
Stock: Magpul PRS
Barrel: 24-in. stainless steel 1:8 twist, .936 diameter heavy barrel, fluted
Sights: N/A
Weight: N/A
Caliber: 5.56 NATO
Magazine: One 30-round PMAG
Features: NiB M16 BCG, APF 15.5-in. T-mod free-float rail, Magpul winter trigger guard.
MSRP: $1,650

223 PISTOL RI-012-5.56X45

Action: semi-auto
Stock: Comes with SIG stabilizing pistol brace
Barrel: 10.5 .223 Wylde, 1:8 twist carbine gas system
Sights: N/A
Weight: N/A
Caliber: .223 Wylde
Magazine: One 30-round PMAG
Features: M16 BCG 9-in. T-mod free-float rail.
MSRP: $1,200

300 BLK PISTOL RI-012-300

Action: semi-auto
Stock: N/A comes with SIG stabilizing pistol brace
Barrel: 10.5-in. 300 BLK, 1:8 twist, pistol gas system
Sights: N/A
Weight: N/A
Caliber: 300 BLK
Magazine: One 30-round PMAG
Features: M16 BCG 9-in. T-mod free-float rail.
MSRP: $1,200

TACTICAL VARMINT 6.5 GRENDEL RI-017

Action: semi-auto
Stock: Magpul ACS mil-spec
Barrel: 18-in. stainless steel 1:8, 6.5 Grendel mid-length gas system
Sights: N/A
Weight: N/A
Caliber: 6.5 Grendel
Magazine: One 25-round
Features: NiB M16 BCG 15.5-in. T-mod free-float rail, Magpul MOE grip.
MSRP: . . . . N/A

.308 CARBINE RI-014

Action: semi-auto
Stock: Magpul MOE 6-position mil-spec
Barrel: 16-in. stainless steel with black finish 1:10 twist rifle-length gas system
Sights: N/A
Weight: N/A
Caliber: .308 Win.
Magazine: One 20-round PMAG
Features: 15.5-in. T-mod free-float rail.
MSRP: $1,100

.308 ENHANCED CARBINE RI-007

Action: semi-auto
Stock: Magpul CTR mil-spec
Barrel: 16-in. stainless steel with black finish 1:10 twist rifle-length gas system
Sights: Magpul Moe BUIS
Weight: N/A
Caliber: .308 Win.
Magazine: One 20-round PMAG
Features: NiB BCG 15.5-in. T-mod free-float rail, ERGO sure grip, AAC 51t flash hider.
MSRP: $1,400

.308 HUNTER RI-008

Action: semi-auto
Stock: Magul MOE Rifle
Barrel: 18-in. stainless steel with black finish, 1:10 twist rifle-length gas system
Sights: N/A
Weight: N/A
Caliber: .308 Win.
Magazine: One 20-round PMAG
Features: NiB BCG 15.5-in. T-mod free-float rail.
MSRP: $1,200

.308 TARGET

Action: semi-auto
Stock: Magpul PRS
Barrel: 20-in. stainless steel with black finish, 1:10 twist rifle-length gas system
Sights: N/A
Weight: N/A
Caliber: .308 Win.
Magazine: One 20-round PMAG
Features: NiB BCG, 15.5-in. T-mod free-float rail, CMC 3.5 lb. flat blade trigger, Harris Benchrest bi-pod, American Defense QD bi-pod adapter, AAC 51t flash hider.
MSRP: .... Black: $1,825, FDE: $1,925

.308 PISTOL RI-015

Action: semi-auto
Stock: N/A comes with SIG stabilizing pistol brace
Barrel: 12.5-in. stainless steel with black finish 1:10 twist mid-length gas system
Sights: N/A
Weight: N/A
Caliber: .308 Win.
Magazine: One 20-round PMAG
Features: 15.5-in. T-mod free-float rail.
MSRP: $1,500

243 FIELD RI-019

Action: semi-auto
Stock: Magpul MOE 6-postion mil-spec
Barrel: 20-in. 1:10 twist rifle-length gas system target crown
Sights: N/A
Weight: N/A
Caliber: .243 Win.
Magazine: One 20-round PMAG
Features: 15.5-in. T-mod free-float rail.
MSRP: $1,300

.243 LRV

Action: semi-auto
Stock: Magpul Moe Rifle
Barrel: 24-in. stainless steel 1:8 twist rifle-length gas system
Sights: N/A
Weight: N/A
Caliber: .243 Win.
Magazine: One 20-round PMAG
Features: NiB BCG, 15.5-in. T-mod free-float rail, CMC 3.5 lb. curved trigger.
MSRP: $1,499

AMERICAN SPIRIT ARMS

ASA-SPR SCR

Action: semi-auto
Stock: 6-position mil-spec receiver extension. Vltor Emod collapsible buttstock
Barrel: 18-in. mid-length gas heavy barrel, 416R stainless steel match, 1:8 RH twist threaded ½x28
Sights: optional flip up sights
Weight: 7.75 lb. unloaded
Overall Length: 35–38.5-in.
Caliber: 5.56x45 NATO
Magazine: 10, 20, 30 round
Features: 7075 side charging receiver with mil-spec 1913 rail, 7075 lower receiver, ERGO Grip, Samson EVO 12-in. rail, ASA 4 lb. single-stage trigger, lifetime warranty, accuracy guarantee ½ to 1 MOA.
MSRP: $1,600

ASA-BBA3 SCR

Action: semi-auto
Stock: 6-position mil-spec dia. receiver extension, Magpul MOE collapsible buttstock
Barrel: 18-in. mid-length gas heavy barrel, 416R stainless steel match, 1:10 RH twist, target crown or threaded 5/8x24
Sights: Optional flip-up sights
Weight: 7.75 lb. unloaded
Overall Length: 31–34.5-in.
Caliber: 5.56x45 NATO
Magazine: 10, 20, 30 round
Features: 7075 side charging receiver with mil-spec 1913 rail, 7075 lower receiver, ERGO Grip, Samson EVO 7-in. rail, ASA 4 lb. single-stage trigger, lifetime warranty, accuracy guarantee ½ to 1 MOA.
MSRP: $1,600

ASA-M4CS1 SCR

Action: semi-auto
Stock: 6-position mil-spec dia. receiver extension, Magpul MOE collapsible buttstock
Barrel: 16-in. carbine-length gas M4 barrel, 4150 CMV M4 feed ramps, 1:7 RH twist, Nitride treated, threaded ½x28
Sights: Optional flip up sights
Weight: 6.5 lb. unloaded
Overall Length: 32–35.5-in.
Caliber: 5.56x45 NATO
Magazine: 10, 20, 30 round
Color Options: Black, OD green, flat dark earth
Features: 7075 side charging receiver with mil-spec 1913 rail, 7075 lower receiver, Samson EVO 10-in. rail, ERGO grip, lifetime warranty, accuracy guarantee ½ to 1 MOA.
MSRP: $1,476

ASA-M4CS2 SCR

Action: semi-auto
Stock: 6-position mil-spec dia. receiver extensions, Magpul MOE collapsible buttstock
Barrel: 16-in. carbine length gas M4 barrel, 4150 CMV M4 feed ramps, 1:7 RH twist, Nitride treated, threaded ½x28
Sights: Optional flip up sights
Weight: 6.5 lb. unloaded
Overall Length: 32–35.5-in.
Caliber: 5.56x45 NATO
Magazine: 10, 20, 30 round
Color Options: Black, OD green, flat dark earth
Features: 7075 side charging receiver with mil-spec 1913 rail, 7075 lower receiver, Midwest Industries Gen 2 drop-in quad rail, ERGO grip, lifetime warranty, accuracy guarantee ½ to 1 MOA.
MSRP: $1,476

ASA-PIS-FT SCR

Action: semi-auto
Stock: Foam covered pistol receiver extension
Barrel: 7.5-in. pistol length gas, 4150 CMV M4 feed ramps, 1:7 RH twist, Nitride treated, threaded ½x28
Sights: Optional flip-up sights
Weight: 5 lb. unloaded
Overall Length: 24-in.
Caliber: 5.56x45 NATO
Magazine: 10, 20, 30 round
Features: 7075 side charging receiver with mil-spec 1913 rail, 7075 lower receiver, Samson EVO 7-in. rail, A2 Grip, lifetime warranty.
MSRP: $1,340

Anderson Manufacturing:
AM15-3G-Elite (3-Gun Elite)

ASA-M4A3 SCR

Action: semi-auto
Stock: 6-position mil-spec dia. receiver extension, Magpul MOE collapsible buttstock
Barrel: 16-in. carbine length gas M4 barrel, 4150 CMV M4 feed ramps, 1:7 RH twist, Nitride treated, threaded ½x28
Sights: Optional flip up sights
Weight: 6.10 lb. unloaded
Overall Length: 32–35.5-in.
Caliber: 5.56x45 NATO
Magazine: 10, 20, 30 round
Color Options: Black, OD green, flat dark earth
Features: 7075 side charging receiver with mil-spec 1913 rail, 7075 lower receiver, Magpul MOE handguard and grip, lifetime warranty, accuracy guarantee ½ to 1 MOA.
MSRP: **$1,300**

ASA-MIDA3 SCR

Action: semi-auto
Stock: 6-position mil-spec dia. receiver extension, Magpul MOE collapsible buttstock
Barrel: 16-in. carbine length gas M4 barrel, 4150 CMV M4 feed ramps, 1:7 RH twist, Nitride treated, threaded ½x28
Sights: Optional flip up sights
Weight: 6.25 lb. unloaded
Overall Length: 32–35.5-in.
Caliber: 5.56x45 NATO
Magazine: 10, 20, 30 round
Color Options: Black, OD green, flat dark earth
Features: 7075 side charging receiver with mil-spec 1913 rail, 7075 lower receiver, Magpul MOE handguard and

grip, lifetime warranty, accuracy guarantee ½ to 1 MOA.
MSRP: **$1,300**

ASA-PIS-9MMFT SCT

Action: semi-auto
Stock: Foam covered pistol receiver extension
Barrel: 7.5-in. pistol barrel, 4140 CMV M4 feed ramps, 1:14 RH twist Nitride treated, threaded ½x28
Sights: Optional flip up sights
Weight: 5.4 lb. unloaded
Overall Length: 24-in.
Caliber: 9x19 NATO
Magazine: 10, 15, 32 round
Features: 7075 side charging receiver with mil-spec 1913 rail, 7075 lower receiver, Samson EVO 7-in. rail, magazine block adaptor, lifetime warranty.
MSRP: **$1,600**

ASA-9MMA3 SCR

Action: semi-auto
Stock: 6-position mil-spec receiver extension standard M4 stock
Barrel: 16-in. barrel, 4140 CMV M4 feed ramps, 1:14 RH twist Nitride treated, threaded ½x28
Sights: Optional flip-up sights
Weight: 6.4 lb. unloaded
Overall Length: 32–35.5-in.
Caliber: 9X19 NATO
Magazine: 10, 15, 32 round
Features: 7075 side charging receiver with mil-spec 1913 rail, 7075 lower receiver, M4 handguards, magazine block adaptor, lifetime warranty.
MSRP: **$1,450**

ASA-20/308-QR SCR

Action: semi-auto
Stock: Rifle receiver extension. Magpul PRS buttstock
Barrel: 20-in. rifle-length gas bull barrel, 416R stainless steel match, 1:10 RH twist, threaded 5/8x24
Sights: Optional flip up sights
Weight: 13.5 lb. unloaded
Overall Length: 41-in.
Caliber: 7.62x51 (.308)
Magazine: 10, 20, 25 round
Features: 7075 side charging receiver with mil-spec 1913 rail, 7075 lower receiver, Samson EVO 15-in. rail, ASA 4 lb. single-stage trigger, bipod, muzzle compensator, lifetime warranty, accuracy guarantee ½ to 1 MOA.
MSRP: **$3,050**

ANDERSON MANUFACTURING

AM15-3G-ELITE (3-GUN ELITE)

Action: semi-auto
Stock: Magpul PRS
Barrel: 18-in. HBAR, 1:8 twist
Sights: Optics ready
Weight: 8.5 lb. without magazine
Caliber: .223 Wylde
Magazine: One 30-round
Features: Forged 7075-T6 receiver, Magpul grip, Anderson's 15-in. EXT free-float forearm, Lantac Dragon 223/556 muzzle brake, Anderson steel adjustable gas block, California-legal available.
MSRP: . . . . **N/A**

Anderson Manufacturing: AM15-LE (M4 LE)

Anderson Manufacturing: AM15-Blackout

Anderson Manufacturing: AM15-Sniper

AM15-LE (M4 LE)

Action: semi-auto
Stock: A2-style stock
Barrel: 16-in. M4 contour chromemoly vanadium, 1:8 twist
Sights: A2-style sights
Weight: 6.4 lb. without magazine
Caliber: 5.56/2.23
Magazine: One 30-round
Features: Forged 7075-T6 receiver, A2-style grip, Anderson EXT free-float forearm, A2-style flash hider and gas block, match-grade trigger and hammer, ambidextrous sling mount, charging handle and buffer tube is 7075-T6 steel.
MSRP: . . . . N/A

AM15-BLACKOUT

Action: semi-auto
Stock: Magpul
Barrel: 16-in. HBAR chromemoly vanadium steel, 1:8 twist
Sights: None, optics ready
Weight: 6.2 lb. without magazine
Caliber: 300 BLK
Magazine: One 30-round
Features: Forged 7075-T6 receiver, buffer tube, and charging handle, Anderson Knight Stalker flash hider, Magpul grip, low-profile gas block, match-grade trigger and hammer, ambidextrous sling mount.
MSRP: . . . . N/A

AM15-SNIPER

Action: semi-auto
Stock: Magpul PRS buttstock
Barrel: 24-in. 416 stainless steel fluted, 1:8 twist
Sights: None, optics ready
Weight: 7.5 lb. without magazine
Caliber: 5.56/.223
Magazine: One 30-round
Features: Forged 7075-T6 receiver, ERGO pistol grip, Anderson EXT free-float forearm, Timney drop-in trigger, tactical charging handle, Harris LMS bipod, low-profile gas block.
MSRP: . . . . N/A

Anderson Manufacturing: AM10-Hunter

Anderson Manufacturing: AM15-7.5 Pistol

AM10-HUNTER

Action: semi-auto
Stock: Molding Solutions Ti7
Barrel: 18-in. HBAR chromoly vanadium, 1:10 twist
Sights: None, optics ready
Weight: 8.9 lb. without magazine
Caliber: .308 Win.
Magazine: One 20-round
Features: Forged 7075-T6 receiver, buffer tube, and charging handle, Anderson Knight Stalker flash hider, Anderson's EXT free-float forearm, low profile gas block, Magpul pistol grip, ambidextrous sling mount, match-grade trigger and hammer.
MSRP: . . . . **N/A**

AM15-7.5 PISTOL

Action: semi-auto
Stock: N/A
Barrel: 7.5-in. M4 contour chromoly vanadium, 1:7 twist
Sights: None, optics ready
Weight: 4.9 lb. without magazine

Caliber: 5.56, .223
Magazine: One 30-round
Features: Pistol buffer tube machined to accept SIG brace, forged 7075-T6 receiver, low-profile gas block, match-grade trigger and hammer, standard charging handle, ambidextrous sling mount, Anderson Knight Stalker flash hider, match-grade trigger and hammer.
MSRP: . . . . **N/A**

ARMALITE

AR-10(T) A-SERIES RIFLE

Action: semi-auto
Stock: Fixed A2 stock, front rounded free-float handguard
Barrel: 20-in. stainless steel, 1:10 twist
Sights: None
Weight: 9.6 lb.
Caliber: .308/7.62x51
Magazine: One 10-round Magpul PMAG

Features: Picatinny rail gas block, forged receivers, upper with Picatinny rail and forward assist, precision two-stage trigger, available in a number of variations.
MSRP: **$1,649**

AR-10 16-IN. TACTICAL RIFLE

Action: semi-auto
Stock: Magpul STR collapsible, 15-in. aluminum tactical KeyMod handguard
Barrel: 16-in. double lapped chrome-lined/chromoly mid-length gas system, 1:11 RH twist, flash suppressor
Sights: MBUS flip-up sights
Weight: 8.4 lb.
Caliber: .308/7.62x51
Magazine: 25-round Magpul PMAG
Features: Two-stage precision trigger, forged flat top mil-spec 1913 rail, lower and upper both made of 7075-T6 aluminum, Raptor ambidextrous charging handle, available in 14-in., 18-in. and California-compliant models.
MSRP: **$1,999**

AR-10 B-SERIES CARBINE

Action: semi-auto
Stock: 6-position collapsible, standard 8-in. handguard
Barrel: 16-in. double lapped chrome-lined/chromoly mid-length gas system, 1:11 RH twist, flash suppressor
Sights: None
Weight: 7.6 lb.
Caliber: .308/7.62x51
Magazine: 20 round
Features: Two-stage precision trigger, forged flat-top mil-spec 1913 rail, lower and upper both made of 7075-T6 aluminum, available in a number of variations.
MSRP: $1,571

M-15 LIGHT TACTICAL CARBINE

Action: semi-auto
Stock: 6-position collapsible, 10-in. aluminum tactical KeyMod handguard
Barrel: 16-in. chrome-lined/chromoly carbine-length gas system, 1:7 RH twist, flash suppressor
Sights: None
Weight: 6 lb.
Caliber: .223/5.56
Magazine: 30-round steel
Features: Single-stage trigger, forged flat-top mil-spec 1913 rail, lower and upper both made of 7075-T6 aluminum, available in 6.8 SPC and 7.62x39 as well as other variations.
MSRP: $999

M-15 18-IN. TACTICAL RIFLE

Action: semi-auto
Stock: 6-position collapsible, 15-in. aluminum tactical KeyMod handguard
Barrel: 18-in. black Cerakoted stainless steel rifle-length gas system, 1:8 RH twist, flash suppressing compensator
Sights: MBUS flip-up sights
Weight: 7.2 lb.
Caliber: .223/5.56
Magazine: 30-round Magpul PMAG
Features: Two-stage precision trigger, forged flat-top mil-spec 1913 rail, lower and upper both made of 7075-T6 aluminum, available in 16-in. and

14-in. versions.
MSRP: $1,699

M-15 DEFENSIVE SPORTING RIFLE

Action: semi-auto
Stock: 6-position collapsible, 6-in. standard handguard
Barrel: 16-in. double-lapped, chrome-lined, chromoly vanadium carbine-length gas system, 1:7 RH twist, flash suppressor
Sights: A2 front sight
Weight: 6.1 lb.
Caliber: .223/5.56
Magazine: 30-round Magpul PMAG
Features: Single-stage trigger, forged flat-top mil-spec 1913 rail, lower and upper both made of 7075-T6 aluminum, available in 16-in. and 14-in. versions.
MSRP: $799

M-15 PISTON

Action: semi-auto, long-stroke piston
Stock: Magpul STR multi-position collapsible, 15-in. free-float piston KeyMod handguard
Barrel: 16-in. Isonite QPQ-treated chromoly, 1:8 RH twist, flash suppressing compensator
Sights: Optics ready
Weight: 7.3 lb.
Caliber: .223/5.56
Magazine: 30-round Magpul PMAG
Features: Two-stage precision trigger, forged flat-top mil-spec 1913 rail, lower and upper both made of 7075-T6 aluminum.
MSRP: $2,249

EAGLE 15

Action: semi-auto
Stock: 6-position collapsible, 6-in. standard handguard
Barrel: 16-in. matte finish, 1:8 RH twist, flash suppressor
Sights: A2 front sight
Weight: 6.5 lb.
Caliber: 5.56
Magazine: 30-round Magpul PMAG
Features: Single-stage trigger, forged flat-top mil-spec 1913 rail, lower and upper both made of 7075-T6 aluminum.
MSRP: $599

EAGLE 15 MISSION FIRST TACTICAL

Action: semi-auto
Stock: 6-position MFT BMS, 6-in. standard handguard
Barrel: 16-in. chromoly, 1:8 RH twist, flash suppressor
Sights: A2 front sight
Weight: 6.7 lb.
Caliber: .223 Wylde
Magazine: 30-round MFT
Features: Single-stage trigger, forged flat-top mil-spec 1913 rail, lower and upper both made of 7075-T6 aluminum.
MSRP: $649

M-15 6-IN. PISTOL

Action: semi-auto
Stock: Arm brace, 6-in. aluminum KeyMod handguard
Barrel: 6-in. double-lapped, chrome-lined, chromoly, 1:7 RH twist, flash suppressing compensator
Sights: MBUS flip-up sights
Weight: 6 lb.
Caliber: .223/5.56
Magazine: 20-round Magpul PMAG
Features: Two-stage precision trigger, forged flat-top mil-spec 1913 rail, lower and upper both made of 7075-T6 aluminum, available in 11.5-in. version.
MSRP: $2,099

ARMSCOR

M1600 SA

Action: semi-auto
Stock: M16-style polymer
Barrel: 18.25-in, 1:6 twist, straight tapered
Sights: Rear peep and A2-style front
Weight: N/A
Caliber: .22LR
Magazine: One 10- or 15-round
Features: Suppressor ready, comes with a 10-round capacity again with optional factory 15-round magazines.
MSRP: $202

BARNES PRECISION MACHINE INC.

BP15 CQB/EBR (CLOSE QUARTERS BATTLE / ENHANCED BATTLE RIFLE)

Action: semi-auto
Stock: Magpul MOE carbine stock / grip.
Barrel: 16-in./18-in. lengths 1:8 twist .223/5.56, 300 BLK–medium/heavyweight contour, mid-length gas system, available in stainless steel or chromoly, both with Nitromet process
Sights: Magpul MBUS
Weight: 7.2 lb.
Caliber: .223, 5.56, 300 BLK
Magazine: One 30-round Magpul
Features: Mil-spec type III hard coat anodized upper & lower, machined from 7075 mil-spec forgings, A4M4 feed ramps USSOC/SOPMOD M4 extractor upgrade, Barnes Precision Machine PSFFRS (Picatinny spec free-float rail system) with proprietary long barrel nut design, for unmatched rigidity of free-float rail system–with four hardened steel sling swivel inserts /bipod mount, Magpul 5/9 slot rail sections, nickel-boron processed bolt carrier group–with Carpenter 158 bolt, USSOC/SOPMOD M4 extractor upgrade, BPMA2 flash hider/breeching tip, users manual, warranty, shipped in a Patriot Cases hard case, Robar NP3 finish upgrade option on all models.
MSRP: **16-in. $1,308; 18-in. $1,341**

BP15 TGMC (THREE GUN MATCH CARBINE)

Action: semi-auto
Stock: ACE SOCOM rifle length stock/Magpul MIAD grip.
Barrel: 16-in./18-in. lengths 1:8 twist .223Wylde Chamber–medium/heavyweight contour, mid-length gas system, available in stainless steel, with Nitromet option.
Sights: None, flat top for optics.
Weight: 7.75 lb.
Caliber: .223/5.56

Magazine: One 30-round Magpul
Features: Mil-spec type III hard coat anodized upper & lower, machined from 7075 mil-spec forgings, A4M4 feed ramps USSOC/SOPMOD M4 extractor upgrade, Barnes Precision Machine PSFFRS (Picatinny spec free-float rail system) with proprietary long barrel nut design for unmatched rigidity of free-float rail system–with four hardened steel sling swivel inserts /bipod mount, Magpul 5/9 slot rail sections, nickel-boron processed bolt carrier group–with Carpenter 158 bolt, USSOC/SOPMOD M4 extractor upgrade, Miculek Style muzzle brake/compensator, HiperFire 24 E/C trigger, MGI style adjustable gas system, users manual, warranty. shipped in a Patriot Cases hard case.
MSRP: . . . **16-in. $1,570; 18-in. $1,581**

BP15 DMR (DESIGNATED MARKSMAN RIFLE)

Action: semi-auto
Stock: Magpul PRS stock, Magpul MIAD grip.
Barrel: Stainless steel 18-in. length, 1:8 twist, .223Wylde chamber–medium/heavyweight contour, mid-length gas system
Sights: None–flat top for optics
Weight: 8.5 lb.
Caliber: .223/5.56
Magazine: 30-round Magpul
Features: Mil-spec type III hard coat anodized upper & lower, machined from 7075 mil-spec forgings, A4M4 feed ramps USSOC/SOPMOD M4 extractor upgrade, Barnes Precision Machine PSFFRS (Picatinny spec free-float rail system) with proprietary long barrel nut design, for unmatched rigidity of free-float rail system–with four hardened steel sling swivel inserts /bipod mount, Magpul 5/9 slot rail sections, nickel-boron processed bolt carrier group–with carpenter 158 bolt, USSOC/SOPMOD M4 extractor upgrade, Miculek style muzzle brake/compensator, HiperFire 24 E/C trigger, MGI style adjustable gas system, users manual, warranty, shipped in a Patriot Cases hard case.
MSRP: **$1,612**

BP15 CQB PISTOL (CLOSE QUARTERS BATTLE PISTOL)

Action: semi-auto
Stock: SIG arm brace /Magpul MOE pistol grip
Barrel: 7.5-in. and 11.5-in. lengths, 1:7 or 1:8 twist .223/5.56 or 300 BLK, pistol-length gas system, chromoly with nitromet process.
Sights: Magpul MBUS
Weight: 6.5 lb.
Caliber: .223/5.56/300 BLK
Magazine: One 30-round Magpul
Features: Mil-spec type III hard coat anodized upper & lower, machined from 7075 mil-spec forgings, A4M4 feed ramps USSOC/SOPMOD M4 extractor upgrade, Barnes Precision Machine PSFFRS (Picatinny spec free-float rail system) with proprietary long barrel nut design, for unmatched rigidity of free-float rail system–with four hardened steel sling swivel inserts/bipod mount, Magpul 5/9 slot rail sections, nickel-boron processed bolt carrier group–with Carpenter 158 bolt, USSOC/SOPMOD M4 extractor upgrade, BPMA2 flash hider/breeching. Users manual/warranty, shipped in a Patriot Cases hard case.
MSRP: **$1,278**

BARRETT REC 7

Action: Gas piston operated
Stock: 6-position stock
Barrel: 16-in. or 8-in. free-floated, hammer-forged, chrome-lined barrel, 1:7 or 1:10 twist
Sights: Aimpoint Micro T-1 or Aimpoint CompM4 optional on some configurations
Weight: 7.62 lb. or 6.05 lb.
Caliber: 5.56mm NATO, 6.8 SPC
Magazine: Two 30-round with beveled magazine well
Features: Patented chrome-lined fluted gas block, one-piece 17-4 stainless piston, anti-tilt bolt carrier, machined from a monolithic block of 8620 steel, carrier features an integral piston strike face, Barrett Enhanced Bolt made from high-strength 9310 steel and is a gas-ring-free design, Nitrided, two-

AR RIFLE MODELS

Battle Rifle Company: BR4 Odin

Battle Rifle Company: 9MM Attache

position, forward-venting gas plug, forged 7075 aluminum upper and lower receivers are type III hard coat anodized, M4 feed ramps machined into the receiver and the barrel extension, mil-spec A2 flash hider, available in numerous configurations with varying barrel lengths and features.
MSRP: . . . . $2,399–$3,075

REC 7 DI

Action: semi-auto, direct impingement
Stock: Magpul MOE 6-position stock, Barrett Rail System with KeyMod,
Barrel: 16-in. or 18-in. match-grade stainless steel barrel, 1:7 or 1:10 twist
Sights: N/A
Weight: 5.5–6.5 lb.
Caliber: 5.56mm NATO, 6.8 SPC, 300 BLK
Magazine: 30 round and 10 round
Features: Magpul MOE furniture, Bravo Company Gunfigher charging handle, ALG Defense ACT trigger,

available in thirty-six configurations with varying barrel lengths and features.
MSRP: . . . . N/A

BATTLE RIFLE COMPANY

BR4 ODIN

Action: semi-auto
Stock: Mission First Tactical (MFT) (Magpul Optional)
Barrel: 14.5-in., 16-in. cryogenically treated barrel
Sights: N/A
Weight: 6.1 lb.
Caliber: 5.56mm standard (optional for 300 BLK)
Magazine: N/A
Features: 12.5-in/15.5-in Odin Works KeyMod rail (w/ one 5-slot. detachable Rail), battle rifle flash suppressor, B.A.D. lever, available with mid-length gas port, nickel-boron bolt carrier group (optional).
MSRP: . . . . N/A

9MM ATTACHE

Action: semi-auto
Stock: N/A
Barrel: N/A
Sights: Flip-up, front and rear
Weight: N/A
Caliber: 9mm
Magazine: N/A
Features: Blow back bolt, Colt SMG configuration with Colt 32-round 9mm straight mag. pistol buffer tube with Nomex cover (optional SIG Brace), single point sling adapter, ERGO pistol grip. Available configured two ways: for civilian use—configured as a pistol under ATF rules—and for law enforcement and military use—which comes with a fully functional integrated suppressor, stock, foregrip and sights.
MSRP: . . . . N/A

Black Dawn Armory: BDR-556 (16BMR)

Black Dawn Armory: BDR-556 (16AFC)

Black Dawn Armory: BDR-556 (16M)

BLACK DAWN ARMORY

BDR-556 (16BMR)

Action: semi-auto
Stock: Magpul MOE collapsible
Barrel: 16-in. M4 profile 1:9 twist
Sights: Magpul BUIS
Weight: 6.6 lb.
Caliber: 5.56
Magazine: One 30-round
Features: Mil-spec type III hard-coat anodized upper & lower, forged 7075-T6 aluminum, ion bong BCG, ERGO Grip, ALG QMS trigger, 12-in. free-float rail, hard case + ACC, lifetime warranty.
MSRP: **$1,289**

BDR-556 (16AFC)

Action: semi-auto
Stock: Magpul MOE collapsible
Barrel: 16-in. M4 profile 1:9 twist
Sights: Magpul BUIS A2 Front Post
Weight: 6.4 lb.
Caliber: 5.56
Magazine: One 30-round
Features: mil-spec type III hard coat anodized upper & lower, forged 7075-T6 aluminum, ERGO Grip, ALG QMS trigger, 9-in. free-float rail, hard case, lifetime warranty.
MSRP: **$1,249**

BDR-556 (16M)

Action: semi-auto
Stock: Magpul MOE collapsible
Barrel: 16-in. M4 profile 1:9 twist
Sights: Magpul BUIS A2 front post
Weight: 6.4 lb.
Caliber: 5.56
Magazine: One 30-round
Features: Mil-spec type III hard-coat anodized upper & lower, forged 7075-T6 aluminum, ERGO Grip, ALG QMS trigger, Magpul carbine rail, hard case, lifetime warranty.
MSRP: **$1,199**

Black Dawn Armory: BDR-556 (20EML)

Black Rain Ordnance: BRO Comp3G 18-in.

Black Rain Ordnance: BRO Force 16-in.

BDR-556 (20EML)

Action: semi-auto
Stock: Magpul MOE Rifle
Barrel: 20-in. M4 profile 1:9 twist
Sights: Magpul BUIS
Weight: 7 lb.
Caliber: 5.56
Magazine: One 30-round
Features: Mil-spec type III hard-coat anodized upper & lower, forged 7075-T6 aluminum, ERGO Grip, ALG QMS trigger, 15-in. free-float rail, hard case, lifetime warranty.
MSRP: **$1,299**

BLACK RAIN ORDNANCE

BRO COMP3G 18-IN.

Action: semi-auto
Stock: Luth AR MBA-1 stock, 17.76-In. SLM M-LOK handguard
Barrel: 18-in. gas fluted stainless barrel
Sights: N/A
Weight: N/A
Caliber: 5.56
Magazine: 30 round
Features: Billet receivers; available in blue titanium, black and Smith's grey; NY and California compliant models available.
MSRP: **$2,299**

BRO FORCE 16-IN.

Action: semi-auto
Stock: UBR stock, 15-in. M-LOK handguard, MOE grip
Barrel: 16-in. Divot mid-length gas stainless barrel, milled gas block
Sights: N/A
Weight: N/A
Caliber: 5.56, 300 BLK
Magazine: 30 round
Features: Billet receivers, BRO-DIT trigger with KNS, adjustable gas block, available in skulls imprint or digi-tan, California compliant model available.
MSRP: **$1,874**

AR RIFLE MODELS

Black Rain Ordnance: BRO Predator 24-in.

Black Rain Ordnance: BRO SBR

Black Rain Ordnance: BRO Spec 15 Carbine

Black Rain Ordnance: BRO Urban 16-in.

BRO PREDATOR 24-IN.

Action: semi-auto
Stock: Magpul PRS stock, M-LOK handguard, MOE grip
Barrel: 25-in. gas fluted stainless barrel
Sights: N/A
Weight: N/A
Caliber: 5.56
Magazine: 30 round
Features: Billet receivers; BRO-DIT trigger with KNS; adjustable gas block; available in OD green, black, and flat dark earth; California compliant model available.
MSRP: **$1,849**

BRO SBR

Action: semi-auto
Stock: Maxim CQB stock, M-LOK handguard, MOE grip
Barrel: 10.5-in. gas stainless barrel
Sights: N/A

Weight: N/A
Caliber: 5.56, 300 BLK
Magazine: 30 round
Features: Billet receivers; BRO-DIT trigger with KNS; adjustable gas block; available in OD green, black, and flat dark earth; California compliant model available.
MSRP: **$2,199**

BRO SPEC 15 CARBINE

Action: semi-auto
Stock: 6-position stock, M-LOK handguard, MOE grip
Barrel: 16-in. M4 4150 chromoly, A2 flash hider
Sights: N/A
Weight: N/A
Caliber: 5.56, 300 BLK
Magazine: 30 round
Features: Forged upper and lower receivers; forged charging handle; Nitride spec bolt carrier group; low-

profile gas block; mil-spec GI trigger; California compliant model available.
MSRP: **$899**

BRO URBAN 16-IN.

Action: semi-auto
Stock: MOE SL stock, M-LOK handguard, MOE grip
Barrel: 16-in. double flute mid-length gas stainless barrel, milled gas block
Sights: N/A
Weight: N/A
Caliber: 5.56
Magazine: 30 round
Features: Billet receivers, BRO-DIT trigger with KNS, adjustable gas block, available in Norguard and black, California compliant model available.
MSRP: **$1,699**

Black Rain Ordnance: BRO Scout

Bravo Company: HSP - The Haley Strategic Jack Carbine

BRO SCOUT

Action: semi-auto
Stock: MFT Minimalist stock, M-LOK handguard, MOE grip
Barrel: 16-in. double flute mid-length gas barrel lightweight profile, slim milled flash suppressor
Sights: N/A
Weight: N/A
Caliber: 5.56, 300 BLK, .308
Magazine: 30-round
Features: Cerakoted billet receivers, BRO-DIT trigger with KNS, adjustable gas block, available in flat dark earth, Smith's grey or OD green, California compliant model available.
MSRP: **$1,699**

BRAVO COMPANY

BCM 300 BLK REECE-16 KMR-A

Action: semi-auto
Stock: adjustable
Barrel: 16.1-in., 1:7 twist, chrome-lined, with M4 feed ramp barrel bolt extension, independent certified mil-spec 11595E steel
Sights: None, full-length top rail
Weight: 6.1 lb.
Caliber: 300 BLK AAC

Magazine: One 30-round
Features: Carbine-length gas system, manganese phosphate barrel finish, bolt machined from mil-spec carpenter No.158 steel, chrome lined carrier, chrome-lined gas key, gas key harder to USGI specs, tool steel extractor, receiver machined from aluminum forgings 7075-T6, staked M4 lock nut, USGI H buffer, BCMGUNFIGHTER grip mod 3, BCMGUNFIGHTER compensator Mod-1 762/300, BCM KMR ALPHA 13 handguard, BCM PNT trigger.
MSRP: **$1,499**

HSP - THE HALEY STRATEGIC JACK CARBINE

Action: semi-auto
Stock: N/A
Barrel: BCM 14.5-in. mid-length gas 1159E w/ permanent BCMGUNFIGHTER compensator Mod 1
Sights: Troy Industries BCM folding battle sights
Weight: N/A
Caliber: 5.56, .223
Magazine: BCM magazine with Magpul follower
Features: BCMGUNFIGHTER pistol grip and charging handle, Joint Force Enterprises Applied HSP disruptive

grey Cerakote, HSP logo laser etched on magwell and upper receiver, ALG Defense ACT trigger, Impact Weapon Components Thorntail mount.
MSRP: **$2,265**

BCM REECE 11 KMR-A PISTOL

Action: semi-auto
Stock: None, USGI H buffer
Barrel: 11.5-in., 1:7 twist, BCM standard government profile
Sights: None, full-length top rail
Weight: 4.9 lb.
Caliber: 5.56/.223
Magazine: One 30-round
Features: BCMGUNFIGHTER pistol grip and charging handle, Joint Force Enterprises Applied HSP disruptive grey Cerakote, HSP logo laser etched on magwell and upper receiver, ALG Defense ACT Trigger.
MSRP: . . . . **BCM RECCE 11 KMR-A: $1,399; BCM RECCE 11 KMR-A ELW Pistol: $1,399; BCM 300 BLK RECCE 9 KMR-A Pistol $1,499; BCM 300 BLK RECCE-12 KMR-A pistol: $1,499**

BCM 300 BLK RECCE 16 KMR-A

Action: semi-auto
Stock: adjustable

Barrel: 16+-in. barrel, BCM enhanced profile with manganese phosphate finish
Sights: None, full-length top rail
Weight: 6.1 lb.
Caliber: 300 BLK AAC or 5.56/.223
Magazine: N/A
Features: BCM PNT trigger, BCM KMR ALPHA 13 handguard, BCMGUNFIGHTER compensator Mod-1, BCM GUNFIGHTER Grip Mod 3, low-profile gas block, staked M4 lock nut, receiver haricot anodized per MIL-A-8625F, type III, class II.
MSRP: .... **BCM 300 BLK RECCE-16 KMR-A: $1,499, BCM RECCE-14 KMR Lightweight: $1,598, BCM RECCE-14 KMR-A FULL PURCHASE: $1,499, BCM RECCE-16 KMR Lightweight: $1,490, BCM RECCE-16 KMR-A (Dark Bronze) FULL PURCHASE: $1,499**

BCM CAR-16LW

Action: Standard carbine-length gas system
Stock: N/A
Barrel: USGI lightweight government profile barrels; independently certified mil-spec 11595E barrel steel; chromelined bore and chamber; manganese phosphate barrel finish on entire barrel
Sights: Mil-spec F-marked forged front sights (.625-in.); taper pinned front sight base
Weight: N/A
Caliber: 5.56mm NATO
Magazine: One included (where legal)
Features: BCM Gunfighter Mod 4 charging handle; M4 feed ramp barrel extension; M4 feed ramp flat top receiver; T-marked upper receivers; bolt machined from mil-spec Carpenter No. 158 steel; shot peened bolt; chrome-lined carrier (AUTO); chrome-lined gas key; gas key hardened to USGI specifications; grade-8 hardened fasteners key; staked per mil-spec; tool steel extractor; BCM extractor spring; black extractor insert; receivers machined from aluminum forgings 7075-T6; receivers hard coat anodize per MIL-A-8625F, type III, class II; BCM mil-spec 7075-T6 receiver extension;

USGI Mold M4 stock staked M4 lock nut; USGI H Buffer (1 USGI tungsten, 2 steel); Magpul MOE enhanced trigger guard; low shelf for RDIAS installation; low shelf for Accu-Wedge use; un-notched hammer compatible with 9mm use; fire controls marked SAFE and SEMI; cable lock; USGI manual; and F.E.T.
MSRP: . . . . **N/A**

BCM M4 CARBINE

Action: Standard carbine-length gas system
Stock: USGI mold M4 stock staked M4 lock nut
Barrel: USGI government profile barrels that are independently certified mil-spec 11595E barrel steel; manganese phosphate barrel finish on entire barrel sights, taper pinned front sight base; mil-spec F-marked forged front sights, Mod 0 does not include rear sight, Mod 1 features detachable 600m carry handle for rear sight, Mod 2 features folding battle sight
Weight: N/A
Caliber: 5.56mm NATO
Magazine: One included (where legal)
Features: BCM Gunfighter; Mod 4 charging handle; M4 feed ramp barrel extension; M4 feed ramp flat top receiver; T-marked upper receivers; chrome-lined bore and chamber; bolt machined from mil-spec Carpenter No. 158 steel; shot peened bolt; chrome-lined carrier (AUTO); chrome-lined gas key; gas key hardened to USGI specifications; grade-8 hardened fasteners key; staked per mil-spec; tool steel extractor; BCM extractor spring; black extractor insert; receivers machined from aluminum forgings 7075-T6; receivers hard coat anodize per MIL-A-8625F, type III, class II; BCM mil-spec 7075-T6 receiver extension; USGI H buffer (1 USGI tungsten, 2 steel); Magpul MOE enhanced trigger guard; low shelf for RDIAS installation; low shelf for Accu-Wedge use; un-notched hammer compatible with 9mm use; fire controls marked SAFE and SEMI; cable lock, manual, and F.E.T.; Mod 0 and 1feature double heat shield

handguards; Mod 2 features tactical handguard system.
MSRP: . . . . **N/A**

BCM MID-16

Action: Mid-length gas system
Stock: USGI Mold M4 stock staked M4 lock nut
Barrel: Government profile barrels; independently certified mil-spec 11595E barrel steel; manganese phosphate barrel finish on entire barrel; Mod 0 does not include rear sight; Mod 2 features folding battle sight
Sights: Taper pinned front sight base; mil-spec F-marked forged front sights
Weight: N/A
Caliber: USGI 5.56mm NATO
Magazine: One included (where legal)
Features: BCM Gunfighter Mod 4 charging handle; M4 feed ramp barrel extension; M4 feed ramp flat top receiver; T-marked upper receivers; chrome-lined bore and chamber; bolt machined from mil-spec Carpenter No. 158 steel; shot peened bolt; chrome-lined carrier (AUTO); chrome-lined gas key; gas key hardened to USGI specifications; grade-8 hardened fasteners key; staked per mil-spec; tool steel extractor; BCM extractor spring; black extractor insert; receivers machined from aluminum forgings 7075-T6; receivers hard coat anodize per MIL-A-8625F, type III, class II; BCM mil-spec 7075-T6 receiver extension; USGI H Buffer (1 USGI Tungsten, 2 steel); Magpul MOE enhanced trigger guard; low shelf for RDIAS installation; low shelf for Accu-Wedge use; un-notched hammer compatible with 9mm use; fire controls marked SAFE and SEMI; cable lock, USGI manual, Mod 0 includes Magpul MOE handguards; Mod 2 carbine includes a drop in tactical handguard system.
MSRP: . . . . **N/A**

BCM A4

Action: Standard rifle-length gas system
Stock: BCM A2 stock with metal buttplate and trapdoor

Bushmaster: XM-15 QRC 91046

Barrel: Independently certified mil-spec 11595E barrel steel; manganese phosphate barrel finish on entire barrel; USGI M16A4 government profile barrels
Sights: Detachable 600m carry handle for rear sight; mil-spec F-marked forged front sights; taper pinned front sight base
Weight: N/A
Caliber: 5.56mm NATO
Magazine: One included (where legal)
Features: Polymer handguards, BCM Gunfighter Mod 4 charging handle; M4 feed ramp barrel extension; M4 feed ramp flat top receiver; T-marked upper receivers; chrome-lined bore and chamber; bolt machined from mil-spec Carpenter No. 158 steel; shot peened bolt; chrome-lined carrier (AUTO); chrome-lined gas key; gas key hardened to USGI specifications; grade-8 hardened fasteners key; staked per mil-spec; tool steel extractor; BCM extractor spring; black extractor insert; receivers machined from aluminum forgings 7075-T6; receivers hard coat anodize per MIL-A-8625F, type III, class II; Magpul MOE enhanced trigger guard; low shelf for RDIAS installation; low shelf for Accu-Wedge use; un-notched hammer compatible with 9mm use; fire controls marked SAFE and SEMI; cable lock; USGI manual; and F.E.T.
MSRP: . . . . N/A

BCM A5

Action: Standard rifle-length gas system
Stock: VLTOR A5 stock
Barrel: Independently certified mil-spec 11595E barrel steel; manganese phosphate barrel finish on entire

barrel; USGI M16A4 government profile barrels
Sights: Does not include a rear sight; optics, or rear-sighting system ready; mil-spec F-marked forged front sights; taper pinned front sight base
Weight: N/A
Caliber: 5.56mm NATO
Magazine: One included (where legal)
Features: Polymer handguards; BCM Gunfighter Mod 4 charging handle; M4 feed; ramp barrel extension; M4 feed ramp flat top receiver; T-marked upper receivers; chrome-lined bore and chamber; bolt machined from mil-spec Carpenter No. 158 steel; shot peened bolt; chrome-lined carrier (AUTO); chrome-lined gas key; gas key hardened to USGI specifications; grade-8 hardened fasteners key; staked per mil-spec; tool steel extractor; BCM extractor spring; black extractor insert; receiver; machined from aluminum forgings 7075-T6; receivers hard coat anodize per MIL-A-8625F, type III, class II; Magpul MOE enhanced trigger guard; low shelf for RDIAS installation; low shelf for Accu-Wedge use; un-notched hammer compatible with 9mm use; fire controls marked SAFE and SEMI; cable lock; USGI manual.
MSRP: . . . . N/A

BCM NFA CARBINES

Action: Standard carbine-length gas system
Stock: USGI mold M4 stock staked M4 lock nut
Barrel: Independently certified mil-spec 11595E barrel steel; manganese phosphate barrel finish on entire barrel; USGI government profile barrels
Sights: Mil-spec F-marked forged front sights; taper pinned front sight base

Weight: N/A
Caliber: 5.56mm NATO
Magazine: One included (where legal)
Features: Optional, select fire (auto or burst), law enforcement/government sales only; BCM Gunfighter Mod 4 charging handle; M4 feed ramp barrel extension; M4 feed ramp flat top receiver; T-marked upper receivers; chrome-lined bore and chamber; bolt machined from mil-spec Carpenter No. 158 steel; shot peened bolt; chrome-lined carrier (auto); chrome-lined gas key; gas key hardened to USGI specifications; grade-8 hardened fasteners key; staked per mil-spec; tool steel extractor; BCM extractor spring; black extractor insert; receivers machined from aluminum forgings 7075-T6; receivers hard coat anodize per MILA-8625F, type III, class II; BCM mil-spec 7075-T6 receiver extension; USGI H buffer (1 USGI tungsten, 2 steel); Magpul MOE enhanced trigger guard; low shelf for RDIAS installation; low shelf for Accu-Wedge use; un-notched hammer compatible with 9mm use; fire controls marked SAFE and SEMI; cable lock; USGI manual.
MSRP: . . . . N/A

BUSHMASTER

XM-15 QRC 91046

Action: semi-auto
Stock: 6-position M4 stock
Barrel: 16-in. superlight 4150 barrel, FNC treated
Sights: Quick detach mount red dot optic
Weight: 5.18 lb.
Caliber: 5.56/.223
Magazine: N/A

Bushmaster: 16-in. Heavy BBL A3 Carbine 90280

Bushmaster: Quad Rail A3 90831

Bushmaster: M4 Type Patrolman's Carbine 90289

Bushmaster: 16-in. Heavy BBL Carbine A2 90212

Features: 7075 forged A3 flat-top upper receiver, 7075 forged lower receiver.
MSRP: $769

XM-15 QRC 91047

Action: semi-auto
Stock: 6-position M4 stock
Barrel: 16-in. superlight 4150 barrel, FNC treated
Sights: Quick-detach mount red dot optic
Weight: 5.18 lb.
Caliber: 5.56/.223
Magazine: One 10-round
Features: 7075 forged A3 flat-top upper receiver, 7075 forged lower receiver.
MSRP: $769

XM-15 QRC 91048

Action: semi-auto
Stock: 6-position M4 stock
Barrel: 16-in. superlight 4150 barrel, FNC treated
Sights: None, optics ready
Weight: 5.18 lb.
Caliber: 5.56/.223
Magazine: N/A

Features: 7075 forged A3 upper receiver, 7075 forged lower receiver.
MSRP: $739

16-IN. HEAVY BBL A3 CARBINE 90280

Action: semi-auto
Stock: 6-position M4 stock
Barrel: 16-in. heavy profile chrome-lined
Sights: None
Weight: 7.3 lb.
Caliber: 5.56/.223
Magazine: N/A
Features: 7075 forged A3 upper receiver, 7075 forged lower receiver.
MSRP: $947

QUAD RAIL A3 90831

Action: semi-auto
Stock: 6-position M4 stock
Barrel: 16-in. M4 profile chrome-lined
Sights: N/A
Weight: 8.2 lb.
Caliber: 5.56/.223
Magazine: N/A
Features: Aluminum free-floating quad rail handguard, 7075 forged A3 flat-top upper receiver, 7075 forged lower receiver.
MSRP: $1,099

M4 TYPE PATROLMAN'S CARBINE 90289

Action: semi-auto
Stock: 6-position M4 stock
Barrel: 16-in. M4 profile chrome-lined
Sights: N/A
Weight: 6.7 lb.
Caliber: 5.56/.223
Magazine: N/A
Features: 7075 forged A3 flat-top upper receiver with detachable carry handle, 7075 forged lower receiver.
MSRP: $947

16-IN. HEAVY BBL CARBINE A2 90212

Action: semi-auto
Stock: 6-position M4 stock
Barrel: 16-in. heavy profile 4150 chrome-lined steel barrel
Sights: N/A
Weight: 7 lb.
Caliber: 5.56/.223
Magazine: N/A
Features: 7075 forged A2 upper receiver with fixed carry handle, 7075 forged lower receiver.
MSRP: $895

20-IN. BARRELED M-19-TYPE RIFLE 90325, 90242

Action: semi-auto
Stock: 6-position M4 stock
Barrel: 20-in. 4150 chome-lined barrel
Sights: N/A
Weight: 8.46–8.78 lb.
Caliber: 5.56/.223
Magazine: N/A
Features: Comes with option for A2 fixed handle upper receiver with 300- to 800-meter rear sight system with ½ MOA windage adjustments, A3 removal handle upper receiver with 300- to 800-meter rear sight system with ½ MOA windage adjustments, A3 upper receiver with Picatinny mounting rail.
MSRP: . . . . $969–$999

M4 TYPE PATROLMAN'S CARBINE M4-A2 90216

Action: semi-auto
Stock: 6-position M4 stock
Barrel: 16-in. M4 profile 4150 chrome-lined steel barrel
Sights: N/A
Weight: 6.7 lb.
Caliber: 5.56/.223
Magazine: N/A
Features: 7075 forged A2 upper receiver with fixed carry handle, 7075 forged lower receiver.
MSRP: $895

MOE M4-TYPE CARBINE 90291

Action: semi-auto
Stock: 6-position MOE stock
Barrel: 16-in. M4 profile 4150 chrome-lined steel barrel
Sights: Magpul back-up sight
Weight: 6.42 lb.
Caliber: 5.56/.223
Magazine: 30-round PMAG
Features: 7075 forged A3 upper receiver, 7075 forged lower receiver, Magpul enhanced trigger guard, MOE handguard and MOE pistol grip.
MSRP: $1,099

16-IN. MOE MID-LENGTH 90827

Action: semi-auto
Stock: 6-position MOE stock
Barrel: 16-in. heavy profile mid-length gas chrome-lined barrel
Sights: Magpul back up sight
Weight: 6.5 lb.
Caliber: 5.56/.223
Magazine: 30-round PMAG
Features: 7075 forged A3 upper receiver, 7075 forged lower receiver, Magpul enhanced trigger guard, MOE handguard and MOE pistol grip.
MSRP: $1,099

MOE DISSIPATOR 90829

Action: semi-auto
Stock: 6-position MOE stock
Barrel: 16-in. chrome-lined barrel
Sights: rifle-length sight, Magpul back-up sight
Weight: 6.42 lb.
Caliber: 5.56/.223
Magazine: 30-round PMAG
Features: 7075 forged A3 upper receiver, 7075 forged lower receiver, Magpul enhanced trigger guard, MOE handguard and MOE pistol grip.
MSRP: $1,298

450 BUSHMASTER 90431

Action: semi-auto
Stock: fixed straight stock
Barrel: 20-in. barrel with 1:24 twist
Sights: N/A
Weight: 8.3 lb.
Caliber: .450 Bushmaster
Magazine: 5 round
Features: Upper and lower receivers machined from mil-spec aluminum forging, ships with chamber flag.
MSRP: $1,299

AR RIFLE MODELS

Bushmaster: 450 Bushmaster Carbine 90425

Bushmaster: Varminter 90641

Bushmaster: Predator 90629

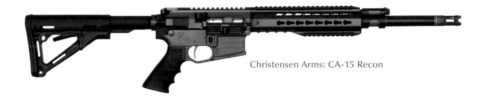

Christensen Arms: CA-15 Recon

450 BUSHMASTER CARBINE 90425

Action: semi-auto
Stock: Fixed straight stock
Barrel: 16-in. barrel with 1:24 twist
Sights: N/A
Weight: 8.1 lb.
Caliber: .450 Bushmaster
Magazine: 5 round
Features: Upper and lower receivers machined from mil-spec aluminum forging, free floating fore-end
MSRP: **$1,299**

VARMINTER 90641

Action: semi-auto
Stock: Vented aluminum fore-end Hogue rubberized pistol grip (black)
Barrel: Fluted 24-in. extra-heavy Bushmaster Varmint barrel (1-in. diameter out to gas block) with 11-degree competition muzzle crown, 1:9 twist on non-chrome-lined barrel, free-floated
Sights: Two 1.25-in. mini-risers for optics mounting

Weight: 8.4 lb.
Caliber: .223
Magazine: 5 round
Features: Ships with chamber flag.
MSRP: **$1,159**

PREDATOR 90629

Action: semi-auto
Stock: Vented aluminum fore-end, Hogue rubberized pistol grip (black)
Barrel: Fluted 20-in. extra-heavy Bushmaster predator barrel (1-in. diameter out to gas block) with 11-degree competition muzzle crown, 1:8 twist on non-chrome-lined barrel, free-floated
Sights: Two 1.25-in. mini-risers for optics mounting
Weight: 8 lb.
Caliber: .223
Magazine: 5 round
Features: Ships with chamber flag.
MSRP: **$1,159**

CHRISTENSEN ARMS

CA-15 RECON

Action: semi-auto, direct impingement or gas piston
Stock: Magpul CTR
Barrel: 416R stainless steel, button-rifled, match-grade, fluted light target contour or carbon fiber-wrapped target contour; 16-in.; 1:8 twist
Sights: N/A
Weight: 5.8-6.2 lb.
Caliber: .204 Ruger, .223 Wylde, 6.5 Grendel, 6.8 SPC, 300 BLK
Magazine: Magpul
Features: Guaranteed sub MOA accuracy; billet machined upper and lower; carbon fiber handguard, match trigger; titanium flash suppressor; black Nitride finished bolt carrier re: direct impingement; nickel-boron coated bolt carrier re: piston system.
MSRP: **$3,395**

Christensen Arms: CA-15 VTac

Christensen Arms: CA-10 DMR

CMMG: Mk3 CBR

CMMG: Mk4 RCE

CA-15 VTAC

Action: semi-auto, direct impingement
Stock: BCM Gunfighter
Barrel: 416R stainless steel, button-rifled, match-grade, fluted light target contour or carbon fiber–wrapped target contour; 16-in.; 1:8 twist, .223 Wylde, 1:7 twist, 300 BLK
Sights: N/A
Weight: 5.3–5.5 lb.
Caliber: .223 Wylde, 300 BLK
Magazine: 30-round Magpul
Features: Sub MOA accuracy guarantee, billet machined upper and lower receivers; carbon fiber handguard—KeyMod or M-LOK; 45 degree safety lever; VTac match trigger—self contained; stainless steel or titanium flash suppressor; black Nitride finished bolt carrier.
MSRP: . . . . **$2,650–$2,850**

CA-10 DMR

Action: semi-auto, direct impingement
Stock: Magpul ACS
Barrel: 18-in. to 24-in., 416R stainless steel, button-rifled, match-grade, fluted light target contour or carbon fiber-wrapped target contour; various twist rates
Sights: N/A
Weight: 7–7.3 lb.
Caliber: .243 Win., 6.5 Creedmoor,

.260 Rem., .308 Win. Match
Magazine: 20-round Magpul
Features: Sub MOA accuracy guarantee, billet machined upper and lower receivers; carbon fiber handguard—KeyMod; oversized bolt release; match trigger; titanium, side baffle muzzlebrake; black Nitride finish finished bolt carrier; various finish options; 20 MOA taper, 1913 mil-spec upper receiver.
MSRP: **$3,799**

CMMG

MK3 CBR

Action: semi-auto
Stock: Magpul ACS-L buttstock
Barrel: 16-in. 416 stainless steel, 1:10 twist, 5/8x24 threaded
Sights: N/A
Weight: 9 lb.
Caliber: .308 Win.
Magazine: 20-round Magpul PMAG
Features: The Mk3 CBR is one of CMMG's premier rifles. The Mk3 CBR features a 16-in. Nitrided 416 stainless steel medium taper profile barrel in

.308 Win. The Mk3 CBR is equipped with CMMG's own SV muzzle brake and RKM15 KeyMod handguard. Every rifle has a Geissele SSA two-stage trigger, Magpul's MOE pistol grip and Magpul ACS-L buttstock installed.
MSRP: **$1,999**

MK4 RCE

Action: semi-auto
Stock: Magpul CTR buttstock
Barrel: 16-in. medium weight tapered profile, 416 stainless steel, 1:7 twist
Sights: N/A
Weight: 6.5 lb.
Caliber: 5.56mm or 300 BLK AAC
Magazine: 30-round Magpul PMAG
Features: The Mk4 RCE is one of CMMG's premiere rifles. The Mk4 RCE features a 16-in. 416 stainless steel medium taper profile barrel available in either 5.56x45mm or 300 BLK. The RCE is equipped with CMMG's own SV muzzle brake and RKM14 KeyMod handguard. Every rifle has a Geissele SSA two-stage trigger and Magpul's MOE pistol grip, MOE trigger guard and CTR buttstock installed.
MSRP: **$1,499**

MK9 T

CMMG: MK9 T

Action: semi-auto
Stock: M4 butt-stock
Barrel: 16-in. medium weight tapered profile, 1:10 twist, M4 profile, SBN
Sights: N/A
Weight: 6.3 lb.
Caliber: 9mm
Magazine: 32 round
Features: When modularity, affordability, and quality are all important the Mk9 T is the rifle of choice. The Mk9 T utilizes CMMG's RKM series of KeyMod free-float hand guards and a Nitrided 4140 chromoly M4 profile barrel.

MSRP: **$1,149**

Colt AR-15A4 Review

I am a long-time user of Colt rifles. As one of Uncle Sam's Misguided Children (USMC), I was issued a Colt M16A2, and that's what I carried and qualified with for most of my eleven-year career. One of my first personally-owned firearms was a Colt AR-15 Sporter Match HBAR rifle, which I still own, and is my only experience with Colt since getting out of the military. In 2004, the Marine Corps retired the A2 and adopted the M16A4. Improvements included a flat-top receiver with removable carry handle and quad-rail handguards made by Knight's Armement Corporation (KAC).

My first impression—even though it's a basic model meant to replicate standard Marine Corps issue—is that it's very well made, which can be seen in the details. For example, the selector switch on many ARs has a little bit of play when in the safe position. The AR-15A4 doesn't have that problem—the selector snaps securely into the safe position with absolutely no play. This is nothing short of a high-quality rifle with all the features you would expect from Colt. One other thing; having become accustomed to AR carbines—it's been a really long time since picking up a full-size AR—I have to say . . . it felt really good.

The AR-15A4 is nearly identical to the M16A4 in every way, with a few notable exceptions. First and most noticeable is the select fire: the M16A4 has burst capabilities, while the AR-15A4 does not. Second, the selector switch is ambidextrous. Another difference is the AR-15A4 has M4 feed ramps, which is not really necessary on a full-size rifle, but definitely doesn't hurt. Less noticeable, inside the lower receiver behind the trigger group and hammer is a sear web built in to prevent illegal modifications. Another difference from the A4 issued to marines is the front handguard. The Marine Corps issues their rifles with KAC quad-rails but, understandably, Colt is not going to equip their rifles with accessories from a competitor, so they went with A2-style handguards.

It comes in 5.56x45 NATO (.223 Remington) and has a chrome lined, 20-inch government profile barrel with 1:7 right hand rifling. It weighs 7.71 pounds and is 39.5 inches in overall length. It has a full-size A2-style stock, GI issue handguards, and comes with a detachable carry handle. The MSRP is $999.

It has a good trigger and trigger reset. It's definitely not an aftermarket trigger, but feels exactly like a government issue trigger…because it is. Some might complain about that, but this is what a grunt cuts his teeth on, and it works. It's not the lightest and smoothest, but its rock solid, dependable, and will get the job done.

AR carbines have taken the market by storm, but there are benefits to the full size AR rifle. The extra barrel length adds weight out front, so muzzle rise is negligible. It's easy to forget how fast follow-up shots are with the full-length rifle. Some would argue that the full-length gas system is also more reliable than carbine length. While technically that could be true, carbine-length ARs are still incredibly reliable, so it's almost a moot point. The longer barrel also means increased muzzle velocity, which equates to better long-range performance. This is why the Marine Corps chose it.

AR RIFLE MODELS

Colt: M.A.R.C. 901 Series AR901-16S

Colt: LE6920

Colt: LE6940

Colt: AR-15A4

Shooting the AR-15A4 is a pleasure. Not that any 5.56/.223 AR has a lot of recoil, but with the reduced muzzle flip of the longer barrel and gas system, this thing can really rock and roll…and stays on target while doing so. It's been a really long time since I've fired a full-size AR and let me tell you: it just *felt right*. Much more so than I thought it would. It really brought back a lot of memories and, more importantly, it reminded me that if tight quarters aren't an issue, the full-size rifle really is a superior weapon. —*Robb Manning*

COLT

M.A.R.C. 901 SERIES AR901-16S

Action: semi-auto
Stock: Adjustable, matte black
Barrel: 16.1-in. heavy chromed 1:12 RH twist
Sights: None
Weight: 8.4 lb.
Caliber: .308 Win.
Magazine: N/A
Features: Direct gas system, locking bolt, California compliant model available.
MSRP: $1,399

LE6940

Action: semi-auto
Stock: Adjustable, matte black
Barrel: 16.1-in. chromed 1:7 RH twist
Sights: Front and rear flip-up, adjustable post front and adjustable for windage in rear

Weight: 6.8 lb.
Caliber: 5.56
Magazine: N/A
Features: Direct gas system, locking bolt, California compliant model available.
MSRP: $1,399

LE6920 SERIES

Action: semi-auto
Stock: Adjustable, matte black
Barrel: 16.1-in. chromed 1:7 RH twist
Sights: Front adjustable post front, flip-up adjustable for windage in rear
Weight: 6.9 lb.
Caliber: 5.56
Magazine: N/A
Features: Direct gas system, locking bolt, available in five configurations including a stripped down model ($799) for optimal personal configuring and three versions in various colors (matte black, gray, and flat dark earth), California compliant model available.
MSRP: . . . . $799–$1,049

AR-15A4

Action: semi-auto
Stock: Fixed, matte black
Barrel: 20-in. chromed 1:7 RH twist
Sights: Front adjustable post, rear adjustable for Windage
Weight: 7.7 lb.
Caliber: 5.56
Magazine: N/A
Features: Direct gas system, locking bolt.
MSRP: $999

COLT COMPETITION

COLT "PRO" MODEL CRP-18

Action: semi-auto, gas-operated, direct impingement
Stock: Magpul CTR 6-position adjustable stock, Colt Competition vented modular float-tube handguard, Magpul MOE grip,
Barrel: 18-in. custom fluted match-grade, air-gaged, polished 416

Colt Competition: Colt "Pro" Model CRP-18

Colt Competition: Colt "Pro" Model CRL-16

Colt Competition: Colt "Pro" Model CRL-20

stainless steel barrel, 6-groove button rifling, 1:8 RH twist, triple-port muzzle brake
Sights: None, full-length integral Picatinny rail for mounting
Weight: 7.22 lb.
Caliber: .223 Rem.
Magazine: 30-round Magpul (10-round available where restricted by law, 10-round fixed available for California)
Features: Geissele two-stage match trigger, low profile adjustable gas block, Colt Competition charging handle with extended tactical latch, forged and precision-fitted upper and lower receivers.
MSRP: **$2,019**

COLT "PRO" MODEL CRP-16

Action: semi-auto, gas-operated, direct impingement
Stock: Magpul CTR 6-position adjustable stock, Colt Competition vented modular float-tube handguard, Magpul MOE grip with extended backstrap.
Barrel: 16-in. custom fluted match-grade, air-gaged, polished 416 stainless steel barrel, 6-groove button rifling, 1:8 RH twist, triple-port muzzle brake
Sights: None, full-length integral Picatinny rail for mounting
Weight: 7 lb.
Caliber: .223 Rem.

Magazine: 30-round Magpul (10-round available where restricted by law, 10-round fixed available for California)
Features: Geissele two-stage match trigger, Magpul enlarged trigger guard, low profile adjustable gas block, Colt Competition charging handle with extended tactical latch, forged and precision-fitted upper and lower receivers.
MSRP: **$1,899**

COLT "PRO" MODEL CRL-20

Action: semi-auto, gas-operated, direct impingement
Stock: Magpul PRS buttstock, JDM float-tube handguard, Magpul MOE grip with extended backstrap
Barrel: 20-in. tapered, heavyweight, air-gaged, polished 416 stainless steel barrel, 6-groove button rifling, 1:10 RH twist, triple-port muzzle brake
Sights: None
Weight: 11.04 lb.
Caliber: .308 Win.
Magazine: 20-round Magpul (10-round available where restricted by law, 10-round fixed available for California)
Features: Geissele two-stage SSA-E match trigger, low profile adjustable gas block, Colt Competition charging handle with extended tactical latch, matched bolt and carrier, CNC-machined and precision-fitted upper and lower receivers.
MSRP: **$2,979**

COLT "PRO" MODEL CRL-16

Action: semi-auto, gas-operated, direct impingement
Stock: Magpul CTR 6-position buttstock, JDM float-tube handguard, Magpul MOE grip with extended backstrap.
Barrel: 16-in. tapered, heavyweight, air-gaged, polished 416 stainless steel barrel, 6-groove button rifling, 1:10 RH twist, triple-port muzzle brake
Sights: None
Weight: 8.67 lb.
Caliber: .308 Win.
Magazine: 20-round Magpul (10-round available where restricted by law, 10-round fixed available for California)
Features: Geissele two-stage SSA-E match trigger, low profile adjustable gas block, Colt Competition charging handle with extended tactical latch, matched bolt and carrier, CNC-machined and precision-fitted upper and lower receivers.
MSRP: **$2,339**

COLT "MARKSMAN" MODEL CRX-16E

Action: semi-auto, gas-operated, direct impingement
Stock: Magpul MOE fixed rifle stock, Colt Competition vented modular float-tube handguard, checkered A2-style finger-groove grip
Barrel: 16-in. custom match-grade "manganese-phospated" 4140

Core Rifle Systems: Core15 Hardcore
System X4 Rifle

chromoly steel barrel, 6-groove button rifling, 1:8 RH twist, twin-port muzzle brake
Sights: None
Weight: 6.68 lb.
Caliber: .223 Rem.
Magazine: 30-round Magpul (10-round available where restricted by law, 10-round fixed available for California)
Features: Colt Competition Match-Target trigger, Magpul enlarged trigger guard, low profile adjustable gas block, Colt Competition charging handle with extended tactical latch, forged and precision-fitted upper and lower receivers.
MSRP: $1,339

COLT "MARKSMAN" MODEL CRX-16

Action: semi-auto, gas-operated, direct impingement
Stock: Carbine-style 4-position stock, Colt Competition vented modular float-tube handguard, checkered A2-style finger-groove grip
Barrel: 16-in. mid-weight custom match-grade "manganese-phospated" 4140 chromoly steel barrel, 6-groove button rifling, 1:8 RH twist, twin-port muzzle brake
Sights: None
Weight: 6.45 lb.
Caliber: .223 Rem.
Magazine: 30-round Magpul (10-round available where restricted by law, 10-round fixed available for California)

Features: Colt Competition Match-Target trigger, Magpul enlarged trigger guard, low profile adjustable gas block, Colt Competition charging handle with extended tactical latch, forged and precision-fitted upper and lower receivers.
MSRP: $1,399

COLT "EXPERT" MODEL CRE-18

Action: semi-auto, gas-operated, direct impingement
Stock: Carbine-style 4-position stock, Colt Competition vented modular float-tube handguard, Hogue rubber finger-groove grip
Barrel: 18-in. mid-weight custom match-grade "manganese-phospated" 4140 chromoly steel barrel, 6-groove button rifling, 1:8 RH twist, twin-port muzzle brake
Sights: None
Weight: 6.92 lb.
Caliber: .223 Rem.
Magazine: 30-round Magpul mag (10-round available where restricted by law, 10-round fixed available for California)
Features: Colt Competition Match-Target trigger, Magpul enlarged trigger guard, low profile adjustable gas block, Colt Competition charging handle with extended tactical latch, forged and precision-fitted upper and lower receivers.
MSRP: $1,599

CORE RIFLE SYSTEMS

CORE15 HARDCORE SYSTEM X4 RIFLE

Action: semi-auto
Stock: Magpul UBR collapsible stock; black hogue rubber grip; CORE15 15-in. aluminum KeyMod rail, machined from 6005 aluminium alloy, in-house sniper grey Cerakote
Barrel: Three options: 18-in. rifle length profile 1:7, 4150 black Nitride finish, fluted; 20-in. 6.5 Grendel, government profile 1:8 twist, 4150 rifle-length gas system, black Nitride finish, fluted; 20-in. 6.5 Grendel, government profile, 1:8 twist, 4150 rifle-length gas system, stainless steel bead blasted finish, fluted
Sights: Leupold MK6 3x18x44 with mount; Magpul MBUS Pro front & rear
Weight: Varies
Caliber: .223/5.56x45mm NATO or 6.5mm Grendel
Magazine: Magpul Gen3 20-round & 30-round; 6.5mm Grendel ACS 25-round
Features: Left or right hand configurable; CORE15 HARDCORE Billet Lower machined from solid 7075-T6 aluminum alloy, in-house sniper grey Cerakote, lo-profile, heavily beveled and relieved magwell oversized integral trigger guard, bullet pictogram safety markings; CORE15 HARDCORE billet upper machined from solid 7075-T6 aluminum alloy, in-house sniper grey Cerakote,

Core Rifle Systems:
Core30 MOE M-Lok

Core Rifle Systems: Core15
TAC 6.5 Grendel Rifle

serialized to match with lower; CORE15 nickel-boron coated M16 chrome lined 8620 steel carrier, magnetic particle inspected bolt (MPI), mil-spec Carpenter 158 steel bolt, chrome lined gas key hardened to USGI specs with grade-8 hardened fasteners, mil-spec staked, tool steel extractor upgrade, extractor spring, M16 profile, shot peened; LanTac Dragon muzzle break; CMC trigger group two-stage 2 lb. break/2 lb. reset; Boyt H44 Compact Rifle/ Carbine case, Otis MSR/AR cleaning kit, Frog Lube Tube, CORE15 welcome kit (manual, warranty registration, CORE15 stickers, dog tags). HARDCORE documentation to include: certificate of authenticity, range log/accuracy guarantee, verification target with serial numbers matching barrel, upper & lower receiver; Atlas BT10 bipod 1913 Picatinny rail mount 4.75-in. to 9-in. adjustable, 5-position.
MSRP: **$5,600**

CORE30 MOE M-LOK

Action: N/A
Stock: Magpul MOE 6-position stock, Magpul MOE mid-length forearm, Magpul MOE grip
Barrel: .308 offerings—CORE30 16-in. 4150 CMV mid-length 1:10 twist 5/8x24 TPI, black Nitride finish; CORE30 18-in. 416R stainless steel match-grade mid-length 1:10 twist 5/8x24. 6.5 Creedmoor offerings—

CORE30 20-in. rifle-length gas system, 1:8 twist, 4150 black Nitride finish; CORE30 20-in. rifle-length gas system, 1:8 twist, 416R fluted stainless steel bead blasted finish; CORE30 22-in. rifle-length gas system, 1:8 twist, 4150 black Nitride finish; CORE30 chrome lined 8620 steel carrier; CORE30 22-in. rifle-length gas system, 1:8 twist, 416R fluted stainless steel bead blasted finish
Sights: N/A
Weight: 8 lb.
Caliber: .308 Win., 6.5mm Creedmoor
Magazine: Magpul 20-round PMAG
Features: CORE30 billet lower CNC machined from solid 7075-T6 aluminum alloy, integral oversized trigger guard, type III hard coat anodized finish; CORE30 billet upper CNC machined from solid 7075-T6 aluminum alloy with 1913 Picatinny rail and laser engraved T-markings; CORE30 billet charging handle V.3; CORE30 low-profile gas block; SureFire SOCOM 3-Prong Flash Hider; CORE15 Hardshell Case; Welcome Kit—owner's manual; CORE15 lifetime warranty registration; stickers; dog tags.
MSRP: . . . . **$1,950–$2,400**

CORE15 TAC 6.5 GRENDEL RIFLE

Action: semi-auto
Stock: Hogue 6-position retractable (mil-spec), CORE15 KeyMod 15-in. rail, Hogue pistol grip

Barrel: CORE15 18-in. government-profile 1:8 twist 4150 rifle-length gas system, black Nitride finish; CORE15 20-in. government profile 1:8 twist 4150 rifle-length gas system, black Nitride finish, fluted; CORE15 18-in. government profile 1:8 twist 4150 rifle-length gas system, bead blasted stainless steel, fluted; CORE15 20-in. government profile 1:8 twist 4150 rifle-length gas system, bead blasted stainless steel, fluted
Sights: N/A
Weight: 6 lb. 5 oz.
Caliber: 6.5mm Grendel
Magazine: ASC 25-round stainless steel magazine
Features: CORE15 mil-spec forged 7075-T6 lower receiver, type III class II hard coat anodized finish, beveled magwell for improved reloading speed, machined chevrons in front of magazine well, bullet pictogram safety markings; CORE15 mil-spec forged 7075-T6 M4 upper receiver, type III class II hard-coat anodized finish, M4 feed ramps, (1913 Picatinny rail flat top) w/ dry lube internal finish and laser engraved T-markings; CORE15 mil-spec carpenter 158 steel bolt, M16 chrome lined 8620 steel carrier, mil-spec staked gas key, tool steel extractor, shot peened; CMC single-stage 3.5 lb. trigger (flat or curved); Lantac Dragon muzzle break; CORE15 oversized trigger guard; CORE15 hardshell case; welcome kit—owner's manual; CORE15 lifetime warranty registration; stickers; dog tags
MSRP: . . . . **$1,490–$1,540**

Daniel Defense: M4 Carbine, V1

Daniel Defense: M4 Carbine, V5

Daniel Defense: M4 Carbine, V5S

DANIEL DEFENSE

M4 CARBINE, V1

Action: Carbine-length direct impingement
Stock: Daniel Defense buttstock and pistol grip with soft touch overmolding
Barrel: Cold hammer forged, chromoly vanadium steel, 16-in. M4 profile, carbine-length gas system, chrome lined, mil-spec heavy phosphate coated, MP tested
Sights: None
Weight: 6.70 lb.
Caliber: 5.56mm NATO
Magazine: 30 round
Handguard: DDM4 rail 12.0 FSP handguard with 1913 Picatinny rail attachment and QD attachment points front and back on both sides
Features: Mil-spec lower receiver with enhanced magazine well, rear receiver QD swivel attachment point, mil-spec upper receiver with indexing marks and M4 feed ramps, mil-spec MP-tested bolt carrier group with properly staked gas key, pinned low-profile gas block, Daniel Defense flash suppressor, custom Daniel Defense full-latch impact plastic case, lifetime satisfaction guarantee, made in the United States.
MSRP: **$1,799**

M4 CARBINE, V5

Action: Mid-length direct impingement
Stock: Daniel Defense buttstock and pistol grip with soft touch overmolding
Barrel: Cold hammer forged, chromoly vanadium steel, 16-in. government profile, mid-length gas system, chrome lined, mil-spec heavy phosphate coated, MP tested
Sights: None
Weight: 6.44 lb.
Caliber: 5.56mm NATO
Magazine: 30 round
Handguard: DDM4 rail 12.0 handguard with 1913 Picatinny rail attachment and QD attachment points front and back on both sides
Features: Mil-spec lower receiver with enhanced magazine well, rear receiver QD swivel attachment point, mil-spec upper receiver with indexing marks and M4 feed ramps, mil-spec MP-tested bolt carrier group with properly staked gas key, pinned low-profile gas block, Daniel Defense flash suppressor, custom Daniel Defense full-latch impact plastic case, lifetime satisfaction guarantee, made in the United States.
MSRP: **$1,689**

M4 CARBINE, V5S

Action: Mid-length direct impingement
Stock: Daniel Defense buttstock and pistol grip with soft touch overmolding
Barrel: Cold hammer forged, chromoly vanadium steel, 14.5-in. government profile, mid-length gas system, chrome lined, mil-spec heavy phosphate coated, MP tested
Sights: None
Weight: 6.23 lb.
Caliber: 5.56mm NATO
Magazine: 30 round
Handguard: DDM4 rail 12.0 handguard with 1913 Picatinny rail attachment and QD attachment points front and back on both sides
Features: Mil-spec lower receiver with enhanced magazine well, rear receiver QD swivel attachment point, mil-spec upper receiver with indexing marks and M4 feed ramps, mil-spec

Daniel Defense: MK12

Daniel Defense:
M4 Carbine, MK18
Factory SBR

Del-Ton: DTI Evolution

MP-tested bolt carrier group with properly staked gas key, pinned low-profile gas block, pinned and welded Daniel Defense flash suppressor, custom Daniel Defense full-latch impact plastic case, lifetime satisfaction guarantee, made in United States.

MSRP: **$1,769**

MK12

Action: Rifle-length direct impingement
Stock: Daniel Defense buttstock and pistol grip with Soft touch overmolding
Barrel: Cold hammer forged, stainless steel, 18-in. MK12 profile, rifle-length gas system, salt bath Nitride treated, MP tested
Sights: None
Weight: 7.41 lb.
Caliber: 5.56mm NATO
Magazine: 20 round
Handguard: DDM4 rail 12.0 handguard with 1913 Picatinny rail attachment and QD attachment points front and back on both sides
Features: Geissele SSA two-stage trigger, mil-spec lower receiver with enhanced magazine well, rear receiver QD swivel attachment point, mil-spec upper receiver with indexing marks and M4 feed ramps, mil-spec

MP-tested bolt carrier group with properly staked gas key, MK12 gas block, Daniel Defense flash suppressor, custom Daniel Defense full-latch impact plastic case, lifetime satisfaction guarantee, made in the United States.

MSRP: **$1,999**

M4 CARBINE, MK18 FACTORY SBR

Action: Carbine-length gas impingement system
Stock: Daniel Defense buttstock and pistol grip with Soft Touch overmolding receiver extension; Daniel Defense RIS II MK18 (free-float)
Barrel: Chromoly vanadium steel, cold hammer–forged, 1:7 twist, 10.3-in. government profile, carbine gas system, chrome lined, MP tested, and mil-spec heavy phosphate coated
Sights: None
Weight: 5.88 lb.
Caliber: 5.56mm NATO
Magazine: 30 round
Features: Low-profile gas block, mil-spec lower receiver with enhanced magazine well, rear receiver QD swivel attachment point, mil-spec upper receiver with indexing marks and A4 feed ramps, mil-spec MP-tested bolt carrier group with properly staked gas key, Daniel

Defense flash suppressor, custom Daniel Defense full-latch impact plastic case, and made in the United States.

MSRP: **$1,749**

DEL-TON

DTI EVOLUTION

Action: semi-auto
Stock: Magpul CTR mil-spec buttstock
Barrel: 16-in., CMV chrome lined, 1:9 twist
Sights: Samson quick-flip dual aperture rear sign; Samson folding front sight
Weight: 6.8 lb.
Caliber: 5.56x45mm
Magazine: One 30-round
Features: A3 mid-length rifle excellent for 3 Gun shooting.

MSRP: **$1,299**

DTI EXTREME DUTY

Action: semi-auto
Stock: M4 five-position reinforced fiber
Barrel: 16-in., hammer forged, chrome lined, 1:7 twist
Sights: Samson quick-flip dual aperture rear sight
Weight: 6.4 lb. empty

Del-Ton: DTI Extreme Duty

Del-Ton: DT Sport OR

Del-Ton: Echo 316 MOE

Del-Ton: Sierra 316 MOE

Del-Ton: Alpha 320H

Caliber: 5.56x45mm
Magazine: One 30-round
Features: A3 carbine with heavy-duty hammer forged barrel built for long life.
MSRP: **$1,100**

DT SPORT OR

Action: semi-auto
Stock: M4 6-position buttstock
Barrel: 16-in., 1:9 twist
Sights: N/A
Weight: 5.6 lb.
Caliber: 5.56 x 45mm
Magazine: One 30-round
Features: Lightweight, A3, optics-ready entry level carbine excellent for first AR or for a woman; also available in standard model (5.6 lb.).
MSRP: **$707**

ECHO 316

Action: semi-auto
Stock: M4, 5-position reinforced fiber
Barrel: 16-in. chromoly vanadium, 1:9 twist
Sights: N/A
Weight: 6.4 lb.
Caliber: 5.56x45mm
Magazine: One 30-round
Features: A3 M4 barreled carbine; California legal model available.
MSRP: **$788**

ECHO 316 MOE

Action: semi-auto
Stock: Magpul MOE polymer stock
Barrel: 16-in., 1:9 twist, chromoly vanadium
Sights: N/A
Weight: 6.8 lb.
Caliber: 5.56x45 mm

Magazine: One 30-round
Features: A3 MOE equipped carbine; also available in heavy-barreled model; available in matte black, flat dark earth, or olive drab finishes.
MSRP: **$858**

SIERRA 316 MOE

Action: semi-auto
Stock: Magpul MOE polymer stock
Barrel: 16-in., 1:9 twist, chromoly vanadium
Sights: N/A
Weight: 7 lb.
Caliber: 5.56x45mm
Magazine: One 30-round
Features: A3 MOE equipped mid-length rifle, also available as Sierra 316H, and A2 mid-length, Sierra 216H.
MSRP: . . . . **$788–$858**

ALPHA 320H

Action: semi-auto
Stock: Standard A2 black Zytel with trap door assembly
Barrel: 20-in., 1:9 twist, chromoly vanadium

Del-Ton: Echo 311/5

Sights: N/A
Weight: 8 lb.
Caliber: 5.56x45mm
Magazine: One 30-round
Features: A3 heavy profile rifle; also available as Alpha 220H (A2 heavy profile rifle) and Alpha 320G (A3 government profile rifle).
MSRP: . . . . $788–$793

ECHO 311/5

Stock: M4, five-position reinforced fiber
Barrel: 11.5-in., 5.5-in. flash hider permanently attached for a total length of 16-in.
Sights: N/A
Weight: 6.6 lb.
Caliber: 5.56x45mm
Magazine: One 30-round
Features: 11.5-in. A3 with 5.5-in. flash hider.
MSRP: $814

DIAMONDBACK

DB15FDE

Action: semi-auto, direct impingement
Stock: ATI Strikeforce stock, Diamondback modified aluminum four rail, A2 style pistol grip
Barrel: 16-in. 4140 chromoly, M4 contour, free-float, 1:9 twist, A2 flash hider
Sights: None
Weight: 6.65 lb.
Caliber: 5.56/.223
Magazine: 30 round
Features: Lower receiver forged 7075-T6 aluminium, upper receiver A3 flat-top forged 7075-T6 aluminum T-marked, flat dark earth coloring, California compliant model available.
MSRP: $1,041

DB15S

Action: semi-auto, direct impingement
Stock: ATI Strikeforce stock, standard two-piece handguard
Barrel: 16-in. 4140 chromoly, M4 contour, free-float, 1:9 twist, A2 flash hider
Sights: A2 front post sight
Weight: 6.65 lb.
Caliber: 5.56/.223
Magazine: 30 round
Features: Lower receiver forged 7075-T6 aluminium, upper receiver A3 flat-top forged 7075-T6 aluminum T-marked, black anodized hard coat finish, California compliant model available.
MSRP: $899

DB15NIB

Action: semi-auto, direct impingement
Stock: Magpul CTR, Diamondback modified aluminum four rail, Magpul MIAD pistol grip
Barrel: 16-in. 4140 chromoly, M4 contour, free-float, 1:9 twist, A2 flash hider
Sights: None
Weight: 6.65 lb.
Caliber: 5.56/.223
Magazine: 30 round
Features: Lower receiver nickel-boron coated forged 7075-T6 aluminium, upper receiver nickel-boron coated A3 flat-top forged 7075-T6 aluminum T-marked, nickel-boron/black anodized hard coat finish, California compliant model available.
MSRP: $1,199

DB15B

Action: semi-auto, direct impingement
Stock: ATI Strikeforce stock,

Diamondback modified aluminum four rail, A2-style pistol grip
Barrel: 16-in. 4140 chromoly, M4 contour, free-float, 1:9 twist, A2 flash hider
Sights: None
Weight: 6.65 lb.
Caliber: 5.56/.223
Magazine: 30 round
Features: Lower receiver nickel-boron coated forged 7075-T6 aluminium, upper receiver nickel-boron coated A3 flat-top forged 7075-T6 aluminum T-marked, black anodized hard coat finish, California compliant model available.
MSRP: $1,019

DB15DCT

Action: semi-auto, direct impingement
Stock: ATI Strikeforce stock, Diamondback modified aluminum four rail, A2-style pistol grip
Barrel: 16-in. 4140 chromoly, M4 contour, free-float, 1:9 twist, A2 flash hider
Sights: None
Weight: 6.65 lb.
Caliber: 5.56/.223
Magazine: Aluminum 30-round
Features: Lower receiver nickel-boron coated forged 7075-T6 aluminium, upper receiver nickel-boron coated A3 flat-top forged 7075-T6 aluminum T-marked, digital camo tan finish, California compliant model available.
MSRP: $1,221

DB15DCG

Action: semi-auto, direct impingement
Stock: ATI Strikeforce stock, Diamondback modified aluminum four rail, A2-style pistol grip
Barrel: 16-in. 4140 chromoly, M4 contour, free-float, 1:9 twist, A2 flash hider
Sights: None
Weight: 6.65 lb.
Caliber: 5.56/.223
Magazine: Aluminum 30-round
Features: Lower receiver nickel-boron coated forged 7075-T6 aluminium, upper receiver nickel-boron coated A3 flat-top, forged 7075-T6 aluminum T marked, digital

DoubleStar: C3

DoubleStar: 3GR

DoubleStar: Midnight Dragon

camo green finish, California compliant model available.
MSRP: **$1,221**

DB15S

Action: semi-auto, direct impingement
Stock: ATI Strikeforce stock, standard two-piece handguard, A2-style pistol grip
Barrel: 16-in. 4140 chromoly, M4 contour, 1:9 twist, A2 flash hider
Sights: A2 front post sight
Weight: 6.65 lb.
Caliber: 5.56/.223
Magazine: 30 round
Features: Lower receiver forged 7075-T6 aluminium, upper receiver A3 flat-top forged 7075-T6 aluminum T-marked, black anodized hard coat finish, no forward assist or dust cover, California compliant model available.
MSRP: **$756**

DB15 PISTOLS

Action: semi-auto, direct impingement
Stock: None
Barrel: 7.5-in. 4140 chromoly, 1:9 twist
Sights: None
Weight: 6.65 lb.
Caliber: 5.56/.223

Magazine: 30 round
Features: Diamondback modified aluminum four rail, A2-style pistol grip, lower receiver forged 7075-T6 aluminium, upper receiver A3 flat-top forged 7075-T6 aluminum T-marked, available in flat dark earth coloring, Diamondback black and Diamondback OD green.
MSRP: . . . . **$899–$914**

DOUBLESTAR

C3

Action: semi-auto
Stock: ACE Ultra Lite
Barrel: 16-in. 4140 chromoly steel lightweight; 1:9 twist
Sights: N/A
Weight: 5.5 lb.
Caliber: 5.56 NATO
Magazine: 20-round PMAG
Features: 9-in. Samson Evolution handguard; DoubleStar Tac Latch charging handle.
MSRP: **$1,499**

3GR

Action: semi-auto

Stock: ACE ARFX
Barrel: 18-in. fluted stainless steel WAG HBAR; 1:8 twist
Sights: N/A
Weight: 7.5 lb.
Caliber: 5.56 NATO
Magazine: 30 round
Features: 15-in. Samson Evolution handguard; ERGO Suregrip pistol grip; CMC trigger group; DSC low-profile gas block; Carlson LE Comp.
MSRP: **$2,039**

MIDNIGHT DRAGON

Action: semi-auto
Stock: ACE ARFX
Barrel: 24-in. Helical fluted stainless steel bull; black Nitride; 1:8 twist
Sights: N/A
Weight: 9.25 lb.
Caliber: 5.56 NATO
Magazine: 5 round
Features: Helical fluted free-float handguard; two-stage trigger; ERGO tactical Pistol grip; DoubleStar Tac Latch charging handle.
MSRP: **$1,649**

DoubleStar: Star-Car

DoubleStar: DS-4

DoubleStar: Patrol Rifle

STAR-CAR

Action: semi-auto
Stock: 6-position adjustable DS-4 buttstock
Barrel: 16-in. chromoly HBAR; 1:9 twist
Sights: N/A
Weight: 6.7 lb.
Caliber: 5.56 NATO
Magazine: 30 round
Features: Standard CAR handguard with heat shield.
MSRP: **$1,326**

DS-4

Action: semi-auto
Stock: 6-position adjustable DS-4 buttstock
Barrel: 16-in. chromoly HBAR; 1:9 twist
Sights: N/A
Weight: 6.3 lb.
Caliber: 5.56 NATO
Magazine: 30 round
Features: Double heat shield DS-4 handguard.
MSRP: **$1,326**

PATROL RIFLE

Action: semi-auto
Stock: 6-position adjustable
Barrel: 16-in. chromoly lightweight; 1:9 twist
Sights: Front sight tower; flip-up rear sight
Weight: 6.35 lb.

Caliber: 5.56 NATO
Magazine: 30-round
Features: DoubleStar 4-rail handguard; Hogue pistol grip; A2 Phantom flash hider.
MSRP: **$1,620**

300 BLK

Action: semi-auto
Stock: 6-position adjustable DS-4 buttstock
Barrel: 16-in. 4140 chromoly steel HBAR; black Nitride; 1:8 twist
Sights: N/A
Weight: 6.7 lb.
Caliber: 300 BLK
Magazine: 30 round
Features: 5/8x24 TPI A2 flash suppressor.
MSRP: **$1,530**

DoubleStar: 300 BLK

DoubleStar: 11.5-in. Mini Dragon

DoubleStar: 10.5-in. Mini Dragon

DoubleStar: 7.5 Mini Dragon

DPMS: TAC 2

11.5-IN. MINI DRAGON

Action: semi-auto
Stock: N/A pistol tube
Barrel: 11.5-in. chromoly HBAR; 1:9 twist
Sights: N/A
Weight: 4.7 lb.
Caliber: 5.56 NATO
Magazine: 30 round
Features: N/A
MSRP: $1,204

10.5-IN. MINI DRAGON

Action: semi-auto
Stock: N/A pistol tube
Barrel: 10.5-in. chromoly HBAR; 1:9 twist
Sights: N/A

Weight: 4.7 lb.
Caliber: 5.56 NATO
Magazine: 30 round
Features: N/A
MSRP: $1,284

7.5 MINI DRAGON

Action: semi-auto
Stock: N/A pistol tube
Barrel: 7.5-in. chromoly HBAR; 1:9 twist
Sights: N/A
Weight: 4.6 lb.
Caliber: 5.56 NATO
Magazine: 30 round
Features: pistol-length free-float handguard.
MSRP: $1331.99

DPMS

TAC 2

Action: semi-auto
Stock: Magpul ACS stock, M111 modular handguard, Magpul MOE pistol grip
Barrel: 16-in. 4150 chrome-lined, rifle length, 1:9 twist, Panther flash hider
Sights: A2 front, Magpul rear
Weight: 8.5 lb.
Caliber: 5.56
Magazine: N/A
Features: Forged 7075-T6 A3 flat-top upper, forged 7075-T6 lower.
MSRP: $1,249

DPMS: TPR

DPMS: Recon

DPMS: Oracle

DPMS: Prairie Panther Brush

TPR

Action: semi-auto
Stock: Magpul MOE stock, M111 modular handguard, Magpul MOE pistol grip
Barrel: 20-in. HBAR bead-blasted 416 stainless, 1:9 twist, AAC Blackout flash hider
Sights: N/A, optics ready
Weight: 7.75 lb.
Caliber: 5.56
Magazine: N/A
Features: Forged 7075-T6 A3 flat-top upper, forged 7075-T6 lower.
MSRP: **$1,249**

RECON

Action: semi-auto
Stock: Magpul MOE stock, mid-length 4-rail free-float handguard, Magpul MOE pistol grip
Barrel: 16-in. HBAR bead blasted 416 stainless steel, 1:9 twist, AAC flash hider
Sights: Magpul front and rear
Weight: 7.65 lb.
Caliber: 5.56
Magazine: N/A
Features: Forged 7075-T6 A3 flat-top upper, forged 7075-T6 lower.
MSRP: **$1,197**

ORACLE

Action: semi-auto
Stock: Pardus composite tube, Glacier Guard handguard, A2 pistol grip
Barrel: 16-in. HBAR 4140 chromoly, 1:9 twist, A2 birdcage flash hider
Sights: N/A
Weight: 8.3 lb.
Caliber: .308/7.62 NATO
Magazine: N/A
Features: Extruded 7029-T6 A3 flat-top upper, billet 7029-T6 lower.
MSRP: **$954**

PRAIRIE PANTHER BRUSH

Action: semi-auto
Stock: A2 stock, carbon-fiber free-float handguard, A2 pistol grip
Barrel: 20-in. lightweight fluted Teflon-coated 416 stainless, 1:8 twist
Sights: N/A, optics ready
Weight: 7.15 lb.
Caliber: .223
Magazine: N/A
Features: Forged 7075-T6 A3 flat-top upper, forged 7075-T6 lower.
MSRP: **$1,849**

KINGS DESERT SHADOW

Action: semi-auto
Stock: Carbon-fiber free-float handguard, A2 pistol grip
Barrel: 20-in. lightweight fluted Teflon-coated 416 stainless, 1:8 twist
Sights: N/A, optics ready
Weight: 7.15 lb.
Caliber: .223
Magazine: N/A
Features: Forged 7075-T6 A3 flat-top upper, forged 7075-T6 lower.
MSRP: **$1,249**

SWEET 16

Action: semi-auto
Stock: A2 fixed stock, aluminum free-float handguard, A2 pistol grip
Barrel: 16-in. bull barrel 416 stainless, 1:9 twist
Sights: N/A, optics ready
Weight: 7.75 lb.
Caliber: .223
Magazine: N/A
Features: Forged 7075-T6 A3 flat-top upper, forged 7075-T6 lower.
MSRP: **$979**

DPMS: AP4 Carbine

DPMS: LBR

BULL 20

Action: semi-auto
Stock: A2 fixed stock, aluminum free-float handguard, A2 pistol grip
Barrel: 20-in. bull barrel, 416 stainless, 1.9 twist
Sights: N/A, optics ready
Weight: 9.5 lb.
Caliber: .223
Magazine: N/A
Features: Forged 7075-T6 A3 flat-top upper, forged 7075-T6 lower.
MSRP: $989

BULL 24

Action: semi-auto
Stock: A2 fixed stock, aluminum free-float handguard, A2 pistol grip
Barrel: 24-in. bull barrel, 416 stainless, 1:9 twist
Sights: N/A, optics ready
Weight: 9.8 lb.
Caliber: .223
Magazine: N/A
Features: Forged 7075-T6 A3 flat-top upper, forged 7075-T6 lower.
MSRP: $999

AP4 CARBINE

Action: semi-auto
Stock: AP4 composite stock, Glacier Guard handguard, A2 pistol grip
Barrel: 16-in. 4150 chrome-lined, 1:9 twist, A2 flash hider
Sights: Rear sight in detachable carry handle

Weight: 7.15 lb.
Caliber: 5.56
Magazine: N/A
Features: Forged 7075-T6 A3 flat-top upper, forged 7075-T6 lower.
MSRP: $945

LBR

Action: semi-auto
Stock: Magpul MOE stock, aluminum vented free-float handguard, A2 pistol grip
Barrel: 16-in. lightweight 416 staineless steel, 1:9 twist, A2 birdcage flash hider
Sights: N/A, optics ready
Weight: 7.25 lb.
Caliber: 5.56
Magazine: N/A
Features: Forged 7075-T6 A3 flat-top upper, forged 7075-T6 lower.
MSRP: $979

3GI

Action: semi-auto
Stock: Magpul CTR stock, V-Tac free-float handguard, Hogue rubber pistol grip
Barrel: 18-in. HBAR Teflon-coated 416 staineless steel, 1:8 twist, Miculek compensator
Sights: Railed gas block, optics ready
Weight: 7.75 lb.

Caliber: 5.56
Magazine: N/A
Features: Forged 7075-T6 A3 flat-top upper, forged 7075-T6 lower.
MSRP: $1,239

300 BLK

Action: semi-auto
Stock: Standard AR-15 stock, M111 mid-length handguard, A2 pistol grip
Barrel: 16-in. heavy 4150 chrome-lined, 1:7 twist, AAC Blackout suppressor adaptor
Sights: A2, optics ready
Weight: N/A
Caliber: 300 BLK
Magazine: N/A
Features: Forged 7075-T6 A3 flat-top upper, forged 7075-T6 lower.
MSRP: $1,149

DREADNAUGHT INDUSTRIES LLC

16-IN 3GUN LIGHT

Action: semi-auto
Stock: Magpul CTR
Barrel: 13.65-in. hammer forged with welded F2 compensator

DSArms: AR-15 ZM4 16-in. WerkerZ V1

Sights: None (A4 flat-top for optics)
Weight: 6.05 pounds
Caliber: .223 Wylde
Magazine: One 30-round
Features: Forged 7075 aluminum upper and lower, gray metallic Cerakote, 12-in carbon fiber fore-end, single-stage trigger, Battle Arms ambi selector, Bravo Company charging handle, stainless bolt carrier with enhanced bolt, Magpul grip, operator's manual and warranty card, soft case.
MSRP: $1,899

18-IN 3GUN MEDIUM

Action: semi-auto
Stock: ACE Skeleton
Barrel: 18-in polygon rifled with F2 compensator
Sights: None (A4 flat top for optics)
Weight: 8.1 lb. (without optics)
Caliber: .223 Wylde
Magazine: One 30-round
Features: Forged 7075 aluminum upper and lower, dark burnt bronze Cerakote, Troy Alpha rail, Geissele Super Dynamic 3Gun trigger, Battle Arms ambi selector, Bravo Company charging handle, stainless bolt carrier with enhanced bolt, Magpul grip, operator's manual and warranty card, soft case.
MSRP: $1,999

JAD-M4

Action: semi-auto
Stock: Magpul CTR
Barrel: 16-in. M4 style chromoly
Sights: YHM folding rear
Weight: 6.5 lb.
Caliber: 5.56 NATO
Magazine: One 30-round

Features: Forged 7075 aluminum upper and lower with type III hard anodized finish, anodized aluminum quad rail fore-end, forged A-frame front sight, tuned trigger, Magpul grip, operator's manual and warranty card, soft case.
MSRP: $849

10-IN. ENTRY

Action: full auto
Stock: Magpul CTR
Barrel: 10-in polygon rifled (SureFire 556K shown for reference)
Sights: Folding tritium (shown with Aimpoint CompM4S for reference only)
Weight: 6.8 pounds (without optics)
Caliber: .223 Wylde
Magazine: One 30-round (60 round shown for reference)
Features: Forged 7075 aluminum upper and lower, Daniel Defense Omega fore-end, tuned full-auto trigger, KNS anti-rotation pin set, Battle Arms ambi selector, PRI charging handle, stainless bolt carrier with enhanced bolt, Magpul grip, operator's manual and warranty card, soft case. Post-86 machine gun for sale to LE/dealers only.
MSRP: $1,899

DSARMS

ZM4 20-IN FLAT TOP RIFLE

Action: semi-auto
Stock: Fixed A2-style stock
Barrel: 20-in 4140 M4 barrel, 1:7 twist
Sights: Forged front sight base with bayonet lug
Weight: N/A
Caliber: 5.56mm

Magazine: 5.56 NATO
Features: Hogue pistol grip, 7075-T6 alloy upper and lower receiver, $1/2$x28 A2 flashider, rifle-length handguards with heat shield, M4 cut A3 flat-top receiver.
MSRP: $820

AR-15 ZM4 16-IN. WERKERZ V1

Action: semi-auto
Stock: B5 Systems SOPMOD stock
Barrel: 16-in. check fluted 1:9 twist mid-length barrel
Sights: None, full-length top rail
Weight: 12 lb.
Caliber: 5.56mm
Magazine: One Magpul PMAG
Features: 4150 steel barrel material, Magpul MOE M-LOK handguards, DSArms enhanced contour delta ring, DSArms steel rail height Picatinny gas block, DSArms forged lightweight enhanced upper receiver, mil-spec M16 cut bolt carrier group, mil-spec forged alloy charging handle, DSArms enhanced trigger guard, Magpul MOE pistol grip.
MSRP: $965

AR-15 ZM4 16-IN. WERKERZ V2 RIFLE

Action: semi-auto
Stock: B5 Systems SOPMOD stock
Barrel: 16-in. HBAR check fluted 1:7 twist carbine, chrome lined 4150 barrel material
Sights: None, full-length top rail
Weight: 12 lb.
Caliber: 5.56mm

DSArms: AR-15 ZM4 M.R.C. "Multi Role Carbine"

Magazine: One Magpul PMAG
Features: Magpul SL series M-LOK handguards, DSArms enhanced contour delta ring, DSArms steel rail height Picatinny gas block, DSArms forged lightweight enhanced upper receiver, DSArms NTFE coated forged steel charging handle, DSArms NTFE coated M16 cut bolt carrier group, DSArms NTFE coated mil-spec 6-position buffer tube, Magpul MOE pistol grip, DSArms enhanced trigger guard, mil-spec semi-auto internals, DSArms 3-prong Trident flash hider.
MSRP: **$1,065**

AR-15 ZM4 M.R.C. "MULTI ROLE CARBINE"

Action: semi-auto
Stock: B5 Systems SOPMOD stock
Barrel: 16-in. HBAR 1:7 twist carbine, Chrome lined 4150 barrel material
Sights: Magpul MBUS front & rear sights included
Weight: 12 lb.
Caliber: 5.56mm
Magazine: One Magpul PMAG
Features: Steel low-profile gas block, 13.5-in. Diamondhead USA VRS-T handguard, BCM Ambi Gunfighter charging handle, DSArms NTFE coated M16 cut bolt carrier group, DSArms NTFE coated mil-spec 6-position buffer tube, Hogue pistol grip, mil-spec semi-auto internals, DSArms 3-prong Trident flash hider.
MSRP: **$1,275**

AR-15 ZM4 16-IN. WAR-Z M4

Action: semi-auto
Stock: B5 Systems SOPMOD stock
Barrel: 16-in. lightweight 1:8 twist mid-length, 416R stainless steel barrel
Sights: ARMS #71 front & rear sights included
Weight: 12 lb.
Caliber: 5.56mm
Magazine: One Magpul PMAG
Features: Steel micro gas block, 15-in. Midwest Industries Gen III stainless steel handguard, DSArms forged lightweight enhanced upper receiver, BCM Ambi Gunfighter charging handle, DSArms NTFE coated M16 cut bolt carrier group, DSArms NTFE coated mil-spec 6-position buffer tube Magpul MIAD pistol grip, DSArms enhanced trigger guard, CMC Triggers #3.5 flat face trigger, Seekins Precision Ambi selector switch, SureFire Pro Comp muzzle device.
MSRP: **$1,495**

16-IN. BARREL, FLATTOP UPPER RECEIVER

Action: semi-auto
Stock: M4 buttstock
Barrel: 16 in. fluted barrel
Sights: N/A
Weight: N/A
Caliber: 5.56mm
Magazine: 30 round
Features: Flat-top upper receiver, standard plastic handguard, Hogue AR-15 grip, Phantom YHM flash hider.
MSRP: **$1,045**

16-IN. BARREL, FLATTOP UPPER RECEIVER

Action: semi-auto
Stock: LMT SOPMOD stock
Barrel: 16-in. barrel
Sights: Fixed A2 front sight
Weight: N/A
Caliber: 5.56mm
Magazine: N/A
Features: YHM 2-piece handguard, Hogue AR-15 grip, McCormick trigger, Magpul trigger guard, Robar NP3.
MSRP: **$1,345**

16-IN. BARREL, FLATTOP UPPER RECEIVER

Action: semi-auto
Stock: M4 or A2 buttstock
Barrel: 16-in. fluted barrel
Sights: Fixed A2 front sight
Weight: N/A
Caliber: 5.56mm
Magazine: 30 round
Features: Flat-top upper receiver, standard plastic handguard, standard A2 grip, standard A2 flash hider.
MSRP: **$800**

Falkor Defense: Blitz AR-15 AMBI SBR

AR 1R A2 UPPER CARBINE RIFLE

Action: semi-auto
Stock: 6-position collapsible stock
Barrel: 16-in. 1:9 twist D4 barrel with A2 flash hider
Sights: Forged front sight base with lug
Weight: 6.25 lb.
Caliber: 5.56mm NATO
Magazine: Detachable
Features: AR 1R A2 upper carbine rifle.
MSRP: $830

AR STANDARD FLAT-TOP RIFLE

Action: semi-auto
Stock: Fixed A2 stock
Barrel: 20-in. 1:9 twist chromoly heavy barrel with A2 flash hider
Sights: Forged front site base with lug
Weight: 9 lb.
Caliber: 5.56mm NATO
Magazine: Detachable
Features: Mil-spec forged 7075-T6 lower receiver, forged flat-top or A2 upper receiver, standard handguard with heat shield, model #DSZM4A4U20.
MSRP: $820

ZM4 FLATTOP CARBINE RIFLE

Action: semi-auto
Stock: 6-position M4 stock
Barrel: 1:9 Nitride barrel with A2 flash hider
Sights: N/A
Weight: N/A
Caliber: 5.56mm NATO
Magazine: N/A
Features: N/A
MSRP: $775

AR STANDARD FLATTOP RIFLE

Action: semi-auto
Stock: A2 stock
Barrel: 1:9 twist chromoly heavy barrel with A2 flash hider
Sights: Forged front sight base with lug
Weight: 9 lb.
Caliber: 5.56mm NATO
Magazine: Detachable
Features: Mil-spec forged 7075-T56 lower receiver, forged flat-top or A2 upper receiver, standard handguard with heat shield.
MSRP: $820

AR CQB MRP CARBINE RIFLE

Action: semi-auto
Stock: Collapsible CAR buttstock
Barrel: 16-in. 1:7 twist chrome lined barrel with threaded A2 flash hider, optional 16-in. stainless steel barrel available
Sights: N/A
Weight: N/A
Caliber: 5.56mm NATO
Magazine: 30 round
Features: DSA forged 7075-T6 lower receiver, LMT-enhanced bolt with dual extractor springs.
MSRP: $2,495

AR 1V A2 UPPER CARBINE RIFLE

Action: semi-auto
Stock: VLTOR collapsible stock
Barrel: 16-in. 1:9 twist D4 barrel with A2 flash hider
Sights: Forged front sight base with lug
Weight: 5.56 lb.
Caliber: 5.56mm NATO
Magazine: Detachable
Features: Mil-spec forged 7075-T6 lower receiver, forged flat-top or A2

carry handle upper receiver, D4 handguard with heat shield.
MSRP: $1,025

AR 1R FLAT-TOP CARBINE RIFLE

Action: semi-auto
Stock: 6-position collapsible stock
Barrel: 1:9 twist D4 barrel with A2 flash hider
Sights: Forged front sight base with lug
Weight: 6.2 lb.
Caliber: 5.56mm NATO
Magazine: Detachable
Features: Mil-spec forged 7075-T6 lower receiver, 4D handguard with heat shield, forged flat-top or A2 carry handle with upper receiver.
MSRP: $825

FALKOR DEFENSE

BLITZ AR-15 AMBI SBR

Action: semi-auto
Stock: Mission First Tactical Minimalist stock
Barrel: 10.5-in. steel barrel, 1:7 twist, carbine gas
Sights: N/A
Weight: 5.75 lb.
Caliber: 5.56
Magazine: One 30-round HEX
Features: Ambidextrous mirrored controls, billet machined bolt/mag, ambi take down pins, QuickSnap dust cover, flared magwell w/magwell grip, Falkor "Fatty" free-float 11.5-in. M-LOK handguard, Falkor R anti-tilt Nitride BCG, Geissele 3.5 lb. Super Dynamic 3Gun trigger, Falkor Mach-15 ambi charging handle, ambi short throw safety selector, Hogue rubber overmold grip, Falkor "Blast Cap" SBR muzzle break.
MSRP: $2,600

Falkor Defense: Breacher 308 AMBI

Falkor Defense: Caitlyn PSR AR-15 AMBI

Falkor Defense: Alpha DMR 308 AMBI

Falkor Defense: Petra Steel .300 Win.

BREACHER 308 AMBI

Action: semi-auto
Stock: Mission First Tactical Battlelink stock
Barrel: 16-in. steel barrel, 1:10 twist, rifle gas
Sights: N/A
Weight: 8.1 lb.
Caliber: .308 Win.
Magazine: 20-round Lancer
Features: Ambidextrous mirrored controls-billet machined bolt/mag, ambi take down pins, QuickSnap dust cover, flared magwell w/magwell grip, 5 Barrier handguard, Falkor anti-tilt Nitride BCG, Geissele Super Dynamic 3Gun (SD-3G) trigger, Falkor Mach-10 ambi charging handle, ambi short throw safety selector, Hogue rubber overmold grip, Falkor "King" muzzle device.
MSRP: **$2,900**

CAITLYN PSR AR-15 AMBI

Action: semi-auto
Stock: Mission First Tactical Battlelink stock
Barrel: 16-in. Proof carbon fiber Wylde chamber 1:8 twist mid-length gas
Sights: N/A

Weight: 6.3 lb.
Caliber: 5.56
Magazine: 30-round HEX
Features: Ambidextrous Mirrored controls-billet machined bolt/mag, ambi take down pins, QuickSnap dust cover, flared magwell w/magwell grip, Falkor R "Tranny" free-float 14.6-in. M-LOK handguard, Falkor anti-tilt Nitride BCG, Geissele SSA-E two-stage trigger, Falkor Mach-15 ambi charging handle, ambi short throw safety selector, Hogue rubber overmold grip, VG6 Epsilon high performance muzzle brake.
MSRP: **$3,299**

ALPHA DMR 308 AMBI

Action: semi-auto
Stock: Luth AR MBA-1 stock
Barrel: 18-in. carbon fiber barrel 1:11 twist
Sights: N/A
Weight: 9 lb.
Caliber: .308 Win.
Magazine: 20-round Lancer
Features: Ambidextrous mirrored controls-billet machined bolt/mag, ambi take down pins, QuickSnap dust cover, flared magwell w/magwell grip,

Falkor "Tranny" free-float 15.4-in. M-LOK handguard, Falkor anti-tilt Nitride BCG, Geissele SSA-E two-stage trigger, Falkor Mach-10 ambi charging handle, ambi short throw safety selector, Hogue rubber overmold grip, VG6 Gamma muzzle break.
MSRP: **$3,900**

PETRA STEEL .300 WIN.

Action: semi-auto
Stock: Luth AR MBA-1 stock
Barrel: 22-in. steel barrel 1:10 twist
Sights: N/A
Weight: 10.8 lb.
Caliber: .300 Win.
Magazine: One 10-round
Features: Ambi take down pins, QuickSnap dust cover, Flared magwell w/magwell grip, Falkor "Tranny" free-float 19-in. M-LOK handguard, Falkor anti-tilt Nitride BCG, Geissele SSA-E two-stage trigger, Falkor Mach-300, ambi charging handle, ambi short throw safety selector, Hogue rubber, overmold grip, Falkor "DS-300" muzzle break.
MSRP: **$4,800**

Falkor Defense: Petra Carbon Fiber .300 Win.

Falkor Defense: Recce .223 Ambi Sporter

FN: 15 Military Collector M16

FN 15 Military Collector M4

PETRA CARBON FIBER .300 WIN.

Action: semi-auto
Stock: Luth AR MBA-1 stock
Barrel: 20-in. PROOF carbon fiber barrel 1:11 twist
Sights: N/A
Weight: 10.3 lb.
Caliber: .300 Win.
Magazine: One 10-round
Features: Ambi take down pins, QuickSnap dust cover, flared magwell w/magwell grip, Falkor "Tranny" free-float 19-in. M-LOK handguard, Falkor anti-tilt Nitride BCG, Geissele SSA-E two-stage trigger, Falkor Mach-300, ambi charging handle, ambi short throw safety selector, Hogue rubber, overmold grip, Falkor "DS-300" muzzle break.
MSRP: **$5,800**

RECCE .223 AMBI SPORTER

Action: semi-auto
Stock: Mission First Battlelink Minimalist stock
Barrel: 16-in. PROOF steel 1:8 twist mid gas

Sights: N/A
Weight: 6.6 lb.
Caliber: 5.56
Magazine: One 30-round HEX
Features: Ambidextrous mirrored controls-billet machined bolt/mag, ambi take down pins, QuickSnap dust cover, flared magwell w/magwell grip, Falkor "Tranny" free-float 14.6-in. M-LOK handguard, Falkor anti-tilt Nitride BCG, Geissele 3.5 lb. Super Dynamic 3Gun trigger, Falkor Mach-15 ambi charging handle, ambi short throw safety selector, Hogue rubber overmold grip, VG6 Epsilon High Performance muzzle break.
MSRP: **$2,350**

FN

15 MILITARY COLLECTOR M16

Action: semi-auto
Stock: Fixed A2 rifle stock
Barrel: 20-in. button-broached chrome-lined, 1:7 RH twist, A2-style compensator

Sights: A2-style front, adjustable rear
Weight: 8.2 lb.
Caliber: 5.56
Magazine: 30-round aluminum
Features: Hard anodized aluminum flat-top receiver.
MSRP: **$1,749**

15 MILITARY COLLECTOR M4

Action: semi-auto
Stock: 6-position stock with sling mount, Knights Armament M4RAS adapter rail with rail covers, M4 pistol grip
Barrel: 16-in. button-broached chrome-lined, 1:7 RH twist, A2-style compensator
Sights: A2-style front, adjustable rear
Weight: 6.6 lb.
Caliber: 5.56
Magazine: 30-round aluminum
Features: Hard anodized aluminum flat-top receiver.
MSRP: **$1,749**

FN: 15 Tactical Carbine

FN: 15 Sporting

FN: 15 DMR

FN: 15 1776

FN: 15 Carbine

15 TACTICAL CARBINE

Action: semi-auto
Stock: Magpul MOE SL buttsock, Magpul MOE grip, Midwest Industries LWM 12-in. handguard with M-LOK
Barrel: 16-in. match-grade cold hammer-forged chrome-lined, 1:7 RH twist, FNH USA three-prong flash hider
Sights: Magpul MBUS sights
Weight: 6.6 lb.
Caliber: 5.56
Magazine: 30-round Magpul PMAG
Features: Hard anodized aluminum flat-top receiver.
MSRP: **$1,479**

15 SPORTING

Action: semi-auto
Stock: Magpul CTR buttstock, Magpul MOE grip, Samson Evolution 15-in. handguard
Barrel: 18-in. match-grade chrome-lined, cold hammer-forged free-floating barrel, 1:8 RH twist, SureFire

ProComp 556 muzzle break
Sights: N/A
Weight: 7.7 lb.
Caliber: .223
Magazine: 30-round Magpul PMAG
Features: flat-top receiver, Timney competition trigger.
MSRP: **$1,749**

15 DMR

Action: semi-auto
Stock: Magpul STR buttstock, Magpul MOE grip, Midwest Industries SSM M-LOK 15-in. handguard
Barrel: 18-in. chrome-lined, cold hammer-forged free-floating barrel, 1:7 RH twist, SureFire ProComp 556 muzzle break
Sights: Magpul MBUS Pro
Weight: 7.2 lb.
Caliber: 5.56
Magazine: 30-round Magpul PMAG
Features: Flat-top receiver, Timney competition trigger.
MSRP: **$1,899**

15 1776

Action: semi-auto
Stock: 6-position stock, oval handguard,
Barrel: 16-in. alloy steel button-broached barrel, 1:7 RH twist, A2-style compensator
Sights: Optics ready
Weight: 6.6 lb.
Caliber: 5.56
Magazine: 30-round Magpul PMAG
Features: Flat-top receiver.
MSRP: **$899**

15 CARBINE

Action: semi-auto
Stock: 6-position stock, oval handguard,
Barrel: 16-in. alloy steel button-broached barrel, 1:7 RH twist, A2-style compensator
Sights: A2-style front sight, removable carry handle with sight
Weight: 6.94 lb.
Caliber: 5.56
Magazine: 30-round aluminum body
Features: Flat-top receiver.
MSRP: **$1,149**

FN: 15 Rifle

FN: 15 MOE SLG

Franklin Armory: BFS Equipped M4 Carbine

Franklin Armory: BFS Equipped M4-HTF R2

15 RIFLE

Action: semi-auto
Stock: Fixed stock, round handguard,
Barrel: 20-in. alloy steel button-broached barrel, 1:7 RH twist, A2-style compensator
Sights: A2-style front sight, removable carry handle with sight
Weight: 7.97 lb.
Caliber: 5.56
Magazine: 30-round aluminum body
Features: Flat-top receiver.
MSRP: **$1,149**

15 MOE SLG

Action: semi-auto
Stock: Magpul MOE SL gray buttstock, Magpul MOE SL gray grip, Magpul MOE SL gray M-LOK carbine handguard
Barrel: 16-in. alloy steel button-broached barrel, 1:7 RH twist, A2-style compensator
Sights: Magpul MBUS rear, A2-style front
Weight: 6.8 lb.
Caliber: 5.56

Magazine: 30-round Magpul PMAG
Features: hard-anodized aluminum flat-top receiver.
MSRP: **$1,199**

FRANKLIN ARMORY

BFS EQUIPPED M4 CARBINE

Action: semi-auto
Stock: M4 design, reinforced six position collapsible, multiple rear sling mounts, angled heel for easier transition, aluminum CAR Receiver extension)
Barrel: 16-in. M4 contour with 1:7 twist, threaded muzzle crown A2 flash Hider
Sights: A2-style front sight
Weight: N/A
Caliber: 5.56 NATO
Magazine: Manufactured from stainless steel, "Marlube" finished, 30-round 5.56 NATO capacity, 10- or 20-round or 10- or 30-round for restricted States, anti-tilt follower

Features: Forged 7075-T6 aluminum and hard coat type III anodized black lower receiver, Franklin Armory Binary Firing System trigger, A2 pistol grip, A4 upper receiver forged from 7075-T6 aluminum, forward assist, salt bath Nitride bolt carrier group, M4 double heat shield handguard with aluminum liners, carbine-length gas system, forged front sight, gas block with integral bayonet lug and front sling swivel.
MSRP: **$1,5254**

BFS EQUIPPED M4-HTF R2

Action: semi-auto
Stock: Mission First tactical battlelink minimalist stock
Barrel: 14.5-in. M4 mid-length contour barrel, revere compensator—pinned and welded compensator to reach 16-in. length
Sights: Magpul MBUS front and rear sights
Weight: N/A
Caliber: 5.56 NATO
Magazine: 30-round Magpul Gen 3 PMAG P30

Franklin Armory: BFS Equipped M4-SBR-L

Franklin Armory: BFS Equipped 3GR-L

Franklin Armory: BFS Equipped XO-26 R2

Features: A4 upper receiver forged from 7075-T6 aluminum, full Picattiny rail, forward assist, salt bath Nitride bolt carrier group, Franklin Armory FST 15-in. M-LOK handguard, Badger Ordnance Gen 2 Tac latch, specialized tension screw, Franklin Armory Binary Firing System trigger, Mission First Tactical EPG 16 grip.
MSRP: . . . . N/A

BFS EQUIPPED M4-SBR-L

Action: semi-auto
Stock: Magpul CTR stock
Barrel: 14.5-in M4 contour barrel, threaded muzzle crown, phantom flash hider pinned and welded, 1:7 twist
Sights: Magpul MBUS front and rear
Weight: N/A
Caliber: 5.56 NATO
Magazine: 30-round Magpul PMAG P30
Features: FSR 13-in. rail system, Franklin Armory Libertas proprietary billet upper receiver, full Picatinny rail, forward assist, salt bath Nitride bolt carrier group, flared magazine well for quick magazine changes, ambidextrous

push button QD sling mounts, integral cold weather trigger guard, serrated memory index point for shooting finger, textured front area for offhand grip, specialized tension screw—eliminates upper/lower play, Franklin Armory Binary Firing System trigger, ERGO ambi sure grip.
MSRP: $2,395

BFS EQUIPPED 3GR-L

Action: semi-auto
Stock: Magpul PRS Stock, with adjustable comb height and length of pull and pica tinny rail section for mounting monopod
Barrel: 18-in. fluted barrel with 1:8 twist, threaded muzzle crown, high efficiency compensator
Sights: N/A
Weight: N/A
Caliber: 5.56 NATO
Magazine: 20- or 30-round Magpul PMAG with anti-tilt follower
Features: FSR 13-in. rail system, full Picatinny rail, ambi tac latch, forward assist, Magpul B.A.D lever, flared magazine well for quick magazine changes, ambidextrous push button

QD sling mounts, integral cold weather trigger guard, serrated memory index point for shooting finger, textured front area for offhand grip, specialized tension screw—eliminates upper/lower play, Franklin Armory Binary Firing System trigger, ERGO ambi sure grip.
MSRP: $2,700

BFS EQUIPPED XO-26 R2

Action: semi-auto
Stock: N/A—padded receiver extension/buffer tube
Barrel: 11.5-in. Barrel with 1:7 twist
Sights: Pop-up front and rear sights
Weight: N/A
Caliber: 5.56 NATO
Magazine: 30-round Magpul PMAG P30
Features: Low profile gas block and carbine-length gas system, Franklin Armory FST M-LOK handguard, toothed flash hider, salt bath Nitride bolt carrier group, forward assist, Ambi sling mount, specialized tension screw, Franklin Armory Binary Firing System trigger, Magpul MIAD grip.
MSRP: $1,865

Franklin Armory: BFS Equipped XO-26-S Salus

Franklin Armory: M4-SBR-M Militia Model

BFS EQUIPPED XO-26-S SALUS

Action: semi-auto
Stock: N/A, padded receiver extension/ buffer tube
Barrel: 11.5-in barrel with 1:7, toothed flash hider, low-profile gas system
Sights: Pop-up front and rear MBUS sights
Weight: N/A
Caliber: 5.56 NATO
Magazine: 30-round Magpul PMAG
Features: Full Picatinny rail, forward assist, salt bath Nitride bolt carrier group, 9-in. KeyMod rail handguard, MFT RSG forward verticle grip, flared magazine well for quick magazine changes, ambidextrous push button QD sling mounts, integral cold weather trigger guard, serrated memory index point for shooting finger textured front area for offhand grip, specialized tension screw, Franklin Armory Binary Firing System trigger, MFT EPG16 grip.
MSRP: **$2,275**

M4-SBR-M MILITIA MODEL

Action: semi-auto
Stock: Magpul CTR stock
Barrel: 14.5-in. barrel with mid-length gas system, threaded muzzle crown, 1:10 twist, 4140 chromoly steel
Sights: Diamondhead front and rear sights
Weight: N/A
Caliber: 7.62x51 NATO, .308 Win.

Magazine: 20-round Magpul PMAG 20 LR/SR Gen 3
Features: Pinned and welded triumvir muzzle device, Franklin Armory Militia Model FSR 14-in. handguard, window cover assembly, forward assist, salt bath Nitride bolt carrier group, direct-impingement gas system, flared magazine well, bilateral QD sling mounts, integral cold weather trigger guard, bilateral serrated memory index point, bilateral safety selector, bilateral bolt release, bilateral magazine release, textured front area for offhand grip, specialized tension screw, Franklin Armory Factory Custom Tuned trigger, ERGO ambi sure grip.
MSRP: **$2,665**

F17-SPR

Action: semi-auto
Stock: Mission First Tactical Battlelink Minimalist stock
Barrel: 18-in. thin Contour barrel, 1:9 twist, 4140 chromoly steel salt bath Nitride chamber, bore, and finish
Sights: N/A
Weight: N/A
Caliber: 17 Win. Super Magnum Rimfire
Magazine: One 10-round (fits standard mag well)
Features: TML-12 free-float and knurled handguard, M-LOK compatible forward slots, forward assist, custom designed 17 WSM bolt carrier group,

gas piston system, specialized tension screw, Franklin Armory Factory Custom Tuned trigger, Mission First Tactical EPG16 grip.
MSRP: **$1,800**

RFS EQUIPPED V1-L

Action: semi-auto
Stock: Magpul PRS stock with adjustable comb height and LOP
Barrel: 24-in full-heavy contour barrel, longitudinal flutes, 11-degree target crown with recessed muzzle crown,1:8 twist
Sights: N/A
Weight: N/A
Caliber: 5.56 NATO
Magazine: 20- or 30-round Magpul PMAG with anti-tilt follower
Features: Franklin Armory free-float handguard (fluted & vented, M-LOK compatible, and an integral bi-pod & tri-pod adapter), free-float fluted & vented handguard, Badger Ordnance Gen 1 tac latch, forward assist, nickel-boron bolt carrier group, flared magazine well for quick magazine changes, ambidextrous push button QD sling mounts, integral cold weather trigger guard, serrated memory index point for shooting finger, textured front area for offhand grip, specialized tension screw— eliminates upper/lower play, Franklin Armory Release Firing System trigger, Magpul MIAD adjustable grip.
MSRP: **$2,480**

Fulton Armory: FAR-15 Predator Varmint Rifle

Fulton Armory

FAR-15 A2 SERVICE RIFLE

Action: semi-auto
Stock: A2
Barrel: Fulton Armory, 20-in. 1:9, HBAR profile, National Match quality, chromoly
Sights: A2
Weight: 8.05 lb.
Caliber: 5.56
Magazine: 10 round (20 round and 30 round optional)
Features: Each gun built to order, available with variety of options, see website for details.
MSRP: **$1,210**

FAR-308 M110 SERVICE RIFLE

Action: semi-auto
Stock: A1 with A2 butt plate
Barrel: Fulton Armory, M110, 20-in. 1:12, stainless steel
Sights: None
Weight: 10.45 lb.
Caliber: .308 Win
Magazine: 10-round, stainless steel, anti-tilt, CrSi spring, black finish (20 round available)
Features: Each gun built to order, available with variety of options, see website for details.
MSRP: **$1,750**

FAR-15 PREDATOR VARMINT RIFLE

Action: semi-auto
Stock: A2 or A1 (Magpul PRS and Magpul UBR optional)
Barrel: Fulton Armory, 24-in. 1:12 bull profile, National Match quality, stainless steel, plain muzzle (1:12 target gray finish, 1:9 stainless steel, and 1:12 target gray finish optional)
Sights: None
Weight: 9.25 lb.
Caliber: 5.56
Magazine: 10 round (20 round and 30 round optional)
Features: Each gun built to order, available with variety of options, see website for details.
MSRP: **$1,249**

FAR-15 PHANTOM RIFLE

Action: semi-auto
Stock: A2 or A1 (Magpul PRS and Magpul UBR optional)
Barrel: Fulton Armory, 20-in. 1:9 HBAR profile, National Match quality, chromoly (Fulton Armory, Krieger, and Douglas in 18 in. and 20 in. chromoly, chrome-lined, stainless steel, and target gray finish in many twists optional)
Sights: None
Weight: 8 lb.
Caliber: 5.56x45mm
Magazine: 10 round (20 round and 30 round optional)
Features: Each gun built to order, available with variety of options, see website for details.
MSRP: **$1,450**

FAR-15 LIBERATOR RIFLE

Action: semi-auto
Stock: A2 or A1 (Magpul UBR optional)
Barrel: Fulton Armory, 20 in. 1:9 HBAR profile, National Match quality, chromoly (Fulton Armory, Krieger, and Douglas in 18-in. and 20-in. chromoly, chrome-lined, stainless steel, and target gray finish in many twists optional).
Sights: None
Weight: 8.1 lb.
Caliber: 5.56
Magazine: 10 round (20 round and 30 round optional)
Features: Each gun built to order, available with variety of options, see website for details.
MSRP: **$1,700**

FAR-15 PEERLESS NM A2

Action: semi-auto
Stock: A2
Barrel: Fulton Armory, 20-in. 1:8 HBAR profile, National Match quality, stainless steel
Sights: Northern Competition National Match NMA2, hooded aperture .040, 1/4xrear, National Match front sight post (.052)
Weight: 9.85 lb.
Caliber: 5.56x45mm
Magazine: 10 round (20 round and 30 round optional)
Features: Each gun built to order, available with variety of options, see website for details.
MSRP: **$1,700**

FAR-308 PHANTOM

Action: semi-auto
Stock: A2 or A1 (Magpul UBR as an option)
Barrel: Fulton Armory, .308 Win. 20-in. 1:12 twist HBAR, National Match quality, stainless steel
Sights: None
Weight: 10 lb.
Caliber: .308 Win or 6.5 Creedmoor

Fulton Armory: FAR-308 Phantom

Fulton Armory: FAR-308 Phantom LTE

GAR Arms: GR-15 A3 16-in. G4 Standard Carbine

Magazine: 10 round (20 round and 30 round optional)
Features: Each gun built to order, available with variety of options, see website for details.
MSRP: $1,800

FAR-308 PHANTOM LTE

Action: semi-auto
Stock: A2 or A1
Barrel: Fulton Armory .308 Win. 18.5-in. 1:10 National Match quality, chrome-lined, lightweight
Sights: None
Weight: 8.11 lb.
Caliber: .308 Win.
Magazine: 10 round (20 round and 30 round optional)
Features: Each gun built to order, available with variety of options, see website for details.
MSRP: $1,850

FAR-308 LIBERATOR

Action: semi-auto
Stock: A2 or A1
Barrel: Fulton Armory, .308 Win, 20-in. 1:12 twist HBAR, National Match quality, stainless steel
Sights: None
Weight: 9.9 lb.

Caliber: .308 Win. or 6.5 Creedmoor
Magazine: 10 round (20 round and 30 round optional)
Features: Each gun built to order, available with variety of options, see website for details.
MSRP: $1,750

FAR-308 LIBERATOR LTE

Action: semi-auto
Stock: A2 or A1
Barrel: Fulton Armory, .308 Win. 18.5-in. 1:10 twist, National Match quality, chrome-lined, lightweight
Sights: None
Weight: 9.5 lb.
Caliber: .308 Win.
Magazine: 10 round (20 round and 30 round optional)
Features: Each gun built to order, available with variety of options, see website for details.
MSRP: $1,750

GAR ARMS

GR-15 A3 16-IN. G4 STANDARD CARBINE

Action: semi-auto
Stock: 6-position collapsible

Barrel: 16-in. chromoly Vanadium, chrome-lined 16-in. carbine length, 1:7 twist, A2 flash hider, Manganese Phosphated, threaded muzzle, G4 contour barrel
Sights: None
Weight: 6.1 lb.
Caliber: 5.56x45
Magazine: 30 round
Features: Standard mil-spec bolt carrier group, Phosphated 8620 steel carrier assembly, chrome lined, standard mil-spec charging handle, carbine-length standard handguards, aluminum delta ring, forged 7075-T6 aluminum, A3 flat top with white T-marks hard coat anodized mil-spec, ejection port cover and round forward assist, right hand ejection, forged 7075-T6 aluminum hard coat anodized mil-spec, aluminum triggerguard, aluminum mag catch button, M4 6-position stock w/ commercial tube.
MSRP: $999

GR-15 A3 20-IN. STANDARD RIFLE

Action: semi-auto
Stock: A2 fixed stock
Barrel: 4150 Vanadium chrome-lined, 20-in. rifle length, 1:7 twist, A2 flash hider, Manganese Phosphated,

GAR Arms: GR-15 A3 16-in. Tactical Carbine

GAR Arms: GR-15 A3 16-in. TAC Defender
10-in. Quad Rails

GAR Arms: GR-15 16-in. A3 TACEVO 7-in. Rail

threaded muzzle
Sights: None
Weight: 6.7 lb.
Caliber: 5.56x45
Magazine: 30 round
Features: Standard mil-spec bolt carrier group, Phosphated 8620 steel carrier assembly, chrome-lined carrier interior, standard mil-spec charging handle, upper receiver: forged 7075-T6 aluminum, A3 flat top with white T-marks, hard coat anodized mil-spec, ejection port cover and round forward assist, right hand ejection, lower receiver: forged 7075-T6 aluminum, hard coat anodized mil-spec aluminum triggerguard, aluminum mag catch button.
MSRP: $1,010

GR-15 A3 16-IN. TACTICAL CARBINE

Action: semi-auto
Stock: M4 6-position commercial tube
Barrel: 16-in. chromoly Vanadium chrome lined, 1:7 twist, A2 flash hider, Manganese Phosphated, threaded

muzzle
Sights: None
Weight: 6.4 lb.
Caliber: 5.56x45
Magazine: 30 round
Features: Standard mil-spec bolt carrier group Phosphated 8620 steel carrier assembly, charging handle: standard mil-spec charging handle, upper receiver: forged 7075-T6 aluminum, A3 flat top with white T-marks, hard coat anodized mil-spec, ejection port cover and round forward assist, right hand ejection, lower receiver: forged 7075-T6 aluminum hard coat anodized mil-spec, aluminum triggerguard, aluminum mag catch button.
MSRP: $1,093

GR-15 A3 16-IN. TAC DEFENDER 10-IN. QUAD RAILS

Action: semi-auto
Stock: M4 6-position commercial tube
Barrel: 16-in. chromoly Vanadium chrome lined, carbine length 1:7 twist, A2 flash hider Manganese Phosphated,

threaded muzzle government contour barrel (M4)
Sights: None
Weight: 6.7 lb.
Caliber: 5.56
Magazine: 30 round
Features: Standard mil-spec bolt carrier group Phosphated 8620 steel carrier assembly, charging handle: standard mil-spec charging handle, upper receiver: forged 7075-T6 aluminum A3 flat top with white T-marks hard coat anodized mil-spec, ejection port cover and round forward assist right hand ejection, lower receiver: forged 7075-T6 aluminum hard coat anodized mil-spec, aluminum triggerguard, aluminum mag catch button.
MSRP: $1,152

GR-15 16-IN. A3 TACEVO 7-IN. RAIL

Action: semi-auto
Stock: M4 collapsible commercial tube, Samsom 7-in. rail
Barrel: 16-in. chromoly Vanadium chrome lined, 1:7 twist, A2 flash hider

GAR Arms: G4 A3 VTAC Defender 9-in. Free Float

GAR Arms: GR-15 A3 16-in. TAC Defender 13.8-in. Quad Rails

manganese phosphated, threaded muzzle
Sights: None
Weight: 6.4 lb.
Caliber: 5.56x45
Magazine: 30-round
Features: Standard mil-spec bolt carrier group, phosphated 8620 steel carrier assembly; charging handle—standard mil-spec; upper receiver—forged 7075-T6 aluminum, A3 flat top with white T-marks, hard coat anodized mil-spec, ejection port cover, round forward assist, right-hand ejection; lower receiver—forged 7075-T6 aluminum hard coat anodized mil-spec, aluminum trigger guard, aluminum mag-catch button.
MSRP: **$1,158**

GR-15 A3 16-IN. TAC DEFENDER 7-IN. QUAD RAILS

Action: semi-auto
Stock: M4 collapsible, commercial tube, Troy Industries 7-in. quad rail, free-float
Barrel: 16-in. chromoly vanadium chrome lined, carbine length, 1:7 twist, A2 flash hider, manganese phosphated, threaded muzzle government contour (M4)
Sights: None

Weight: 6.7 lb.
Caliber: 5.56x45
Magazine: 30 round
Features: Standard mil-spec bolt carrier group, phosphated 8620 steel carrier assembly; charging handle—standard mil-spec; upper receiver—forged 7075-T6 aluminum, A3 flat top with white T-marks, hard coat anodized mil-spec, ejection port cover, round forward assist, right-hand ejection; lower receiver—forged 7075-T6 aluminum hard coat anodized mil-spec, aluminum trigger guard, aluminum mag-catch button.
MSRP: **$1,160**

G4 A3 VTAC DEFENDER 9-IN FREE-FLOAT

Action: semi-auto
Stock: M4 collapsible stock, Troy Industries VTAC 9-in. rail
Commercial Tube
Barrel: 16-in. chromoly vanadium, chrome lined, carbine length, 1:7 twist, A2 flash hider, manganese phosphated, threaded muzzle, government contour (M4)
Sights: None
Weight: 6.7 lb.
Caliber: 5.56x45
Magazine: 30 round
Features: Standard mil-spec bolt

carrier group, phosphated 8620 steel carrier assembly; charging handle—standard mil-spec; upper receiver—forged 7075-T6 aluminum, A3 flat top with white T-marks, hard coat anodized mil-spec, ejection port cover, round forward assist, right-hand ejection; lower receiver—forged 7075-T6 aluminum hard coat anodized mil-spec, aluminum trigger guard, aluminum mag-catch button.
MSRP: **$1,180**

GR-15 A3 16-IN. TAC DEFENDER 13.8-IN. QUAD RAILS

Action: semi-auto
Stock: M4 6-position commercial tube
Barrel: 16-in. chromoly vanadium, chrome lined, carbine length, 1:7 twist, A2 flash hider, manganese phosphated, threaded muzzle, government contour (M4)
Sights: None
Weight: 6.9 lb.
Caliber: 5.56x45
Magazine: 30 round
Features: Standard mil-spec bolt carrier group, phosphated 8620 steel carrier assembly; charging handle—standard mil-spec; upper receiver—forged 7075-T6 aluminum, A3 flat top

GAR Arms: GR-15 TBB16 A3 16-in. SS Bison (Bull) Barrel

GAR Arms: A3 16-in. TACTC Tactical Carbine

with white T-marks, hard coat anodized mil-spec, ejection port cover, round forward assist, right-hand ejection; lower receiver—forged 7075-T6 aluminum, A3 flat top with white T-marks, hard coat anodized mil-spec, ejection port cover, round forward assist, right-hand ejection; lower receiver—forged 7075-T6 aluminum hard coat anodized mil-spec, aluminum trigger guard, aluminum mag-catch button.

MSRP: $1,191

GR-15 TBB16 A3 16-IN. SS BISON (BULL) BARREL

Action: semi-auto
Stock: A2 standard
Barrel: 16-in. stainless steel bull barrel, 1:8 twist
Sights: None
Weight: 8.7 lb.
Caliber: .223 Rem.
Magazine: 20 round
Features: Standard mil-spec bolt carrier group, phosphated 8620 steel carrier assembly; charging handle—standard mil-spec; upper receiver—forged 7075-T6 aluminum, A3 flat top with white T-marks, hard coat anodized mil-spec, ejection port cover, round forward assist, right-hand ejection; lower receiver—forged 7075-T6 aluminum, A3 flat top with white

T-marks, hard coat anodized mil-spec, ejection port cover, round forward assist, right-hand ejection; lower receiver—forged 7075-T6 aluminum hard coat anodized mil-spec, aluminum trigger guard, aluminum mag-catch button.

MSRP: $1,205

TBB20 GR-15 A3 20-IN. SS BISON (BULL) BARREL

Action: semi-auto
Stock: A2 standard stock, rifle-length, free-float aluminum handguards
Barrel: 20-in. stainless steel bull barrel, 1:8 twist
Sights: None
Weight: 9.7 lb.
Caliber: .223 Wylde
Magazine: 20 round
Features: Standard mil-spec bolt carrier group, phosphated 8620 steel carrier assembly; charging handle—standard mil-spec; upper receiver—forged 7075-T6 aluminum, A3 flat top with white T-marks, hard coat anodized mil-spec, ejection port cover, round forward assist, right-hand ejection; lower receiver—forged 7075-T6 aluminum hard coat anodized mil-spec, aluminum trigger guard, aluminum mag-catch button.

MSRP: $1,217

A3 16-IN. TACTC TACTICAL CARBINE

Action: semi-auto
Stock: TAPCO M4 6-position, commercial tube, TAPCO INTRAFUSE carbine length, TAPCO ertical grip with bipod., aluminum delta ring
Barrel: 16-in. chromoly vanadium, chrome lined, carbine length, 1:7 twist, A2 flash hider, manganese phosphated, threaded muzzle, government contour (M4)
Sights: None
Weight: 6.9 lb.
Caliber: 5.56x45
Magazine: 30 round
Features: Standard mil-spec bolt carrier group, phosphated 8620 steel carrier assembly; charging handle—standard mil-spec; upper receiver—forged 7075-T6 aluminum, A3 flat top with white T-marks, hard coat anodized mil-spec, ejection port cover, round forward assist, right-hand ejection; lower receiver—forged 7075-T6 aluminum hard coat anodized mil-spec, aluminum trigger guard, aluminum mag-catch button.

MSRP: $1,223

GAR Arms: ORHS Optics Ready Hunter Carbine

GAR Arms: 20-in. ORHS Optics Ready Hunter Rifle

GAR Arms: GR-15 A3 16-in. TACPB Carbine

ORHS OPTICS READY HUNTER CARBINE

Action: semi-auto
Stock: A2 standard
Barrel: 16-in. chrome 4150 chromoly vanadium, non-threaded muzzle chrome, 1:7, 1:8, or 1:9 twist, manganese phosphated
Sights: None
Weight: 6.5 lb.
Caliber: 5.56x45
Magazine: 10 round
Features: Standard mil-spec bolt carrier group, phosphated 8620 steel carrier assembly; charging handle—standard mil-spec; upper receiver—forged 7075-T6 aluminum, A3 flat top with white T-marks, hard coat anodized mil-spec, ejection port cover, round forward assist, right-hand ejection; lower receiver—forged 7075-T6 aluminum hard coat anodized mil-spec, aluminum trigger guard, aluminum mag-catch button.
MSRP: **$1,360**

20-IN. ORHS OPTICS READY HUNTER RIFLE

Action: semi-auto
Stock: A2 standard
Barrel: 20-in. 4140 chromoly nonthreaded muzzle, nonchrome lined, 1:7, 1:8, or 1:9 twist, manganese phosphated
Sights: None
Weight: 6.8 lb.
Caliber: 5.56x45
Magazine: One 10-round
Features: Standard mil-spec bolt carrier group, phosphated 8620 steel carrier assembly; charging handle—standard mil-spec; upper receiver—forged 7075-T6 aluminum, A3 flat top with white T-marks, hard coat anodized mil-spec, ejection port cover, round forward assist, right-hand ejection; lower receiver—forged 7075-T6 aluminum hard coat anodized mil-spec, aluminum trigger guard, aluminum mag-catch button.
MSRP: **$1,371**

GR-15 A3 16-IN. TACPB CARBINE

Action: semi-auto
Stock: Magpul MOE fixed, Troy Alpha free-float handguard
Barrel: 16-in. 4150 chromoly vanadium non-threaded muzzle, 1:7 twist
Sights: Troy M4 tritium folding sights (front & rear)
Weight: 6.6 lb.
Caliber: 5.56x45
Magazine: 30 round
Features: Standard mil-spec bolt carrier group, phosphated 8620 steel carrier assembly; standard mil-spec charging handle with tactical latch; upper receiver—forged 7075-T6 aluminum, A3 flat top with T-marks, lower receiver—forged 7075-T6 aluminum hard coat anodized mil-spec, aluminum trigger guard, aluminum mag-catch button.
MSRP: **$1,687**

GAR Arms: GR-15 A3 16-in. Zombie Hunter ZTAC Tactical Carbine

GAR Arms: GR-15 16-in. MTCSS Tactical Sniper Rifle

GAR Arms: GR-15 A3 16-in. TACE Carbine

GR-15 A3 16-IN. ZOMBIE HUNTER ZTAC TACTICAL CARBINE

Action: semi-auto
Stock: ERGO PRO 8-position stock, collapsible, ERGO quad rails
Barrel: 16-in. 4150 chromoly vanadium, chrome lined, 1:7 twist, A2 flash hider
Sights: Front and rear adjustable flip-up sights
Weight: 6.9 lb.
Caliber: 5.56x45
Magazine: 30 round
Features. Standard mil-spec bolt carrier group, phosphated 8620 steel carrier assembly; charging handle—standard mil-spec; upper receiver—forged 7075-T6 aluminum, A3 flat top with white T-marks, hard coat anodized mil-spec, ejection port cover, round forward assist, right-hand ejection; lower receiver—forged 7075-T6 aluminum hard coat anodized mil-spec, aluminum trigger guard, aluminum mag-catch button.
MSRP: **$1,723**

GR-15 16-IN. MTCSS TACTICAL SNIPER RIFLE

Action: semi-auto
Stock: Magpul PRS adjustable, 9-in. mid-length Daniel Defense free-float quad rail
Barrel: 16-in. mid-length stainless steel, 1:8 twist, phantom flash hider
Sights: None
Weight: 7.5 lb.
Caliber: 5.56x45
Magazine: 30 round
Features: Mil-spec bolt carrier group; chromed 8620 steel carrier assembly; mil-spec charging handle with tactical latch; upper receiver—forged 7075-T6 aluminum A3 flat top with white marks, hard coat anodized mil-spec, ejection port cover, round forward assist; lower receiver—forged 7075-T6 aluminum hard coat anodized mil-spec, Magpul aluminum trigger guard, aluminum mag-catch button with Magpul B.A.D. lever.
MSRP: **$1,800**

GR-15 A3 16-IN. TACE CARBINE

Action: semi-auto
Stock: Magpul ACS 6-position collapsible, Midwest Industries carbine-length free-float quad rail
Barrel: 16-in. 4150 chromoly vanadium, chrome lined, 1:7 twist, Midwest Industries flash hider, parkerized finish
Sights: Midwest industries folding sight, tower gas block, ERS flip-up rear sight adjustable windage and elevation
Weight: 6.5 lb.
Caliber: 5.56x45
Magazine: 30 round
Features: Standard mil-spec bolt carrier group, phosphated 8620 steel carrier assembly; standard mil-spec charging handle with tactical latch, handguards; upper receiver—forged 7075-T6 aluminum A3 flat top with white marks, hard coat anodized mil-spec, ejection port cover, round forward assist; lower receiver—forged 7075-T6 aluminum hard coat anodized mil-spec, aluminum trigger guard, and aluminum mag-catch button.

GAR Arms: GR-15 A3 16-in. TACDE7 7-in. Rails

Heckler & Koch: MR556A1

High Standard: Enforcer 300

MSRP: **$1,845**

GR-15 A3 16-IN. TACDE7 7-IN. RAILS

Action: semi-auto
Stock: Troy Ind. CQB 6-position collapsible, Troy Inustries 7-in. rail, free-float handguards
Barrel: 16-in. 4150 chromoly vanadium, chrome lined, 1:7 twist, Vortex flash hider
Sights: YHM flip-up front sight tower gas block, YHM flip-up rear sight
Weight: 6.4 lb.
Caliber: 5.56x45
Magazine: 30 round
Features: Mil-spec bolt carrier group; chromed 8620 steel carrier assembly; mil-spec charging handle with tactical latch; upper receiver—forged 7075-T6 aluminum A3 flat top with white marks, hard coat anodized mil-spec, ejection port cover, round forward assist; lower receiver—forged 7075-T6 aluminum hard coat anodized mil-spec, Magpul aluminum trigger guard, aluminum mag-catch button.
MSRP: **$1,884**

HECKLER & KOCH

MR556A1

Action: semi-auto
Stock: Adjustable buttstock, 6-positions, 96mm of travel
Barrel: 16.5-in.
Sights: Diopter front and rear
Weight: 9.10 lb. w/ empty magazine
Caliber: 5.56x45mm
Magazine: 30-round steel magazine (will fit all standard AR magazines)
Features: Gas-operated, short-stroke piston; sight radius is 14.6-in.; trigger pull is 7.64 lb. (note: new rail).
MSRP: **$3,399**

HIGH STANDARD

ENFORCER

Action: semi-auto
Stock: 6-position adjustable, various colors
Barrel: 16-in. M4 style barrel with A2 flash hider, 1:9 twist
Sights: N/A
Weight: N/A

Caliber: 5.56/.223
Magazine: 30-round Magpul PMAG
Features: Aluminum forged 7075-T6 upper and low receivers; free-float aluminum quad rail; carbine length; Picatinny gas block; Magpul MOE vertical grip; Magpul MOE enhanced trigger guard, ambidextrous single-point sling adapter.
MSRP: **$1,050**

ENFORCER 300

Action: semi-auto
Stock: M4-style adjustable 6-position stock
Barrel: 16-in. medium-heavy barrel with A2 flash hider; 1:8 twist
Sights: N/A
Weight: N/A
Caliber: 300 BLK AAC
Magazine: 30-round Magpul PMAG
Features: Aluminum forged 7075-T6 upper and low receivers; free-float aluminum quad rail; carbine length; Picatinny gas block; Magpul MOE vertical grip; Magpul MOE enhanced trigger guard; ambidextrous single-point sling adapter.
MSRP: **$1,099**

High Standard: Crusader

High Standard: Lone Star

High Standard: HSA-15

CRUSADER

Action: semi-auto
Stock: M4-style 6-position adjustable stock
Barrel: 16-in. M4 barrel (hard chrome bore) with A2 flash hider, 1:7 twist
Sights: N/A
Weight: N/A
Caliber: 5.56/.223
Magazine: 30-round Magpul PMAG
Features: Aluminum forged 7075-T6 upper and low receivers; free-float aluminum quad rail; carbine length; Picatinny gas block; Magpul MOE vertical grip; Magpul MOE enhanced trigger guard; ambidextrous single-point sling adaptor; ambidextrous safety.
MSRP: . . . . **N/A**

LONESTAR

Action: semi-auto
Stock: Magpul MOE carbine stock
Barrel: 16-in. M4 barrel; hard chrome bore; 1:7 twist
Sights: Magpul MBUS front and rear flip-up sights
Weight: N/A
Caliber: N/A
Magazine: 30-round Magpul PMAG
Features: 10.25-in enhanced quad rail; aluminum forged 7075-T6 upper and low receivers; hard coat anodized finish and Lone Star special edition laser engraving; A2 front sight base and A2 flash hider; Diamondhead VR-S "T" 10.25-in free-floating Versa handguard system; low-profile gas block; two-stage trigger; ambidextrous safety, Magpul MOE pistol grip; Magpul MOE enhanced trigger guard; ambidextrous single-point sling adapter.
MSRP: **$1,299**

HSA-15, FLAT-TOP RIFLE

Action: semi-auto
Stock: A2-style, polymer
Barrel: 20-in. lightweight, 1:10 twist
Sights: Standard front sight tower
Weight: 6.1 lb. (without magazine and ammunition)
Caliber: 6x45 (6mm .223)
Magazine: 20 round (1 standard)
Features: Limited lifetime warranty for manufacturing and material defects.
MSRP: $863

HSA-15, RIFLE A2, MODEL TX6500

Action: semi-auto
Stock: A2-style, polymer
Barrel: 20-in.
Sights: Standard front sight tower, A2 adjustable rear sight
Weight: 6.8 lb. (without magazine and ammunition)
Caliber: .223 (5.59x45mm)
Magazine: 30 round (1 standard)
Features: Limited lifetime warranty for manufacturing and material defect; USGI profile; 1:7 or 1:9 twist; CMV 4140 or 4150 material; A2 flash hider; fixed carry handle.
MSRP: $880

HSA-15, FLAT-TOP RIFLE, MODEL TX6550

Action: semi-auto
Stock: A2-style, polymer
Barrel: 20-in.
Sights: Standard front sight tower, none rear (options available)
Weight: 6.5 lb. (without magazine and ammunition)
Caliber: .223 (5.59x45mm)
Magazine: 30 round (1 standard)
Features: Limited lifetime warranty for manufacturing and material defect; USGI profile; 1:7 or 1:9 twist; CMV 4140 or 4150 material; A2 flash hider.
MSRP: $840

HSA-15, CARBINE A2, MODEL TX6501

Action: semi-auto
Stock: M4 (6-position), polymer
Barrel: 16-in.
Sights: Standard front sight tower, A2 adjustable rear sight
Weight: 6.4 lb. (without magazine and ammunition)
Caliber: .223 (5.59x45mm)
Magazine: 30 round (1 standard)
Features: Limited lifetime warranty for manufacturing and material defect— USGI profile, 1:7 or 1:9 twist; CMV

High Standard: HSA-15, Flat-Top Carbine, Model TX6551

HM Defense: HM15F-300

4140 material; A2 flash hider; fixed carry handle.
MSRP: **$875**

HSA-15, FLAT-TOP CARBINE, MODEL TX6551

Action: semi-auto
Stock: M4 (6-position), polymer
Barrel: 16-in.
Sights: Standard front-sight tower, (options available for rear)
Weight: 6.1 lb. (without magazine and ammunition)
Caliber: .223 (5.59x45mm)
Magazine: 30 round (1 standard)
Features: Limited lifetime warranty for manufacturing and material defect—USGI profile, 1:7 twist; CMV 4140 material; A2 flash hider.
MSRP: **$840**

HSA-15, TACTICAL RIFLE FLAT-TOP, MODEL TX6570

Action: semi-auto
Stock: A2-style, polymer
Barrel: 24-in. fluted barrel, chromoly
Trigger: Two-stage trigger
Sights: None
Weight: 9.8 lb. (without magazine and ammunition)
Caliber: .223 (5.56x45mm)
Magazine: 20 round (1 standard)

Features: Limited lifetime warranty for manufacturing and material defect; USGI profile; 1:8 twist; chromoly vanadium 4140 material; A2 flash hider; Picatinny gas block.
MSRP: **$1,250**

HSA-15, NATIONAL MATCH RIFLE, MODEL TX6570

Action: semi-auto
Stock: A2-style, polymer
Barrel: 20-in. free-float barrel, stainless steel
Trigger: Two-stage trigger
Sights: None
Weight: 16 lb. (without magazine and ammunition)
Caliber: .223 (5.59x45mm)
Magazine: 20 round (1 standard)
Features: Limited lifetime warranty for manufacturing and material defect; 1:8 twist
Other: Leather sling.
MSRP: **$1,238**

HSA-15, MODEL TX9551

Action: semi auto
Stock: M4 (6-position), polymer
Barrel: 16-in. barrel
Sights: Standard front sight tower; rear options available
Weight: 6.4 lb. (without magazine and ammunition)

Caliber: 9mm
Magazine: 30 round (1 standard)
Features: Limited lifetime warranty for manufacturing and material defect; USGI profile, 1:7 twist—CMV 4140 material, A2 flash hider.
MSRP: **$975**

HSA-15, MODEL TX9501

Action: semi-auto
Stock: M4 (6-position), polymer
Barrel: 16-in. fluted barrel
Sights: Standard front sight tower; A2 adjustable rear sights
Weight: 6.1 lb. (without magazine and ammunition)
Caliber: 9mm
Magazine: 30 round (1 standard)
Features: Limited lifetime warranty for manufacturing and material defect—USGI profile; 1:7 twist; chromoly vanadium 4140 material; A2 flash hider; fixed carry handle.
MSRP: **$1,007**

HM DEFENSE

HM15F-300

Action: semi-auto
Stock: Magpul MOE black color stock; 12-in. black type III anodized Picatinny rail, Magpul MOE black grip

HM Defense: HM15-SPFCR-556-LR

Barrel: 16-in. 300 BLK 416 stainless spiral fluted barrel, CNC machined FH-CR-V30 black flash hider
Sights: None
Weight: 6 lb. 9.5 oz.
Caliber: 300 BLK
Magazine: Magpul PMAG
Features: 7075 full-forged rifle; black colored type III; hard anodized; CNC machined steel gas block; pistol-length gas system.
MSRP: . . . . **N/A**

HM15-SPFCR-556-LR

Action: semi-auto
Stock: Black Magpul MOE stock; Magpul MOE black grip,
Barrel: 16-in. chromoly spiral fluted triple honed HBAR; 1:8 twist l, CNC machined V1-556 black flash hider
Sights: None
Weight: 6 lb. 9.8 oz.
Caliber: 5.56 NATO/.223
Magazine: 30-round Magpul Gen 2 PMAG
Features: Full billet upper and lower; Black type III hard anodized; 14-in. black Picatinny rail; CNC machined steel gas block; carbine gas system.
MSRP: . . . . **N/A**

HULDRA ARMS

MARK IV 5.45X39 CARBINE

Action: semi-auto, gas piston
Stock: Mil-spec 6-position buttstock, M4 handguards, A2 grip
Barrel: 16-in. chromoly vanadium 4150 melonite coated and lined barrel with 1:8 RH twist; melonited A2 flash hider

Sights: N/A
Weight: 6.2 lb.
Caliber: 5.45x39
Magazine: Magazine included
Features: Dry film lubed upper receiver, single-stage trigger.
MSRP: **$1,015**

MARK IV 5.56 CARBINE

Action: semi-auto, gas piston
Stock: Mil-spec 6-position buttstock, M4 handguards, A2 grip
Barrel: 16-in. chromoly vanadium 4150 melonite coated and lined barrel with 1:7 RH twist; M4 feed ramps, A2 flash hider
Sights: N/A
Weight: 6.1 lb.
Caliber: 5.56
Magazine: Magazine included
Features: Dry-film lubed upper receiver; single-stage trigger.
MSRP: **$950**

MARK IV 5.56 TACTICAL ELITE

Action: semi-auto, gas piston
Stock: Vltor IMOD mil-spec stock; free-float extended quad rail; ERGO Ambi grip
Barrel: 16-in. chromoly vanadium 4150 melonite coated and lined government-contour barrel with 1:7 RH twist; M4 feed ramps; A2 flash hider
Sights: N/A
Weight: 6.1 lb.
Caliber: 5.56
Magazine: Magazine included
Features: Dry-film lubed, T-marked upper receiver; 4.5-lb. JP single-stage trigger.
MSRP: **$1,450**

MARK IV TACTICAL EVO 14.5-IN.

Action: semi-auto, gas piston
Stock: Magpul CTR stock, Samson Evolution Series 6061-T6 aluminum fore-end
Barrel: 14.5-in. chromoly vanadium 4150 melonite coated and lined government contour barrel with 1:7 RH twist; M4 feed ramps; reduced radius elongated and permanently fixed flash hider
Sights: N/A
Weight: 6.6 lb.
Caliber: 5.56
Magazine: Magazine included
Features: Dry-film lubed, T-marked upper receiver, single-stage trigger.
MSRP: **$1,300**

5.56 X-PRE 2

Action: semi-auto, gas piston
Stock: Luth MBA-1 stock; Mega Arms MKM free-float KeyMod fore-arm; Magpul MOE-K2 grip
Barrel: 18-in. chromoly vanadium 4150 melonite coated and lined ultralight match-grade barrel with 1:8 RH twist; Adams Arms JET compensator
Sights: N/A
Weight: 7.45 lb.
Caliber: 5.56
Magazine: Six magazines included
Features: Mega Arms MKM upper; 7075-T6 aluminum lower; Hipertouch 24 3G trigger; includes tactical gun case.
MSRP: **$1,500**

Integrity Arms: JARD J21

INTEGRITY ARMS

300 BLK AR PISTOL

Action: semi-auto
Stock: SIG arm brace on rear
Barrel: 12.5-in. melonite; chambered in 300 BLK (7.62X35); 1:7 twist; pistol gas
Sights: N/A
Weight: N/A
Caliber: 5.56
Magazine: N/A
Features: Integrity Arms Premium; MPI tested 9310 bolt; shot peen; S7 extractor; M16 type Noveske KX5 muzzle brake; mil-spec single-stage trigger (4–6 lb. break) with KNS Gen ST pins; ambidextrous safety; ERGO grip with aggressive texture.
MSRP: **$1,249**

BASIC M4 CARBINE

Action: semi-auto
Stock: Magpul MOE (mil-spec)
Barrel: 16-in. 4150 chromoly vanadium steel; Wylde chamber; 1:7 twist; M4 feed ramps; carbine gas
Sights: A2-style front sight
Weight: N/A
Caliber: 5.56
Magazine: One 30-round
Features: M16 type bolt carrier group; MPI tested; 9310 alloy bolt; shot peen per mil-spec; S7 tool steel extractor; 8620 carrier; chrome lined carrier and gas key; 100 percent U.S. made; grade-8 fasteners; mil-spec single-stage (5–7 lb. break) trigger.
MSRP: **$849**

BATTLE WORN SIDE CHARGING CARBINE— WYLDE CHAMBER

Action: semi-auto
Stock: VLTOR IMOD Clubfoot, mil-spec
Barrel: 4150 chromoly vanadium; mid gas melonite w/ 5R rifling and Wylde Chamber
Sights: N/A
Weight: N/A
Caliber: 5.56/.223
Magazine: One 30-round
Features: Non-reciprocating side charging handle, Integrity Arms matching 7075-T6 billet combo; side charging upper; Integrity Arms premium M16/MPI BCG w/ S7 tool steel extractor; Integrity Arms slim KeyMod rail, 12-in. free-floating handguard; mil-spec single-stage (4–6 lb. break) trigger; ERGO ambidextrous Suregrip pistol grip.
MSRP: **$1,399**

SIDE-CHARGING AR PISTOL, WYLDE CHAMBER

Action: semi-auto
Stock: N/A
Barrel: 10.5-in. Wylde Chamber (.223 or 5.56) melonite Treated (QPQ) carbine gas, M4 ramps; 1:8 twist
Sights: N/A
Weight: N/A
Caliber: 5.56/.223
Magazine: One 30-round
Features: Integrity 7075-T6 billet machined, side charging, non-reciprocating upper; Integrity Arms Premium M16/MPI BCG w/ S7 tool steel extractor, deluxe pistol buffer tube w/tungsten filled heavy buffer, quick-detach end plate, ALG Defense QMS trigger group w/ KNS Anti-Walk pins; Hogue soft rubber grip w/ beavertail, dark earth; Troy Industries 11-in. Bravo Rail handguard; Troy Industries Claymore muzzle brake.
MSRP: **$1,300**

ULTRALIGHT FIGHTING CARBINE (UFC)

Action: semi-auto
Stock: Magpul MOE 6-position collapsible, mil-spec
Barrel: 16-in. mil-spec 4150 steel, melonite treated, Wylde Chamber (.223/5.56); 5R rifling, mid-length gas system
Sights: Magpul Gen2 MBUS front/rear
Weight: N/A
Caliber: 5.56/.223
Magazine: One 30-round Magpul PMAG
Features: 7075-T6 forged upper/lower; upper has T-markings and M4 ramps; Integrity Arms Premium M16/MPI BCG bolt carrier group with S7 tool steel extractor, Integrity Arms rifle Length carbon fiber free-float rail.
MSRP: **$1,249**

JARD

J21

Action: semi-auto
Stock: None
Barrel: 7 in.
Sights: None
Weight: 4 lb.
Caliber: .22 LR
Magazine: N/A
Features: N/A
MSRP: . . . . **$714–$762**

AR RIFLE MODELS

JARD: J16

JARD: J22

JP Rifles: SCR-11

JP Rifles: PSC-11

JP Rifles: CTR-02

J16

Action: semi-auto
Stock: AR style
Barrel: 16-in.
Sights: None
Weight: 6 lb.
Caliber: .223 Wylde
Magazine: N/A
Features: Right side charging handle; left folding stock.
MSRP: **$1,014**

J22

Action: semi-auto
Stock: AR style
Barrel: 16-in.
Sights: None
Weight: 6 lb.
Caliber: .223 Wylde
Magazine: N/A
Features: Right side charging handle; left folding stock.
MSRP: **$734**

JP RIFLES

SCR-11

Action: Side-charge semi-auto

Stock: Selectable; A2, Tactical Intent TI-7 or Magpul MOE standard
Barrel: 14.5–22-in. JP Supermatch barrel with Thermo-Fit installation and JP compensator
Sights: None
Weight: Base 6.6 lb.
Caliber: .223 Wylde, 5.56 NATO, 6.5 Grendel or 300 BLK
Magazine: One 10-round
Features: 7075-T6 billet aluminum side-charge upper and lower receiver; MK III handguard system; JP adjustable gas system; JP operating system including JP bolt carrier and JP EnhancedBolt assembly; JP fire control package; fully customizable w/ pre-built configurations available.
MSRP: . . . . **$2,699 (base), $2,744 (as shown)**

PSC-11

Action: Dual-charge semi-auto
Stock: Selectable; A2, tactical intent TI-7 or Magpul MOE standard
Barrel: 14.5–22-in. JP Supermatch barrel with Thermo-Fit installation and JP compensator

Sights: None
Weight: Base 6.7 lb.
Caliber: .223 Wylde, 5.56 NATO, 6.5 Grendel or 300 BLK
Magazine: One 10-round
Features: 7075-T6 billet aluminum dual-charge upper receiver; 7075-16 billet forged lower receiver; MK III handguard system; JP adjustable gas system; JP operating system including JP bolt carrier and JP EnhancedBolt assembly; JP fire control package; fully customizable w/ pre-built configurations available.
MSRP: . . . . **$2,699 (base), $2,814 (as shown)**

CTR-02

Action: Top-charge semi-auto
Stock: Selectable; A2, Tactical Intent TI-7 or Magpul MOE standard
Barrel: 14.5–22-in. JP Supermatch barrel with Thermo-Fit installation and JP compensator
Sights: None
Weight: Base 6.6 lb.
Caliber: .223 Wylde, 5.56 NATO, 6.5 Grendel, or 300 BLK
Magazine: One 10-round
Features: 7075-T6 billet aluminum top-charge upper and lower receiver; MK III handguard system; JP adjustable gas system; JP operating system including JP bolt carrier and JP

JP Rifles: JP-15

JP Rifles: GMR-13

JP Rifles: LRP-07

JP Rifles: PSC-12

EnhancedBolt assembly; JP fire control package; fully customizable w/ pre-built configurations available.
MSRP: . . . . $2,499 (base), $2,544 (as shown)

JP-15

Action: Top-charge semi-auto
Stock: Selectable; A2, Tactical Intent TI-7 or Magpul MOE standard
Barrel: 14.5–22-in. JP Supermatch barrel with Thermo-Fit installation and JP compensator
Sights: None
Weight: Base 6.3 lb.
Caliber: .223 Wylde, 5.56 NATO, 6.5 Grendel, or 300 BLK
Magazine: One 10-round
Features: 7075-T6 billet aluminum top-charge upper and lower receiver; MK III handguard system; JP adjustable gas system; JP operating system including JP bolt carrier and JP EnhancedBolt assembly; JP fire control package; fully customizable w/ pre-built configurations available.
MSRP: . . . . $1,999 (base), $2,264 (as shown)

GMR-13

Action: Top-charge semi-auto or dual-charge semi-auto

Stock: Selectable; A2, Tactical Intent TI-7 or Magpul MOE standard
Barrel: 14.5–16-in. JP Supermatch barrel with Thermo-Fit installation and JP compensator
Sights: None
Weight: Base 6.8 lb.
Caliber: 9mm
Magazine: One 10-round
Features: 7075-T6 billet or forged aluminum dual- or top-charge upper receiver; 7075-T6 billet aluminum lower receiver; MK III handguard system; JP operating system including JP 9mm and JPSCS-9mm; JP fire control package; fully customizable w/ pre-built configurations available.
MSRP: . . . . $1,499 (base), $1,549 (as shown)

LRP-07

Action: Side-charge semi-auto
Stock: Selectable; A2, Tactical Intent TI-7 or Magpul MOE standard
Barrel: 14.5–22-in. JP Supermatch barrel with Thermo-Fit installation and JP compensator
Sights: None
Weight: Base 7.9 lb.
Calibers: .308 Win.; .260 Rem.; 6.5 Creedmoor
Magazine: One 10-round

Features: 7075-T6 billet aluminum side-charge upper and lower receiver; MK III handguard system; JP adjustable gas system; JP operating system including JP bolt carrier and JP EnhancedBolt assembly; JP fire control package; fully customizable w/ pre-built configurations available.
MSRP: . . . . $3,299 (base), $3,844 (as shown)

PSC-12

Action: Dual-charge semi-auto
Stock: Selectable; A2, Tactical Intent TI-7 or Magpul MOE standard
Barrel: 14.5–22-in. JP Supermatch barrel with Thermo-Fit installation and JP compensator
Sights: None
Weight: Base 8.1 lb.
Caliber: .308 Win.; .260 Rem.; 6.5 Creedmoor
Magazine: One 10-round
Features: 7075-T6 billet aluminum dual-charge upper and lower receivers; 7075-T6 billet forged lower receiver; MK III handguard system; JP adjustable gas system; JP operating system including JP bolt carrier and JP EnhancedBolt assembly; JP fire control package; fully customizable w/ pre-built configurations available.
MSRP: . . . . $3,499–$3,549

JP Rifles: MR-10

JP Rifles: JP-22

Kavod Custom: KVD-15 Alef

Kavod Custom: KVD-15 Bet

MR-10

Action: Short-throw bolt action
Stock: Magpul PRS
Barrel: 24-in. JP Supermatch cryogenically treated 6-groove barreled action w/ JP compensator
Sights: None
Weight: 12.1 lb.
Calibers: .308 Win.; 6.5 Creedmoor; .260 Rem.
Magazine: Two 10-round
Features: 20 MOA mil-spec-1913 Picatinny base; extra-long JP modular handguard; 1–3 lb. trigger.
MSRP: **$3,999**

JP-22

Action: Top-, side-, or dual-charge semi-auto
Stock: Selectable; A2, Tactical Intent TI-7 or Magpul MOE standard
Barrel: 18-in. JP Supermatch barrel with Thermo-Fit installation and JP compensator
Sights: None
Weight: Base 6.6 lb.
Caliber: .22 LR
Magazine: One 10-round
Features: 7075-T6 billet or forged aluminum dual, side or top charge upper and lower receiver; MK III handguard system; JP operating system including JP rimfire bolt; JP fire control package; Fully customizable w/ pre-built configurations available.
MSRP: . . . . **$1,349–$1,524**

Kavod Custom

KVD-15 ALEF

Action: semi-auto
Stock: Black Magpul MOE rifle
Barrel: 16-in. stainless steel 1:7 twist; medium profile; mid-length gas; hreaded ½x28
Sights: None
Weight: 6.5 lb.
Caliber: 5.56mm
Magazine: Two 30-round Magpul PMAG
Features: Nickel-boron M16 bolt carrier group; Troy Industries 15-in. Alpha/VTAC handguard with three rail stubs; black Magpul trigger guard and MOE rifle stock; Bravo Company Mod3 charging handle; Hogue rubber grip; fully-shrouded gas system; available 3.5 lb. two-stage trigger.
MSRP: **$1,180**

KVD-15 BET

Action: semi-auto
Stock: Black Magpul MOE (mil-spec)
Barrel: 16-in. stainless steel 1:8 twist; heavy profile, carbine-length gas; threaded ½-in.x 28
Sights: None
Weight: 6.5 lb.
Caliber: 5.56mm
Magazine: Two 30-round Magpul PMAG
Features: Nickel-boron M16 bolt carrier group; Odin Works 15-in. sport rail handguard with one rail stub; black Magpul trigger guard, MOE stock and MOE+ rubber grip; Bravo Company Mod3 charging handle; fully-shrouded gas system; available 3.5 lb. two-stage trigger.
MSRP: **$1,200**

KVD-15 GIMEL

Action: semi-auto
Stock: Black B5 Systems Bravo (mil-spec)
Barrel: 16-in. stainless steel; 1:8 twist; medium profile; mid-length gas; threaded ½x28
Sights: None
Weight: 6.5 lb.

Kavod Custom: KVD-15 Gimel

Lancer: L15 Competition

Lancer: L15 Outlaw

Lancer: L15 Patrol

Caliber: 5.56mm
Magazine: Two 30-round Magpul PMAG
Features: Nickel-boron M16 bolt carrier group; Parallax Tactical 13-in. free-float super-slim rail; black LWRC trigger guard and B5 Systems Bravo stock; Bravo Company Mod3 charging handle; fully-shrouded gas system; available 3.5-lb. two-stage trigger.
MSRP: **$1,160**

LANCER

L15 COMPETITION

Action: semi-auto
Stock: Lancer carbon fiber stock
Barrel: Mid-weight 16-in. CHF chrome lined barrel

Sights: N/A
Weight: 7.7 lb.
Caliber: .223
Magazine: 20-round smoke and 30-round smoke Lancer L5AWM
Features: Lancer carbon fiber handguard.
MSRP: **$2,138**

L15 OUTLAW

Action: semi-auto
Stock: Lancer carbon fiber stock (LCS)
Barrel: Mid-weight 17-in. Bartlein barrel
Sights: N/A
Weight: 6.25 lb.
Caliber: .223
Magazine: 20-round smoke and 30-round smoke Lancer L5AWM

Features: Lancer carbon fiber handguard.
MSRP: **$2,854**

L15 PATROL

Action: semi-auto
Stock: B5 Bravo
Barrel: Mid-weight 16-in. CHF chrome lined barrel
Sights: N/A
Weight: 6.5 lb.
Caliber: .223
Magazine: 30-round smoke Lancer L5AWM
Features: Lancer carbon fiber handguard.
MSRP: **$1,894**

Lancer: L15 Patrol Professional

Lancer: L15 Sporter

Lancer: L15 Super Competition

Lancer: L30 Heavy Metal

L15 PATROL PROFESSIONAL

Action: semi-auto
Stock: FAB GL
Barrel: Mid-weight 14.5 in. CHF chrome lined barrel
Sights: N/A
Weight: 6.5 lb.
Caliber: .223
Magazine: 20-round smoke and 30-round smoke Lancer L5AWM
Features: Lancer carbon fiber handguard.
MSRP: **$1,908**

L15 SPORTER

Action: semi-auto
Stock: F93 Pro Stock
Barrel: Mid-weight 16-in. CHF chrome lined barrel
Sights: N/A
Weight: 7.4 lb.
Caliber: .223
Magazine: 30-round smoke Lancer L5AWM
Features: Lancer carbon fiber handguard.
MSRP: **$1,687**

L15 SUPER COMPETITION

Action: semi-auto
Stock: Lancer carbon fiber stock
Barrel: Mid-weight 17-in. Bartlein stainless steel barrel
Sights: N/A
Weight: 7.5 lb.
Caliber: .223
Magazine: 20-round smoke and 30-round smoke Lancer L5AWM
Features: Lancer carbon fiber handguard.
MSRP: **$2,698**

L30 HEAVY METAL

Action: semi-auto
Stock: Lancer Carbon Fiber Stock (LCS)
Barrel: 18-In. White Oak barrel
Sights: N/A
Weight: 9.5 lb.
Caliber: .308
Magzine: 10-round smoke and 20-round smoke Lancer L5AWM
Features: Lancer carbon fiber handguard.
MSRP: **$3,345**

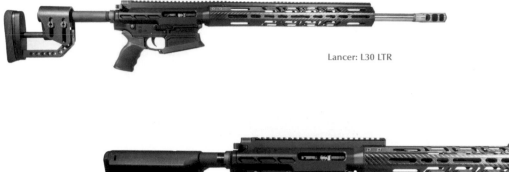

Lancer: L30 LTR

Lancer: L30 MBR

L30 LTR

Action: semi-auto
Stock: KFS TACMOD
Barrel: 24-in. Bartlein stainless barrel
Sights: N/A
Weight: 12.5 lb.
Caliber: .308 or 6.5
Magzine: 10-round smoke and
20-round smoke Lancer L5AWM
Features: Lancer carbon fiber
handguard; LTR is available in
7.62X51 (.308) or 6.5 Creedmoor.
MSRP: **$4,199**

L30 MBR

Action: semi-auto
Stock: B5 Sopmod
Barrel: 16-in. black Nitride barrel
Sights: N/A
Weight: 9.0 lb.
Caliber: .308
Magzine: 10-round smoke and
20-round smoke Lancer L5AWM
Features: Lancer carbon fiber
handguard.
MSRP: **$2,559**

KNIGHTS ARMAMENT

SR-15 CQB MOD 2

Action: semi-auto
Stock: URX4 handguard, 6-position
stock
Barrel: 11.5-in. hammer-forged
chrome-lined barrel; 1:7 twist; three-
prong flash hider
Sights: Flip-up sights
Weight: 6.1 lb.
Caliber: 5.56
Magazine: N/A
Features: Two-state match trigger,
ambidextrous controls.
MSRP: . . . . **N/A**

SR-15 E3 CARBINE MOD 2

Action: semi-auto
Stock: URX4 handguard, 6-position
stock
Barrel: 14.5-in. hammer-forged
chrome-lined barrel; 1:7 twist; three-
prong flash hider
Sights: Flip-up sights
Weight: 6.4 lb.
Caliber: 5.56
Magazine: N/A
Features: Two-state match trigger,
ambidextrous controls.
MSRP: . . . . **N/A**

SR-15 E3 MOD 2

Action: semi-auto
Stock: URX4 handguard; 6-position
stock
Barrel: 16-in. hammer-forged chrome-
lined barrel; 1:7 twist; three-prong
flash hider
Sights: Flip-up sights
Weight: 6.55 lb.
Caliber: 5.56
Magazine: N/A
Features: Two-state match trigger,
ambidextrous controls.
MSRP: . . . . **N/A**

SR-15 LPR MOD 2

Action: semi-auto
Stock: URX4 handguard, 6-position
stock
Barrel: 18-in. stainless steel barrel; 1:7
twist; three-prong flash hider
Sights: Flip-up sights
Weight: 7.4 lb.
Caliber: 5.56
Magazine: N/A
Features: Two-state match trigger,
ambidextrous controls.
MSRP: . . . . **N/A**

SR-25 E2 ACC

Action: semi-auto
Stock: URX4 handguard; 6-position
stock
Barrel: 16-in. 5R cut; chrome-lined
barrel; 1:10 twist; 7.62 QDC flash
suppressor
Sights: Flip-up sights
Weight: 8.4 lb.
Caliber: 7.62 NATO/.308
Magazine: N/A
Features: Two-state match trigger;
ambidextrous controls.
MSRP: . . . . **N/A**

SR-25 E2 APC

Action: semi-auto
Stock: URX4 handguard; 6-position
stock
Barrel: 16-in. 5R cut; chrome-lined
barrel; 1:10 twist, 7.62 QDC flash
suppressor

LaRue Tactical: PredatOBR 556

LaRue Tactical: OBR 556

LaRue Tactical: PredatAR 556

Sights: Flip-up sights
Weight: 9 lb.
Caliber: 7.62 NATO/.308
Magazine: N/A
Features: Two-state match trigger; ambidextrous controls.
MSRP: . . . . **N/A**

SR-25 E2 APR

Action: semi-auto
Stock: URX4 handguard; 6-position stock
Barrel: 20-in. 5R cut, chrome-lined barrel, 1:10 twist, 7.62 QDC flash suppressor
Sights: Flip-up sights
Weight: 10.5 lb.
Caliber: 7.62 NATO/.308
Magazine: N/A
Features: Two-state match trigger, ambidextrous controls.
MSRP: . . . . **N/A**

SR-30

Action: semi-auto
Stock: URX4 handguard; 6-position stock
Barrel: 9.5-in. chrome lined barrel; 1:7 twist, QDC flash suppressor
Sights: Flip-up sights
Weight: 6.2 lb.
Caliber: 300 BLK
Magazine: N/A
Features: Two-state match trigger, ambidextrous controls.
MSRP: . . . . **N/A**

LaRue Tactical

PREDATOBR 556

Action: semi-auto
Stock: LaRue RAT Stock
Barrel: 14.5-in, 16-in., 18-in., 20-in., 1:8 twist, Rearden steel
Sights: None (mil-spec-1913 flat-top for optics)
Weight: 8 lb. (16-in. model)
Caliber: 5.56
Magazine: Two 30-round
Features: The handguards extend out to suit a larger range of shooting styles. The zero-MOA upper rail provides room for weapon-mounted night-vision day/night combinations. Both the upper and lower are CNC-machined from billet aluminum. All barrels are threaded in ½x28, with an A2 flash hider attached (other muzzle devices can be added at an additional cost).
MSRP: **$2,245**

OBR 556

Action: semi-auto
Stock: LaRue RAT Stock
Barrel: 12-in., 16-in., 18-in., 20-in., 1:8 twist, Rearden steel
Sights: None (mil-spec-1913 flat-top for optics)
Weight: 8.2 lb. (16-in. model)
Caliber: 5.56
Magazine: Two 30-round

Features: The LaRue OBR 556 (Optimized Battle Rifle) was built using a newly designed upper receiver platform. Both the upper and lower are CNC-machined from billet. The upper-rail provides generous room for all issue weapon-mounted night-vision day/night combinations (suitable for 5.56mm). The built-in cant provides correct ballistic orientation for inline night vision combinations. The mil-spec-1913 side rails are detachable, so that they can be configured for Vis, IR illuminators, etc., or left off. The bottom rails are also detachable, and can be positioned anywhere along the entire lower length, for the interface of mil-spec-1913 equipped bipods, grips, tripod mounts, etc.
MSRP: **$2,245**

PREDATAR 556

Action: semi-auto
Stock: LaRue RAT Stock
Barrel: 16-in., 18-in., 1:8 twist, Rearden steel
Sights: None (mil-spec-1913 flat-top for optics)
Weight: 7.17 lb. (16-in. model)
Caliber: 5.56
Magazine: One 30-round
Features: The PredatAR takes the OBR 5.56 design and lightens it. By contouring the barrel, skeletonizing the handguard, lowering and simplifying the upper rail, and using a low-profile gas block, LaRue reduced roughly two pounds from the standard OBR 5.56 rifle. The zero-MOA upper rail provides plenty of room for weapon-mounted night-vision day/ night combinations. The PredatAR barrels are Wylde chambered and feature polygonal rifling. All barrels

AR Rifle Models • **117**

LaRue Tactical: PredatOBR 7.62

LaRue Tactical: OBR 76.2

LaRue Tactical: PredatAR 76.2

are threaded in ½x28, with an A2 flash hider attached. Each rifle ships with one, 3-in. long, mil-spec-1913 detachable rail section.

MSRP: **$1,807**

PREDATOBR 7.62

Action: semi-auto
Stock: LaRue RAT Stock
Barrel: 14.50-in., 16-in., 18-in., 20-in., 1:10 twist, Rearden steel
Sights: None (mil-spec-1913 flat-top for optics)
Weight: 9.5 lb. (16-in. model)
Caliber: 7.62
Magazine: Two 20-round
Features: The PredatOBR 7.62 is designed for those who are searching for a hybrid cross between the OBR and PredatAR 7.62mm NATO rifles. The PredatOBR takes the OBR 7.62 design, and lightens it in every possible way. The handguards on the PredatOBR extend out to suit a larger range of shooting styles. The zero-MOA upper rail provides room for weapon-mounted night-vision day/ night combinations. Both the upper and lower are CNC-machined from

billet aluminum. All barrels are threaded in 5/8x24.

MSRP: **$3,370**

OBR 7.62

Action: semi-auto
Stock: LaRue RAT stock
Barrel: 16-in., 18-in., 20-in., 1:10 twist, Rearden steel
Sights: None (mil-spec-1913 flat-top for optics)
Weight: 9.75 lb. (16-in. model)
Caliber: 7.62
Magazine: Two 20-round
Features: Both the upper and lower are CNC-machined from billet, for the optimum fit and consistency. The upper rail provides generous room for all weapon-mounted night-vision day/ night combinations (suitable for 7.62mm). The built-in cant provides correct ballistic orientation for all inline night vision combinations. The mil-spec-1913 side rails are detachable, so that they can be configured for Vis/IR illuminators, or left off to keep rails pristine, without the need for bulky rail covers. The bottom rails are also detachable, and

can be positioned anywhere along the entire lower length.

MSRP: **$3,370**

PREDATAR 7.62

Action: semi-auto
Stock: LaRue RAT stock
Barrel: 16-in., 18-in., 1:10 twist, Rearden steel
Sights: None (mil-spec-1913 flat-top for optics)
Weight: 8 lb. (16-in. model)
Caliber: 7.62
Magazine: Two 20-round
Features: By contouring the barrel, skeletonizing the handguard, lowering and simplifying the upper rail, and using a low-profile gas block, weight is reduced by roughly two pounds from the standard OBR 7.62 rifle. The handguards extend out 14-in. to suit a larger range of shooting styles. The zero-MOA upper rail provides room for weapon-mounted night-vision day/ night combinations. Both the upper and lower are CNC-machined from billet 7075-T6. All barrels are threaded in 5/8x24, with an A2 flash hider attached (other muzzle devices can be added at an additional cost).

MSRP: **$2,932**

AR RIFLE MODELS

Les Baer: .264 LBC-AR Super Varmint Model

Les Baer: M4 Flattop Model (Law Enforcement Model)

Les Baer: Mid-Length Monolith .308 semi-auto SWAT Model

Les Baer: NRA Match Rifle

LES BAER

.264 LBC-AR SUPER VARMINT MODEL

Action: semi-auto
Stock: Fixed stock, round handguard
Barrel: N/A
Sights: None
Weight: N/A
Caliber: .264 LBC-AR
Magazine: Two 14-round
Features: Bipod.
MSRP: . . . . **N/A**

M4 FLATTOP MODEL (LAW ENFORCEMENT MODEL)

Action: semi-auto
Stock: 4-position stock, free-float handguard
Barrel: LBC bench rest 416 R stainless steel barrel with precision cut rifling (1:9 twist standard, optional twists available including 1:12 or 1:8); 16-in. length standard
Sights: none
Weight: N/A

Caliber: .223
Magazine: 20 round
Features: LBC forged and precision machined upper and lower receivers (available with or without forward assist upper); Picatinny-style flat top rail; Geissele two-stage trigger, Versa-Pod; soft case.
MSRP: . . . . **N/A**

MID-LENGTH MONOLITH .308 SEMI-AUTO SWAT MODEL

Action: semi-auto
Stock: Magpul PRS stock, LBC custom grip
Barrel: LBC bench rest 416R stainless steel 16-in. barrel with precision cut rifling, 1:10 twist
Sights: None
Weight: N/A
Caliber: .308
Magazine: Two 20-round
Features: No forward assist; precision bolt chromed; Geissele two-stage trigger; Versa-Pod and adaptor; soft rifle case; integral trigger guard bowed at bottom for glove wear.
MSRP: . . . . **N/A**

NRA MATCH RIFLE

Action: semi-auto
Stock: Fixed stock; precision-machined adjustable free-float handguard; LBC custom grip
Barrel: LBC bench rest 416 R stainless steel barrel with precision cut rifling (1:8 twist standard, optional twists available, including 1:7) 30-in. length standard
Sights: RM-1 rear sight, Anshutz Globe front sight with aperture
Weight: N/A
Caliber: .223
Magazine: 20 round
Features: Geissele two-stage trigger; forged and precision machined upper and lower; Picatinny-style flat-top rail; available with or without forward assist upper; chromed bolt, chromed extractor; soft case.
MSRP: . . . . **N/A**

.223 SUPER VARMINT MODEL

Action: semi-auto
Stock: Precision machined adjustable

Les Baer: .223 Super Varmint Model

Les Baer: .223 Super Match Model

Les Baer: .308 semi-auto Match Rifle

free-float handguard with locking ring; LBC custom grip with extra material under the trigger guard corner barrel; LBC bench rest 416 R stainless steel barrel with precision-cut rifling (1:9 twist standard, optional twists available, including 1:12, 1:8, 1:7); 20-in. length standard (18-in., 22-in., and 24-in. optional)

Sights: N/A
Weight: N/A
Caliber: .223; .264 LBC-AR, 6x45mm
Magazine: 20 round
Features: Forged and precision machined upper and lower receivers; Picatinny-style flat-top rail; National Match carrier; Geissele two-stage trigger group; aluminum gas block with Picatinny rail top; scope package available.
MSRP: . . . . **N/A**

.223 SUPER MATCH MODEL

Action: semi-auto
Stock: 4-position free-float handguard with integral Picatinny rail system, custom grip with extra material under the trigger guard corner
Barrel: Benchrest 416 R stainless steel barrel with precision-cut rifling (1:9 twist standard, optional twists available including 1:12, 1:8, 1:7); 20-in. length standard (18-in., 22-in., and 24-in. optional)
Sights: None
Weight: N/A
Caliber: .223; .204 Ruger
Magazine: 20 round
Features: Forged and precision machined upper and lower receivers; Picatinny-style flat top rail, National Match carrier; Geissele two-stage trigger group; aluminum gas block; Versa-Pod installed; scope package available.
MSRP: . . . . **N/A**

.308 SEMI-AUTO MATCH RIFLE

Action: semi-auto
Stock: Fixed, precision machined free-float handguard with lock ring
Barrel: Benchrest 416R stainless steel barrel with precision cut rifling, 1:10 twist
Sights: None
Weight: N/A
Caliber: .308
Magazine: Two 20-round
Features: Upper and lower receivers machined 7075-T6-51 premium billet; no forward assist; Picatinny-style flat-top-rail; chrome bolt; chrome extractor; Geissele two-stage trigger; steel gas block with Picatinny rail on top; custom grip with extra material under the trigger guard; integral trigger guard is bowed on the bottom to allow wearing gloves; Harris bipod.
MSRP: . . . . **N/A**

Lewis Machine & Tool

LM308MWSE

Action: semi-auto
Stock: SOPMOD buttstock
Barrel: 16-in. chrome lined; 1:10 twist
Sights: LMT tactical adjustable rear and tactical front
Weight: 10.02 lb.
Caliber: .308 (7.62x51)
Magazine: Original stoner AR-10 compatible
Features: Standard semi-auto bolt carrier group; tactical charging handle assembly; two-stage trigger group; ambi safety selector; ambi mag release.
MSRP: $3,153
California Legal: $3,203

LM308MWSF

Action: semi-auto
Stock: SOPMOD buttstock
Barrel: 16-in.; 1:11 5R twist; ultra-match blackened stainless steel
Sights: LMT tactical adjustable rear and tactical front
Weight: 10.02 lb.
Caliber: .308 (7.62x51)
Magazine: Original stoner AR-10 compatible
Features: Standard semi-auto bolt carrier group; tactical charging handle assembly; two-stage trigger group; ambi safety selector; ambi mag release.
MSRP: $3,565
California Legal: $3,615

LM308COMP16– COMPLIANT .308 (EAST COAST COMPLIANT)

Action: semi-auto
Stock: SOPMOD buttstock
Barrel: 16-in. chrome lined, 1:10 twist .308 target style
Sights: LMT tactical adjustable rear and tactical front
Weight: 10.02 lb.
Caliber: .308 (7.62x51)
Magazine: Original stoner AR-10 compatible
Features: Standard semi-auto bolt carrier group; tactical charging handle assembly; two-stage trigger group;

ambi safety selector; ambi mag release.
MSRP: $3,153

CQB16

Action: semi-auto
Stock: SOPMOD buttstock
Barrel: 16-in.; chrome-lined; 1:7 twist
Sights: LMT tactical adjustable rear and tactical front
Weight: 7.4 lb.
Caliber: .223 (5.56mm)
Magazine: Standard AR-15 type
Features: Standard semi-auto bolt carrier group; tactical charging handle assembly; Defender lower; standard trigger group.
MSRP: $2,205
California Legal: $2,225

STD16

Action: semi-auto
Stock: SOPMOD buttstock
Barrel: 16-in.; chrome-lined; 1:7 twist
Sights: Fixed AR front; tactical adjustable rear
Weight: 6.78 lb.
Caliber: .223 (5.56mm)
Magazine: Standard AR-15 type
Features: Standard semi-auto bolt carrier group; tactical charging handle assembly; Defender lower; and standard trigger group.
MSRP: $1,674
California Legal: $1,694

SPM16

Action: semi-auto
Stock: Gen 2 collapsing
Barrel: 16-in.; chrome-lined; 1:7 twist
Sights: Fixed AR front; tactical adjustable rear
Weight: 6.78 lb.
Caliber: .223 (5.56mm)
Magazine: Standard AR-15 type
Features: Standard semi-auto bolt carrier group; tactical charging handle assembly; Defender lower; and standard trigger group.
MSRP: $1,460
California Legal: $1,480

COMP16 (COMPLIANT)

Action: semi-auto
Stock: SOPMOD buttstock
Barrel: 16-in.; chrome-lined; 1:7 twist; target style
Sights: Fixed AR front; tactical adjustable rear
Weight: 7.4 lb.
Caliber: .223 (5.56mm)
Magazine: Standard AR-15 type
Features: Standard semi-auto bolt carrier group; tactical charging handle assembly; Defender lower; and standard trigger group.
MSRP: $2,205

CQB16 6.8

Action: semi-auto
Stock: SOPMOD buttstock
Barrel: 16-in.; chrome lined; 1:7 twist; target style
Sights: LMT tactical adjustable rear and tactical front
Weight: 7.45 lb.
Caliber: 6.8
Magazine: Standard AR-15 type
Features: Standard semi-auto bolt carrier group; tactical charging handle assembly; Defender lower; and standard trigger group.
MSRP: $2,307
California Legal: $2,327

CQBPS16

Action: semi-auto
Stock: SOPMOD buttstock
Barrel: 16-in.; chrome lined; 1:7 twist; target style
Sights: LMT tactical adjustable rear and tactical front
Weight: 7.9 lb.
Caliber: .223 (5.56mm)
Magazine: Standard AR-15 type
Features: Piston semi-auto bolt carrier group; tactical charging handle assembly; Defender lower; and standard trigger group.
MSRP: $2,488
California Legal: $2,508

CQBPS 6.8

Action: semi-auto
Stock: SOPMOD buttstock
Barrel: 16-in.; chrome lined; 1:7 twist; target style
Sights: LMT tactical adjustable rear and tactical front

LWRC: IC Enhanced Individual Carbine

LWRC: IC SPR Individual Carbine—Special Purpose Rifle

LWRC: IC A2 Individual Carbine

Weight: 7.9 lb.
Caliber: 6.8
Magazine: Standard AR-15 type
Features: Piston semi-auto bolt carrier group; tactical charging handle assembly; Defender lower; and standard trigger group.
MSRP: **$2,633**
California Legal: $2,653

LWRC

IC ENHANCED INDIVIDUAL CARBINE

Action: LWRCI patented short stroke gas-piston, semi-auto
Stock: LWRCI adjustable compact stock
Barrel: 14.7-in.; 16.1-in. LWRCI NiCorr treated cold hammer forged spiral fluted barrel; 1:7 RH rifling
Sights: LWRCI skirmish BUIS
Weight: 7.1 lb.
Caliber: 5.56 NATO
Magazine: One 10- and 30-round Magpul PMAG
Features: Monoforge upper receiver with integrated rail base; 9-in. user-configurable rail system; 2-position adjustable gas block to switch between suppressed and unsuppressed shooting; LWRCI Enhanced Fire Control Group; oversized trigger guard allows for use

with gloves; LWRCI ambidextrous charging handle; nickel-boron coated bolt carrier for unparalled wear resistance, corrosion resistance, and permanent lubricity; Magpul MOE+ grip; integrated quick-detach LWRCI ambidextrous sling mount; available in anodized black and FDE, OD green and patriot brown LWRCI Cerakote finish options.
MSRP: $2,499 black, $2,649 FDE/OD green/patriot brown cerakote

IC SPR INDIVIDUAL CARBINE—SPECIAL PURPOSE RIFLE

Action: LWRCI patented short stroke gas-piston, semi-auto
Stock: LWRCI adjustable compact stock with integrated sling attachment point
Barrel: 14.7-in., 16.1-in. LWRCI NiCorr treated cold hammer forged spiral fluted barrel; 1:7 RH rifling
Sights: LWRCI Skirmish BUIS
Weight: 7.1 lb.
Caliber: 5.56 NATO
Magazine: One 10- and 30-round Magpul PMAG
Features: Monoforge upper receiver with integrated rail base; 12-in. user configurable rail system; LWRCI Enhanced Fire Control Group; oversized trigger guard allows for use

with gloves; dual control fully ambidextrous lower receiver includes bolt catch and release; magazine release and fire control access from both sides of the rifle; LWRCI ambidextrous charging handle; nickel-boron coated bolt carrier for unparalled wear resistance, corrosion resistance and permanent lubricity; Magpul MOE+ grip; integrated quick-detach LWRCI ambidextrous sling mount; available in anodized black and FDE, OD green and patriot brown LWRCI Cerakote finish options.
MSRP: $2,349 black, $2,499 FDE/OD green/patriot brown cerakote

IC A2 INDIVIDUAL CARBINE

Action: LWRCI patented short stroke gas-piston, semi-auto
Stock: LWRCI adjustable compact stock
Barrel: 14.7-in., 16.1-in. LWRCI NiCorr treated cold hammer forged spiral fluted barrel; 1:7 RH rifling
Sights: LWRCI Skirmish BUIS
Weight: 7.3 lb.
Caliber: 5.56 NATO
Magazine: One 10- and 30-round Magpul PMAG
Features: Monoforge upper receiver with integrated rail base; 9-in. quad rail System user configurable rail system; LWRCI railskins enhance shooting performance; LWRCI Enhanced Fire Control Group; oversized trigger guard allows for use with gloves; dual control fully ambidextrous lower receiver includes bolt catch and release, magazine release and fire control access from

LWRC: SIX8 A2

LWRC: SIX8 SPR Special Purpose Rifle

LWRC: SIX8 UCIW—
Ultra Compact
Individual Weapon

both sides of the rifle; LWRCI ambidextrous charging handle; nickel-boron coated bolt carrier for unparalled wear resistance; corrosion resistance and permanent lubricity; LWRCI A2 birdcage flash hider; Magpul MOE+ grip; available in anodized black and FDE, OD green and patriot brown LWRCI Cerakote finish options.
MSRP: $2,249 black, $2,399 FDE/OD green/patriot brown cerakote

SIX8 A2

Action: LWRCI patented short stroke gas-piston, semi-auto
Stock: LWRCI adjustable compact stock with integrated sling attachment point, 9-in. ARM-R quad rail system
Barrel: 10.5-in., 12.7-in., 14.7-in., 16.1-in., LWRCI NiCorr treated cold hammer forged spiral fluted barrel, 1:10 RH rifling
Sights: LWRCI Skirmish BUIS
Weight: 6.5 lb., 6.8 lb., 7.0 lb., 7.3 lb.
Caliber: 6.8 SPC
Magazine: Magpul magazine with high visibility follower
Features: Proprietary upper and lower receivers optimized for the 6.8 SPC cartridge; enlarged ejection port; Advanced Combat Bolt in 6.8 features a fully supported bolt face, dual extractor springs and claw extractor

that provide 20 percent more purchase on the case rim; LWRCI Enhanced Fire Control Group; LWRCI ambidextrous charging handle; LWRCI high efficiency flash hider; Magpul MOE+ grip; available in anodized black and FDE, OD green and patriot brown LWRCI Cerakote finish options.
MSRP: $2,249 black, $2,399 FDE/OD green/patriot brown cerakote

SIX8 SPR SPECIAL PURPOSE RIFLE

Action: LWRCI patented short stroke gas-piston, semi-auto
Stock: LWRCI adjustable compact stock with integrated sling attachment point; 12-in. user-configurable rail system
Barrel: 14.7-in. or 16.1-in. LWRCI NiCorr treated cold hammer forged spiral fluted barrel; 1:10 RH rifling
Sights: LWRCI Skirmish BUIS
Weight: 7.25 lb., 16.1-in.
Caliber: 6.8 SPC
Magazine: Magpul magazine with high visibility follower
Features: Proprietary upper and lower receivers optimized for the 6.8 SPC cartridge; enlarged ejection port; Advanced Combat Bolt in 6.8 features a fully supported bolt face, dual extractor springs and claw extractor that provide 20 percent more purchase

on the case rim; LWRCI Enhanced Fire Control Group; LWRCI ambidextrous charging handle; LWRCI high efficiency flash hider; Magpul MOE+ grip; available in anodized black and FDE, OD green and patriot brown LWRCI Cerakote finish options.
MSRP: $2,499 black, $2,649 FDE/OD green/patriot brown cerakote

SIX8 UCIW—ULTRA COMPACT INDIVIDUAL WEAPON

Action: LWRCI patented short stroke gas-piston, semi-auto
Stock: LWRCI adjustable ultra compact stock with integrated sling attachment point; 7-in. Picatinny quad rail
Barrel: 8.5-in. LWRCI NiCorr treated cold hammer forged spiral fluted barrel; 1:10 RH rifling
Sights: LWRCI Skirmish BUIS
Weight: 6.25 lb.
Caliber: 5.56 NATO
Magazine: One 10- and 30-round Magpul
Features: Proprietary upper and lower receivers optimized for the 6.8 SPC cartridge; LWRCI vertical folding grip; enlarged ejection port allows unhindered ejection of 6.8 casings; Advanced Combat Bolt; LWRCI Enhanced Fire Control Group; LWRCI ambidextrous charging handle; LWRCI high efficiency flash hider; Magpul MOE+ grip; available in anodized black and FDE, OD green and patriot brown LWRCI Cerakote finish options.
MSRP: $2,249 black, $2,399 FDE/OD green/patriot brown cerakote

AR RIFLE MODELS

LWRC: SIX8 PISTOL

LWRC: R.E.P.R.—Rapid Engagement Precision Rifle

LWRC: M6 SL—Stretch Lightweight

SIX8 PISTOL

Action: LWRCI patented short-stroke gas-piston, semi-auto
Stock: LWRCI adjustable compact stock; full Picatinny quad rail
Barrel: 8.5-in. LWRCI NiCorr treated cold hammer forged spiral fluted barrel; 1:10 RH rifling
Sights: LWRCI Skirmish BUIS
Weight: 6.25 lb.
Caliber: 6.8 SPC
Magazine: Magpul with high visibility follower
Features: Proprietary upper and lower receivers optimized for the 6.8 SPC cartridge; enlarged ejection port allows unhindered ejection of 6.8 casings; LWRCI pistol buffer tube; Advanced Combat Bolt in 6.8 features a fully supported bolt face, dual extractor springs and claw extractor that provide 20 percent more purchase on the case rim; LWRCI Enhanced Fire Control Group; LWRCI ambidextrous charging handle; LWRCI high efficiency flash hider; LWRCI rail skins; Magpul MOE+ grip; available in anodized black and FDE, OD green, and patriot brown LWRCI Cerakote finish options.
MSRP: $2,149 black, $2,299 FDE/OD green/patriot brown cerakote

R.E.P.R.—RAPID ENGAGEMENT PRECISION RIFLE

Action: LWRCI patented short-stroke gas-piston, semi-auto
Stock: B5 SOPMOD stock adjustable, 12.5-in. modular rail system
Barrel: 16-in. LWRCI NiCorr treated cold hammer forged spiral fluted barrel; 1:10 RH rifling
Sights: LWRCI Skirmish BUIS
Weight: 9.3 lb.
Caliber: 7.62 NATO
Magazine: One 10- to 20-round Magpul PMAG
Features: Removable top-rail with 100 percent return to zero; upper and lower receivers machined from billet aluminum; 2-position adjustable gas block for easy switch from normal to suppressed shooting side-mounted, nonreciprocating charging handle; Geissele SSA two-stage trigger; nickel-boron coated bolt carrier for unparalled wear resistance, corrosion resistance and permanent lubricity; Magpul MOE+ grip; LWRCI A2 birdcage flash hider; available in anodized black and FDE, OD green and patriot brown LWRCI Cerakote finish options.
MSRP: $3,600 black, $3,750 FDE/OD green/patriot brown cerakote

M6 SL—STRETCH LIGHTWEIGHT

Action: LWRCI patented short stroke gas-piston, semi-auto
Stock: LWRCI carbine stock
Barrel: 14.7-in., 16.1-in. LWRCI NiCorr treated cold hammer forged barrel; 1:7 RH rifling
Sights: fixed A-frame front sight, LWRCI rear sight
Weight: 6.6 lb.
Caliber: 5.56 NATO
Magazine: One 10- to 30-round Magpul PMAG
Features: Magpul MOE furniture; MOE, mid-length handguard; MOE pistol grip; light contour barrel; EXO (nickel-boron) plated advanced combat bolt; one-piece EXO coated carrier; EXO-coated enhanced fire control group; available in anodized black and FDE, OD green, and patriot brown LWRCI Cerakote finish options.
MSRP: $1,675 black, $1,775 FDE/OD green/patriot brown cerakote

MGI

MARCK 15 BASE SYSTEM

Action: semi-auto
Stock: 6-position telescoping buttstock with MGI logo
Barrel: 16-in.
Sights: Optics ready
Weight: 6 lb. 8 oz.
Caliber: 5.56mm
Magazine: 30 round
Features: Modular lower receiver with a 5.56mm magazine well; QCB-C upper receiver; 16-in. barrel. Simple as changing just a bolt and barrel on this system, the user will be able to fire

MHT Defense:
Shootrite Katana

Mossberg: MMR Hunter

Mossberg: MMR Tactical

eight-plus calibers, including .22 rimfire, .223 or 5.56, 6.5 Grendel, 6.8 SPC, .450 Thumper, .458 SOCOM, .50 Beowulf, and the 300 BLK.
MSRP: **$1,299**

MHT DEFENSE

SHOOTRITE KATANA

Action: semi-auto
Stock: Magpul MOE fixed, or Magpul SL carbine stock
Barrel: 16-in., 1:7 twist; lightweight profile; rifle-length gas system; chrome chamber/bore
Sights: Fixed, with Daniel Defense A1.5 rear, or Magpul folding front and rear
Weight: 5 lb. 14 oz.
Caliber: 5.56
Magazine: 30 round

Features: Bolt group HP/MPI tested; nickel-boron; ALG ACT trigger; custom flat-top upper and lower machined by MHT; PRI rifle-length handguard; MechArmor ambi charging handle; assembled one at a time with custom features available; available in FDE, black, or OD green; Agile sling; soft carry case; autographed copy of *The Book of Two Guns* by Tiger McKee.
MSRP: **$1,850**

MOSSBERG

MMR HUNTER

Action: semi-auto
Stock: A2-style buttstock, slender checkered, aluminum tubular free-floating fore-end
Barrel: Free floating, 20-in., 1:9 twist

Sights: None
Weight: 7 lb.
Caliber: .223 Rem. (5.56mm)
Magazine: 5 round
Features: Direct-impingement gas system; A4 flat-top upper with Picatinny rail; single-stage trigger; Stark SE-1 pistol grip; shell deflector ramp behind ejection port; available in black, Mossy Oak Treestand, or Mossy Oak Brush.
MSRP: . . . . **$1,028–$1,127**

MMR TACTICAL

Action: semi-auto
Stock: Picatinny-vented quad rail free-float forearm with plastic rail covers; 6-position collapsible buttstock; mil-spec receiver extension (buffer tube) and fixed stock versions
Barrel: Free-floating 16.25-in., 1:9 twist; removable A2-style muzzle brake
Sights: Picatinny rail front and rear sight system, optional A2-style sights
Weight: 7–7.5 lb.
Caliber: .223 Rem. (5.56mm)
Magazine: Optional 10- and 30-round
Features: Direct-impingement gas system; single-stage trigger, Picatinny rail flat-top upper; Stark SE-1 pistol grip with storage compartment; available in eight configurations; black phosphate/anodized aluminum finishes.
MSRP: . . . . **$987–$1,028**

Mossberg: 715T Flat Top (formerly Tactical .22)

Nemo: Omen/ASP .300 Win. MSR

Nemo: Omen/Match 2.0

Nemo: Omen/Match 7mm Rem

Nemo: Omen/Pratka

715T FLAT TOP (FORMERLY TACTICAL .22)

Action: semi-auto
Stock: Black, Realtree MAX-5, Mossy Oak Brush, or Muddy Girl synthetic stock; 6-position adjustable stock that offers a 10.5–14.25-in. LOP or fixed LOP stock
Barrel: 16.25-in. + A2-style muzzle brake
Sights: Rail-mounted adjustable front/rear
Weight: 5.25–5.75 lb.
Caliber: .22
Magazine: Available in either 10-round or 25-round capacity
Features: Quad rail fore-end; sling mounts; removeable/adjustable sights; full-length top rail for ease of adding optics; scoped combo versions available.
MSRP: . . . . $366–$509

715T CARRY HANDLE (FORMERLY TACTICAL .22)

Action: semi-auto
Stock: Black synthetic, 6-position adjustable stock that offers a 10.5–14.25-in. LOP or fixed LOP stock
Barrel: 18-in.
Sights: A2-style adjustable front/rear
Weight: 5.25 lb.
Caliber: .22
Magazine: Available in 10- and 25-round capacity

Features: Quad rail fore-end; sling mounts; integrated A2-style carry handle with rear sight and includes an optional handle-mount Picatinny rail that allows versatility in mounting scopes and other optics while providing the clearance necessary to utilize the open sights.
MSRP: $308

NEMO

OMEN/ASP .300 WIN. MSR

Action: semi-auto
Stock: Magpul MOE stock and cheek riser; NEMO integrated free-floating handguard; enhanced pistol grip
Barrel: 16-in. 416 stainless barrel, 1:8 twist
Sights: N/A
Weight: 9.4 lb.
Caliber: .300 Win.
Magazine: Two NEMO 14-round polymer, 10-round available
Features: 7075 billet aluminum machined receivers with hard-anodized finish, nickel-boron bolt carrier group, steel side charge handle, Geissele SSA-E two-stage trigger, NEMO muzzle brake.
MSRP: . . . . N/A

OMEN/MATCH 2.0

Action: semi-auto
Stock: MAKO adjustable SSR-25 sniper buttstock; NEMO integrated free-floating M-LOK handguard with hard anodized finish, enhanced pistol grip
Barrel: 22-in. fluted 416 stainless barrel, 1:8 twist
Sights: N/A
Weight: 10.9 lb.
Caliber: .300 Win.
Magazine: Two NEMO 14-round polymer, 10-round available
Features: 7075 billet aluminum machined receivers with hard-anodized finish; nickel-boron bolt carrier group; steel side charge handle; Geissele SSA-E two-stage trigger; NEMO muzzle brake.
MSRP: . . . . N/A

OMEN/MATCH 7MM REM

Action: semi-auto
Stock: Magpul PRS buttstock; NEMO integrated free-floating M-LOK handguard with hard anodized finish; enhanced pistol grip
Barrel: 24-in. 416 stainless barrel, 1:9 twist

Nemo: Omen/Watchman

Nemo: MS 300

Nemo: Tango 2

Sights: N/A
Weight: 12.6 lb.
Caliber: 7mm Rem.
Magazine: Two NEMO 14-round polymer, 10-round available
Features: 7075 billet aluminum machined receivers with hard-anodized finish; nickel-boron bolt carrier group; steel side charge handle; Geissele SSA-E two-stage trigger, NEMO muzzle brake; available in a Match .338 Win. version as well.
MSRP: . . . . N/A

OMEN/PRATKA

Action: semi-auto
Stock: Mission First Tactical Battlelink Minimalist buttstock; NEMO integrated free-floating M-LOK handguard with hard anodized finish; enhanced pistol grip
Barrel: 20-in. ultra-lightweight 416 stainless barrel, 1:8 twist
Sights: N/A
Weight: 9.5 lb.
Caliber: .300 Win.
Magazine: Two NEMO 14-round polymer, 10-round available
Features: 7075 billet aluminum machined receivers with hard-anodized finish; nickel-boron bolt carrier group; steel side charge handle; Geissele SSA-E two-stage trigger; NEMO muzzle brake; available in carbine-length (Omen/Recon) model as well.
MSRP: . . . . N/A

OMEN/WATCHMAN

Action: semi-auto
Stock: Magpul PRS buttstock, NEMO integrated free-floating M-LOK handguard with hard anodized finish; enhanced pistol grip
Barrel: 24-in. PROOF research carbon fiber barrel, 1:8 twist
Sights: N/A
Weight: 11 lb.
Caliber: .300 Win.
Magazine: Two NEMO 14-round polymer, 10-round available
Features: 7075 billet aluminum machined receivers with hard-anodized custom tiger stripe finish; nickel-boron bolt carrier group; steel side charge handle; Geissele SSA-E two-stage trigger; NEMO muzzle brake; available in carbine-length (Omen/Recon) model as well.
MSRP: . . . . N/A

MS 300

Action: semi-auto
Stock: Mission First Tactical Battlelink Minimalist buttstock, free-floating KeyMod handguard, Hogue overmolded pistol grip
Barrel: 7.5-in. NEMO 416 stainless steel
Sights: Troy Micro sights
Weight: 6.5 lb.
Caliber: 300 BLK

Magazine: 30-round polymer
Features: 7075 billet aluminum machined receivers with hard-anodized custom tiger stripe finish; nickel-boron bolt carrier group; BCM Gunfighter charging handle; Geissele SD-C trigger; suppressor ready; foam-lined case.
MSRP: . . . . N/A

TANGO 2

Action: semi-auto
Stock: Mission First Tactical Battlelink Minimalist buttstock, free-floating KeyMod handguard, Hogue overmolded pistol grip
Barrel: 16-in. NEMO 416 stainless steel
Sights: Troy Micro sights
Weight: 7 lb.
Caliber: 5.56/.223
Magazine: 30-round polymer
Features: 7075 billet aluminum machined receivers with hard-anodized custom tiger stripe finish; nickel-boron bolt carrier group; Geissele SSA-E two-stage trigger; NEMO flash hider; foam-lined case; SBR version available as well as size and caliber configurations in .308, 300 BLK, and 7.62x39.
MSRP: . . . . N/A

Noveske: 13.7-in. Gen III Infidel 5.56mm

Noveske: Shorty Basic SBR Rifle

Noveske: Gen I Light Recce Basic MOE 300 BLK

Noveske: Recce Basic Rifle

NOVESKE

13.7-IN. GEN III INFIDEL 5.56MM

Action: semi-auto, mid-length gas system
Stock: Magpul STR stock, NSR handguard, MIAD pistol grip
Barrel: 13.7-in. 5.56mm stainless barrel, 1:7 twist polygonal rifling
Sights: Noveske Signature back-up iron sights
Weight: N/A
Caliber: 5.56mm
Magazine: 30 round
Features: Gen III precision machined billet receiver; hard coat type III anodizing; ALG Defense ACT trigger; available in FDE version as well.
MSRP: **$2,595**

SHORTY BASIC SBR RIFLE

Action: semi-auto, carbine-length gas system
Stock: Magpul CTR stock; Magpul MOE grip; M4-type handguard
Barrel: 10.5-in. cold hammer–forged, 1:7 twist
Sights: Noveske Signature Back-Up Iron Sights
Weight: N/A
Caliber: 5.56
Magazine: 30 round
Features: Extended feed ramps; flat-top upper receiver; forged lower.
MSRP: **$1,710**

GEN I LIGHT RECCE BASIC MOE 300 BLK

Action: semi-auto, mid-length gas system
Stock: Magpul CTR stock; Magpul MOE grip; MOE carbine length handguard
Barrel: 16-in. cold hammer–forged barrel, 1:7 twist
Sights: Rear Magpul MBUS sight
Weight: N/A
Caliber: 300 BLK
Magazine: 30 round
Features: Extended feed ramps; flat-top upper receiver; forged lower.
MSRP: **$1,557**

RECCE BASIC RIFLE

Action: semi-auto, mid-length gas system
Stock: Magpul CTR stock; Magpul MOE grip; M4-type handguard
Barrel: 16-in. cold hammer–forged barrel, 1:7 twist
Sights: Rear Noveske BUIS
Weight: N/A
Caliber: 5.56, 300 BLK
Magazine: 30 round
Features: Extended feed ramps; Gen I forged flat-top upper receiver; forged lower; MOD 4 Gunfigher charging handle; ALG Defense ACT trigger.
MSRP: **$1,730**

16-IN. ROGUE HUNTER

Action: semi-auto, carbine-length gas system
Stock: Magpul CTR stock; Magpul MOE grip, NSR free floating handguard
Barrel: 16-in. lightweight contour stainless steel barrel, 1:7 twist
Sights: Noveske Signature BUIS optional
Weight: N/A

Noveske: 16-in. Rogue Hunter

Noveske: Gen III Rifle

Caliber: 5.56, 300 BLK
Magazine: 30 round
Features: Extended feed ramps low-profile gas block pinned to barrel; Gen I forged upper receiver; forged lower; MOD 4 Gunfighter charging handle; A2 or AAC 51T Blackout flash suppressor also available in 18-in. model.
MSRP: . . . . 1,825–$1,845

GEN III RIFLE

Action: semi-auto, carbine-length gas system
Stock: Magpul STR carbine stock; MIAD grip, NSR free-floating handguard
Barrel: 16-in. stainless steel or cold-hammer forged barrel, 1:7 twist
Sights: Noveske Signature BUIS optional
Weight: N/A
Caliber: 5.56, 300 BLK
Magazine: 30 round
Features: Extended feed ramps; low-profile gas block pinned to barrel; Gen III machined billet upper and lower; Raptor ambidextrous charging handle; AAC Blackout NM or AAC 51T Blackout flash suppressor. Also available in similar variations including a 10.5-in. and 18-in. model.
MSRP: . . . . $2,505–$2,595

OLYMPIC ARMS

K10—PISTOL CAL 10MM

Action: Blowback-operated semi-auto action
Stock: M4 Fiberite, 6-point collapsible
Barrel: 16-in., button rifled, 416 stainless steel with a 1:16 twist

Sights: A2 w/ fully adjustable rear sight; elevation adjustable post w/ bayonet lug front sight
Weight: 6.73 lb.
Caliber: 10mm
Magazine: Accepts polymer pistol caliber, one polymer pistol caliber included
Features: Receiver material—7075-T6 aluminum forged, machined by Olympic Arms; receiver finish—black matte anodized receiver with parkerized steel parts; handguard—Fiberite carbine-length caps; long-life non-chromed bore; pistol-caliber flash suppressor; also available with flat-top uppers and optics-ready flat tops
MSRP: $1,007

K40—PISTOL CA L .40 S&W

Action: Blowback-operated semi-auto action
Stock: M4 aluminum, 6-point collapsible
Barrel: 16-in., button rifled, 416 stainless steel with a 1:16 twist
Sights: A2 w/ fully adjustable rear sight; elevation adjustable post w/ bayonet lug front sight.
Weight: 6.73 lb.
Caliber: .40 S&W
Magazine: Accepts polymer pistol caliber, one polymer pistol caliber included
Features: Receiver material—7075-T6 aluminum forged, machined by Olympic Arms; receiver finish—black matte anodized receiver with parkerized steel parts; handguard—Fiberite carbine-length caps; long-life non-chromed bore; pistol-caliber flash suppressor; also available with flat-top uppers and optics-ready flat tops. Also

available in .45 ACP and 9mm for same price point.
MSRP: $1,007

K4B—AR-15 RIFLE

Action: Gas-operated semi-auto
Stock: A2 w/ trapdoor
Barrel: 20-in., button rifled, 4140 chromoly steel with 1:9 twist
Sights: Fully adjustable rear sight; elevation adjustable post w/ bayonet lug front sight
Weight: 8.51 lb.
Caliber: 5.56mm NATO
Magazine: N/A
Features: A2 upper; receiver material—7075-T6 aluminum forged receivers machined by Olympic Arms; receiver finish—black matte anodized receivers, parkerized steel parts; handguard; Fiberite rifle-length caps; long-life non-chromed bore; A2 flash suppressor.
MSRP: $969

K8—TARGETMATCH

Action: Gas-operated semi-auto
Stock: A2 w/ trapdoor
Barrel: 20-in. bull, button rifled, 416 stainless steel with a 1:9 twist
Sights: N/A
Weight: 8.5 lb.
Caliber: 5.56mm NATO
Magazine: N/A
Features: Receiver material—7075-T6 aluminum forged recievers, machined by Olympic Arms; receiver finish—black matte anodized receiver with parkerized steel parts; flat top w/ Picatinny rails; gas block w/ Picatinny

Olympic Arms: K8—Targetmatch

Olympic Arms: K23P—AR-15 Pistol

rails; handguard: free-floating aluminum tube w/ knurled surface; long-life non-chromed bore; crowned muzzle.

MSRP: **$909**

K8-MAG—TARGETMATCH MAGNUM

Action: Gas-operated semi-auto action
Stock: N/A
Barrel: 24-in. bull, button rifled, 4140 chromoly steel with a 1:10 twist (or 1:8 depending on WSSM)
Sights: N/A
Weight: 9.41 lb.
Calibers: WSSM .223, .243, .25, .300 OSSM
Magazine: One 6-round for WSSM
Features: Receiver material: 7075-T6 aluminum Forged receivers machined by Olympic Arms. Receiver finish: black matte anodized receivers, Parkerized steel parts. Flat top w/ Picatinny rails. Gas block w/ Picatinny rails. Handguard: free-floating aluminum tube w/ knurled surface. long-life non-chromed bore; crowned muzzle.

MSRP: **$1,364**

K8 TARGETMATCH IN 6.8 SPC

Action: Gas-operated semi-auto
Stock: A2 with trapdoor
Barrel: 20-in. stainless steel button cut with 1:10 twist rate
Sights: N/A
Weight: 8.5 lb.
Caliber: 6.8 Rem. SPC
Magazine: N/A
Features: Receiver material—7075-T6 aluminum forged recievers, machined by Olympic Arms; receiver finish— black matte anodized receiver with parkerized steel parts; flat top with Picatinny rails; gas block with Picatinny rails; handguard—free-floating aluminum tube with knurled surface; crowned muzzle.

MSRP: **$1,034**

PLINKER PLUS 20

Action: Gas-operated semi-auto
Stock: A2 with trapdoor
Barrel: 20-in., button rifled, 4140 chromoly steel with a 1:9 twist
Sights: Elevation adjustable post with bayonet lug front sight; A1 with adjustable windage only rear sight
Weight: 8.46 lb.
Caliber: 5.56mm NATO
Magazine: N/A
Features: Receiver material—7075-T6 aluminum forged recievers, machined by Olympic Arms; receiver finish— black matte anodized receiver with parkerized steel parts; handguard— Fiberite rifle length caps; long-life non-chromed bore; A2 flash suppressor.

MSRP: **$844**

UM-1P—ULTRAMATCH

Action: Gas-operated semi-auto
Stock: A2 with trapdoor
Barrel: 24-in. bull Ultramatch, broachcut, 416 stainless steel with a 1:10 twist
Sights: N/A
Weight: N/A
Caliber: .223 Rem.
Magazine: 9.46 lb.
Features: Receiver material— 7075-T6 aluminum forged recievers, machined by Olympic Arms; receiver finish—black matte anodized receiver with parkerized steel parts; flat top with Picatinny rails; gas block with Picatinny rails; handguard—free-floating aluminum tube with knurled surface; long-life non-chromed bore; crowned muzzle; AC4 Pneumatic Recoil Buffer; Harris S-series Bipod installed; ERing and EXring system, hand-selected premium receivers; Williams set trigger; standard with a 24-in.

Ultramatch broach-cut bull barrel and available with an optional 20-in. Ultramatch broach-cut bull barrel at no additional cost.

MSRP: **$1,624**

K23P—AR-15 PISTOL

Action: Gas-operated semi-auto
Stock: N/A
Barrel: 6.5-in., button rifled, 4140 chromoly steel with a 1:7 twist
Sights: Fully-adjustable rear sight; elevation adjustable post—no bayonet lug front sight
Weight: 5.12 lb.
Caliber: 5.56mm NATO
Magazine: N/A
Features: Receiver material—7075-T6 aluminum forged receivers, machined by Olympic Arms; receiver finish— black matte anodized receiver with parkerized steel parts; A2 upper; handguard—free-floating aluminum tube with knurled surface; long-life non-chromed bore; A2 flash suppressor; padded receiver extension tube.

MSRP: **$974**

K23P 9MM

Action: Blow-operated semi-auto
Stock: N/A
Barrel: 6.5-in. AR-15 pistol barrel with 1:16 twist
Sights: Fully adjustable rear sight; elevation adjustable post—no bayonet lug front sight
Weight: 5.12 lb.
Caliber: 9mm

Precision Reflex Inc. (PRI): Mark 12 Mod O Gen III

Magazine: N/A
Features: Receiver material—7075-T6 aluminum forged receivers, machined by Olympic Arms; receiver finish—black matte anodized receiver with parkerized steel parts; A2 upper; handguard—free-floating aluminum tube with knurled surface; long-life nonchromed bore; A2 flash suppressor.
MSRP: $929

PRECISION REFLEX INC. (PRI)

MARK 12 MOD O GEN III

Action: semi-auto 5.56 AR-15
Stock: (include material and style if applicable) B5 6-position butt-stock with A PRi rifle-length carbon fiber fore-arm.
Barrel: (need length, any other pertinent details) 18-in. Douglas stainless steel barrel with a 1:7 twist
Sights: PRI flip-up front sight gas block and PRi flip-up rear sight
Weight: N/A
Caliber: 5.56 NATO
Magazine: One 10-round PRI steel
Features: MOA Accuracy, mil-spec type III hard coat anodized upper & lower; A4M4 feed ramp; forged rigid 7075 aluminum; rifle-length carbon-fiber fore-arm with heat shield; full-length top rail and AE Brake and color; operator's manual and warranty card; hard case.
MSRP: $1,931

PRIMARY WEAPONS SYSTEMS

MK107 RIFLE

Action: semi-auto
Stock: Magpul MOE stock and grip
Barrel: 7.75-in.
Sights: Magpul MBUS
Weight: 5 lb. 13 oz.
Caliber: .223 Wylde or 7.62x39
Magazine: Magpul or CProducts
Features: The PWS long-stroke piston system combines the agility of the AR-15 with the reliability of the AK-47 into a sleek and efficient design. A floating piston head, detachable for charging handle replacement, is attached directly to the operating rod, which in turn is securely attached to the carrier. With only one moving assembly, the PWS long-stock system offers a lighter recoil impulse, while at the same time proving increased longevity and durability. Our four-position adjustable gas block restricts gasses, rather than venting them from the side. This allows the unused gas to exit from the front of the gun, rather than the sides of the gas block, resulting in a more quiet operation. The MK107 was designed specifically for CQB requirements and as a replacement option for the MP5 Style weapon. Utilizing only the highest quality barrel blanks, PWS barrels are turned in house then Isonite QPQ treated for hardness and corrosion resistance.
MSRP: $1,949

MK109 RIFLE

Action: semi-auto
Stock: Magpul MOE stock and grip
Barrel: 9.75-in.
Sights: Magpul MBUS
Weight: 6 lb. 1 oz.
Caliber: 300 BLK
Magazine: Magpul
Features: The PWS long-stroke piston system combines the agility of the AR-15 with the reliability of the AK-47 into a sleek and efficient design. A floating piston head, detachable for charging handle replacement, is attached directly to the operating rod, which in turn is securely attached to the carrier. With only one moving assembly, the PWS long-stock system offers a lighter recoil impulse, while at the same time proving increased longevity and durability. Our four-position adjustable gas block restricts gasses, rather than venting them from the side. This allows the unused gas to exit from the front of the gun, rather than the sides of the gas block, resulting in a more quiet operation. Utilizing only the highest quality barrel blanks, PWS barrels are turned in house then Isonite QPQ treated for hardness and corrosion resistance.
MSRP: $1,949

MK110 RIFLE

Action: semi-auto
Stock: Magpul MOE stock and grip
Barrel: 10.75-in.
Sights: Magpul MBUS
Weight: 6 lb. 3 oz.
Caliber: .223 Wylde

Magazine: Magpul
Features: The PWS long-stroke piston system combines the agility of the AR-15 with the reliability of the AK-47 into a sleek and efficient design. A floating piston head, detachable for charging handle replacement is attached directly to the operating rod, which in turn is securely attached to the carrier. With only one moving assembly, the PWS long-stock system offers a lighter recoil impulse, while at the same time proving increased longevity and durability. Our four-position adjustable gas block restricts gasses, rather than venting them from the side. This allows the unused gas to exit from the front of the gun, rather than the sides of the gas block, resulting in a more quiet operation. The MK110 came shortly after and sports a barrel typically associated with suppressor manufacturer's minimum recommended barrel length. Utilizing only the highest quality barrel blanks, PWS barrels are turned in house then Isonite QPQ treated for hardness and corrosion resistance.
MSRP: $1,949

MK112 RIFLE

Action: semi-auto
Stock: Magpul MOE stock and grip
Barrel: 12.75-in.
Sights: Magpul MBUS
Weight: 6 lb. 6 oz.
Caliber: .223 Wylde
Magazine: Magpul
Features: The PWS long-stroke piston system combines the agility of the AR-15 with the reliability of the AK-47 into a sleek and efficient design. A floating piston head, detachable for charging handle replacement, is attached directly to the operating rod, which in turn is securely attached to the carrier. With only one moving assembly, the PWS long-stock system offers a lighter recoil impulse, while at the same time proving increased longevity and durability. Our four-position adjustable gas block restricts gasses, rather than venting them from the side. This allows the unused gas to exit from the front of the gun, rather than the sides of the gas block,

resulting in a more quiet operation. Utilizing only the highest quality barrel blanks, PWS barrels are turned in house then Isonite QPQ treated for hardness and corrosion resistance.
MSRP: $1,949

MK114 RIFLE

Action: semi-auto
Stock: Magpul MOE stock and grip
Barrel: 14.5-in.
Sights: Magpul MBUS
Weight: 6 lb. 9 oz.
Caliber: .223 Wylde
Magazine: Magpul
Features: The PWS long-stroke piston system combines the agility of the AR-15 with the reliability of the AK-47 into a sleek and efficient design. A floating piston head, detachable for charging handle replacement, is attached directly to the operating rod, which in turn is securely attached to the carrier. With only one moving assembly, the PWS long-stock system offers a lighter recoil impulse, while at the same time proving increased longevity and durability. Our four-position adjustable gas block restricts gasses, rather than venting them from the side. This allows the unused gas to exit from the front of the gun, rather than the sides of the gas block, resulting in a more quiet operation. Due to NFA regulations, PWS MK114 rifle muzzle devices are permanently pinned to ensure the overall length of the 16-in. Utilizing only the highest quality barrel blanks, PWS barrels are turned in house then Isonite QPQ treated for hardness and corrosion resistance.
MSRP: $1,949

MK116 RIFLE

Action: semi-auto
Stock: Magpul MOE stock and grip
Barrel: 16-in.
Sights: Magpul MBUS
Weight: 6 lb. 13 oz.
Caliber: .223 Wylde
Magazine: Magpul
Features: The PWS long-stroke piston system combines the agility of the AR-15 with the reliability of the AK-47

into a sleek and efficient design. A floating piston head, detachable for charging handle replacement, is attached directly to the operating rod, which in turn is securely attached to the carrier. With only one moving assembly, the PWS long-stock system offers a lighter recoil impulse, while at the same time proving increased longevity and durability. Our four-position adjustable gas block restricts gasses, rather than venting them from the side. This allows the unused gas to exit from the front of the gun, rather than the sides of the gas block, resulting in a more quiet operation. Utilizing only the highest quality barrel blanks, PWS barrels are turned in house then Isonite QPQ treated for hardness and corrosion resistance.
MSRP: $1,949

MK116 RIFLE

Action: semi-auto
Stock: Magpul MOE stock and grip
Barrel: 16-in.
Sights: Magpul MBUS
Weight: 6 lb. 10 oz.
Caliber: 300 BLK
Magazine: Magpul
Features: The PWS long-stroke piston system combines the agility of the AR-15 with the reliability of the AK-47 into a sleek and efficient design. A floating piston head, detachable for charging handle replacement, is attached directly to the operating rod, which in turn is securely attached to the carrier. With only one moving assembly, the PWS long-stock system offers a lighter recoil impulse, while at the same time proving increased longevity and durability. Our four-position adjustable gas block restricts gasses, rather than venting them from the side. This allows the unused gas to exit from the front of the gun, rather than the sides of the gas block, resulting in a more quiet operation. Utilizing only the highest quality barrel blanks, PWS barrels are turned in house then Isonite QPQ treated for hardness and corrosion resistance.
MSRP: $1,949

AR RIFLE MODELS

Primary Weapons Systems: MK212 Rifle

MK118 RIFLE

Action: semi-auto
Stock: Magpul MOE stock and grip
Barrel: 18-in.
Sights: Magpul MBUS
Weight: 7 lb. 2 oz.
Caliber: .223 Wylde
Magazine: Magpul
Features: The PWS long-stroke piston system combines the agility of the AR-15 with the reliability of the AK-47 into a sleek and efficient design. A floating piston head, detachable for charging handle replacement, is attached directly to the operating rod, which in turn is securely attached to the carrier. With only one moving assembly, the PWS long-stock system offers a lighter recoil impulse, while at the same time proving increased longevity and durability. Our four-position adjustable gas block restricts gasses, rather than venting them from the side. This allows the unused gas to exit from the front of the gun, rather than the sides of the gas block, resulting in a more quiet operation. Utilizing only the highest quality barrel blanks, PWS barrels are turned in house then Isonite QPQ treated for hardness and corrosion resistance.
MSRP: $1,949

DI-10 PISTOL

Action: semi-auto
Stock: Magpul MOE Grip
Barrel: 10.75-in.
Sights: None
Weight: 6 lb.
Caliber: .223 Wylde
Magazine: Magpul

Features: With the success of the MK1 and MK2 rifle series and a DI accessory line designed to reliably enhance any AR platform, PWS' next logical step was to supply customers with the best DI AR-15 rifle available. The smallest barrel recommended for suppressor use, the DI10-P ships with a SIG Sauer SB15 stabilizing brace and is classified as a pistol by the NFA. Utilizing only the highest quality barrel blanks, PWS DI barrels are turned in house, then Isonite QPQ treated for hardness and corrosion resistance.
MSRP: $1,599

DI-14 RIFLE

Action: semi-auto
Stock: Magpul MOE grip and stock
Barrel: 14.5-in.
Sights: None
Weight: 6 lb. 7 oz.
Caliber: .223 Wylde
Magazine: Magpul
Features: With the success of the MK1 and MK2 rifle series and a DI accessory line designed to reliably enhance any AR platform, PWS' next logical step was to supply customers with the best DI AR-15 rifle available. The shortest Modern Musket rifle, the DI14 has a permanently pinned muzzle device in accordance with NFA regulations. The DI-14 retains lethal capability out to 500 meters with varying types of ammunition. Utilizing only the highest quality barrel blanks, PWS DI barrels are turned in house then Isonite QPQ treated for hardness and corrosion resistance.
MSRP: $1,499

DI-16 RIFLE

Action: semi-auto
Stock: Magpul MOE grip and stock
Barrel: 14.5-in.
Sights: None
Weight: 6 lb. 12 oz.
Caliber: .223 Wylde
Magazine: Magpul
Features: With the success of the MK1 and MK2 rifle series and a DI accessory line designed to reliably enhance any AR platform, PWS' next logical step was to supply customers with the best DI AR-15 rifle available. Utilizing only the highest quality barrel blanks, PWS DI barrels are turned in house then Isonite QPQ treated for hardness and corrosion resistance.
MSRP: $1,499

MK212 RIFLE

Action: semi-auto
Stock: Magpul MOE grip and stock
Barrel: 12.75-in.
Sights: Magpul MBUS
Weight: 8 lb. 6 oz.
Caliber: .308 Match
Magazine: Magpul
Features: The PWS long-stroke piston system combines the agility of the AR-15 with the reliability of the AK-47 into a sleek and efficient design. A floating piston head, detachable for charging handle replacement, is attached directly to the operating rod, which in turn is securely attached to the carrier. With only one moving assembly, the PWS long-stock system offers a lighter recoil impulse, while at the same time proving increased longevity and durability. Our four-position adjustable gas block restricts

Primary Weapons Systems: MK214 Rifle

Primary Weapons Systems: MK216 Rifle

Primary Weapons Systems: MK220 Rifle

gasses, rather than venting them from the side. This allows the unused gas to exit from the front of the gun, rather than the sides of the gas block, resulting in a more quiet operation. Utilizing only the highest quality barrel blanks, PWS barrels are turned in house then Isonite QPQ treated for hardness and corrosion resistance.
MSRP: **$2,599**

MK212 PISTOL

Action: semi-auto
Stock: Magpul MOE grip
Barrel: 12.75-in.

Sights: Magpul MBUS
Weight: 8 lb. 9 oz.
Caliber: .308 Match
Magazine: Magpul
Features: The PWS long-stroke piston system combines the agility of the AR-15 with the reliability of the AK-47 into a sleek and efficient design. A floating piston head, detachable for charging handle replacement, is attached directly to the operating rod, which in turn is securely attached to the carrier. With only one moving assembly, the PWS long-stock system offers a lighter

recoil impulse, while at the same time proving increased longevity and durability. Our four-position adjustable gas block restricts gasses, rather than venting them from the side. This allows the unused gas to exit from the front of the gun, rather than the sides of the gas block, resulting in a more quiet operation. Utilizing only the highest quality barrel blanks, PWS barrels are turned in house then Isonite QPQ treated for hardness and corrosion resistance.
MSRP: **$2,599**

MK214 RIFLE

Action: semi-auto
Stock: Magpul MOE grip and stock
Barrel: 14.5-in.
Sights: Magpul MBUS
Weight: 8 lb. 8 oz.
Caliber: .308 Match
Magazine: Magpul
Features: The PWS long-stroke piston system combines the agility of the AR-15 with the reliability of the AK-47 into a sleek and efficient design. A floating piston head, detachable for charging handle replacement, is attached directly to the operating rod, which in turn is securely attached to the carrier. With only one moving assembly, the PWS long-stock system offers a lighter recoil impulse, while at the same time proving increased longevity and durability. Our four-position adjustable gas block restricts gasses, rather than venting them from the side. This allows the unused gas to exit from the front of the gun, rather than the sides of the gas block, resulting in a more quiet operation. SR-25 pattern upper and lower forged receivers are also available for purchase in DI configuration from PWS. The MK214 with pinned muzzle device, is a lightweight compact and ultra-portable battle rifle lethal capability. Utilizing only the highest quality barrel blanks, PWS barrels are turned in house then Isonite QPQ treated for hardness and corrosion resistance.
MSRP: **$2,599**

MK216 RIFLE

Action: semi-auto
Stock: Magpul MOE grip and stock
Barrel: 16-in.
Sights: Magpul MBUS
Weight: 8 lb. 10oz
Caliber: .308 Match
Magazine: Magpul
Features: The PWS long-stroke piston system combines the agility of the AR-15 with the reliability of the AK-47 into a sleek and efficient design. A floating piston head, detachable for charging handle replacement, is

attached directly to the operating rod, which in turn is securely attached to the carrier. With only one moving assembly, the PWS long-stock system offers a lighter recoil impulse, while at the same time proving increased longevity and durability. Our four-position adjustable gas block restricts gasses, rather than venting them from the side. This allows the unused gas to exit from the front of the gun, rather than the sides of the gas block, resulting in a more quiet operation. SR-25 pattern upper and lower forged receivers are also available for purchase in DI configuration from PWS. Utilizing only the highest quality barrel blanks, PWS barrels are turned in house then Isonite QPQ treated for hardness and corrosion resistance.
MSRP: **$2,599**

MK220 RIFLE

Action: semi-auto
Stock: Magpul MOE grip and stock
Barrel: 20-in.
Sights: Magpul MBUS
Weight: 8 lb. 10oz
Caliber: .308 Match
Magazine: Magpul
Features: The PWS long-stroke piston system combines the agility of the AR-15 with the reliability of the AK-47 into a sleek and efficient design. A floating piston head, detachable for charging handle replacement, is attached directly to the operating rod, which in turn is securely attached to the carrier. With only one moving assembly, the PWS long-stock system offers a lighter recoil impulse, while at the same time proving increased longevity and durability. Our four-position adjustable gas block restricts gasses, rather than venting them from the side. This allows the unused gas to exit from the front of the gun, rather than the sides of the gas block, resulting in a more quiet operation. SR-25 pattern upper and lower forged receivers are also available for purchase in DI configuration from PWS. Utilizing only the highest quality barrel blanks, PWS barrels are

turned in house then Isonite QPQ treated for hardness and corrosion resistance.
MSRP: **$2,599**

MK107—MK116 (MK1 PLUS BARREL LENGTH) AND MK212 THROUGH MK216

Action: Push rod, long-stroke piston
Stock: Magpul MOE stock, MOE grip, XT rail panels (high-impact polymer)
Barrel: 416 stainless, Isonite-treated (68Rc hardness)
Sights: Magpul MBUS flip-up sights
Weight: MK107—5 lb. 14 oz.; MK110—6 lb. 8 oz.; MK112—6 lb. 12 oz.; MK114—6 lb. 13 oz.; MK116—6 lb. 15 oz.; MK212—8 lb. 6 oz.; MK214—8 lb. 10 oz.; MK216—8 lb. 13 oz.
Caliber: MK107—5.56 and 7.62x39; MK109—300 BLK; MK110—5.56; MK112—5.56; MK114—5.56 and 7.62x39; MK116—5.56
Magazine: MK1—30-round PMAG where allowed, MK2—20-round PMAG where allowed
Features: Enhanced charging handle; enhanced bolt carrier group muzzle devise standard for most models.
MSRP: . . . . **$1,550–$2,296**

QUALITY ARMS

ODIN

Action: semi-auto
Stock: Magpul MOE 6-position collapsible stock
Barrel: 16-in. M4 profile with a 1:9 twist
Sights: Primary Arms red dot with cantilever mount; front and rear A.R.M.S. flip-up sights
Weight: N/A
Caliber: 5.56K
Magazine: 30-round Magpul
Features: Quality Arms forged mil-spec lower receiver; standard M3/M4 forged mil-spec upper receiver; winter trigger guard; Odin free-float fore-end; 4.5 lb. single-stage trigger Magpul MOE 6-position collapsible stock; nickel plated bolt and carrier; Magpul grip; 30-round Magpul magazine; black soft tactical case; Quality Arms USB flash

Quality Arms: Odin

Quality Arms: Grendel

drive with warranty and instructional information.

MSRP: **$1,1495**

BATTLESTORM

Action: semi-auto
Stock: Battlelink 6-position collapsible stock with storage
Barrel: 16-in. Free floated M4 profile barrel with a 1:9 twist
Sights: Front and rear RTS 45 degree off-set sights; Primary Arms 1-4x24 optical red dot scope
Weight: N/A
Caliber: 5.56
Magazine: 30-round Magpul
Features: Quality Arms forged mil-spec lower receiver Standard M3/M4 forged mil-spec upper receiver; 16-in. free floated M4 profile barrel with a 1:9 twist; free-float lightweight Midwest Industries Gen 2 12-in. fore-end; low-profile gas block; ergonomic pistol grip for better fire control; Battle Blades knife and scabbard; winter trigger guard; single-point sling end plate; 4.5-lb. single-stage trigger;

nickel plated trigger, hammer and bolt and carrier; black soft tactical case; Quality Arms USB flash drive with warranty and instructional information.

MSRP: **$1,895**

THOR

Action: semi-auto
Stock: Magpul STR stock
Barrel: 16-in. free floated M4 profile
Sights: front and rear flip-up sights
Weight: N/A
Caliber: 5.56
Magazine: One-30 round Magpul
Features: Quality Arms forged mil-spec lower receiver; Magpul k-grip; Troy Industries Alpha rail; 4.5 lb. single-stage trigger; nickel-plated trigger, hammer, bolt, and carrier; black soft tactical case Quality Arms USB flash drive with warranty and instructional information.

MSRP: **$1,235**

AMBI GEN 2—SIDE CHARGING

Action: semi-auto
Stock: Magpul ACS 6-position collapsible stock
Barrel: 16-in. match-grade free-floated medium contour stainless barrel with a 1:9 twist
Sights: Front and rear A.R.M.S. flip-up sight
Weight: N/A
Caliber: 5.56
Magazine: 30-round Magpul
Features: Quality Arms forged mil-spec lower receiver; Quality Arms custom billet 7075 aluminum ambidextrous upper receiver; ambidextrous side charging handles; ambidextrous safety and magazine release; Midwest Industries Gen2 fore-end; 4.5 lb. single-stage trigger; nickel-plated trigger, hammer, bolt, and carrier; black soft tactical case; Quality Arms USB flash drive with warranty and instructional information.

MSRP: **$1,495**

Quentin Defense: Billet AR Style Pistol

GRENDEL

Action: semi-auto
Stock: Magpul ACS 6-position collapsible stock
Barrel: 16-in., 18-in., 20-in. match-grade; free-floated medium contour, stainless barrel
Sights: Front and rear A.R.M.S. flip-up sights
Weight: N/A
Caliber: 6.5 Grendel
Magazine: One 10-round, one 26-round
Features: Quality Arms forged mil-spec lower receiver; Standard M3/M4 forged mil-spec upper receiver Troy VTAC series tactical free-float rail; 4.5 lb. single-stage trigger; nickel-plated trigger, hammer, bolt, and carrier; scope and mounts not included; black soft tactical case; Quality Arms USB flash drive with warranty and instructional information.
MSRP: $1,595

BIG BORE 50

Action: semi-auto
Stock: ACE skeleton stock
Barrel: Available 16- or 18-in. barrels
Sights: A.R.M.S. flip-up front and rear sights
Weight: N/A
Caliber: .50-cal Beowulf
Magazine: One 10-round
Features: Quality Arms forged mil-spec lower receiver; Quality Arms new 7075 side-charging billet upper receiver; nickel-plated trigger, hammer,

bolt, and carrier; Midwest Industries Gen 2 free-float fore-end; Stark pistol grip with integrated winter trigger guard; black soft tactical case; Quality Arms USB flash drive with warranty and instructional information.
MSRP: $1,895

HUNTER

Action: semi-auto
Stock: ACE skeleton stock
Barrel: 18- and 20-in. match-grade, free-floated medium contour, stainless steel
Sights: None, optics ready
Weight: N/A
Caliber: 6.5 Grendel
Magazine: One 10-round, one 26-round
Features: Quality Arms forged mil-spec lower receiver; Quality Arms new 7075 side-charging billet upper receiver; Midwest Industries Gen 2 free-float rail; 4.5 lb. single-stage trigger; nickel plated trigger, hammer, bolt and carrier; mount and bipod not included; black soft tactical case; Cerakote coating in three-color camo; Quality Arms USB flash drive with warranty and instructional information.
MSRP: $1,895

QUENTIN DEFENSE

BILLET AR STYLE PISTOL

Action: semi-auto
Stock: Billet pistol receiver extension

Barrel: 7.5-in. Wilson barrel; 1:9 CM
Sights: None, optics ready
Weight: N/A
Caliber: 5.56
Magazine: None
Features: Billet upper and lower receivers, mil-spec M16 bolt carrier group, QD 7-side free-float KeyMod rail; A2 flash hider.
MSRP: $1,149

R GUNS

A1 7-IN.

Action: semi-auto
Stock: N/A
Barrel: 5.56x45mm NATO, 1:9 twist pistol
Sights: A-frame front sight
Weight: N/A
Caliber: 5.56
Magazine: N/A
Features: Quad rail; free-float handgun; Vortex flash suppressor.
MSRP: $895

A1 RIFLE 16-IN. FLUTED

Action: semi-auto
Stock: M4 carbine stock
Barrel: 5.56x45mm 1:9 twist; ½x28 TPI muzzle thread; .750-in. barrel; chromoly (CVM) National match-grade
Sights: Black A-frame front sight
Weight: N/A
Caliber: 5.56

Magazine: 30 round
Features: A2 grip, IMI defense (MRS) modular rail system; handguard; A2 flash suppressor; A2 suppressor; hard case.
MSRP: $795

A1 RIFLE 16-IN. HEAVY BARREL

Action: semi-auto
Stock: Type III black fiber light A1 carbine stock
Barrel: 5.56x45mm 1:9 twist; ½x28 TPI muzzle thread; .635-in.; chromoly (CVM) National match-grade barrel
Sights: A-frame font sight
Weight: N/A
Caliber: 5.56
Magazine: 30 round
Features: A2 grip; A1 handguard; black, A2 flash suppressor; hard case.
MSRP: $750

A1 RIFLE 16-IN. LW PENCIL BARREL

Action: semi-auto
Stock: Type III black fiber light; A1 carbine stock
Barrel: 5.56x45mm 1:9 twist; ½x28 TPI muzzle thread; .635-in.; chromoly (CVM) National match-grade barrel
Sights: A-frame front sight
Weight: N/A
Caliber: 5.56
Magazine: 30 round
Features: A2 grip; carbine handguard; black three-prong flash suppressor; hard case.
MSRP: $750

RIFLE A3 16-IN. SUPER BULL

Action: semi-auto
Stock: Magpul PRS rifle stock
Barrel: Fluted 5.56x45mm 1:9 twist; .936-in.; chromoly (CVM) National match-grade barrel
Sights: None, optics ready
Weight: N/A
Caliber: 5.56
Magazine: 30 round

Features: Type III black 14.5-in. free-float handguard, MOE grip; MOE trigger guard, all black; hard case.
MSRP: $950

A3 RIFLE 20-IN. FLUTED

Action: semi-auto
Stock: Type III black IMI Defense SRS-1 rifle stock
Barrel: 5.56x45mm 1:9 twist; ½x28 TPI muzzle thread; .635-in.; chromoly (CVM) National match-grade barrel
Sights: YHM flip-up front sight
Weight: N/A
Caliber: 5.56
Magazine: One 10-round
Features: IMI CG-1 grip; quad rail free-float handguard; black Vortex flash suppressor.
MSRP: $875

RIFLE 16-IN. HB 6.8 SPC

Action: semi-auto
Stock: Magpul MOE rifle stock
Barrel: 1:11 twist chromoly barrel (CVM) National match-grade
Sights: YHM flip-up front sight
Weight: N/A
Caliber: 6.8 Grendel
Magazine: PRI 25-round
Features: Type III OD green KeyMod handguard; Euro grip, OD green; A2 flash hider; hard case.
MSRP: $875

A3 RIFLE

Action: semi-auto
Stock: Type III, black, IMI Defense SRS-1 rifle stock
Barrel: 20-in. fluted barrel; .204 ruger 1:12 twist; ½x28 TPI muzzle thread; .750-in barrel; chromoly (CVM) National match-grade barrel
Sights: Black YHM flip-up front sight
Weight: N/A
Caliber: .204 Ruger
Magazine: One 10-round
Features: IMI CG-1 grip quad rail free-float handguard; Vortex flash suppressor.
MSRP: $875

RIFLE A3

Action: semi-auto
Stock: IMI Defense TS-1 carbine stock
Barrel: 18-in. HB 7.62x39mm 1:10 twist; chromoly barrel (CVM) National match-grade
Sights: YHM flip-up front sight; Magpul MOE flip-up rear sight
Weight: N/A
Caliber: 7.62x39
Magazine: 30 round
Features: Type III IMI Defense (MRS) modular rail system, handguard; IMI CG-1 grip; IMI Defense trigger guard; A2 flash hider; hard case.
MSRP: $895

RIFLE A3

Action: semi-auto
Stock: Grip; Magpul PRS target stock
Barrel: 20-in. Harris stainless steel fluted ultra target National Match barrel; 7.62x51mm NATO chamber 1:10 RH twist; M4 feed ramps
Sights: None, optics ready
Weight: N/A
Caliber: 7.62x51
Magazine: 20-round IMI Defense
Features: 7075-T6 machined billet A3 upper and lower receiver; mil-spec anodized hard coat type II, black; nickel-boron bolt assembly; BTE single-stage 3.5 lb. trigger; target; slab side quad rail; free-float handguard (S-RGQ); hard case.
MSRP: $2,600

RIFLE A3

Action: semi-auto
Stock: Magpul MOE rifle stock
Barrel: 20-in. 7.62x51mm 1:10 twist; National Match 416 stainless steel fluted; 5/8x24 TPI muzzle thread; .750-in. barrel
Sights: None, optics ready
Weight: N/A
Caliber: 7.62x51
Magazine: 20-round IMI Defense
Features: 7075-T6 billet slab side upper assembly; mil-spec hard coat anodized type III 14.5-in. free-float handguard; MOE grip, YHM flash suppressor; hard case.
MSRP: $1,650

Rebel Arms Corp: Rebel Raptor Pistol

R&J Firearms: R&J Premium

R&J FIREARMS

ORC (OPTICS READY CARBINE)

Action: semi-auto
Stock: Com-spec M4-style adj. stock; carbine tube free-float handguard
Barrel: 16-in. phosphate 1:8 M4 barrel; A2 flash hider
Weight: N/A
Calibers: 5.56/.223; 7.62x39; 300 BLK; .502 T-Sabre
Magazine: One 10-round
Features: Nitride M16 BCG, stainless hammer+trigger set; RR&J Firearms 7075 lower; A3 upper with M4 ramps; add $149 for thread and brake option.
MSRP: . . . .$799 (5.56/.223), $899 (7.62x39, 300 BLK), $1,599 (.502 T-Sabre)

R&J PREMIUM

Action: semi-auto
Stock: IMI Defense adj. stock; 13-in. premium free-float handguard
Barrel: 16-in. QPQ treated 1:7 M4 barrel; choice of R&J Firearms Keg muzzle break or Crown muzzle brake
Weight: N/A
Caliber: 5.56/.223, 7.62x39, 300 BLK, .502 T-Sabre

Magazine: One 10-round
Features: RR&J Firearms 7075 billet upper and lower set; NiB M16 BCG; stainless hammer+trigger set; add $149 for thread and brake option.
MSRP: . . . . $1,299 (5.56/.223), $1,399 (7.62x39, 300 BLK), $1,599 (.502 T-Sabre)

R&J QUAD CLASSIC

Action: semi-auto
Stock: Mil-spec M4-style adj. stock; 12-in. classic free-float quad rail handguard (10-in. and 7-in. available)
Barrel: 16-in. QPQ treated 1:7 M4 barrel; A2 flash hider
Weight: N/A
Caliber: 5.56/.223, 7.62x39, 300 BLK, .502 T-Sabre
Magazine: One 10-round
Features: R&J Firearms 7075 billet upper and lower set; Nitride M16 BCG; stainless hammer+trigger set; add $149 for thread and brake option.
MSRP: . . . . . $999 (5.56/.223), $1,099 (7.62x39, 300 BLK), $1,599 (.502 T-Sabre)

R&J FIREARMS PATROL

Action: semi-auto
Stock: Mil-spec M4 style adj. stock; carbine M4 style two-piece handguard

Barrel: 16-in. phosphate 1:8 M4 barrel; A2 flash hider
Weight: N/A
Caliber: 5.56/.223, 7.62x39, 300 BLK, .502 T-Sabre
Magazine: One 10-round
Features: R&J Firearms 7075 billet upper and lower set; Nitride M16 BCG; stainless hammer+trigger set; add $149 for thread and brake option.
MSRP: . . . .$899 (5.56/.223), $999 (7.62x39, 300 BLK), $1,599 (.502 T-Sabre)

REBEL ARMS CORP

REBEL RAPTOR PISTOL

Action: semi-auto
Stock: SB-15 pistol stabilizing brace; SLR 10-in. Solo KeyMod handguard; Mission First Tactical ENGAGE AR-15/ M16 pistol grip
Barrel: 10.5-in. Rebel Arms 4150 CMV Nitride premium barrel; 1:7 twist; M4SD Tactical compensator
Sights: Optics ready
Weight: 5.2 lb.
Caliber: 5.56
Magazine: Two 30-round Hexmag HX30 polymer

Rebel Arms Corp: RBR-15 Mod II S

Rebel Arms Corp: LIghtning Mod II

Features: Aluminum forged upper receiver; Mod II lower made of 7075 aluminum alloy forging; mil-spec fire control group; Nitride bolt carrier; Cerakote finish; low-profile gas block; soft case.
MSRP: $1,589

REBEL RAPTOR ELITE PISTOL

Action: semi-auto
Stock: SB-15 pistol stabilizing brace; SLR 10-in. Solo KeyMod handguard; Mission First Tactical ENGAGE AR-15/M16 pistol grip
Barrel: 10.5-in. Rebel Arms 4150 CMV Nitride premium barrel; 1:7 twist; Griffin Armament M4SD Paladin muzzle brake
Sights: MBUS Pro
Weight: 5.2 lb.
Caliber: 5.56
Magazine: Four 30-round Hexmag HX30 polymer
Features: Aluminum forged upper receiver; Mod II lower made of 7075 aluminum alloy forging; Hiperfire Hipertouch 24E fire control group; Nitride bolt carrier; enhanced buffer system; Cerakote finish; SN-ACH (Suppressor Normalized Ambidextrous Charging Handle); low-profile gas block; soft case.
MSRP: $2,140

RBR-15 MOD II S

Action: semi-auto
Stock: Mission First Tactical Battlelink Minimalist stock; SLR 15-in. Solo KeyMod handguard; Mission First Tactical ENGAGE AR-15/M16 pistol grip
Barrel: 14.5-in. Rebel Arms 4150 CMV Nitride premium barrel; 1:7 twist; M4SD-II muzzle brake
Sights: Optics ready
Weight: 6.6 lb.
Caliber: 5.56
Magazine: Two 30-round Hexmag HX30 polymer
Features: Aluminum forged upper receiver; Mod II lower made of 7075 aluminum alloy forging; mil-spec fire control group; Nitride bolt carrier; Cerakote finish; low-profile gas block; soft case.
MSRP: $1,615

RBR-30

Action: semi-auto
Stock: Mission First Tactical Battlelink Utility stock; SLR 15-in. Solo KeyMod handguard; Mission First Tactical ENGAGE AR-15/M16 pistol grip
Barrel: 16-in. 416R stainless steel, 1:10 twist; Griffin 30SD muzzle brake
Sights: Optics ready
Weight: 8.2 lb.
Caliber: .308
Magazine: Two 30-round Hexmag HX30 polymer
Features: Giessele SSA fire control group; Nitride bolt carrier; anodized finish; low-profile gas block; soft case.
MSRP: $2,700

RCR-15 COMPETITION RIFLE

Action: semi-auto
Stock: LUTH-AR MBA Modular buttstock; SLR 16.5-in. Solo Ultra Lite KeyMod handguard; Mission First Tactical ENGAGE AR-15/M16 pistol grip
Barrel: 18-in. 416R stainless steel barrel; 1:7 twist; M4SD-II muzzle brake
Sights: Optics ready
Weight: 6.4 lb.
Caliber: 5.56
Magazine: Two 30-round Hexmag HX30 polymer
Features: Aluminum forged upper receiver; Mod II lower made of 7075 aluminum alloy forging; Hiperfire 24 3G trigger; Nitride bolt carrier; BCMGunfigher Mod IV medium latch charging handle; Cerakote finish; low-profile gas block; soft case.
MSRP: $2,140

RBR-15 MOD II

Action: semi-auto
Stock: Mission First Tactical Battlelink Utility stock; SLR 15-in. Solo KeyMod handguard; Mission First Tactical ENGAGE AR-15/M16 pistol grip
Barrel: 16-in. Rebel Arms 4150 CMV Nitride premium barrel; 1:7 twist; M4SD-II muzzle brake
Sights: Optics ready
Weight: 6.6 lb.
Caliber: 5.56
Magazine: Two 30-round Hexmag HX30 polymer
Features: Aluminum forged upper receiver; Mod II lower made of 7075 aluminum alloy forging; mil-spec fire control group; Nitride bolt carrier; Cerakote finish; low-profile gas block; soft case.
MSRP: $1,615

LIGHTNING MOD II

Action: semi-auto
Stock: Mission First Tactical Battlelink Minimalist stock; SLR 12-in. Solo KeyMod handguard; Mission First Tactical ENGAGE AR-15/M16 pistol grip
Barrel: 16 in. Rebel Arms 4150 CMV Nitride premium barrel; 1:7 twist; Griffin M4SD-II muzzle brake
Sights: Optics ready
Weight: 6.25 lb.
Caliber: 5.56

Magazine: Two 30-round Hexmag HX30 polymer
Features: Aluminum forged upper receiver; Mod II lower made of 7075 aluminum alloy forging; mil-spec fire control group; Nitride bolt carrier; Cerakote finish; low-profile gas block; soft case.
MSRP: $1,510

RED X ARMS

RXA15 3G RIFLE

Action: semi-auto
Stock: Magpul UBR buttstock assembly
Barrel: 18-in. 416R stainless steel HBAR barrel; 5.56 NATO, 1:8 twist; button rifled
Sights: None, optics ready
Weight: N/A
Caliber: 5.56 NATO
Magazine: One 30-round window PMAG
Features: 5-in. Samson evolution rail system; mid-length gas system with a .750 low-profile gas block; RXA stainless steel tactical gill muzzle brake; RXA M16 hybrid bolt carrier group with a 9310 steel MPI tested bolt; BCM MOD 4 charging handle; RXA certified 7075-T6 aluminum lower; hard coat anodized; class III, Rock River two-stage National Match trigger; RXA mil-spec lower parts kit with enhanced trigger guard and MFT G2 grip; 42-in. tactical soft case; owners manual; available in black; lifetime warranty.
MSRP: $1,200

16-IN. RXA15 5.56 NATO STAINLESS M4 MOE RIFLE

Action: semi-auto
Stock: Magpul MOE 6-position collapsible stock; free floating carbine-length RXA quad rail
Barrel: 16-in. 416 stainless steel M4 barrel chambered in 5.56; 1:9 twist; button rifled; ½x28 threads with stainless steel A2 compensator
Sights: None, optics ready
Weight: N/A
Caliber: 5.56 NATO

Magazine: One 30-round PMAG
Features: Carbine gas system; 7075-T6 forged aluminum flat-top upper receiver with M4 feed ramps; black hard coat anodized and T-marked; top rail gas block; M16 bolt carrier group; standard mil-spec 7075-T6 aluminum charge handle; 7075-T6 forged aluminum lower receiver; available in black, FDE, and OD green.
MSRP: $1,049

RXA15 5.56 NATO STAINLESS HBAR RIFLE

Action: semi-auto
Stock: 6-position collapsible stock
Barrel: 16-in. 416 stainless steel HBAR barrel chambered in 5.56 NATO, 1:9 twist; button rifled; ½x28 threads with stainless steel A2 compensator
Sights: None, optics ready
Weight: N/A
Caliber: 5.56
Magazine: One 30-round PMAG black
Features: Carbine gas system; 7075-T6 forged aluminum flat-top upper receiver with M4 feed ramps; black hard coat anodized and T-marked; free-floating carbine-length RXA modular handguard made from 6000 series aluminum and black hard coat anodized; M16 bolt carrier group; standard mil-spec charge handle; 7075-T6 forged aluminum lower receiver; soft tactical rifle case.
MSRP: $849

RXA15 300 BLK NITRIDE COATED HBAR RIFLE

Action: semi-auto
Stock: 6-position collapsible stock
Barrel: 6-in. 4150 CMV HBAR barrel, Nitride coated, 1:7 twist; button rifled; ½x28 threads with stainless steel A2 compensator
Sights: None, optics ready
Weight: N/A
Caliber: 300 BLK
Magazine: One 30-round PMAG black
Features: Carbine gas system; 7075-T6 forged aluminum flat-top upper receiver with M4 feed ramps; black hard coat anodized and T-marked; free-floating carbine-length RXA modular handguard made from 6000

series aluminum and black hard coat anodized; M16 bolt carrier group; standard mil-spec charge handle; 7075 T6 forged aluminum lower receiver; soft tactical rifle case with mag pouches.
MSRP: $999

REVOLUTION ARMS
REV ARMS—R.K.S.—5.56 S.E.L. 16-IN. RIFLE UPPER

Action: semi-auto, mid-length gas impingement system
Stock: KeyMod handguard
Barrel: 1:7 twist; proprietary target crown; A2 flash hider
Sights: N/A
Weight: N/A
Caliber: 5.56
Magazine: N/A
Features: REV R.K.S., three Picatinny rail sections; built in QD compatibility 4150 CMV, black Nitride; .750 steel gas block; black Nitride, forged, mil-spec upper receiver; hand trued receiver face dust cover and forward assist; slick side upper available upon request; mil-spec charging handle hand fitted; black Nitride BCG.
MSRP: $695

REV ARMS— WATCHMAN—16-IN. .223 WYLDE UPPER

Action: semi-auto
Stock: Magpul MOE handguard
Barrel: 4150 CMV barrel, 1:9 twist; 11 target crown, A2 flash hider
Sights: N/A
Weight: N/A
Caliber: .223 Wylde
Magazine: N/A
Features: Colors in FDE, OD green, and Magpul Grey; M4 profile; black Nitride finish; pinned FSB carbine-length gas impingement system; forged mil-spec upper receiver; hand trued receiver face; mil-spec charging handle; hand fitted, chrome lined, manganese phosphate BCG; NiB, and TiN BCG also available.
MSRP: $625

Remington: R-25 GII

Remington: R-15 VTR Predator MOE Fixed Stock

RND 1000

REMINGTON

R-25 GII

Action: semi-auto
Stock: Vented carbon fiber modular free-float tube, Hogue rubber pistol grip; skeletonized stock with recoil pad
Barrel: 20-in. Teflon-coated 416 stainless steel barrel
Sights: None
Weight: 7 5/8 lb.
Caliber: 7.62x51mm
Magazine: 5 round
Features: Forged, anodized, Teflon-coated 7075 upper and lower receivers.
MSRP: $1,697

R-15 VTR PREDATOR MOE FIXED STOCK

Action: semi-auto
Stock: Fixed stock, Magpul grip
Barrel: 18-in. carbon steel barrel with 1:9 twist; AAC 51 Tooth Blackout muzzle break
Sights: None
Weight: 6.75 lb.
Caliber: .223 Rem.
Magazine: 5 round

RENO GUNS & RANGE (AKA BATTLE BORN GUNS)

BB-16 DIRECT IMPINGEMENT 16-IN. A-FRAME

Action: semi-auto
Stock: Magpul stock, Magpul Handguard, Hogue Grip
Barrel: 16-in. M4 contour; 1:9 twist; chrome lined
Sights: Magpul rear sight
Weight: 8 lb.
Caliber: 5.56mm
Magazine: One 30-round PMAG
Features: Billet lower; matched upper.
MSRP: $1,299

BB-16 DIRECT IMPINGEMENT 16-IN. RAIL GASBLOCK

Action: semi-auto
Stock: Magpul stock; Magpul handguard; Hogue grip

Features: Magpul trigger guard, Mossy Oak Brush finish.
MSRP: $1,229

Barrel: 16-in. M4 contour; 1:9 twist; chrome lined
Sights: Optics ready
Weight: 8 lb.
Caliber: 5.56mm
Magazine: One 30-round PMAG
Features: Billet lower; matched upper.
MSRP: 1,300

BB-16 DIRECT IMPINGEMENT 10.5-IN. RAIL GASBLOCK SBR

Action: semi-auto
Stock: Magpul stock; Magpul handguard; Hogue grip
Barrel: 10.5-in. M4 contour; 1:9 twist; chrome lined
Sights: Optics ready
Weight: 7 lb.
Caliber: 5.56mm
Magazine: One 30-round PMAG
Features: Billet lower; matched upper.
MSRP: $1,300

RND

RND 400

Action: Gas operated, semi-auto
Stock: Synthetic A2-style stock
Barrel: Steel; 18–26-in.
Sights: N/A
Weight: 9.5 lb.
Caliber: .223 (5.56mm NATO)
Magazine: N/A
Features: RND CNC machined matched upper and lower receivers; hard black anodized with a black or gray gun coat; integral Picatinny rail; speed lock hammer; 3.5 lb. trigger pull; titanium firing pin; free-floating handguard.
MSRP: $2,195

RND 800

Action: Piston gas-operated, semi-auto
Stock: Adjustable stocks
Barrel: 20–26-in. free-floating supermatch
Sights: N/A
Weight: 11 lb.
Caliber: .308 (7.62mm NATO)
Magazine: MIA .308
Features: RND CNC-machined matched upper and lower receivers; left sided non-reciprocating charging

RND 3000

handle; hard black anodized with black or gray gun coat; integral Picatinny rail; speed lock hammer; titanium firing pin; oversized charging handle; oversized bolt face; 3.5 lb. trigger pull; modular handguard.
MSRP: **$3,795**

RND 1000

Action: Piston gas-operated, semi-auto
Stock: Fully adjustable stock
Barrel: 20–26-in. free-floating supermatch
Sights: N/A
Weight: 11 lb.
Caliber: .300 Win. Short Magnum
Magazine: Double stack, single feed
Features: RND CNC machined matched upper and lower receivers; left sided, non-reciprocating charging handle; hard black anodized with black or gray gun coat; integral Picatinny rail; speed lock hammer; 3.5 lb. trigger pull; RND integrated buffer system; modular handguard.
MSRP: **$3,895**

RND 2000

Action: Piston gas-operated, semi-auto
Stock: Fully adjustable
Barrel: 20–26-in. free-floating supermatch
Sights: N/A
Weight: 14 lb.
Caliber: .338 Lapua Magnum
Magazine: Double stack, single feed
Features: RND CNC machined matched upper and lower receivers; left sided non-reciprocating charging handle; hard black anodized with

black or gray gun coat; integral Picatinny rail; speed lock hammer; 3.5 lb. trigger pull; RND integrated buffer system; modular handguard.
MSRP: **$4,795**

RND 2100

Action: Piston gas-operated, semi-auto
Stock: Fully adjustable
Barrel: 20–26-in. free-floating supermatch
Sights: N/A
Weight: 14 lb.
Caliber: .300 Rem. Ultra Mag
Magazine: Double stack, single feed
Features: RND CNC machined matched upper and lower receivers; left sided non-reciprocating charging handle; hard black anodized with black or gray gun coat; integral Picatinny rail; speed lock hammer; 3.5 lb. trigger pull; RND integrated buffer system; modular handguard.
MSRP: **$4,795**

RND 2500

Action: Piston gas-operated, semi-auto
Stock: Fully adjustable stock
Barrel: 26-in. free-floating supermatch
Sights: N/A
Weight: 18 lb.
Caliber: .408 CheyTac
Magazine: Double stack, single feed
Features: RND CNC machined matched upper and lower receivers; left sided non-reciprocating charging handle; hard black anodized with black or gray gun coat; integral Picatinny rail; speed lock hammer; 3.5

lb. trigger pull; RND integrated buffer system; modular handguard.
MSRP: **$10,500**

RND 2600

Action: Piston gas-operated, semi-auto
Stock: Fully adjustable
Barrel: 20–26-in. free-floating supermatch
Sights: N/A
Weight: 18 lb.
Caliber: .375
Magazine: Double stack, single feed
Features: RND CNC machined matched upper and lower receivers; left sided non-reciprocating charging handle; hard black anodized with black or gray gun coat, integral Picatinny rail; speed lock hammer; 3.5 lb. trigger pull; RND integrated buffer system; modular handguard.
MSRP: **$10,500**

RND 3000

Action: Piston gas-operated, semi-auto
Stock: Fully adjustable
Barrel: 26-in. free-floating supermatch
Sights: N/A
Weight: 28 lb.
Caliber: BMG .50 caliber
Magazine: Double stack, single feed
Features: Left sided non-reciprocating charging handle; hard black anodized with black or gray gun coat; integral Picatinny rail; speed lock hammer; 3.5 lb. trigger pull; modular handguard.
MSRP: **$11,500**

RND PISTOL

Action: Gas-operated, semi-auto
Stock: N/A
Barrel: 7.5-in.
Sights: N/A
Weight: 9.5 lb. (steel barrel)
Caliber: .223 (5.56mm NATO)
Magazine: N/A
Features: RND CNC machined matched upper and lower receivers; hard black anodized with a black or gray gun coat; integral Picatinny rail; speed lock hammer; 3.5 lb. trigger pull; titanium firing pin; free-floating handguard.
MSRP: **$1,800**

Rock River Arms: Predator HP

Rock River Arms: Fred Eichler Series Predator .223

Rock River Arms: LAR-40 Mid-Length A4

ROCK RIVER ARMS

PREDATOR HP

Action: semi-auto
Stock: RRA Operator A2 and A2
Barrel: 20-in. bead-blasted stainless steel HBAR; 1:10 twist, cryo treated
Sights: None (A4 flat-top for optics)
Weight: 8.6 lb.
Calibers: .308/7.62mm, 7mm-08, and .243
Magazine: One 10-round
Features: RRA winter trigger guard; RRA's limited lifetime warranty.
MSRP: . . . . **$1,690–$1,740**

FRED EICHLER SERIES PREDATOR .223

Action: semi-auto
Stock: RRA Operator A2 or 6-position
Barrel: 1:9 twist; 16-in. mid-length chromoly cryogenically treated barrel
Sights: None (A4 flat-top for optics)
Weight: 7.5 lb.
Caliber: .223
Magazine: One 10-round and one 20-round (where legal)
Features: RRA winter trigger guard;

RRA's limited lifetime warranty; one- or two-stage RRA trigger available.
MSRP: **$1,510**

PDS PISTOL—LP2110

Action: semi-auto
Stock: Hogue rubber pistol grip
Barrel: 1:9 twist; 8-in. chromoly
Sights: None (A4 flat-top for optics)
Weight: 5 lb.
Caliber: 5.56mm NATO chamber for 5.56mm and .223
Magazine: One mag, number of rounds N/A
Features: A2 flash hider; RRA two-stage trigger.
MSRP: . . . . **$1,335–$1,460**

PDS CARBINE

Action: semi-auto
Stock: Hogue pistol grip and RRA side-folding 6-position tactical CAR stock
Barrel: 16-in. chromoly, 1:9 twist
Sights: None
Weight: 7.4 lb.
Caliber: 5.56mm NATO chamber for 5.56mm and .223

Magazine: One, number of rounds N/A
Features: Two-stage match and A2 flash hider.
MSRP: . . . . **$1,595–$1,750**

LAR-40 MID-LENGTH A4

Action: semi-auto
Stock: RRA tactical CAR stock; Hogue grip
Barrel: 1:16 twist, 16-in. chromoly
Sights: None (A4 flat-top for optics)
Weight: 7.5 lb., 7.1 lb.
Caliber: .40 S&W chamber
Magazine: One, number of rounds N/A
Features: 5/8x32 thread; single-stage trigger.
MSRP: **$1,260**

LAR-6.8 MID-LENGTH A4

Action: semi-auto
Stock: RRA 6-postion
Barrel: 16-in. chromoly, 1:10 twist
Sights: None (A4 flat-top for optics)
Weight: 7.5 lb., 7.1 lb.
Caliber: 6.8mm Rem. SPC II chamber
Magazine: One, number of rounds N/A
Features: 5/8x24 thread.
MSRP: **$1,055**

Rock River Arms: LAR-6.8 Coyote Carbine

Rock River Arms: LAR-8 Standard A4

LAR-6.8 COYOTE CARBINE

Action: semi-auto
Stock: Hogue rubber grip/ RRA operator CAR stock barrel; 16-in. chromoly HBAR; 1:10 twist
Sights: None (A4 flat-top for optics)
Weight: 7 lb.
Caliber: 6.8mm Rem. SPC II chamber
Magazine: One, number of rounds N/A
Features: Smith Vortex flash hider, 5/8x24 thread.
MSRP: $1,310

PREDATOR PURSUIT MID-LENGTH

Action: semi-auto
Stock: Hogue pistol grip and A2 buttstock
Barrel: 20-in/16-in. air gauged heavy match stainless steel; 1:8 twist; cryo-treated
Sights: None (A4 flat-top for optics)
Weight: 8.1 lb., 7.2 lb.
Caliber: .223 Wylde chamber for 5.56mm and .223
Magazine: One, number of rounds N/A
Features: Forged RRA LAR-15 lower and forged A4 upper.
MSRP: $1,340

COYOTE RIFLE, COYOTE CARBINE

Action: semi-auto
Stock: Hogue pistol grip and operator A2
Barrel: 20-in/16-in. chromoly HBAR; 1:9 twist
Sights: None
Weight: 8.4 lb., or 7.0 lb.
Caliber: .223 Wylde/ 5.56mm NATO chamber for 5.56mm and .223
Magazine: One, number of rounds N/A

Features: Two-stage match and winter trigger guard.
MSRP: $1,300

LAR-40 7-IN. A4 PISTOLS

Action: semi-auto
Stock: Hogue rubber grip
Barrel: 7-in. chromoly, 1:16 twist
Sights: A2 front sight, no sights
Weight: 4.8 lb.
Caliber: .40 S&W chamber
Magazine: One, number of rounds N/A
Features: Single-stage trigger; RRA aluminum free-float tube; A2 flash hider.
MSRP: $1,260

LAR-6.8 CAR A4

Action: semi-auto
Stock: Available RRA 6-postion tactical CAR stock
Barrel: 16-in. chromoly; 1:10 twist
Sights: A2/ no sights (A4 flat-top for optics)
Weight: 7.5 lb., 7.1 lb.
Caliber: 6.8mm Rem. SPC II chamber
Magazine: One, number of rounds N/A
Features: A2 flash hider and 5/8x24 thread.
MSRP: . . . . . $995–$1,010, $960–$975

LAR-8 ELITE OPERATOR

Action: semi-auto
Stock: RRA operator CAR stock
Barrel: 16-in. chromoly; 1:10 twist; cryogenically-treated
Sights: RRA flip-front sight gas block
Weight: 9.1 lb.
Caliber: .308/7.62x51mm NATO chamber
Magazine: One, number of rounds N/A

Features: RRA flip-front sight gas block; Hogue grip; RRA two-stage trigger, cryogenically-treated barrel; RRA LAR-8 advanced half quad with three ladder rail covers; RRA operator CAR stock.
MSRP: $1,740

LAR-8 MID-LENGTH A4

Action: semi-auto
Stock: RRA 6-position tactical CAR stock
Barrel: 16-in. chromoly, 1:10 twist; cryogenically-treated
Sights: A4 features gas block sight base
Weight: A2 weighs 8.5 lb. and the A4 weighs 8.1 lb.
Caliber: .308/7.62x51mm NATO chamber
Magazine: One, number of rounds N/A
Features: Cryogenically-treated barrel; Hogue grip; RRA tactical CAR Stock, RRA two-stage trigger.
MSRP: $1,335

LAR-8 STANDARD A4

Action: semi-auto
Stock: A2 buttstock
Barrel: 20-in. chromoly; 1:10 twist; cryogenically-treated
Sights: A2 features front-sight housing with rail/A4 features gas block sight base
Weight: A2 weighs 9.4 lb. and the A4 weighs 9.0 lb.
Caliber: .308/7.62x51mm NATO chamber
Magazine: One, number of rounds N/A
Features: Cryogenically-treated barrel; RRA two-stage trigger, Hogue grip.
MSRP: $1,370

AR RIFLE MODELS

Rock River Arms: LAR-8 Standard Operator

Rock River Arms: LAR-8 Varmint A4

Rock River Arms: LAR-9 Mid-Length A4

LAR-8 STANDARD OPERATOR

Action: semi-auto
Stock: RRA Operator A2 stock
Barrel: 20-in. chromoly; 1:10 twist; cryogenically-treated
Sights: RRA flip-front sight gas block
Weight: 9 lb.
Caliber: .308/7.62x51mm NATO chamber
Magazine: One, number of rounds N/A
Features: RRA flip-front sight gas block; RRA two-stage trigger; Hogue grip; RRA operator A2 stock; RRA LAR-8 advanced half quad with three ladder rail covers; cryogenically treated barrel.
MSRP: **$1,790**

LAR-8 VARMINT A4

Action: semi-auto
Stock: A2 buttstock
Barrel: 20-in. or 26-in. bull stainless steel; 1:10 twist; cryogenically treated
Sights: None
Weight: 20-in. is 10.4 lb. /26-in. is 11.6 lb.
Caliber: .308/7.62x51mm NATO chamber
Magazine: One, number of rounds N/A
Features: Cryogenically treated air gauged stainless steel bull barrel; RRA aluminum free-float tube; RRA two-stage trigger and RRA winter trigger guard; Hogue grip.
Model #: 20-in. 308A1520 / 26-in. 308A1560.
MSRP: . . . **20-in. $1,655/26-in. $1,660**

LAR-9 7 A4 PISTOLS

Action: semi-auto
Stock: No stock
Barrel: 7-in. chromoly; 1:10 twist; A1 flash hider with ½x36 thread
Sights: A2 features an A2 front sight
Weight: A4 weighs 4.8 lb.
Caliber: 9mm Luger
Magazine: One, number of rounds N/A
Features: Hogue grip; single-stage trigger; RRA aluminum free-float tube; pistol-length handguard.
MSRP: **$1,320**

LAR-9 10.5-IN. A2 & A4 PISTOLS

Action: semi-auto
Stock: no stock
Barrel: 10.5-in. chromoly; 1:10 twist; A1 flash hider; ½x36 thread
Sights: RRA quad rail free-float; RRA flip-front sight Gas block
Weight: A4 weighs 4.9 lb.
Caliber: 9mm Luger
Magazine: One, number of rounds N/A
Features: Hogue grip, single-stage trigger, R-4 handguard.
MSRP: **$1,205**

LAR-9 CAR A4

Action: semi-auto
Stock: RRA 6-position tactical CAR stock
Barrel: 16-in. chromoly; 1:10 twist/A1 flash hider; ½x36 thread

Sights: Optional gas block sight, flip-up front sight
Weight: A4 weighs 7.1 lb.
Caliber: 9mm Luger
Magazine: One, number of rounds N/A
Features: Hogue grip; RRA tactical CAR stock.
MSRP: **$1,180**

LAR-9 MID-LENGTH A4

Action: semi-auto
Stock: RRA 6-position tactical CAR stock
Barrel: 16-in. chromoly; 1:10 twist, A1 flash hider. ½x36 thread
Sights: N/A
Weight: A4 weighs 7.1 lb.
Caliber: 9mm Luger
Magazine: One, number of rounds N/A
Features: Hogue grip, RRA tactical CAR stock.
MSRP: **$1,180**

LAR-15 7-IN. A2 & A4 PISTOLS

Action: semi-auto
Stock: None
Barrel: 7-in. chromoly; 1:9 twist; A2 flash hider; ½x28 thread
Sights: A2 pistol has an A2 front sight
Weight: A2 pistol weighs 5.1 lb. and the A4 pistol weighs 5 lb.
Caliber: 5.56mm NATO chamber for 5.56mm & .223 cal.
Magazine: One, number of rounds N/A
Features: Hogue rubber pistol grip; RRA aluminum free-float tube, pistol length.
MSRP: A2 pistol is $955 and A4 pistol is $990

LAR-15 10.5-IN. A4 PISTOLS

Action: semi-auto
Stock: None

AR RIFLE MODELS

Barrel: 10.5-in. chromoly; 1:7 twist; A2 flash hider; ½x28 thread
Sights: RRA quad rail free-float; flip-front sight gas block and RRA stand alone rear sight
Weight: A4 pistol weighs 5.2 lb.
Caliber: 5.56mm NATO chamber for 5.56mm & .223 cal.
Magazine: One, number of rounds N/A
Features: Single-stage trigger; Hogue rubber pistol grip; R-4 handguard; 26.5-in.
MSRP: $1,055

LAR-15 ATH CARBINE ADVANCED TACTICAL HUNTER

Action: semi-auto
Stock: RRA operator CAR stock
Barrel: 18-in. heavy match stainless steel; 1:8 twist; cryo-treated
Sights: N/A
Weight: 7.6 lb.
Caliber: .223 Wylde chamber for 5.56mm and .223 cal.
Magazine: One, number of rounds N/A
Features: RRA tactical muzzle brake; cryogenically treated 18-in. heavy match stainless steel barrel; RRA two-stage trigger; RRA operator CAR stock; ERGO SureGrip; RRA Winter trigger guard; RRA advanced half quad free-float mid-length handguard with three ladder rail covers; low-profile gas block.
MSRP: $1,370

LAR-15 CAR A4

Action: semi-auto
Stock: A2 buttstock or 6-position tactical CAR stock
Barrel: 16-in. chromoly; 1:9 twist; A2 flash hider
Sights: Front sight housing with bayonet lug; RRA tactical carry handle or RRA Dominator EOTech mount
Weight: A2 weighs 7.5 lb. and the A4 weighs 7.1 lb.
Caliber: 5.56mm NATO chamber for 5.56mm and .223 cal.
Magazine: One, number of rounds N/A
Features: RRA two-stage trigger; CAR-length gas system.

MSRP: . . . . .with chromoly barrel—$1,065; with chrome lined chromoly barrel—$1,105

LAR-15 COYOTE CARBINE

Action: semi-auto
Stock: RRA operator A2 stock
Barrel: 16-in. chromoly HBAR; 1:9 twist
Sights: None
Weight: 7.2 lb.
Caliber: 5.56mm NATO chamber for 5.56mm & .223 cal.
Magazine: One, number of rounds N/A
Features: RRA operator CAR Stock Hogue grip; RRA two-stage match trigger and winter trigger guard; Hogue free-float tube CAR-length gas system; 16-in. chromoly HBAR with Smith Vortek flash hider.
MSRP: $1,300

LAR-15 COYOTE RIFLE

Action: semi-auto
Stock: RRA operator A2 stock
Barrel: 20-in. chromoly HBAR; 1:9 twist
Sights: Free-float rail
Weight: 8.4 lb.
Caliber: .223 Wylde chamber for 5.56mm & .223 cal.
Magazine: One, number of rounds N/A
Features: 20-in. chromoly HBAR with Smith Vortex flash hider; Hogue free-float tube; rifle-length gas system; RRA two-stage match trigger and winter trigger guard; Hogue grip; RRA operator A2 stock.
MSRP: $1,345

LAR-15 ELITE CAR A4

Action: semi-auto
Stock: RRA 6-position tactical CAR stock
Barrel: Either a 16-in. chromoly barrel, 1:9 twist or a chrome lined 16-in. chromoly barrel, 1:9 twist
Sights: A2 carry handle assembly, tactical carry handle assembly or a Dominator EOTech mount
Weight: 7.7 lb.
Caliber: 5.56mm NATO chamber for 5.56 and .223 cal.

Magazine: One, number of rounds N/A
Features: Side mount sling swivel; mid-length handguard, mid-length gas system; RRA tactical CAR stock; RRA two-stage trigger, Hogue grip.
MSRP: . . . . .with chromoly barrel, $1,065; with chrome lined chromoly barrel, $1,105

LAR-15 ELITE CAR A4

Action: semi-auto
Stock: RRA 6-position tactical CAR stock
Barrel: 16-in.; chromoly; 1:9 twist
Sights: Optional
Weight: 7.7 lb.
Caliber: 5.56mm NATO chamber for 5.56mm and .223 cal.
Magazine: One, number of rounds N/A
Features: Side mount sling swivel; mid-length handguards; mid-length gas system; RRA two-stage trigger; RRA tactical CAR stock; Hogue grip.
MSRP: $1,065

LAR-15 ELITE COMP

Action: semi-auto
Stock: RRA operator CAR stock
Barrel: Chrome-lined 16-in. chromoly; 1:9 twist
Sights: RRA flip-front sight gas block assembly; A.R.M.S. #40L low-profile flip-up rear sight
Weight: 8.4 lb.
Caliber: 5.56mm NATO chamber for 5.56mm and .223 cal.
Magazine: One, number of rounds N/A
Features: RRA operator CAR stock; ERGO SureGrip; RRA two-stage trigger and RRA winter trigger guard; RRA half quad free-float with full-length top rail and three ladder rail covers; chrome-lined barrel with RRA tactical muzzle brake; RRA flip-front sight gas block assembly; mid-length gas system; A.R.M.S. #40L low-profile flip-up rear sight.
MSRP: $1,515

Rock River Arms: LAR-15 Elite Comp

Rock River Arms: LAR-15 Operator Series
Entry Tactical

LAR-15 ENTRY TACTICAL

Action: semi-auto
Stock: RRA 6-position tactical CAR stock
Barrel: With either a 16-in. chromoly R-4 barrel 1:9 twist, or a chrome-lined 16-in. chromoly R-4 barrel, 1:9 twist
Sights: Either an A2 carry handle assembly, tactical carry handle assembly, or Dominator EOTech Mount
Weight: 7.5 lb.
Caliber: 5.56mm NATO Chamber for 5.56mm and .223 cal.
Magazine: One, number of rounds N/A
Features: RRA tactical CAR stock; Hogue grip; RRA two-stage trigger; R-4 handguard; R-4 barrel profile; CAR-length gas system; side mount sling swivel.
MSRP: . . . . .with chromoly R-4 barrel—$1,065; with chrome lined chromoly R-4 barrel—$1,105

LAR-15 MID-LENGTH A4

Action: semi-auto
Stock: 6-position tactical CAR stock
Barrel: 16-in. chromoly; 1:9 twist, A2 flash hider
Sights: Choices of front sight housing with bayonet lug, no sight, A2 carry handle assembly, RRA tactical carry handle, RRA Dominator EOTech mount
Weight: A2 weighs 7.5 lb. and the A4 weighs 7.1 lb.
Caliber: 5.56mm NATO chamber for 5.56mm and .223 cal.
Magazine: One, number of rounds N/A
Features: RRA two-stage trigger, CAR-length gas system.
MSRP: $1,035

LAR-15 NM A2 & NM A4

Action: semi-auto
Stock: A2 buttstock
Barrel: 20-in. air gauged heavy match stainless steel; 1:8 twist; cryotreated
Sights: Match ½x½ min, .040 hooded aperture rear sight and match .050 post front sight
Weight: 9.7 lb.
Caliber: .223 Wylde chamber for 5.56mm and .223 cal.
Magazine: One, number of rounds N/A
Features: Free-float thermo mold handguard; match front and rear sights; cryogenically treated air gauged heavy match stainless steel barrel; RRA two-stage chrome trigger group.
MSRP: NM A2, $1,335; NM A4, $1,415

LAR-15 OPERATOR SERIES ELITE COMP

Action: semi-auto
Stock: RRA operator CAR stock
Barrel: 16-in. chromoly; 1:9 twist
Sights: RRA flip-front sight gas block assembly; A.R.M.S. #40L low-profile flip-up rear sight
Weight: 8.4 lb.
Caliber: 5.56mm NATO chamber for 5.56mm and .223 cal.
Magazine: One, number of rounds N/A
Features: RRA operator CAR stock; ERGO SureGrip; RRA half-quad free-float; RRA two-stage trigger and winter trigger guard; RRA tactical brake.
MSRP: $1,515

LAR-15 OPERATOR SERIES ENTRY TACTICAL

Action: semi-auto
Stock: RRA operator CAR stock
Barrel: 16-in. chromoly R-4, 1:9 twist
Sights: Front sight housing with bayonet lug
Weight: 7.5 lb.
Caliber: 5.56mm NATO chamber for 5.56mm and .223 cal.
Magazine: One, number of rounds N/A
Features: RRA operator CAR stock; ERGO SureGrip; R-4 handguard; R-4 barrel profile; RRA tactical brake.
MSRP: $1,105

LAR-15 OPERATOR SERIES TACTICAL CAR A4

Action: semi-auto
Stock: RRA operator CAR stock
Barrel: 16-in. chromoly; 1:9 twist
Sights: Front sight housing with bayonet lug
Weight: 7.5 lb.
Caliber: 5.56mm NATO chamber for 5.56mm and .223 cal.
Magazine: One, number of rounds N/A
Features: RRA operator CAR stock; Hogue rubber grip; R-4 handguard;

Rock River Arms: LAR-40 CAR A4

RRA two-stage trigger and winter trigger guard; RRA tactical brake.
MSRP: **$1,105**

LAR-15 PREDATOR PURSUIT MID-LENGTH

Action: semi-auto
Stock: A2 buttstock
Barrel: 16-in. air gauged heavy match stainless steel; 1:8 twist; cryotreated
Sights: RRA deluxe extended free-float rail with low-profile gas block mid-length gas system
Weight: 7.1 lb.
Caliber: .223 Wylde chamber for 5.56mm and .223 cal.
Magazine: One, number of rounds N/A
Features: Cryogenically treated 16-in. stainless steel heavy match barrel; RRA aluminum free-float tube mid-length gas system; Hogue grip.
MSRP: **$1,305**

LAR-15 PREDATOR PURSUIT RIFLE

Action: semi-auto
Stock: A2 buttstock
Barrel: 20-in. air gauged heavy match stainless-steel; 1:8 twist; cryo-treated
Sights: RRA extended free-float rail with low profile gas block, rifle-length gas system
Weight: 8.1 lb.
Caliber: .223 Wylde chamber for 5.56mm and .223 cal.
Magazine: One, number of rounds N/A
Features: Hogue grip; RRA aluminum free-float tube rifle-length gas system; cryogenically treated 20-in. stainless steel heavy match barrel.
MSRP: **$1,340**

LAR-15 STANDARD A4

Action: semi-auto
Stock: A2 stock
Barrel: 20 in. chromoly HBAR, 1:9 twist

Sights: Choices of front sight housing with bayonet lug or A2 carry handle assembly
Weight: A2 weighs 8.6 lb. and the A4 weighs 8.2 lb.
Caliber: .223 Wylde chamber for 5.56mm and .223 cal.
Magazine: One, number of rounds N/A
Features: RRA two-stage trigger.
MSRP: **$1,010**

LAR-15 VARMINT A4

Action: semi-auto
Stock: A2 butt stock
Barrel: Air gauged stainless steel, 1:8 twist, cryo-treated
Sights: None
Weight: Depending on model chosen
Caliber: .223 Wylde chamber for 5.56mm and .223 cal.
Magazine: One, number of rounds N/A
Features: RRA aluminum free-float tube; cryogenically treated air gauged stainless steel bull barrel in 16-, 18-, 20-in. Rock River Arms LAR-15 Tactical CAR UTE2, and 24-in.; RRA two stage match trigger and RRA winter trigger guard; Hogue grip.
MSRP: 16-in, $1,255; 18-in, $1,270; 20-in, $1,285; 24-in, $1,295

LAR-15 VARMINT EOP

Action: semi-auto
Stock: A2 butt stock
Barrel: Air gauged stainless steel; 1:8 twist, cryo-treated
Sights: None
Weight: Depending on model chosen
Caliber: .223 Wylde chamber for 5.56mm and .223 cal.
Magazine: One, number of rounds N/A
Features: Cryogenically treated air gauged stainless steel bull barrel in 16-, 18-, 20-, and 24-in.; RRA aluminum free-float tube; Hogue grip.

MSRP: $1,100–$1,340, depending on features selected

LAR-40 CAR A4

Action: semi-auto
Stock: RRA 6-position tactical CAR stock
Barrel: 16-in. chromoly; 1:16 twist A2 flash hider; 5/8x32 thread
Sights: Front sight housing with bayonet lug
Weight: A2 is 7.5 lb. /A4 is 7.1 lb.
Caliber: .40 S&W chamber
Magazine: One, number of rounds N/A
Features: Hogue grip; RRA tactical CAR stock.
MSRP: **$1,260**

LAR-458 CAR A4

Action: semi-auto
Stock: A2 buttstock
Barrel: 16-in. chromoly bull barrel, 1:14 twist
Sights: RRA aluminum free-float tube; CAR-length gas system
Weight: 7.6 lb.
Caliber: .458 SOCOM chamber
Magazine: One, number of rounds N/A
Features: Chromoly bull barrel; RRA aluminum free-float tube CAR-length gas system; RRA two-stage trigger.
MSRP: **$1,220**

LAR-458 TACTICAL CARBINE

Action: semi-auto
Stock: RRA NSP 6-Position CAR stock
Barrel: 16-in. chromoly bull barrel; 1:14 twist
Sights: None
Weight: 7.8 lb.
Caliber: .458 SOCOM chamber
Magazine: One, number of rounds N/A
Features: RRA two-stage trigger; RRA aluminum free-float tube; mid-length gas system; chromoly bull barrel.
MSRP: **$1,415**

AR RIFLE MODELS

Ruger AR-556 Review

I don't know if it was intentional, but Ruger's timing was impeccable. In 2009, during the height of the AR boom, Ruger released the SR-556, a gas piston operated AR. People were buying ARs at any price; which was good, because the SR-556 commands a $2,000 price tag—pretty typical for a piston AR. Sales have cooled off a bit—and by cooled off I mean ARs are being sold by the half-truckload, as compared to the whole-truckload—and consumers are looking for well-priced ARs. To fill that need, in 2014, Ruger released the AR-556, with an MSRP of $799. The street price is in the $699 range, but is frequently seen on sale for less. In keeping with the spirit of the Ruger American Rifle, this is a real bargain—you're getting a lot of performance for a fair price.

It's a basic AR, without a lot of the bells and whistles found in the over-$1,000 rifles—but then it also has some things that aren't so basic. Like the M4 feed ramps for reliable feeding. Also, the oversized trigger guard for gloves. Plus, it's chambered in 5.56 NATO, so you can use it with that or a .223 Remington. Ruger also did a good job on the milled A2-style front sight/gas block. It has serrations on the rear surface to eliminate glare, plus a QD (quick detach) socket and bayonet lug. One of my pet peeves is when ARs don't come with a forward assist (FA), and for a time many budget ARs didn't have an FA. However, Ruger got this right—the AR-556 does.

The barrel is medium contoured, 16.1 inches in length and cold hammer forged for durability and accuracy, and with a carbine-length gas system. The 1:8 twist is rated for bullet sizes ranging from 35 to 77 grains, though it really excels in the sweet spot of 55 and 62 grains. It's topped with a Ruger flash hider, and is threaded at .5x28 for installing other muzzle devices and suppressors.

The front grips are reminiscent of those found on a standard length AR rifle, not the mil-spec carbine—they're round, not oval, and are smaller in circumference. Ruger accomplishes this by ditching the aluminum heat shields. I was leery about this at first, but after dumping two mags in about 15 seconds, I'm no longer as concerned. Ruger makes the grips of heat-resistant glass-filled nylon. While the barrel was hot enough to be untouchable, the grip was barely warm.

One of my favorite things about this rifle is Ruger's Delta Ring. I've been wrestling with mil-spec Delta Rings for over two and a half decades now, and I hate it. On older, worn rifles, it can be a piece of cake. On a new one, it can be nearly impossible. I've even bought a tool to remove them, but it's never around when I actually want to remove the grips. Ruger changes all of that with a threaded barrel nut and a screw-on Delta Ring. To remove the handguards, simply unscrew the Delta Ring, no fuss. The nice thing is that it's compatible with General Issue (GI) carbine grips and any aftermarket pop-in grips that fit mil-spec delta rings.

Another plus is the rear sight. It's a quick deploy polymer sight, very reminiscent of Magpul—it's solid, dependable, and works well. I'm a fan of these type sights because you can fold them out of the way and mount an optical sight but, if that breaks or for whatever reason, you can remove it and flip up your backup sights. Plus, I like that Ruger included the sights—I've bought ARs at two to three times this price that had nothing. I like an AR that is ready to rock out of the box.

I fired well over 240 rounds through this rifle my first trip to the range, and it's definitely a shooter. I was shooting American Eagle AR5.56 Fresh Fire Packs of XM855 62 Grain FMJ, thanks to Federal Ammunition. The rifle function was nearly flawless—out of everything I shot, I had one round that didn't fire. It had a dimple on the primer, but no ignition. I re-chambered it and it fired no problem. Most of the rounds were fired rapid fire, at a six-inch metal gong target sitting out 50 yards. Once I got the sights on target, the rifle hit it every time unless the shooter got sloppy. After my initial testing back in 2014, I purchased that rifle and have put a lot of rounds through it, never with any problems. It's been very reliable, just as much so as the $1,000-plus and $2,000-plus ARs that I own. Heck, it's been as reliable as the bolt-action rifles that I own.

—*Robb Manning*

Ruger: AR-556

Ruger: SR-556 Takedown

from 7075-T6 aluminum forging, 9130 alloy steel bolt, milled gas block, chrome-plated bolt carrier, single-stage trigger.
MSRP: **$799**

SR-556 TAKEDOWN

Action: semi-auto
Stock: Magpul SL collapsible buttstock, Magpul MOE grip, KeyMOd handguard
Barrel: 16.1-in. precision-rifled cold hammer-forged mil-spec 41V45 chromoly-vanadium barrel with 1:8 RH twist, Ruger flash suppressor

RUGER

AR-556

Action: semi-auto
Stock: Black synthetic, 6-position M4 collapsible, glass-filled nylong handguards, ergonomic grip
Barrel: 16.1-in. medium contour cold hammer-forged barrel with 1:8 RH twist
Sights: Front—adjustable post, rear—adjustable Ruger Rapid Deploy folding rear sight
Weight: 6.5 lb.
Caliber: 5.56
Magazine: 30-round Magpul PMAG
Features: Flat-top upper receiver made

Ruger: SR-762

Ruger: SR-22

Sights: Front and rear folding iron sights
Weight: 7.1 lb.
Caliber: 5.56
Magazine: Three 30-round Magpul PMAG
Features: Takedown barrel removable without tools; chrome-plated, two-stage piston; Ruger Elite 452 two-stage trigger, carry case.
MSRP: $2,199

SR-762

Action: semi-auto
Stock: 6-position M4-style collapsible stock, rounded Ruger lightweight adaptable handguard, Hogue monogrip
Barrel: 16.1-in. precision-rifled cold hammer-forged mil-spec 41V45 chromoly-vanadium fluted barrel with 1:10 RH twist, Ruger flash suppressor
Sights: Front and rear folding backup iron sights
Weight: 8.6 lb.
Caliber: .308 Win.
Magazine: Three 20-round Magpul PMAG
Features: Patented chrome two-stage piston; Ruger Elite 452 two-stage trigger, carry case.
MSRP: $2,349

SR-22

Action: semi-auto
Stock: Fixed buttstock (model 1236) or collapsible buttstock (model 11134) depending on version, rounded mid-length handguard, Hogue monogrip
Barrel: 16.12-in. precision-rifled cold hammer-forged alloy steel barrel with 1:16 RH twist
Sights: Rapid Deploy folding backup

sights
Weight: 6.5 lb.
Caliber: .22 LR
Magazine: One 10-round detachable rotary
Features: Picatinny rail optic mount, barrel support block.
MSRP: $709

SEEKINS PRECISION

BATTLEFIELD SERIES SPBRV3

Action: semi-auto
Stock: Magpul MOE
Barrel: 14.5-in. stainless steel 416R match-grade
Sights: None
Weight: 6.5 lb.
Caliber: .223 Wylde, 300 BLK
Magazine: One 30-round
Features: Upper and lower receivers CNC machined from 7075-T6 aluminum forgings, exceeds mil-spec requirements and performance, MCSR hand guard (Modular Combat Suppressor Rail), type III class II hard coat anodized finish, match-grade 14.5-in. stainless steel barrel, M4 feed ramps, melonited gas block, gas tube and M16 bolt carrier group, pin and weld seekins melonited flash hider.
MSRP: $1,425

COMBAT BILLET SERIES SPCBRV1

Action: semi-auto
Stock: Magpul MOE
Barrel: 16-in. stainless steel 416R match-grade

Sights: None
Weight: 7.2 lb.
Caliber: .223 Wylde, 300 BLK
Magazine: One 30-round
Features: Upper and lower receivers CNC machined from solid 7075-T6 Billet aluminum, aggressive unique styling only offered on Seekins precision billet receivers, exceeds mil-spec requirements and performance, BAR hand guard quad rail system, type III class II hard coat anodized finish, match-grade stainless steel barrel, M4 feed ramps, melonited adjustable gas block, gas tube and M16 bolt carrier group, seekins melonited flash hider.
MSRP: $1,850

PRO SERIES SPROV3

Action: semi-auto
Stock: Magpul STR
Barrel: 8-in. or 16-in. stainless steel 416R match-grade
Sights: None
Weight: 7.5 lb.
Caliber: .223 Wylde, 300 BLK
Magazine: One 30-round
Features: Billet upper, SP223 billet ambi lower, 8-in. or 16-in. match-grade stainless steel barrel, Seekins precision melonite coated flash hider 16-in. only, MCSR KeyMod hand guard, ambidextrous bolt release and selector switch, melonited adjustable gas block, gas tube and M16 bolt carrier group, ERGO grip tactical deluxe pistol grip.
MSRP: $1,995

SIG Sauer: 516 Patrol

SIG Sauer: M400

SIG Sauer: 716 Patrol

PRO SERIES SPRO3G AND 3GL

Action: semi-auto
Stock: Magpul STR
Barrel: 14.5-in.—3GL or 18-in.—3G stainless steel 416R match-grade
Sights: None
Weight: 8.50 lb.—3G or 7 lb.—3GL
Caliber: .223 Wylde, 300 BLK
Magazine: One 30-round
Features: iRMT-R billet upper, SP223 billet ambi lower, 14.5-in or 18-in. match-grade stainless steel barrel, Seekins Precision ATC (Advanced Tactical Compensator) muzzle brake threaded in ½x28, SP3Rv3 KeyMod free-float precision rifle hand guard, CMC single stage trigger, ambidextrous bolt release and selector switch, melonited adjustable gas block, gas tube and M16 bolt carrier group, ERGO grip tactical deluxe pistol grip.
MSRP: **$2,250**

SIG SAUER

M400

Action: semi-auto
Stock: Standard M4 type
Barrel: 16-in. chrome lined and phosphate coated
Sights: Adjustable front post, dual aperture w/ 300–600m capability.

Adjustable for windage and elevation.
Weight: 5.95 lb.
Caliber: 5.56x45mm NATO
Magazine: 30-round aluminum
Features: Military grade, chrome-lined barrel, flat-top upper with M1913 accessory rail.
MSRP: **$1,065**

516 PATROL

Action: semi-auto
Stock: Magpul MOE adjustable stock
Barrel: 16-in. free-floating chrome-lined and phosphate coated
Sights: Flip-up metallic
Weight: 7.3 lb.
Caliber: 5.56x45mm NATO
Magazine: M16 type
Features: Short-stroke pushrod gas system, 3-position adjustable gas valve (4-position optional), free-floating, military-grade, chrome-lined barrel, free-floating aluminum M1913 quad rail fore-end, flat-top upper with M1913 accessory rail.
MSRP: **$1,599**

716 PATROL

Action: semi-auto
Stock: Magpul ACS adjustable
Barrel: 16-in. free-floating chromelined and phosphate coated
Sights: Flip-up metallic
Weight: 9.3 lb.
Caliber: 7.62x51mm NATO
Magazine: 20-round Magpul PMAG
Features: Short-stroke pushrod gas

system, 4-position adjustable gas valve, free-floating, military-grade, chromelined barrel, free-floating aluminum M1913 quad rail fore-end, flat-top upper with M1913 accessory rail.
MSRP: **$1,866**

S&W

M&P 15 SPORT

Action: semi-auto
Stock: 6-position telescopic. 35-in. extended overall length, 32-in. collapsed
Barrel: 16-in., 4140 steel, 1:8 twist, 5R rifling
Sights: Adjustable A2 post front sight, adjustable dual aperture Magpul folding MBUS rear sight
Weight: 6.5 lb.
Caliber: 5.56mm NATO
Magazine: 30-round detachable PMAG
Features: Durable, corrosion-resistant barrel, chromed gas key and bolt carrier, gas operated, single-stage trigger. Available in state-compliant models.
MSRP: **$739**

M&P 15T

Action: semi-auto
Stock: 6-position telescopic, 35-in. extended overall length, 32-in. collapsed
Barrel: 16-in., 4140 steel, 1:8 twist, 5R rifling
Sights: Folding Magpul (MBUS) front and rear

S&W: M&P 15 Sport

S&W: M&P 15T

Weight: 6.85 lb.
Caliber: 5.56mm NATO
Magazine: 30-round detachable PMAG
Features: 10-in. patent pending, antitwist, free-floating quad rail; corrosion-resistant barrel; chromed bolt carrier and gas key. Gas operated. Single-stage trigger. Available in state-compliant models.
MSRP: $1,159

M&P 15

Action: semi-auto
Stock: 6-position telescopic. 35-in. extended overall length. 32-in. stock collapsed
Barrel: 16-in., 4140 steel, 1:9 twist
Sights: Adjustable A2 post front sight, adjustable dual aperture rear sight
Weight: 6.74 lb.
Caliber: 5.56mm NATO
Magazine: 30-round detachable PMAG

Features: Solid handguard; chromed barrel, gas key and bolt carrier; gas-operated; removable carry handle; single-stage trigger.
MSRP: $1,249

M&P 15X

Action: semi-auto
Stock: 6-position telescopic. 35-in. extended overall length. 32-in. stock collapsed Barrel: 16-in., 4140 steel, 1:9 twist
Sights: Adjustable A2 post front sight, adjustable folding Troy battle sight
Weight: 6.74 lb.
Caliber: 5.56mm NATO
Magazine: 30-round detachable PMAG
Features: Quad rail handguard; chromed barrel, gas key and bolt carrier; gas-operated; single-stage trigger.
MSRP: $1,379

M&P 15TS

Action: semi-auto
Stock: Magpul MOE. 34-in. extended overall length. 31-in. stock collapsed
Barrel: 16-in. 4140 steel, 1:7 twist
Sights: Folding Magpul (MBUS) front and rear.
Weight: 6.5 lb.
Caliber: 5.56mm NATO
Magazine: 30-round detachable PMAG
Features: Troy TRX Extreme handguard; permanent Smith Vortex flash hider; chromed barrel, gas key and bolt carrier; gas-operated; single-stage trigger.
MSRP: $1,569

M&P 15 MOE MID

Action: semi-auto
Stock: Magpul MOE
Barrel: 16-in., 4140 steel, 1:9 twist

S&W: M&P 15

S&W: M&P 15X

S&W: M&P 15TS

Sights: Folding Magpul (MBUS) rear sight, adjustable A2 post front sight
Weight: 6.5 lb.
Caliber: 5.56mm NATO
Magazine: 30-round detachable PMAG
Features: Mid-length gas system, co-branded, forged lower design, Magpul MOE grip; Magpul MOE handguard; corrosion-resistant barrel, chromed gas key and bolt carrier; single-stage trigger; available in black and flat dark earth finish, patented S&W enhanced flash hider, integrated trigger guard design, forward serrated edge of magwell.
MSRP: **$1,249**

M&P 15 VTAC II (VIKING TACTICS MODEL)

Action: semi-auto
Stock: VLTOR IMod 6-position telescopic. 35-in. extended overall length, 32-in. stock collapsed
Barrel: 16-in., 4150 CMV steel, 1:8 twist
Sights: None
Weight: 6.28 lb.
Caliber: 5.56mm NATO
Magazine: 30-round detachable PMAG
Features: Mid-length gas system, S&W patented enhanced flash hider; VTAC/Troy 13-in. TRX handguard; corrosion-resistant barrel; chromed gas key and bolt carrier; Geissele Super V Trigger, two adjustable Picatinny-style rails; VTAC padded 2-point tactical sling, VTAC LPSM low profile sling mount.
MSRP: **$1,949**

M&P 15OR (OPTICS READY)

Action: semi-auto
Stock: 6-position telescopic. 35-in. extended overall length. 32-in. stock collapsed
Barrel: 16-in., 4140 steel, 1:9 twist
Sights: None
Weight: 6.5 lb.
Caliber: 5.56mm NATO
Magazine: 30-round detachable
Features: Chromed barrel, gas key and bolt carrier; solid handguard; Picatinny gas block; gas operated.
MSRP: **$1,069**

S&W: M&P 15 MOE Mid

S&W: M&P 15 VTAC II (Viking Tactics Model)

S&W: M&P 15OR (Optics Ready)

S&W: MM&P 15PC (Performance Center)

M&P 15PC (PERFORMANCE CENTER)

Action: semi-auto
Stock: A2 buttstock
Barrel: 20-in., stainless steel, 1:8 twist
Sights: None
Weight: 8.2 lb.
Caliber: 5.56 NATO
Magazine: One 10-round detachable
Features: Chromed gas key and bolt carrier; solid full-float Yankee Hill handguard; gas operated; available in black or Realtree Advantage Max-1; two-stage trigger.
MSRP: $1,589 Camo and $1,549 Black

M&P 15-300 WHISPER

Action: semi-auto
Stock: 6-position telescopic. 35-in. extended overall length. 32-in. stock collapsed
Barrel: 16-in., 4140 steel, 1:7 twist
Sights: None
Weight: 6.38 lb.
Caliber: .300 Whisper/300 BLK
Magazine: One 10-round detachable
Features: Threaded barrel; A2-style flash hider, corrosion-resistant barrel; chromed gas key and bolt carrier; solid handguard; available in black or Realtree APG finish.
MSRP: $1,119

M&P 10

Action: semi-auto
Stock: 6-position telescopic. 40.9-in. extended overall length. 37.6 in stock collapsed
Barrel: 18-in., 4140 steel, 1:10 twist
Sights: None
Weight: 7.71 lb
Caliber: .308 Win/7.62x51
Magazine: 10- and 20-round detachable
Features: Ambidextrous magazine catch, bolt catch, safety selector; patented S&W enhanced flash hider; Gas block with integral Picatinny-style rail, QD sling swivel attachment point; solid handguard; chromed gas key and bolt carrier; Available in state-compliant models and black and camo finish.
MSRP: . . . . $1,619–$1,729

M&P15-22

Action: semi-auto, blow back
Stock: 6-position CAR stock. 33.75-in. extended overall length, 32.5-in. collapsed
Barrel: 16.5-in. barrel, 1:15 twist, carbon steel

Sights: Adjustable A2 post front sight, adjustable dual aperture rear sight.
Weight: 5.5 lb.
Caliber: .22 LR
Magazine: One 10-round and one 25-round detachable
Features: Available in multiple finishes including Realtree APG camo, black, Harvest Moon Orange, Purple Platinum, Pink Platinum and Tan/Black polymer upper and lower receiver, threaded barrel availability. Magpul and state-compliant model options.
MSRP: . . . . $499–$609

M&P15-22 PERFORMANCE CENTER (PC)

Action: semi-auto, blow back
Stock: 6-position Vltor adjustable.35.75-in. extended overall length, 32.5-in. collapsed.
Barrel: 18-in. heavy barrel, 1:15 twist, carbon steel
Sights: Adjustable A2 post front sight, adjustable dual aperture rear sight
Weight: 5.5 lb.
Caliber: .22 LR
Magazine: One 10-round detachable
Features: Polymer upper and lower

S&W: M&P 15-300 Whisper

S&W: M&P 10

S&W: M&P15-22 Performance Center (PC)

Stag Arms: Model 1

receiver, threaded barrel, match-grade precision barrel and chamber, matchgrade trigger, ambidextrous load-assist button, ladder-style handguard covers, overmolded Hogue grip. Non-threaded barrel and state-compliant model availability.

MSRP: **$789**

STAG ARMS

MODEL 1 AND 1L

Action: semi-auto, direct impingement
Stock: 6-position collapsible
Barrel: 16-in. chrome lined 1:9 twist 4140 government profile
Sights: Detachable carry handle/front post
Weight: 7 lb.
Caliber: 5.56mm NATO
Magazine: 30 round
Features: Forged and mil-spec type III hard coat anodized upper, forged and mil-spec—type III hard coat anodized lower, right-handed safety, standard magazine release, standard pistol grip, single-stage trigger, left handed model available (model 1L) with left handed safety. NEW! Stag Arms is now offering most of their rifles with a durable Cerakote finish. The rifle colors available from the top to bottom are Gun Metal Grey, Desert Tan, Burnished Bronze, and Forest Green.

MSRP: **$949**

MODEL 2 AND 2L

Action: semi-auto, direct impingement
Stock: 6-position collapsible
Barrel: 16-in. chrome-lined 1:9 twist 4140 government profile
Sights: Midwest ERS rear flip sight/ front post
Weight: 6.5 lb.
Caliber: 5.56mm NATO
Magazine: 30 round
Features: Forged and mil-spec type III hard coat anodized upper, forged and mil-spec—type III hard coat anodized lower, right-handed safety, standard magazine release, standard pistol grip, single-stage trigger, left-handed model available (model 2L) with left-handed safety. NEW! Stag Arms is now offering most of their rifles with a durable Cerakote finish. The rifle colors available from the top to bottom are Gun Metal Grey, Desert Tan, Burnished Bronze, and Forest Green.

MSRP: **$940**

MODEL 2T AND 2TL

Action: semi-auto, direct impingement
Stock: 6-position collapsible
Barrel: 16-in. chrome-lined 1:9 twist 4140 government profile
Sights: A.R.M.S. 40L/front post
Weight: 6.8 lb.
Caliber: 5.56mm NATO

Stag Arms: Model 1L

Stag Arms: Model 2

Stag Arms: Model 2L

Stag Arms: Model 2TL

Stag Arms: Model 2T

Magazine: 30 round
Features: Forged and mil-spec type III hard coat anodized upper, forged and mil-spec—type III hard coat anodized lower, right-handed safety, standard magazine release, standard pistol grip, single-stage trigger, left-handed model available (model 2TL) with left-handed safety. NEW! Stag Arms is now offering most of their rifles with a durable Cerakote finish. The rifle colors available from the top to bottom are Gun Metal Grey, Desert Tan, Burnished Bronze, and Forest Green.
MSRP: **$1,130**

MODEL 3 AND 3L

Action: semi-auto, direct impingement
Stock: 6-position collapsible
Barrel: 16-in. chrome-lined 1:9 twist 4140 government profile
Sights: No rear, railed gas block front

Weight: 6.1 lb.
Caliber: 5.56mm NATO
Magazine: 30 round
Features: Forged and mil-spec type III hard coat anodized upper, forged and mil-spec—type III hard coat anodized lower, right-handed safety, standard magazine release, standard pistol grip, single-stage trigger, left-handed model available (model 3L) with left-handed safety. NEW! Stag Arms is now offering most of their rifles with a durable Cerakote finish. The rifle colors available from the top to bottom are Gun Metal Grey, Desert Tan, Burnished Bronze, and Forest Green.
MSRP: **$895**

MODEL 4 AND 4L

Action: semi-auto, direct impingement
Stock: A2

Barrel: 20-in. chromoly 4140 **heavy profile**
Sights: Detachable carry handle, front post
Weight: 6.1 lb.
Caliber: 5.56mm NATO
Magazine: 20 round
Features: Forged and mil-spec type III hard coat anodized upper, forged and mil-spec—type III hard coat anodized lower, right-handed safety, standard magazine release, standard pistol grip, single-stage trigger, left-handed model available (model 4L) with left-handed safety. NEW! Stag Arms is now offering most of their rifles with a durable Cerakote finish. The rifle colors available from the top to bottom are Gun Metal Grey, Desert Tan, Burnished Bronze, and Forest Green.
MSRP: **$1,015**

Stag Arms: Model 3

Stag Arms: Model 3L

Stag Arms: Model 4

Stag Arms: Model 4L

Stag Arms: Model 5

Stag Arms: Model 5L

MODEL 5 AND 5L

Action: semi-auto, direct impingement
Stock: 6-position collapsible
Barrel: 16-in. 1:11 twist 6-groove stainless steel heavy profile
Sights: Detachable carry handle, front post
Weight: 6.4 lb.
Caliber: 6.8SPC SPEC2
Magazine: 25 round
Features: Forged and mil-spec—type III hard coat anodized upper, forged and mil-spec—type III hard coat anodized lower, right-handed safety, standard magazine release, standard pistol grip, single-stage trigger, lefthanded model available (model 5L) with left-handed safety. NEW! Stag Arms is now offering most of their rifles with a durable Cerakote finish.

The rifle colors available from the top to bottom are Gun Metal Grey, Desert Tan, Burnished Bronze, and Forest Green.
MSRP: **$1,045**

MODEL 6 AND 6L

Action: semi-auto, direct impingement
Stock: A2
Barrel: 24-in. 1:8 twist stainless steel heavy bull profile
Sights: No rear/gas block front
Weight: 10 lb.
Caliber: 6.8SPC SPEC2
Magazine: 25 round
Features: Forged and mil-spec—type III hard coat anodized upper, forged and mil-spec—type III hard coat anodized lower, right-handed safety, standard magazine release, standard pistol grip, single-stage trigger, lefthanded model available (model 6L)

with left-handed safety. NEW! Stag Arms is now offering most of their rifles with a durable Cerakote finish. The rifle colors available from the top to bottom are Gun Metal Grey, Desert Tan, Burnished Bronze, and Forest Green.
MSRP: **$1,055**

MODEL 7 AND 7L

Action: semi-auto, direct impingement
Stock: A2
Barrel: 20.77-in. 1:11 twist 4-groove stainless steel heavy profile
Sights: No rear/gas block front
Weight: 7.8 lb.
Caliber: 6.8SPC SPEC2
Magazine: 5 round
Features: Forged and mil-spec—type

Stag Arms: Model 6

Stag Arms: Model 6L

Stag Arms: Model 7

Stag Arms: Model 7L

Stag Arms: Model 8

Stag Arms: Model 8L

III hard coat anodized upper, forged and mil-spec—type III hard coat anodized lower, right-handed safety, standard magazine release, Hogue pistol grip, single-stage trigger, lefthanded model available (model 7L) with left-handed safety. NEW! Stag Arms is now offering most of their rifles with a durable Cerakote finish. The rifle colors available from the top to bottom are Gun Metal Grey, Desert Tan, Burnished Bronze, and Forest Green.

MSRP: **$1,055**

MODEL 8 AND 8L

Action: semi-auto, gas piston
Stock: 6-position collapsible
Barrel: 16-in. chrome-lined 1:9 twist 4140 government profile
Sights: Midwest SPLP rear flip sight/ Midwest flip-front sight
Weight: 7.8 lb.
Caliber: 5.56mm NATO
Magazine: 30 round
Features: Forged and mil-spec—type

III hard coat anodized upper, forged and mil-spec—type III hard coat anodized lower, right-handed safety, standard magazine release, standard pistol grip, single-stage trigger, lefthanded model available (model 7L) with left-handed safety. NEW! Stag Arms is now offering most of their rifles with a durable Cerakote finish. The rifle colors available from the top to bottom are Gun Metal Grey, Desert Tan, Burnished Bronze, and Forest Green.

MSRP: **$1,145**

TACTICAL FIREARMS SOLUTIONS, LLC

GENESIS

Action: semi-auto
Stock: Collapsible Mission First "Minimalist" Stock
Barrel: 16-in., 5.56 NATO, 1:7 twist,

mid-length gas system, chrome-lined 16-in., .223 Wylde, 1:8 twist, mid-length gas system, chrome-lined
Sights: N/A
Weight: Sub-7 lb.
Caliber: 5.56 NATO, 300 BLK, .458 SOCOM
Magazine: 30-round Magpul PMAG
Features: Nickel-boron plating on all aluminum parts which reduces friction, eliminates the need for oil, cleans easier, and greatly reduces part wear. Finished in our new patented NiB Dark, NiB Smoke, and NiB Battleworn finishes, NiB full auto bolt carrier, Elf match trigger (optional upgrade), enhanced parts kit, Magpul K+ grip, lightweight slim M-LOK 15-in. rail, TFS custom "Leveler" muzzle brake, 7075 billet aluminum receiver set. Includes a mid-length 5.56 barrel and an adjustable gas block. Exterior can be finished in many custom Cerakote patterns. We also make the "Revelation" AR-10, .308 and the more cost friendly forged

Texas Black Rifle Co.: 1836 Bravo AR-15

Texas Black Rifle Co.: 1836P Bravo AR-15 Pistol

Tactical Firearms Solutions, LLC: TFS Genesis

"Exodus" rifle.
MSRP: $1,800–$2,200 depending on configuration

TEXAS BLACK RIFLE CO.

1836 AR-15

Action: semi-auto
Stock: Magpul ACS-L mil-spec
Barrel: TBRC 16-in. 1:7 twist Nitride
Sights: N/A
Weight: 10.25 lb.
Caliber: 5.56/.223 or 300 BLK
Magazine: N/A
Features: TBRC M16 bolt carrier group, TBRC 11.4-in. ARS lightweight KeyMod rail, CMC flat bow, 3.5 lb. drop-in. trigger, MOE trigger guard & grip.
MSRP: **$1,559**

1836 BRAVO AR-15

Action: semi-auto
Stock: Magpul MOE mil-spec
Barrel: 16-in. 1:7 twist Nitride carbine-length gas with low-profile gas block
Sights: N/A
Weight: 9.75 lb.
Caliber: 5.56—mid-length gas, 300 BLK—pistol-length gas system
Magazine: N/A
Features: TBRC M16 bolt carrier Group, TBRC ARS KeyMod rail.
MSRP: **$995**

1836P BRAVO AR-15 PISTOL

Action: semi-auto
Stock: N/A
Barrel: 7.5-in. 1:7 twist Nitride pistol-length gas with low-profile gas block
Sights: N/A
Weight: 8.5 lb.
Caliber: 5.56 or 300 BLK
Magazine: N/A
Features: TBRC ARS KeyMod rail, TBRC M16 bolt carrier group, pistol-length gas system.
MSRP: **$949**

TNW FIREARMS

AERO SURVIVAL PISTOL

Action: semi-auto
Stock: N/A
Barrel: 8-in.
Sights: Flip-up iron sights
Weight: 5.5 lb.
Caliber: .357 SIG, .40 S&W, .45 ACP, 10mm, 9mm
Magazine: Glock-style pistol magazine
Features: Available in Hard Anodized Black, Dark Earth, OD Green, and Variegated Tiger Green and Pink, machined from aircraft aluminum, available with a threaded barrel.
MSRP: **$799**

AERO SURVIVAL RIFLE

Action: semi-auto

Stock: Adjustable
Barrel: 16.25-in.
Sights: Included 4X scope
Weight: 5.5 lb.
Caliber: 9mm, .40 S&W, .45 ACP, 10mm, .357 SIG
Magazine: Glock-style magazine
Features: Upper and lower rails, direct blow back, sliding safety and integrated child trigger lock, made of machined aircraft aluminum.
MSRP: . . . . **N/A**

SDI PISTOL

Action: semi-auto
Stock: N/A
Barrel: 10.5-in.
Sights: N/A
Weight: 5.5 lb.
Caliber: 5.56, 7.62x39, 300 BLK
Magazine: Standard AR magazine
Features: Billet aluminum upper and lower, hard black anodized, included rear sling attachment point.
MSRP: **$995**

SDI RIFLE

Action: semi-auto
Stock: Adjustable
Barrel: 16.2-in.
Sights: N/A
Weight: 8 lb.
Caliber: 5.56, .223, 7.62x39, 300 BLK
Magazine: Standard AR magazine
Features: Included quad rail and billet upper, uses gas-impingement system.

MSRP: **$995**

TRIDENT ARMS

AR-9 GLOCK PATTERN DEDICATED 9MM AR CARBINE—TAG91316

Action: semi-auto
Stock: Magpul MOE mil-spec stock
Barrel: Green Mountain 16-in. threaded machine gun–rated barrel
Sights: N/A
Weight: N/A
Caliber: 9mm
Magazine: 33-round glock pattern
Features: Billet aluminum dedicated Colt pattern 9mm lower, Vltor Mur-1S upper, Troy Alpha, or Bravo Rail system, Magpul MOE grip.
MSRP: . . . . **N/A**

Trident Arms: AR-9 Glock Pattern Dedicated 9mm AR Carbine—TAG91316

Trident Arms: AR-15 Carbine w/ Vltor MUR/1A Upper

AR-15 CARBINE W/A4 UPPER AND TROY ALPHA OR BRAVO RAIL SYSTEM TA15556A41316

Action: semi-auto
Stock: Magpul CTR mil-spec stock
Barrel: 16-in. 4140 5.56 threaded barrel, .750 micro gas block and A2 comp/flash hider
Sights: N/A
Weight: N/A
Caliber: 5.56, .223
Magazine: 30-round alloy w/ anti-tilt green follower
Features: A4 upper with forward assist, Magpul MOE Grip, Troy Alpha, or Bravo Rail system, Triden Arms TA-15 lower.
MSRP: . . . . **N/A**

AR-15 CARBINE W/VLTOR MUR/1A UPPER

Action: semi-auto
Stock: Magpul CTR mil-spec stock
Barrel: 16-in. 4140 5.56 threaded barrel, .750 micro gas block and A2 comp/flash hider
Sights: N/A
Weight: N/A
Caliber: 5.56/.223
Magazine: 30-round Magpul PMAG
Features: Magpul MOE Grip, Troy

Alpha or Bravo Rail system, Vltor MUR/1A (w/ forward assist) upper, Trident Arms TA-15 lower.
MSRP: . . . . **N/A**

AR-15 CARBINE W/A4 INTIMIDATOR 556 UPPER

Action: semi-auto
Stock: Magpul CTR mil-spec stock
Barrel: 16-in. 4140 5.56 threaded Barrel, .750 micro gas block
Sights: N/A
Weight: N/A
Caliber: 5.56/.223
Magazine: 30-round allow magazine w/ anti-tilt green follower
Features: Trident Arms TA-15 lower, A4 (w/ forward assist) upper, YHM Phantom flash hider, reconfigurable free-float Picatinney Rail system w/ aggressive fore-end cap, Magpul MOE grip.
MSRP: . . . . **N/A**

AR-15 CARBINE W/A2 RAPTOR 556 UPPER

Action: semi-auto
Stock: Magpul CTR mil-spec stock
Barrel: 16-in. 4140 5.56 threaded barrel, front sight post w/ gas block
Sights: A2-style front and rear carry-handle sight
Weight: N/A

Caliber: 5.56, .223
Magazine: 30-round allow magazine w/ anti-tilt green follower
Features: Trident Arms TA-15 lower, A2 (w/ forward assist) upper, reconfigurable Picatinney Rail system, Magpul MOE grip.
MSRP: . . . . **N/A**

300 BLK

Action: semi-auto
Stock: Magpul CTR mil-spec stock
Barrel: 16-in. threaded .300 4140 blackout barrel, .750 micro gas block
Sights: N/A
Weight: N/A
Caliber: .300 AAC Blackout
Magazine: 30-round Magpul PMAG
Features: Trident Arms TA-15 lower, Vltor MUR/1A (w/ forward assist) upper, Troy Alpha or Bravo Rail system, Magpul MOE grip.
MSRP: . . . . **N/A**

VIGILANT ARMS

VIGILANT ARMS VA15

Action: semi-auto
Stock: standard A2
Barrel: 16-in. government contour
Sights: Flat top, optics ready
Weight: 6 lb.

Trident Arms: AR-15 Carbine w/ A4 Intimidator 556 Upper

Trident Arms: AR-15 Carbine w/ A2 Raptor 556 Upper

VLtor Weapon Systems: TS3 Carbine

Caliber: 5.56
Magazine: One 30-round
Features: Mil-spec forged hard coat anodized upper and lower, M4 feed ramp, rail height gas block, Magpul handguard, Magpul pistol grip, enhanced trigger guard, ambi sling plate.
MSRP: **$1,100**

VLTOR WEAPON SYSTEMS

TS3 CARBINE

Action: semi-auto
Stock: Vltor LOP adjustable, collapsible stock
Barrel: Noveske hammer forged, chrome lined, 15-in., 1:7 twist barrel with mid-length gas system. Vltor compensator (VC-A1) permanently attached to the barrel, making the barrel length a legal 16.25-in.
Sights: Diamondhead USA, flip-up "Classic" combat sights
Weight: 7 lb. 7 oz.
Caliber: 5.56 NATO
Magazine: N/A
Features: Vltor VIS-2A-AK polylithic/free-float upper receiver assembly with 10-in. rail section and bolt assist, EMod w/ A5 enhancement kit (Enhanced Mod-stock) featuring

integral rubber buttpad, multiple sling attachments, and storage for up to eight AA-batteries or nine 3-volt lithium batteries. A5 receiver extension offers seven different stock placements, Geissele Hi-Speed National Match, DMR Trigger/Hammer Assembly, Bravo Company USA, Gunfighter Charging Handle (BCM-GFH-556-MOD4) designed by Vitor, TangoDown SCAR Rail Panels and BattleGrip (BG-16).
MSRP: **$2,495**

VWS PRAETORIAN

Action: semi-auto
Stock: VLTOR IMOD stock
Barrel: Noveske stainless steel
Sights: Diamondhead front and rear
Weight: N/A
Caliber: 5.56
Magazine: N/A
Features: LTOR lower receiver with oversized mag release and side saddle sling plate, VLTOR VIS extended mid-length monolithic upper with forward assist and KeyMod system, VLTOR seven position A5 receiver extension with VLTOR A5H2 5.3 oz. buffer with

VLtor Weapon Systems: VWS Praetorian

VLtor Weapon Systems: VWS-XVI Defender

VLtor Weapon Systems: VWS-XVI Warrior

rifle spring, Geiselle SSA trigger, VLTOR low-profile gas block with Nitride surface finish, TangoDown pistol grip, VLTOR/ Bravo Company Mod 4 Gunfighter charging handle, VLTOR VC-A2 flash hider, VLTOR castle nut and endplate, five-piece Picatinny rail section.

MSRP: . . . . **N/A**

VWS-XVI DEFENDER

Action: semi-auto
Stock: VLTOR IMOD stock
Barrel: 16-in.
Sights: Flip-up front and rear sights
Weight: N/A
Caliber: 5.56
Magazine: Two 30-round
Features: VLTOR lower receiver with oversized mag release and side saddle sling plate, VLTOR MUR-1A upper receiver with forward assist, VLTOR

Freedom Rail in 15-in. length with KeyMod system, VLTOR low-profile gas block, TangoDown pistol grip, VLTOR/ Bravo Company Mod 4 Gunfighter charging handle, VLTOR six-position A5 receiver extension with mil-spec rifle spring and VLTOR A5H2 buffer, VLTOR VC-A2 flash hider, VLTOR castle nut, and endplate.

MSRP: **$1,559**

VWS-XVI WARRIOR

Action: semi-auto
Stock: VLTOR EMOD stock
Barrel: Noveske chrome-lined barrel, 16-in.
Sights: Front and rear flip-up sights
Weight: N/A
Caliber: 5.56
Magazine: Two 30-round
Features: VLTOR lower receiver with oversized mag release and side saddle

sling plate, VLTOR VIS rifle-length monolithic upper with forward assist and KeyMod system, VLTOR seven-position A5 receiver extension with VLTOR A5H2 5.3 oz. buffer with rifle spring, Geiselle DMR trigger, VLTOR low profile gas block, TangoDown pistol grip, VLTOR/ Bravo Company Mod 4 Gunfighter charging handle, VLTOR VC-A2 flash hider, VLTOR castle nut and endplate.

MSRP: **$2,359**

WAR SPORT

LVOA-C

Action: semi-auto
Stock: B5 Systems Enhanced SOPMOD Bravo stock
Barrel: WS 14.7-in. (16.2-in. overall when pin and welded with comp), 1:8 RH QPQ Melonite
Sights: Magpul MBUS Pro front and rear sights
Weight: 8 lb.
Caliber: .223 Rem./5.56mm NATO
Chamber: .223 Wylde chamber
Magazine: 30 round
Features: Cerakote finish, forged 7075 aluminum upper and lower receiver,

War Sport: LVOA-C

War Sport: LVOA-S

War Sport: LVOA-SP

War Sport: GPR

War Sport rail, CMC 3.5lb single-stage flat trigger, War Sport Top Hat compensator, B.A.D. ambidextrous 50-degree safety selector, Norgon ambidextrous mag release, ambidextrous charging handle, War Sport flash drive with all manuals and warranty information. Ships in a hard case including a Hexmag 30-round magazine.
MSRP: **$3,050**

LVOA-S

Action: semi-auto
Stock: B5 Systems Enhanced SOPMOD Bravo stock
Barrel: WS 11.75-in., 1:8 RH QPQ Melonite
Sights: Magpul MBUS Pro front and rear sights
Weight: 7.5 lb.
Caliber: .223 Rem./5.56mm NATO
Chamber: .223 Wylde chamber
Magazine: 30 round
Features: Cerakote finish, forged 7075 aluminum upper and lower receiver,

War Sport rail, CMC 3.5 lb. single-stage flat trigger, War Sport Top Hat compensator, B.A.D. ambidextrous 50-degree safety selector, Norgon ambidextrous mag release, ambidextrous charging handle, War Sport flash drive with all manuals and warranty information. Ships in a hard case including a Hexmag 30-round magazine.
MSRP: **$3,050**

LVOA-SP

Action: semi-auto
Stock: Sig SB-15 brace
Barrel: WS 11.75-in., 1:8 RH QPQ Melonite
Sights: Magpul MBUS Pro front and rear sights
Weight: 7 lb.
Caliber: .223 Rem./5.56mm NATO
Chamber: .223 Wylde chamber
Magazine: 30 round
Features: Cerakote finish, forged 7075 aluminum upper and lower receiver, War Sport rail, CMC 3.5 lb. single-

stage flat trigger, War Sport Top Hat compensator, B.A.D. ambidextrous 50-degree safety selector, Norgon ambidextrous mag release, ambidextrous charging handle, War Sport flash drive with all manuals and warranty information. Ships in a hard case including a Hexmag 30-round magazine.
MSRP: **$3,050**

GPR

Action: semi-auto
Stock: B5 Systems SOPMOD Bravo stock
Barrel: WS 14.7-in. (16.2-in. overall when pin and welded with comp), 1:8 RH QPQ Melonite
Sights: Magpul MBUS rear sight, A2 front sight post
Weight: 6.5 lb.
Caliber: .223 Rem./5.56mm NATO
Chamber: .223 Wylde chamber
Magazine: 30 round
Features: Cerakote finish, forged 7075 aluminum upper and lower receiver,

War Sport: GPR-E

Wilson Combat: Paul Howe Tactical Carbine

Wilson Combat: Recon Tactical

Wilson Combat: SBR Tactical

B5 Systems mid-length handgaurd, ALG Defense trigger, War Sport GP compensator, B.A.D. ambidextrous 90-degree safety selector, Norgon ambidextrous mag release, ambidextrous charging handle, War Sport flash drive with all manuals and warranty information. Ships in a hard case including a Hexmag 30 round magazine.

MSRP: **$1,650**

GPR-E

Action: semi-auto
Stock: B5 Systems SOPMOD Bravo Stock
Barrel: WS 14.7-in. (16.2-in. overall when pin and welded with comp), 1:8 RH QPQ Melonite
Sights: Magpul MBUS Pro front and rear sights
Weight: 7.5 lb.
Caliber: .223 Rem./5.56mm NATO
Chamber: .223 Wylde chamber
Magazine: 30 round
Features: Cerakote finish, forged 7075 aluminum upper and lower receiver, War Sport rail, Geissele SSA trigger, War Sport GP compensator, B.A.D. ambidextrous 90-degree safety selector, Norgon ambidextrous mag release, ambidextrous charging

handle, War Sport flash drive with all manuals and warranty information. Ships in a hard case including a Hexmag 30-round magazine.

MSRP: **$2,250**

WILSON COMBAT

PAUL HOWE TACTICAL CARBINE

Action: semi-auto
Stock: Wilson/Rogers Super Stoc
Barrel: 14.7-in. + perm flash hider, 16.1-in. total
Sights: Daniel Defense fixed front
Weight: 6.25 lb.
Caliber: 5.56mm
Magazine: One 10-, 20-, and 30-round
Features: The Paul Howe Tactical Carbine is built from the thirty years of tactical experience that Retired Master Sergeant Paul Howe has learned as an operator and trainer in selecting his ultimate all-around tactical rifle.

MSRP: . . . . **N/A**

RECON TACTICAL

Action: semi-auto
Stock: Wilson/Rogers Super Stoc
Barrel: 16-in.
Sights: N/A
Weight: 7 lb.
Caliber: 5.56mm, 6.8 SPC, 300 BLK, 7.62x40 WT, .458 SOCOM
Magazine: One 10-, 20-, and 30-round
Features: The heart of every Recon Tactical is our Wilson Combat match-grade medium weight stainless steel barrel designed for accuracy and sustained high rates of fire. Loaded with Wilson Combat custom features and accessories, this popular model has never been better.

MSRP: . . . . **N/A**

SBR TACTICAL

Action: semi-auto
Stock: Wilson/Rogers Super Stoc
Barrel: 11.3-in.
Sights:
Weight: 6 lb. 5 oz.
Caliber: 5.56mm, 6.8 SPC, 300 BLK, 7.62x40 WT
Magazine: One 10-, 20-, and 30-round
Features: Tuned for reliability, the

Wilson Combat: Recon SR Tactical

Wilson Combat: Tactical Lightweight

Wilson Combat SBR (Short Barreled Rifle) Tactical is our smallest custom AR rifle. Highly portable, the SBR Tactical comes with the muzzle device of your choice.
MSRP: . . . . **N/A**

RECON SR TACTICAL

Action: semi-auto
Stock: Wilson/Rogers Super Stoc
Barrel: 14.7-in.
Sights: N/A
Weight: 6 lb. 10 oz.
Caliber: 5.56mm, 6.8 SPC, 300 BLK, 7.62x40 WT, .458 SOCOM
Magazine: One 10-, 20-, and 30-round
Features: The Recon SR (Suppressor Ready) is the ideal package for a tactical shooter who wants the shortest possible suppressed AR-15 rifle that isn't classified as an NFA registered weapon. The Recon SR has an extra long 14-in. TRIM rail for a seamless mating to our Whisper Suppressor and extra real estate for preferred rail mounted accessories. The Recon SR has a 14.7-in. medium weight barrel and features a permanently mounted Rapid Thread attachment that attaches to our Wilson Combat Whisper Suppressor. A permanently attached Accu-Tac flashider is available for

locales where owning a suppressor is not an option.
MSRP: . . . . **N/A**

TACTICAL LIGHTWEIGHT

Action: semi-auto
Stock: Wilson/Rogers Super Stoc
Barrel: 16-in. lightweight
Sights: N/A
Weight: 6 lb. 11 oz.
Caliber: 5.56mm, 6.8 SPC, 300 BLK, 7.62x40 WT, .458 SOCOM
Magazine: One 10-, 20-, and 30-round
Features: Designed to be the lightest possible multi-use tactical carbine in the Wilson Combat rifle family. Comes standard with a collapsible stock, ERGO pistol grip, free floated aluminum handguard and match-grade lightweight barrel.
MSRP: . . . . **N/A**

WINDHAM WEAPONRY

300 BLK RIFLE

Action: semi-auto, gas impingement system
Stock: Hogue 6-position telestock
Barrel: 16-in. medium profile. chrome-lined with Diamondhead "T" brake,

1:7 RH twist
Sights: None—ready for accessory sights, optics, scope
Weight: 6.95 lb.
Caliber: 300 BLK, 7.62x35mm
Magazine: One 30-round
Features: Diamondhead VRS-T 13.5-in. free-float fore-end, 2 Q.D sling swivels included, Hogue Beavertail pistol grip.
MSRP: **$1,680**

300 BLK SRC

Action: semi-auto, gas impingement system
Stock: 6-position telescoping buttstock with Windham Weaponry logo
Barrel: 16-in. heavy profile, chrome-lined with A2 flash suppressor, 1:7 RH twist
Sights: None—ready for accessory sights, optics, scope
Weight: 6.15 lb.
Caliber: 300 BLK, 7.62x35mm
Magazine: One 30 round
Features: M4 double heat shield handguards, A2 black plastic grip.
MSRP: **$1,056**

18-IN. .308 WITH FREE-FLOAT FORE-END

Action: semi-auto, gas impingement

system
Stock: 6-position telescoping buttstock with Windham Weaponry logo
Barrel: 18-in. fluted, chrome-lined with A2 flash suppressor, 1:10 RH twist
Sights: None—ready for optics or other type accessory sights
Weight: 8.05 lb.
Caliber: .308 Win., 7.62x51mm
Magazine: One 20-round Magpul PMAG
Features: Midwest KeyMod 15-in. handguard, Q.D. sling swivel, Hogue pistol grip.
MSRP: $1,708

16-IN. .308 WITH FREE-FLOAT FORE-END

Action: semi-auto, gas impingement system
Stock: 6-position telescoping buttstock with Windham Weaponry logo
Barrel: 16.5-in. medium profile, chrome-lined with A2 flash suppressor, 1:10 RH twist
Sights: None—ready for optics or other type accessory sights
Weight: 7.65 lb.
Caliber: .308 Win., 7.62x51mm
Magazine: One 20-round Magpul PMAG
Features: Midwest KeyMod 15-in. handguard, Q.D. sling swivel, Hogue pistol grip.
MSRP: $1,645

.308 SRC

Action: semi-auto, gas impingement system
Stock: 6-position telescoping buttstock with Windham Weaponry logo
Barrel: 16.5-in. medium profile, chrome-lined with A2 flash suppressor, 1:10 RH twist
Sights: None—ready for accessory sights, optics, scope
Weight: 7.55 lb.
Caliber: .308 Win., 7.62x51mm
Magazine: One 20-round Magpul PMAG
Features: Mid-length tapered shielded hand guards, Hogue overmolded pistol grip.

MSRP: $1,413

18-IN. .308 HUNTER WITH NUTMEG HARDWOOD STOCK/FORE-END

Action: semi-auto, gas impingement system
Stock: Nutmeg finish laminated hardwood, matching two-piece fore-end
Barrel: 18-in. fluted medium profile, chrome-lined w/ A2 flash suppressor/ 1:10 RH twist
Sights: None—ready for optics or other type accessory sights
Weight: 8.05 lb.
Caliber: .308 Win., 7.62x51mm
Magazine: One 5-round
Features: Receivers in hard coat Coyote Brown anodize finish, Q.D. sling swivel, Hogue overmolded pistol grip. Optional: 18-in. .308 Hunter with Pepper Hardwood stock, Model: R18FFTWS-1-308 Same features as immediately above but with Electroless Nickel Receiver finish and Pepper Hardwood stock/fore-end.
MSRP: $1,587

.308 TIMBERTEC CAMO SRC

Action: semi-auto, gas impingement system
Stock: 6-position telescoping buttstock with Timbertec camo finish
Barrel: 16.5-in. medium profile, chrome-lined with A2 flash suppressor, 1:10 RH twist
Sights: None—ready for accessory sights, optics, scope
Weight: 7.55 lb.
Caliber: .308 Win., 7.62x51mm
Magazine: One 20-round Magpul PMAG
Features: Mid-length tapered shielded Timbertec camo finish hand guards, stark pistol grip w/ Timbertec camo finish, receivers w/ Timbertec camo finish.
MSRP: $1,533

7.62X39MM SRC

Action: semi-auto, gas impingement

system
Stock: 6-position telescoping buttstock with Windham Weaponry logo
Barrel: 16-in., chrome-lined with A2 flash suppressor, 1:9 RH twist
Sights: None—ready for accessory sights, optics, scope
Weight: 6.15 lb.
Caliber: 7.62x39mm
Magazine: One 30-round
Features: M4 double heat shielded hand guards, A2 black plastic pistol grip.
MSRP: $1,056

VEX-SS WOOD STOCKED SERIES

Action: semi-auto, gas impingement system
Stock: Laminated Hardwood—Nutmeg Finish, matching fore-end
Barrel: 20-in. stainless steel—fluted—matte finish—w/ sling stud finish, 1:8 RH twist
Sights: None—ready for optics
Weight: 8.35 Lb.
Caliber: .223 Rem.
Magazine: One 5-round
Features: Receivers in hard coat Coyote Brown anodize finish, Hogue pistol grip. Optional: VEX-SS with Pepper Hardwood stock, Model: R20FSSFTWS-EN-1; Same features as immediately above but with Electroless nickel receiver finish and pepper hardwood stock/fore-end.
MSRP: $1,480

VEX-SS CAMO SERIES C1—SNOW CAMO

Action: semi-auto, gas impingement system
Stock: Solid A2 stock with sling swivel & snow camo coating
Barrel: 20-in. stainless steel—fluted—matte finish, 1:8 RH twist
Sights: None—ready for optics
Weight: 8.2 lb.
Caliber: .223 Rem.
Magazine: One 5-round
Features: Receivers, A2 pistol grip, knurled, vented aluminum free-float

fore-end all with Snow camo finish. Optional: VEX-SS with TrueTimber camo, Model: R20FSSFTWS-C6 same features as immediately above but with TrueTimber camo finish receivers, stock & free-float fore-end.

MSRP: $1,470

VEX-SS VARMINT EXTERMINATOR STANDARD MODEL

Action: semi-auto, gas impingement system
Stock: Skeleton stock with sling swivel
Barrel: 20-in. stainless steel—fluted—matte finish, 1:8 RH twist
Sights: None—ready for optics
Weight: 8.20 Lb.
Caliber: .223 Rem.
Magazine: One 5-round
Features: Knurled, vented aluminum free-float fore-end, Hogue overmolded pistol grip.

MSRP: $1,295

CDI

Action: semi-auto, gas impingement system
Stock: Magpul MOE 6-position telestock
Barrel: 16-in. M4 profile, chrome-lined with Vortex flash suppressor, 1:9 RH twist
Sights: Diamondhead dual aperture flip-up sight, Diamondhead front flip-up sight
Weight: 7.025 lb.
Caliber: .223 Rem., 5.56mm NATO
Magazine: One 30-round
Features: Diamondhead free-float fore-end w/ Magpul AFG angled grip, Magpul MOE black pistol grip w/ storage compartment.

MSRP: $1,680

DISSIPATOR M4

Action: semi-auto, gas impingement system
Stock: 6-position telescoping buttstock with Windham Weaponry logo
Barrel: 16-in. M4 profile, chrome-lined with A2 flash suppressor, 1:9 RH

twist
Sights: A4 detachable carry handle with A4 dual aperture elevation & windage adjustable: 300–600m, adjustable height square post in A2 standard base
Weight: 7.2 lb.
Caliber: .223 Rem., 5.56mm NATO
Magazine: One 30-round
Features: Rifle-length heat shielded hand guards, A2 black plastic grip, functional low-profile gas block under rifle-length hand guards gives rifle-length sight radius. Also: WW "Dissipator" Hvy Bbl, Model: R16DA4T, specs similar to above with heavy profile barrel.

MSRP: $1,192

MPC

Action: semi-auto, gas impingement system
Stock: 6-position telescoping buttstock with Windham Weaponry logo
Barrel: 16-in. M4 profile, chrome-lined with A2 flash suppressor, 1:9 RH twist
Sights: A4 detachable carry handle with A4 dual aperture elevation & windage adjustable: 300–600m, adjustable height square post in A2 standard base
Weight: 6.85 lb.
Caliber: .223 Rem., 5.56mm NATO
Magazine: One 30-round
Features: M4 double heat shielded hand guards, A2 black plastic grip. Also: WW "HBC" Hvy Bbl, Model: R16A4T, specs similar to above with heavy profile barrel.

MSRP: $1,086; heavy barrel version $1,096

SRC

Action: semi-auto, gas impingement system
Stock: 6-position telescoping buttstock with Windham Weaponry logo
Barrel: 16-in. M4 profile, chrome-lined with A2 flash suppressor, 1:9 RH twist
Sights: None—ready for accessory sights, optics
Weight: 6.3 lb.

Caliber: .223 Rem., 5.56mm NATO
Magazine: One 30-round
Features: M4 double heat shielded hand guards, A2 black plastic grip. Options: Timbertec camo SRC Model R16M4FTT-C3 /specs same as SRC above with TiberTec camo finish on fore-end, receivers, pistol grip, telestock; True Timber Snowfall camo SRC Model R16M4FTT-C2, specs same as SRC above with True Timber Snowfall camo finish on fore-end, receivers, pistol grip, telestock; Muddy Girl camo SRC, Model: R16M4FTT-C4, specs same as SRC above with Muddy Girl camo finish on fore-end, Receivers, pistol grip, telestock.

MSRP: . . . $1,040; Timbertec $1,160; True Timber $1,160; Muddy Girl $1,160

CARBON FIBER SRC

Action: semi-auto, gas impingement system
Stock: 6-position telescoping buttstock with Windham Weaponry logo
Barrel: 16-in. M4 profile, chrome-lined with A2 flash suppressor, 1:9 RH twist
Sights: None—ready for accessory sights, optics
Weight: 5.85 lb.
Caliber: .223 Rem., 5.56mm NATO
Magazine: One 30-round
Features: Receivers molded of carbon fiber composite, M4 double heat shielded handguards, A2 black plastic grip.

MSRP: $846

20-IN. GOV'T. TYPE RIFLE

Action: semi-auto, gas impingement system
Stock: A2 solid stock with trapdoor storage compartment
Barrel: 20-in. government A2 profile chrome-lined with A2 flash suppressor, 1:7 RH twist
Sights: Rear: A4 dual aperture elevation & windage adjustable—300–600m
Front: Adjustable height square post in A2 standard base

Weight: 7.7 lb.
Caliber: .223 Rem., 5.56mm NATO
Magazine: One 30-round
Features: A4 detachable carry handle on flat-top receiver, rifle-length fiberglass hand guards with heats hields, A2 black plastic grip.
MSRP: **$1,192**

WAY OF THE GUN PERFORMANCE CARBINE

Action: semi-auto, gas impingement system
Stock: Magpul MOE telescoping buttstock
Barrel: 20-in. government A2 profile, chrome-lined with A2 flash suppressor, 1:7 RH twist
Sights: None—ready for accessory sights or optics on upper rec. rail or fore-end rail
Weight: 6.3 lb.
Caliber: .223 Rem., 5.56mm NATO
Magazine: One 30-round
Features: Flat-top upper receiver w/ BCM charging handle & CMC trigger, Midwest Industries 15-in. free-float stainless steel KeyMod fore-end w/ BCM Gunfighter MOD2 pistol grip w/ storage compartment, receiver laser engraved with Way of the Gun logo, Frank Proctor "Way of the Gun" Instructional CD.
MSRP: **$1,795**

RP11SFS-7 PISTOL

Action: semi-auto, gas impingement system
Stock: AR pistol-type w/ foam sleeve & WW laser engraved logo
Barrel: 11.5-in. heavy profile, chrome-lined with A2 flash suppressor, 1:7 RH twist
Sights: Mil-spec 1913 rail ready for accessory sights/optics
Weight: 5.65 lb.
Caliber: .223 Rem., 5.56mm NATO
Magazine: One 30-round
Features: Midwest Industries 10-in. stainless steel KeyMod free-float w/ 2-in. rail segment. A2 black plastic grip.
MSRP: **$1,264**

300 BLK PISTOL

Action: semi-auto, gas impingement system
Stock: AR pistol type w/ foam sleeve & WW laser engraved logo—includes a Q.D. endplate and Q.D. sling swivel
Barrel: 9-in. heavy profile, chrome-lined with A2 flash suppressor, 1:7 RH twist
Sights: Mil-spec 1913 rail ready for accessory sights/optics
Weight: 4.85 lb.
Caliber: 300 BLK
Magazine: One 30-round

Features: 7.25-in. carbine free-float vented fore-end with Q.D. swivel stud, Hogue overmolded rubber pistol grip, Magpul enhanced trigger guard in lower, laser engraved caliber designation on upper receiver.
MSRP: **$1,160**

XTREME MACHINING

BASIC XR-15

Action: semi-auto
Stock: N/A
Barrel: 16.25-in., chromoly, cut-rifled, 1:7 twist,
Sights: Optional detachable front and rear adjustable iron sights; Picatinny rail for mounting scope/red dot sights
Weight: 7.5 lb.
Caliber: 5.56mm NATO
Magazine: One 30-round
Features: Two-stage trigger, 4.5 lb. pull, comes with extra magazine, locking front sling swivel, 1.25-in. nylon sling, detachable carry handle.
MSRP: . . . . **N/A**

ENHANCED XR-15

Action: semi-auto
Stock: Quad rail or vented tubular free-floating handguard, VLTOR Sniper Stock or Magpul PRS, adjustable for length of pull and cheekpiece height
Barrel: 24- or 26-in. 416 stainless steel, cut-rifled barrel with target

YHM (Yankee Hill Machine) Burnt Bronze Specter XL

The author on the range with the YHM Burnt Bronze Specter XL billet carbine.

When Yankee Hill Machine first came out with their Model 57 Specter designed AR, I was working as an editor at *Gun Digest* magazine. It was YHM's first billet carbine and another example of a company stepping out from the design limitations of the mil-spec world. I had to try one. When I called to request, the marketing rep on the other end suggested I hold tight for one they were building, a variation of the Model 57 that he felt would be really cool looking in the magazine.

When the rifle came, he was dead-on correct. I opened the box and in front of me was a beautiful Cerakoted

Burnt Bronze Specter XL carbine, the coloration and sharp lines of which challenged the usual "black" gun personality of the platform and threatened to convert those AR holdouts who claimed ARs were ugly and didn't compare to more traditional, wood-stocked firearms. This gun was a beauty. The burnt bronze coloration on the billet and slant-front nearly full-length handguard was enough to make it stand out from the crowd.

The rifle was machined from 7075-T6 aluminum and, along with the front slant handguard that hides the gas block (hence the Specter moniker), is a nice looking change of pace from standard ARs. It uses a carbine-length DI system and is chambered in 5.56 NATO, 6.8 SPC II, and 300 BLK. The YHM Specter Length SLR-Slant handguard provides accessory rails at twelve, three, six, and nine o'clock positions, but leaves most of the grip smooth for a comfortable hold. The exclusive ball-cut barrel is patterned so that even though material is removed to reduce its weight, it retains its strength. It also features the newly designed YHM Slant Series Muzzle Break to align visually and performance-wise with the handguard and EZ Pull take down pins.

On the range, with its upgraded features and two-stage trigger (5-pound pull), the rifle handles and shoots as beautifully as it looks, pulling surrounding shooters over to inquire what type of AR it was. It tips the scales at 7.76 pounds but handles as nimbly as a rifle beneath the 7-pound threshold. It's one model that black-model weary AR owners will definitely want to check out.

—*Doug Howlett*

Yankee Hill Machine: YHM-8820
5.56mm Black Diamond Specter XL

crown, 1:7 RH twist
Sights: Picatinny rail for mounting scope/red dot sights
Weight: 10.5 lb.
Caliber: .223 Rem.
Magazine: Two 30-round
Features: Single-stage or two-stage trigger, 2 lb. pull.
MSRP: **$1,650**

YANKEE HILL MACHINE

YHM-8820 5.56MM BLACK

DIAMOND SPECTER XL

Action: YHM low-profile gas block
Stock: Adjustable carbine stock
Barrel: 16-in. threaded & diamond fluted, chromoly vanadium, steel barrel, heat treated to RC 25–32, 1:9 or 1:7 twist
Sights: YHM Q.D.S. flip-front sight, YHM Q.D.S. flip-rear sight (YHM-5040)
Weight: 7.1 lb.
Caliber: 5.56
Magazine: One 30-round

Features: All mil-spec internal parts, mil-spec forged 7075-T6 aluminum YHM lower receiver and flat-top upper receiver, T-marked upper receiver, diamond fluting, mil-spec bolt carrier assembly, forward assist, YHM Phantom 5c2 flash hider/compensator, YHM Specter XL length diamond handguard.
MSRP: **$1,525**

YHM-8810 5.56MM BLACK DIAMOND SPECTER

Yankee Hill Machine: YHM-8810
5.56mm Black Diamond Specter

Action: YHM low-profile gas block
Stock: Adjustable carbine stock
Barrel: 16-in. threaded & diamond fluted, chromoly vanadium steel barrel, heat treated to RC 25–32, 1:9 or 1:7 twist
Sights: YHM same plane flip sights
Weight: 6.9 lb.
Caliber: 5.56mm
Magazine: One 30-round
Features: All mil-spec internal parts, mil-spec forged 7075-T6 aluminum YHM lower receiver and flat-top upper receiver, T-marked upper receiver, diamond fluting, mil-spec bolt carrier assembly, forward assist, YHH Phantom 5c2 flash hider/compensator, YHM Specter XL length diamond handguard.
MSRP: **$1,407**

YHM-8800 5.56MM BLACK DIAMOND CARBINE

Action: semi-auto
Stock: Adjustable carbine stock
Barrel: 16-in. threaded & diamond fluted, chromoly vanadium steel barrel, heat treated to RC 25–32, 1:9 or 1:7 twist
Sights: YHM same plane flip-front sight gas block mounted, YHM same plane flip-rear sight
Weight: 6.7 lb.
Caliber: 5.56mm
Magazine: One 30-round
Features: All mil-spec internal parts, mil-spec forged 7075-T6 aluminum YHM lower receiver and flat-top upper receiver, T-marked upper receiver, diamond fluting, mil-spec bolt carrier

assembly, forward assist, YHH Phantom 5c2 flash hider/compensator, YHM carbine-length diamond handguard.
MSRP: **$1,369**

YHM-8530 5.56MM S.L.R. SMOOTH SPECTER XL

Action: YHM low-profile gas block
Stock: Adjustable carbine stock
Barrel: 16-in. Threaded & Diamond Fluted, chromoly vanadium steel barrel, heat treated to RC 25–32, 1:9 or 1:7 twist
Sights: YHM Q.D.S. flip-front sight, YHM Q.D.S. flip-rear sight YHM-5040
Weight: 7.1 lb.
Caliber: 5.56mm
Magazine: One 30-round
Features: All mil-spec internal parts, mil-spec forged 7075-T6 aluminum YHM lower receiver and flat-top upper receiver, T-marked upper receiver, diamond fluting, mil-spec bolt carrier assembly, forward assist, YHM Phantom 5c2 flash hider/compensator, YHM Specter XL length lightweight handguard.
MSRP: **$1,725**

5.56MM S.L.R. SMOOTH SPECTER

Action: YHM low-profile gas block
Stock: Adjustable carbine stock
Barrel: 16-in. threaded & diamond fluted, chromoly vanadium steel barrel, heat treated to RC 25–32, 1:9

or 1:7 twist
Sights: YHM Q.D.S. flip-front sight, YHM Q.D.S. flip-rear sight YHM-5040
Weight: 6.9 lb.
Caliber: 5.56mm
Magazine: One 30-round
Features: All mil-spec internal parts, mil-spec forged 7075-T6 aluminum YHM lower receiver and flat-top upper receiver, T-marked upper receiver, diamond fluting, mil-spec bolt carrier assembly, forward assist, YHM Phantom 5c2 flash hider/compensator, YHM mid-length lightweight handguard.
MSRP: **$1,700**

5.56MM LIGHTWEIGHT CARBINE

Action: semi-auto
Stock: Adjustable carbine stock
Barrel: 16-in. threaded & diamond fluted, chromoly vanadium steel barrel, heat treated to RC 25–32, 1:9 or 1:7 twist
Sights: YHM flip rear sight, YHM flip-front sight tower
Weight: 6.7 lb.
Caliber: 5.56mm
Magazine: One 30-round
Features: All mil-spec internal parts, mil-spec forged 7075-T6 aluminum YHM lower receiver and flat-top upper receiver, T-marked upper receiver, diamond fluting, mil-spec bolt carrier assembly, forward assist, YHH Phantom 5c2 flash hider/compensator, YHM carbine-length lightweight

Yankee Hill Machine: YHM-8830
5.56mm Black Diamond Rifle

Yankee Hill Machine: YHM-8600
5.56mm Entry Level Rifle

handguard, YHM forearm endcap.
MSRP: **$1,361**

YHM-8200 5.56MM SMOOTH CARBINE

Action: semi-auto
Stock: Adjustable carbine stock
Barrel: 16-in. threaded & diamond fluted, chromoly vanadium steel barrel, heat treated to RC 25–32, 1:9 or 1:7 twist
Sights: YHM same plane flip-rear sight, YHM barrel mounted front flip-front tower
Weight: 6.4 lb.
Caliber: 5.56mm
Magazine: One 30-round
Features: All mil-spec internal parts, mil-spec forged 7075-T6 aluminum YHM lower receiver and flat-top upper receiver, T-marked upper receiver, diamond fluting, mil-spec bolt carrier assembly, forward assist, YHM Phantom 5c2 flash hider/compensator, YHM Extended carbine-length smooth handguard.
MSRP: **$1,472**

5.56MM CUSTOMIZABLE CARBINE

Action: semi-auto
Stock: Adjustable carbine stock barrel: 16-in. chromoly vanadium steel barrel, heat treated to RC 25–32, 1:9 or 1:7 twist
Sights: YHM flip-rear sight, YHM flip-front sight tower
Weight: 6.3 lb.
Caliber: 5.56mm
Magazine: N/A
Features: All mil-spec internal parts, mil-spec forged 7075-T6 aluminum YHM lower receiver and flat-top upper receiver, T-marked upper receiver, diamond fluting, mil-spec bolt carrier assembly, forward assist, YHH Phantom 5c2 flash hider/compensator, YHM carbine-length customizable handguard, YHM forearm endcap.
MSRP: **$1,366**

5.56MM ENTRY LEVEL CARBINE

Action: semi-auto
Stock: Adjustable carbine stock
Barrel: 16-in. chromoly vanadium steel barrel, heat treated to RC 25–32, 1:9 or 1:7 twist
Sights: None
Weight: 6.4 lb.
Caliber: 5.56mm
Magazine: N/A

Features: All mil-spec internal parts, mil-spec forged 7075-T6 aluminum YHM lower receiver and flat-top upper receiver, T-marked upper receiver, diamond fluting, mil-spec bolt carrier assembly, forward assist, YHH Phantom flash hider, YHM carbine-length handguard, YHM single rail gas block.
MSRP: **$1,186**

YHM-8830 5.56MM BLACK DIAMOND RIFLE

Action: semi-auto
Stock: A2 stock
Barrel: 20-in. threaded & diamond fluted, chromoly vanadium steel barrel, heat treated to RC 25–32, 1:9 or 1:7 twist
Sights: None
Weight: 6.4 lb.
Caliber: 5.56mm
Magazine: One 30-round
Features: All mil-spec internal parts, mil-spec forged 7075-T6 aluminum YHM lower receiver and flat-top upper receiver, T-marked upper receiver, diamond fluting, mil-spec bolt carrier assembly, forward assist, YHM Phantom flash hider, YHM rifle-length Black Diamond handguard, YHM

Yankee Hill Machine: YHM-8800-68
6.8 SPC II Black Diamond Carbine

Yankee Hill Machine: YHM-8200-68
6.8 SPC II Smooth Carbine

single rail gas block, two YHM mini scope risers.

MSRP: **$1,445**

YHM-8600 5.56MM ENTRY LEVEL RIFLE

Action: semi-auto
Stock: A2 stock
Barrel: 20-in. chromoly vanadium steel barrel, heat treated to RC 25–32, 1:9 or 1:7 twist
Sights: None
Weight: 6.6 lb.
Caliber: 5.56mm
Magazine: One 30-round
Features: All mil-spec internal parts, mil-spec forged 7075-T6 aluminum YHM lower receiver and flat-top upper receiver, T-marked upper receiver, mil-spec bolt carrier, assembly, forward assist, YHM rifle-length free-float tube lightweight handguard, YHM railed gas block, two YHM mini risers.

MSRP: **$1,311**

YHM-8830-68 6.8 SPC II BLACK DIAMOND

SPECTER XL RIFLE

Action: semi-auto
Stock: A2 Trapdoor stock
Barrel: 20-in. diamond fluted, chromoly vanadium steel barrel, heat treated to RC 25–32, 1:10 twist
Sights: None
Weight: 6.4 lb.
Caliber: 6.8mm SPC II
Magazine: One 30-round
Features: All mil-spec internal parts, mil-spec forged 7075-T6 aluminum YHM lower receiver and flat-top upper receiver, T-marked upper receiver, diamond fluting, mil-spec bolt carrier assembly, forward assist, YHM Rifle length Black Diamond handguard, YHM railed gas block.

MSRP: **$1,498**

YHM-8800-68 6.8 SPC II BLACK DIAMOND CARBINE

Action: semi-auto
Stock: Adjustable carbine stock
Barrel: 16-in. threaded & diamond fluted, chromoly vanadium steel

barrel, heat treated to RC 25–32, 1:10 twist
Sights: YHM same plane flip sights
Weight: 6.4 lb.
Caliber: 6.8 SPC II
Magazine: One 30-round
Features: All mil-spec internal parts, mil-spec forged 7075-T6 aluminum YHM lower receiver and flat-top upper receiver, T-marked upper receiver, diamond fluting, mil-spec bolt carrier assembly, forward assist, YHM .30-cal 5C2 flash hider/compensator, YHM carbine-length Black Diamond handguard.

MSRP: **$1,579**

YHM-8200-68 6.8 SPC II SMOOTH CARBINE

Action: semi-auto
Stock: Adjustable carbine stock
Barrel: 16-in. threaded & diamond fluted, chromoly vanadium steel barrel, heat treated to RC 25–32, 1:10 twist
Sights: YHM barrel mounted flip-front sight tower, YHM flip-rear sight
Weight: 6.4 lb.
Caliber: 6.8 SPC II

Magazine: One 30-round
Features: All mil-spec internal parts, mil-spec forged 7075-T6 aluminum YHM lower receiver and flat-top upper receiver, T-marked upper receiver, diamond fluting, mil-spec bolt carrier assembly, forward assist, YHM .30-cal 5C2 flash hider/compensator, YHM Extended carbine-length Smooth handguard.
MSRP: $1,525

YHM-8600-68 6.8 SPC II ENTRY LEVEL RIFLE

Action: semi-auto
Stock: A2 stock
Barrel: 20-in. chromoly vanadium steel barrel, heat treated to RC 25–32, 1:10 twist
Sights: None
Weight: 6.6 lb.
Caliber: 6.8 SPC II
Magazine: One 30-round
Features: All mil-spec internal parts, mil-spec forged 7075-T6 aluminum YHM lower receiver and flat-top upper receiver, T-marked upper receiver, mil-spec bolt carrier assembly, forward assist, YHM rifle-length smooth handguard, single-rail gas block, two YHM mini scope risers.
MSRP: $1,354

YHM-8820-300 300 BLK BLACK DIAMOND SPECTER XL

Action: semi-auto
Stock: Adjustable carbine stock
Barrel: 16-in. threaded & diamond fluted, chromoly vanadium steel barrel, heat treated to RC 25–32, 1:9 twist
Sights: YHM same plane flip-front sight, YHM Q.D.S. flip-rear sight YHM-5040
Weight: 6.9 lb.
Caliber: 300 BLK
Magazine: One 30-round
Features: All mil-spec internal parts, mil-spec forged 7075-T6 aluminum YHM lower receiver and flat-top upper receiver, T-marked upper receiver, diamond fluting, 300 BLK bolt carrier assembly, forward assist, YHM .30Cal 5C2 flash hider/

compensator, YHM Specter XL length Black Diamond handguard, low-profile gas block.
MSRP: $1,579

300 BLK S.L.R. SMOOTH SPECTER XL

Action: semi-auto
Stock: Adjustable carbine stock
Barrel: 16-in. threaded & diamond fluted, chromoly vanadium steel barrel, heat treated to RC 25–32, 1:9 twist
Sights: YHM Q.D.S. flip-up sights YHM-5040
Weight: 7.1 lb.
Caliber: 300 BLK
Magazine: One 30-round
Features: All mil-spec internal parts, mil-spec forged 7075-T6 aluminum YHM lower receiver and flat-top upper receiver, T-marked upper receiver, diamond fluting, 300 BLK bolt carrier assembly, forward assist, YHM .30 cal. 5C2 flash hider/compensator, YHM Specter length S.L.R. smooth handguard, YHM low-profile gas block.
MSRP: $1,806

HRC-200 YHM HUNT READY RIFLE CAMOUFLAGE

Action: semi-auto
Stock: A2 trapdoor buttstock
Barrel: 20-in. fluted barrel with low-profile gas block on rifle-gas system
Sights: Bushnell 3x9x40 sighted at 100 yards Realtree Ap
Weight: 6.6
Caliber: 5.56mm, 6.8mm
Magazine: One 5-round
Features: Mil-spec forged 7075-T6 aluminum YHM lower receiver and flat-top upper receiver, mil-spec bolt carrier assembly, forward assist, Grovtec Realtree AP sling, Realtree AP Bushnell Banner 3-9X40mm scope with Circle-X reticule, YHM AR-Tall scope rings, two 3-in. modular rails for mounting accessories to the rifle-length hand guard, available in an all-black model as well.
MSRP: . . . . **5.56mm Hunt Ready Camouflage Rifle. 1:7 or 1:9 $1,563; 6.8 SPC II Hunt Ready Camouflage**

Rifle 1:10 $1,605

HRC-160 YHM HUNT READY CARBINES

Action: semi-auto
Stock: 6-position collapsible stock
Barrel: 16-in. threaded and fluted barrel with low-profile gas block
Sights: Bushnell 3-9x40 Sighted at 100 yards Realtree Ap
Weight: 6.6
Caliber: 5.56mm, 6.8mm, 300 BLK
Magazine: One 5-round
Features: Mil-spec forged 7075-T6 aluminum YHM lower receiver and flat-top upper receiver, mil-spec bolt carrier assembly, forward assist, Grovtec Realtree AP sling, Realtree AP Bushnell Banner 3-9X40mm scope with Circle-X reticule, YHM AR-Tall scope rings, two 3-in. modular rails for mounting accessories to the handguard, available in an all-black model as well.
MSRP: . . . . **5.56mm Hunt Ready Camouflage Rifle. 1:7 or 1:9 $1,531; 6.8 SPC II Hunt Ready Camouflage Rifle 1:10 $1,584; 300 BLK Hunt Ready Camouflage 1:8 $1,584**

TODD JARRETT COMPETITION SERIES

Action: semi-auto
Stock: Ace carbine stock
Barrel: 16-in. Threaded & Diamond Fluted, chromoly vanadium steel barrel, heat treated to RC 25–32, chrome-lined
Sights: YHM Q.D.S. flip-front sight, YHM Q.D.S. flip-rear sight hooded YHM-5040-H
Weight: N/A
Caliber: 5.56, 6.8 SPC II, 300 BLK
Magazine: One 30-round
Features: All mil-spec internal parts, mil-spec forged 7075-T6 aluminum YHM lower receiver, mil-spec forged 7075-T6 aluminum YHM flat-top upper receiver, T-marked upper receiver, YHM Phantom 5C2 flash hider/compensator, YHM low-profile gas block, Command Arms ergonomic grip, mil-spec bolt carrier assembly, forward assist. Available in rifle-, mid-, and carbine-length hand guard.
MSRP: $2,007

5. D-I-Y Rifles

ORDERING A CUSTOM RIFLE

From ordering a custom-built gun to your exact speci-fications to buying the parts and building one from the ground up in your garage, one of the things that makes the AR such an incredible weapon system is the ability to customize it any way you like. Very few of the 90-plus parts cannot be changed out for a customized part. In fact, where the traditional gun market seems to be dominated by large scale firearms manufacturers with custom gun makers in the minority and on the extreme high-end of cost, the AR market, while there are plenty of mainline and off-the-shelf models available (as evidenced in the previous chapter), custom gun makers are abundant. Why? Because the modularity of the AR lends itself so well for small builders

to produce high-performing rifles and compete with the big boys.

Wilson Combat, not exactly a "small" company, but one renowned for building quality combat-inspired firearms—both production and custom, as well as best-in-class aftermarket accessories—has a really nice "Custom AR Rifle Builder" program in which buyers fill out the form on the Wilson website dictat-ing exactly what they want in a rifle. Then, Wilson Combat builds it to those specs. What's better is the personal attention they deliver to the build. Wilson Combat will contact you and walk you through the build, but it's important to understand what you want beforehand. Their process is refined, yet still fairly rep-resentative of the considerations you would need to make when ordering a custom rifle from any builder.

KEY CONSIDERATIONS

The very first thing you'll need to do is figure out what you're going to be using the rifle for, and what your needs are. Is it going to be for home and/or personal defense? If yes, this means it may need to be used in tight quarters, with shots being at close range. You won't convince a judge and jury it was self-defense if you shot someone from the middle of an alfalfa field from 375 yards away. Other uses include but aren't limited to competition, hunting, or perhaps just something to plink with at the range.

⌃ Before having a rifle custom built, first determine if it shall be used for hunting (above), high-volume target shooting (right), or some other purpose.

You will also want to decide on a caliber. This will be dictated primarily by what kind of role it is going to fill. The most common caliber of course for a traditional AR is the 5.56/.223 Rem. Since most people don't decide to get their feet wet in the world of ARs by getting a custom gun, odds are you probably already own an AR, and statistically speaking, there's a good chance it's a 5.56/.223 Rem. There's more 5.56 ammo on the market than any other rifle caliber, so it's easy to find and almost always readily available. A third option to the .223 Rem. and 5.56 NATO, is a rifle chambered in .223 Wylde, which allows the rifle to shoot both 5.56 and .223 Rem., including cartridges with the long 80-grain bullets. Other AR caliber options include .204 Ruger, 6.8 SPC, .300 Blackout, 6.5 Grendel, .458 SOCOM, .450 Bushmaster, plus dozens more. If you're looking for a large-frame AR, then the .308 Winchester is a great choice. There are even ARs now chambered

in 7.62x39 Soviet, though I don't see that one being offered in a custom rifle.

Another big decision will be the barrel. Aside from the caliber, you'll need to determine barrel material composition, what length you want, the twist rate, gas length and barrel profile. The two predominant barrel materials used are Chromoly and Stainless Steel. Chromoly is what the military uses and is great for most applications. Stainless makes for a better barrel—in durability and accuracy—but is more expensive. Most custom guns will be stainless. Barrel length is going to determine accuracy at distance. Longer barrels are going to be more accurate at longer ranges—such as competitive shooting and varmint hunting—and shorter barrels will be more maneuverable. Eighteen-inch to 20-inch barrels are considered full-length rifles, while 16-inch barrels are carbine length for civilians. Barrels that are 14.5, 12.5 and 10.5 inches are for

Short Barreled Rifles and require an NFA stamp to own unless converted to a pistol.

Twist rate is going to largely determine the size of the bullet that you're going to be able to shoot. The three most common rates are 1:7 (fastest twist), 1:8, and 1:9 (slowest). The faster the twist rate the more the bullet will be stabilized during flight, and the heavier the bullet that can be stabilized. Using a 1:7 twist can stabilize a 55-grain bullet and one that's 70 grains plus. Whereas a 1:9 twist rate is best used for 55 grain bullets. Some people using it for self-defense applications prefer a slower twist rate because the bullet is less stable in flight and will cause the bullet to tumble upon impact. 18 and 20 inch barrels will have a rifle-length gas system, as the AR system was originally intended. Barrels that are 10.5 inches and 12.5 inches will have a carbine-length system. Barrels that are 14.5 inches and 16 inches can have either carbine or mid-length gas systems. If given the choice, there aren't many benefits to choosing the carbine-length gas system over the mid-length. The mid-length gas system is easier on the parts and smoother shooting.

The last part to the barrel equation is fluted or non-fluted. Fluted barrels offer less weight and faster heat dissipation. Fluted barrels also offer less weight in your wallet and faster money dissipation—they are more expensive.

The next part of the custom build is the type of rail and rail length. Wilson Combat offers 7.3-, 9.3-, 10.4-, 12.6-, and 13.8-inch rails. Aside from the obvious route of putting a carbine-length rail on a carbine, mid length on a mid-length gas system, and rifle length on a rifle, you can put just about any length rail on whichever length of rifle that you have. The key, however, is that at a minimum the rail needs to be as long as the gas system. But, if you want to put a rifle length rail on a carbine, go for it. That's becoming more common now, for a couple of reasons—first, people want as much rail space as they can get in order to attach accessories without affecting their grip, and second, shooters want to be able to grab as far forward as possible with their weak-side hand, for better stability and control when firing.

The trigger unit is also an important consideration. Mil-spec triggers, good enough for the Marines and other U.S. military forces, are a fine choice when building your rifle, though the smooth feel of a high-end trigger makes shooting that much sweeter. When making a determination on what kind of trigger to put in your custom gun, it's important to again look at what you're going to use it for. If you're using it for home defense you don't want to put a 2-pound match trigger on it, for safety reasons. A light trigger in a controlled environment is fine, but a self-defense situation is the opposite of a controlled situation. A great option for home/self defense is a tactical trigger. Tactical triggers are generally going to have a little heavier pull than a match trigger, but it has a quick reset for fast follow-

⌃ Fiberglass or polymer fore-end are comfortable to hold and lightweight, making a hunting AR more comfortable to carry and shoot. But with no points to add accessories, it will be a poor choice for someone who wishes to add a light, vertical grip or other tactical item.

⌃ Mil-spec triggers, good enough for the Marines and other U.S. military forces, are a fine choice when building your rifle, though the smooth feel of a high-end trigger makes shooting that much sweeter.

up shots. Somewhere in the middle is the 3Gun trigger, which is a balance of the two—light enough for good accuracy, yet with a fast reset. Velocity Triggers (velocitytriggers.com) makes easy-to-drop-in trigger assemblies expressly for AR rifles that perform great and are very reasonably priced, while Timney Triggers are legendary for their aftermarket performance.

Another key consideration is determining the type of receivers—upper and lower—that you want. There are two different types: billet or forged. Billet has been machined, whereas forged is smashed into shape while it's hot. Forged receivers are the most common, are the cheapest to produce, and for a long time thought of as being stronger. They're also mil-spec. Billet receivers are more expensive, but more pleasing to the eye. They can be made just as strong as forged receivers by adding thickness. In reality, the strength issue of forged vs. billet has been overhyped. Back in the day some of the first billet receivers that hit the market were terribly flawed, which gave billet a bad name and tainted them for many. In truth, a receiver doesn't need to be indestructible, evidence of this is in the polymer receivers now on the market. Choosing which type of receiver you want will usually determine which manufacturer you go with, as most do one or the other. Choosing one company over another will dictate the other customization you can do.

Once you figure out what you want, ordering a custom AR is a cinch. Custom gunmakers generally have phone-in customer service that will walk you through the order, and some have forms on their website that you print, fill out and send in. Whichever way you go, it's easy, and even if you're new to ARs, most companies that build custom guns offer plenty of help and assistance. The AR that you receive is going to surprise you with performance—I would put my Wilson Combat up against any bolt-action rifle. Aside from that, there is also a pride in ownership that you don't get from off-the-shelf ARs, but can only be attained from providing the input when ordering a custom AR, or from building your own.

BUILD YOUR OWN

Because no other firearm offers the versatility and component availability of the AR platform, it is the perfect gun for the true do-it-yourselfer to construct in his or her own home. Best of all, with the simplicity of the gun's design and the availability of resources to help guide your efforts, you don't need a gunsmith's understanding of firearms to pull off your own build.

To simplify matters, do-it-yourselfers can buy everything they need in a single kit, or they can buy a completed lower receiver and assemble the upper along with the rest of the rifle or buy a completed upper and build the lower. They even have the option of buying a completed lower and upper and simply dressing them up with the furniture and accessories they prefer by putting them together. Remember, even when building an AR from scratch, the lower receiver housing still must be purchased through a licensed gun dealer. If purchasing the lower over the internet or through a mail-order supplier, it will have to be shipped to a dealer in your area who can handle the paperwork and legally transfer the lower into your possession. Most FFLs holders will perform this service for as little as $25 to $40 depending on where you live to cover the costs the dealer incurs by issuing the background check and filing the papers.

Like everything else there is to know or discuss about these rifles, there is no shortage of resources, either online or available for purchase, to guide the do-it-yourselfer in his project. Brownell's (www.brownells.com), one of the nation's most recognized suppliers of gunsmithing tools and gun parts, has a number of resources such as free online step-by-step videos, a parts checklist and even their patent-pending AR-15 Builder (www.ar15builder.com). AR15.com also has

≫ The versatility and component availability of the AR platform make it the perfect gun for the true do-it-yourselfer.

⩘ AR-15s are actually easy guns to build with the right tools, parts, and instruction.

a tool that allows you to select the parts needed for a build in their online tool Gunstruction (http: /www. ar15.com/gunstruction).

Regarding Brownell's AR-15 Builder, the site allows a user to shop and select the various parts of the rifle they want and then drag each item onto a mock-up panel that lets them see what the gun will actually look like. Log-in (it's free) and you can save the online build and use it as a checklist or wish list for when you're ready to start buying the parts for your gun. Complete linked information on each product, along with current pricing, allows the amateur gun builders to easily select exactly what they want and keep the overall project within their budgets. Even if you have no plans of building an AR anytime soon, it's a fun tool to play with and begin building your dreams if nothing else!

"Think it. Build it. That's our theme," said former Brownell's public relations manager Larry Weeks soon after the tool was created. "Tools like the AR Builder let you assemble a gun through pictures first to determine exactly what you need and make sure it is within your budget." Weeks, who says he is no expert tech on ARs or any other type of gun for that matter, has built a number of ARs of his own.

"And I've made just about every mistake there is to make in the process," he laughs. "But the truth is, ARs are really easy to build and if a person does run into a problem putting theirs together, they can simply call one of our gun techs on the phone. They can usually walk the person through the problem."

Lou Correa, a former sailor in the U.S. Navy who currently works as a member of the sales team at Bob's Gun Shop (bobsgunshop.com) in Norfolk, Virginia, didn't get into AR rifles until he began competing in 3Gun competitions back around 2004.

"An AR is the ideal gun to have in 3Gun. That's what got me interested. I saw from other guys I was competing against how easy it was to put one together, so I decided to try it myself," Correa says. The AR's modular system is what makes it so simple to work on. Parts are standardized, so an amateur builder has countless options from different companies to choose from, meaning a person can get something made from the type of materials and in the price point they want or can afford.

"There are really very few parts that go into making it," he says. "If you wanted to make a 1911, there are four or five times as many parts." When Correa started his own build, he could have turned to the gunsmiths he worked with for guidance, but instead, he found all the information he needed on a website called AR15. com (noted earlier in this chapter)—a site that has steadily grown from a simple mail list back in 1994 to a full-blown online phenomenon among AR and other modern sporting rifle enthusiasts today.

AR15.com and Additional Resources

"AR15.com provides blow-by-blow directions right there on their site," says Correa. "That's the easiest way to do it." In fact, it has been the way to do it for

⩘ Resources abound for the do-it-yourselfers, from manuals and books to websites such as brownells.com or AR15.com.

a number of people. Since Correa first did his builds, AR15.com has come out with their Gunstruction tool, which helps make the process even easier.

Edward Avila, who owns AR15.com with his brothers Juan and Jorge, left the Army in the early 1990s and was looking for information on ARs but couldn't find it. He had used the guns in the military and being familiar with them, wanted to keep shooting them as a reservist and then as a civilian. Absent any readily available information and with the internet as a tool of the masses still in its infancy, Avila decided to begin a site to gather and share the information that he hadn't been able to find anywhere else.

Online forums as we know them had yet to evolve, so the site had its genesis as a mailing list where people would sign up to receive information. When members of the list group had a question or wanted to share something they had found or learned, they emailed it out to everybody else on the list.

"Over time, we began to identify some key experts on the list. Anytime somebody had a question, these same guys would almost always have an answer. We realized there were some very knowledgeable guys out there," Avila says. "The more valuable the information that got shared, the more it attracted an increasing number of readers." Sometime around 1996 or 1997, as websites became more common and more and more people went online, AR15.com migrated to a regular website where the information on the mailing list could be shared on a forum. That format provides the backbone of AR-15.com's wealth in resources

⌃ The AR lower is the one part regulated by the ATF and includes the serial number used for their records.

today. Whether a person is just learning about ARs and has a general question, already has one but is seeking information about an accessory or certain model, or needs help or insight on calibers, specific loads, building problems or anything else, it can be found in the easily categorized forums of the site. Aside from ARs, there are also sections or threads dedicated to information on AKs, FALs, pistols, training, competitions and the outdoors. But ARs remain the backbone.

"Everyone wants to have what the military is using and the military continues to use the AR because it is such an adaptable platform," Avila says. "The AR-15 remains the hot platform over all others." The site averages 3 million hits a day (yes, a day) and at any given time, there are anywhere from 4,000 to more than 5,000 people logged onto the site. The AR15.com name has become so recognizable among serious fans of the rifle that the company began actually selling AR parts and accessories—first from other companies and then under the AR15.com brand as well. Since around 2011, the company has been selling AR15. com branded complete billet lowers based on a design Magpul came out with several years before as a short-run special for the website.

In addition to the resources available on AR15.com or Brownells.com (the gun parts supplier also has a complete printable checklist of the items needed to build your rifle), companies such as Midway U.S.A., another large mail-order and online parts supplier, offers step-by-step instructions on building an upper receiver including required tools and parts. The company's online GunTec Dictionary can also be helpful with providing the meaning to general firearms terms that you may need to understand as you read over rifle-building directions. In that vein, the NRA Firearms Sourcebook is a reference no gunowner should be without, whether they ever plan on building their own rifle or not.

There are two other great books for understanding the details, operation, care and construction of the AR rifle. The first is The AR-15 Complete Owner's Guide by Walt Kuleck with Scott Duff and the second is Kuleck's follow-up book, The AR-15 Complete Assembly Guide, which he wrote with Clint McKee. The books were initially published in 2000 and 2002, respectively, at the height of the Clinton Assault Weapons Ban. So some thoughts on the outlook and future of tactical arms in civilian hands were much bleaker than what has actually transpired. But the detail the authors go into and abundant photographs illustrating every step in assembling and understanding the function of an AR remains spot on and as relevant as ever—even with the technological advancements in production and materials over the past decade. The essential AR remains the same.

Necessary Tools

Depending on the level of build you expect to put into creating your AR, there are a number of tools you will need, many of them that you probably already own.

"You can do virtually anything on the gun with less than perfect tools," says Weeks. Brownells AR-15/M16 Critical Tool Kit has most of the AR essential tools that a builder might need, but likely won't have in their tool box at home. The kit includes a .223 armorer's wrench for tightening or removing barrels from the upper receiver, a lower receiver vice block that clamps the lower into a vice when working on it and protects the lower from damage, an action block for holding the upper receiver in a vice without damage, a pivot pin detent depressor for installing the spring loaded

detent to remove the pivot pin free of the upper, a pivot pin detent installation tool and a bolt catch pin punch designed to remove the bolt catch pivot pin. Additional gunsmithing tools that may be helpful include a pin block for removing a front site, a handguard removal tool if using delta rings to hold the handguards in place and a headspace gauge, also known as a go-no go gauge, to ensure the headspace is correct from inside the chamber to the face of the bolt.

"A lot of guys will build the lower themselves, because it doesn't require as many special tools," says Avila. "Upper receivers take more work and need more tools." He says for a guy who plans on building only one AR, it probably isn't very cost effective when compared to buying pre-built uppers and lowers. However, for the guy who anticipates making changes and upgrades through the years, it can be well worth the investment.

⌃ An armorer's wrench is an essential tool for removing or installing AR barrels.

A checklist of tools Brownell's recommends for the repair and assembly of ARs follows:

__Ballpeen Hammer
__Nylon/Brass Hammer
__Bit Driver Screwdriver
__Torx Bit Set
__Hex Bit Set
__Flat Head Bits
__Philips Head Bits
__Needle Nose Pliers
__Upper Receiver Vise Block
__Lower Receiver Vise Block
__Rifle Bench Block
__Bench Mat
__Bench Vise
__Padded Vice Jaws
__Roll Pin Holders (Numbers 1, 2, 3 & 4)
__Roll Pin Punches (Numbers 1, 2, 3 & 4)

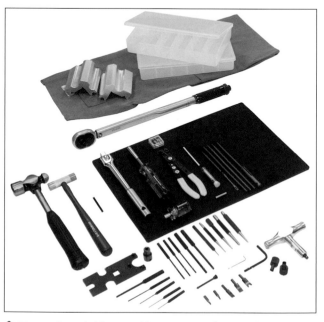

⌃ Many tools needed for assembling your own rifle are probably already around your home.

__Armorer's Wrench
__Handguard Removal Tool
__Buttstock Tool for collapsible stocks only

Barrel Specific Tools Include:
__½-inch drive Torque Wrench
__3/32-inch Taper Starter Punch
__1/8-inch Flat Punch
__Staking Punch
__Sight Adjustment Tool (for A-1/A-2 style sights)
__Gas Tube Alignment Pin
__Snap Ring Pliers
__Breaker Bar
__Strap Wrench

Upper Receiver Specific Tools
__Headspace Gauge
__Rear Sight Elevation Tool
__Sight Adjustment Tool
__Ejector Removal Tool

Lower Receiver Specific Tools
__Punch for trigger installation
__Pivot Pin Detent Installation Tool
__Bolt Catch Pin Punch
__AR-15 Hammer Trigger Jig
__Hammer Trigger Drop Block

Crucial Considerations

Many of the tools listed above may already be in your tool box. For others you may be able to just wing it. (Who hasn't made due with the wrong tool in lieu of making that extra trip to Lowe's or Home Depot. Besides, isn't necessity the mother of invention?) However, there are a number of required tools that are an absolute must to do the job without destroying the various parts of the rifle. Obviously, the cost of such items can add up quickly to more than several hundred dollars or more, depending on what you already have and don't have. So if you're looking to build a single rifle in order to save money, you may want to keep that in mind and factor that into to the total cost of the build.

In fact, tools notwithstanding, the cost of the individual parts of a gun that you plan to build can eas-

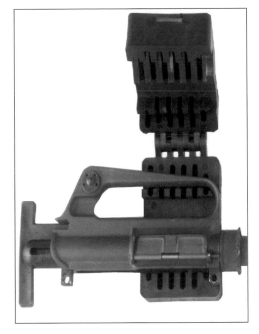

⌃ An action block (left) works as a vice to hold receivers for gunsmithing and construction purposes.

ily exceed the cost of some base model ARs on the market.

"At the time (I built my AR), it was cheaper to build one than to buy one," says Correa. But now, that's not necessarily the case, even with the surge in AR sales witnessed following the 2008 election of Barack Obama as president and his subsequent re-election in 2012. Fears that he would lead an anti-gun charge inspired those surges in sales, which ultimately drove the cost of an average AR up significantly. But with

⌃ Want to build a gun, but need a little personal help? Partner up with a local gunsmith and see what he will charge to do some of the work.

no significant gun control legislation ever developing, combined with an oversaturation of product availability in response to the spikes in sales, prices leveled off overall in 2014-15 and even at the time of this book's writing, many models could be had for under $1,000, some well under $1,000 in the $500 to $700 range. With another presidential election looming in 2016 and the very real threat that Hillary Clinton—who has said she will make gun control legislation a part of her platform—the industry could see sales of the guns surge to unprecedented numbers by the end of the year.

Looking at several random variations of completed uppers, lowers, collapsible buttstocks, iron sights and magazines at the lower end of the price spectrum can still run you close to $1,000. Conversely, if you go completely top shelf, parts to build your own gun and accessorize it can quickly soar above the $2,000 mark, right at the price point of some high-quality complete AR packages. So cost shouldn't be the only motivator for building a rifle.

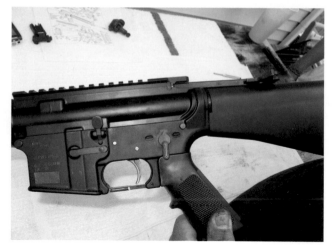

In the end, the decision on whether to build your own rifle can't be one based on price, but rather on purpose. If you love to tinker and build, constructing your own AR may well be the ultimate expression of responsibility and self-reliance.

6. Outfitting Your Rig

*A*sk anyone who already owns or who is in the market for an AR what the number-one reason the platform appeals to them and almost universally—besides the fact they are so bad ass—you will hear them say they really like that they can easily customize the gun to their exact preferences. Indeed, in the post-2008 and 2012 election buying frenzies (both after the election and re-election of Barack Obama) it is estimated more than 2.5 million of the guns were sold in the years immediately following President Obama's victory. Indeed, a look at the FBI's NICS (National Instant Criminal Background Check System) statistics show background checks spiking after the election; the government racked up more than 400,000 more background checks in November 2008 and in December 2008 what was seen in the previous months. While handguns are still the number-one category of firearm sold, anyone you talk to in the industry agrees where rifles are concerned, the AR was

and remains king. In fact, according to BATFE figures, 3.1 million rifles were manufactured in the United States in 2012 and 3.9 million were built in 2013. That compares to 1.7 million in 2008, the year President Obama was elected. You can bet many of these were ARs.

While sales of AR-style and other tactical rifles should continue to enjoy a steady uptick, the fact is, a lot of American gunowners now own an AR-style rifle, and as a result, it makes sense that the next big thing (or actually current big thing) is to to customize the rifle and outfit with better rails, better grips, a better buttstock, improved optics and more. More than one accessory manufacturer and user has dubbed the AR "the ultimate Erector Set" for adults.

The build factor was certainly a large part of the appeal for AR owner and shooting enthusiast Chris Castle, who serves as vice president of AScIS, an environmental services and information technology firm that serves both the government and commercial clients from its headquarters in Virginia Beach, Virginia. Castle actually started the business in the 1990s as a young computer programmer and systems administrator with the purpose of serving small local businesses by installing and maintaining computer networks. He's always been a type of hands-on, technical guy who likes to take things apart and put them back together to see how they work and, more importantly, to see if he can make them work better. Although he grew up in a family of hunters, he did not hunt himself. But he was interested in firearms, an interest that only grew as he became older and made more friends who served in the military. He became close friends with a member of the Navy SEALs, who would take him out shooting, and from that, a casual interest in the shooting sports grew even stronger. As then-president Bill Clinton worked in concert with anti-gun groups to devise more restrictions such as the Assault Weapons Ban that bore his name in the 1990s, Castle was appalled.

"A friend and I decided we better get out ahead of the curve before more firearms were restricted," he says. So they both went out and bought handguns and got their concealed carry permits. His first gun was an H&K Tactical pistol in .45 caliber.

"I shot that for awhile and really enjoyed it, but I am a technical guy by nature and wanted a more technical weapon. The AR was a natural next step," Castle says from his spacious, orderly office. His desk, however, was covered with his Bushmaster AR and a host of accessories that he purchased over the years. The cleanliness and order of his office is reflective of a man who is precise and detail oriented. No project or purchase is made without thinking it clearly through. It is those qualities that brought him to join the ranks of millions of other AR owners.

"As I started getting more into guns and doing more research, I kept coming back to the AR. I found it would have a low learning curve since it is so easy

⌃ Accessorizing your rifle with optics, lasers, lights, grips, or more is one of the key attractions to owning an AR-15.

OUTFITTING YOUR RIG

to operate and maintain, yet it still had a technical complexity to it in that it is a modern design that really appeals to me. The military aspect of it, to me, was really cool. I also wanted something that I could do things with more than just shoot and with the way you can customize these rifles that really appealed to me" says Castle. "Best of all, with me still just learning about shooting rifles, it was a known platform that I could find plenty of help and resources in learning about it and training on it."

Bought during the ban, Castle's Bushmaster is absent any bayonet lug and the compensator is welded onto the barrel and can't be removed—that is, until he swaps out the barrel. But he has indulged in the purchase of countless other accessories, something that has become a side hobby along with taking it to the range whenever he gets the chance. In fact, just some of the things he has outfitted his rifle with are a Leupold Mark 4 CQT scope, an ARMS S.I.R.S. rail system, a Surefire rail-mounted light, a Knight Armaments Front Grip, a Versa Bi-Pod, a collapsible stock to replace the pre-ban fixed stock, a number of 30-round mags and even a 100-round Beta C Mag for some serious high-volume trigger time at the range. Castle is like many shooters, who once they own an AR or two, the next natural step is to customize it. But where to start on your own gun? Here's a look at some of the top types of accessories available for your rifle and considerations that need to be made in selecting them.

RAILS/HANDGUARDS

"The first thing a guy wants to do when he buys (an AR) is put a rail on them," says former SEAL Senior Chief

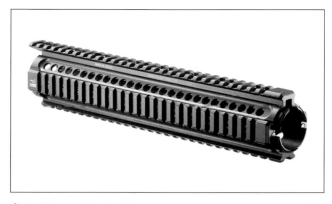

⌃ A rail is one of the first things you may want to swap out on your rifle.

Dave "Jonzy" Jones. Aside from the rifle itself, the rails are the foundation of every other accessory that will be attached to an AR. If they fail, the whole house of cards tumbles and you're in trouble.

Hard-mounted, solid handguards with rails (for our purposes here, the terms handguard and rails are synonymous) can require an armorer or gunsmith to install, or at the very least, take some specific tools and a little know-how to swap out. These fore-end or handguard designs incorporate the rails right into the guard and can't be taken on or off like one fitted with threaded holes designed to accept individual Picatinny rails. Two-piece handguards or rails, which are much more easily installed and designed to replace the plastic handguards that are commonly standard furniture for basic production AR models, can be swapped out by simply snapping them into place where the original handguards were. These two-piece designs attach near the barrel nut by pulling down the delta ring and up behind the gas block (more on this later in this chapter). From a combat standpoint, the two-piece rail can move and flex as the gun heats up during high volume shooting. They also attach at multiple points along the barrel, which ultimately can affect accuracy. For that reason, more of today's shooters prefer free-floating barrels and guards.

For most shooters, many modern ARs come with fore-ends and flat-top uppers that allow for the easy attachment of various sized Picatinny rails. These rails are affordable, easily installed and provide more versatility to customizing your AR to suit the accessories you want to install. Picatinny rails were designed to provide a standard way in which to attach optics, lasers, lights, sights and any other manner of accessories. Made an official standard of the U.S. military in 1995, Picatinny rails are similar to the traditional Weaver style rail, but the grooves are .206 inch wide and have a consistent width from center to center of .394 inch. The grooves in Weaver-style rails don't always have consistent center-to-center widths. Most Weaver-style attachments will fit a Picatinny rail, but not all Picatinny rail attachments will fit a Weaver mount.

In deciding on which rails to go with, there is no shortage of offerings. For flat-top rifle designs there are full-length rails that extend from the front of the upper receiver all the way to or past the gas block depending on the configuration, and there are a number of additional lengths from as short as 2 inches on up to 12, with additional common length rails available in 3, 4, and 6 inches. While being held to the same standard, rails do have a number of configurations to help you mount optics and other accessories, as well as rail risers to provide more elevation to optics, lasers and lights; extended risers that provide for the forward mounting of optics to offer more eye relief; and low-profile rails that allow for virtual flush mounting between fore-end and receiver.

The trend seems to suggest that shorter rails are the way to go. John Chvala, co-owner of ATI (atigunstocks. com), says logic also has a lot to do with that trend.

"There's really no need for a full length rail," Chvala says. "Once people find a good position for an optic or other accessory that is usually where it stays. Shooters are not constantly moving them around." Shorter rails on the handguard also equates to better comfort in the hands unless using a vertical grip, but more on that in a moment.

Jason Jackson, of Artisan Defense (artisandefense. com), is teaming up with Tom Dougherty of Taccfour Defense to develop and market a line of new handguards and a patent pending barrel nut that are lighter, don't require special effort to align and can be tightened with an adjustable wrench (no special tools needed). It also locks together with their rails for perfect alignment and a firm fit.

Jackson cites four things every AR owner will want to consider when swapping out rails to improve a rifle's feel and performance. They are generally looking for one that:

1. Is free floating; where the rail only contacts the upper receiver/barrel nut and doesn't make contact with the barrel past that point. This improves the barrels accuracy and protects the hands better from heat build-up in high-volume shooting situations or training.
2. Has improved accessory mounting capabilities. Most shooters will want their rail to have room or contain enough Picatinny rails, KeyMod or M-LOK mounting options to outfit the gun with a number of accessories designed to improve the gun's utility.
3. Reduces, not adds, weight to your rig.
4. Improves ergonomics—if the rail doesn't improve the overall feel and grip of the gun when shooting, why buy it?

Additionally, Jackson says buyers should consider whether or not the barrel nut requires special tools to install it (most require a special wrench or gunsmith's knowledge to fasten), whether it has anti-rotation features built into it to prevent rotating should the barrel nut comes loose and hamper the concentricity of the rail to barrel. In other words, some barrel nuts and rails, once installed, may be slightly off center of the barrel, which can ultimately affect proper aim and overall performance.

And note that not all handguards come with rails or even permit the mounting of them, though most

⌃ Artisan Defense and Taccfour Defense have teamed up to develop a line of new handguards and a barrel nut that are lighter, don't require special effort to align and can be tightened with an adjustable wrench.

will. The earlier M16s had a triangular handguard that later gave way to the rounded design we see today. AR handguards are designed to allow heat to escape the barrel and promote cooling, while protecting the hands from that heat dissipation so that the gun doesn't become too hot to hold.

Various styles of handguards, made of aluminum, polymer, or carbon fiber, incorporate fixed rails that can only be swapped out with a complete fore-end change, though you can buy rail covers to place over

 FAB Defense offers a variety of forward grip options including the PTK Instinctive Pointing Foregrip (top image) and the simplified VTS-Versatile Tactical Support, which allows for various forward grip positioning. The LWRC AR (bottom image) features a rail that has a full length Picatinny along the top and a shortened Picatinny rail on the bottom for quick attachment of accessories.

them for a better, more comfortable grip. Shooters can also attach a vertical grip which attaches via the bottom Picatinny rail and can actually help improve muzzle flip—the tendency of recoil to drive the barrel upward. Bare rails on the hands when shooting can "feel like cheese graters" according to one shooter, so tactical gloves, some sort of fore-end grip such as a vertical grip or ergonomic pointing grip, such as FAB Defense's PTK, are almost a necessity. Other handguard models simply include threaded holes in which to attach individual rails for precise placement of accessories.

Handguards come in free-float models or two-piece models. Free-float handguards are a single tube design that attach with a replacement barrel nut where the barrel attaches to the receiver. They require more work and tools and unless you are a real do-it-yourselfer, you might be better off letting a gunsmith tackle this one, unless you opt for a barrel nut like Artisan Defense offers. Two piece handguards are designed to replace the plastic ones that commonly come on stock model rifles and can easily replace the removed handguards with a minimal effort. When shopping fore-ends or handguards, or quad rails as they are called when encircled with four Picatinny rails at the 12, 3, 6, and 9 o'clock positions, it's important to know what length you will need: rifle length, midlength or carbine length. Typically a rifle-length guard fits a rifle with a 20-inch barrel, a mid-length guard fits a firearm with a 16-inch to 18-inch barrel and carbine length rifles have barrels that are 16 inches in length or less.

In 2011, ATI introduced a 15-inch 8-sided Aluminum Free-Float Fore-end that gives the shooter eight planes on which to install rails in the 12, 1:30, 3, 4:30, 6, 7: 30, 9, and 10:30 positions. It is still a popular option. Rails can be attached in 45-degree increments for a multitude of accessory arrangement or sighting angles. They also introduced their FS8 Nose Cone, which attaches to the front of the fore-end, looks rugged and is functional by providing support when anchored into a corner, door jam or fence for support when shooting. As manufacturers and engineers work to provide eager consumers with even more configurations for AR handguards, production models are coming out with unique free-float designs.

⌃ Shooters have virtually limitless sighting options available for everything from close quarters shooting to long-range target acquisition. This Meprolight red dot offers rapid target sighting for target, hunting and self-defense purposes.

Sighting Systems

In both competitive shooting and hunting circles, it's rare to find the rifleman who does not install some sort of scope or optical aid to his firearm, particularly since the real intent of shooting with a rifle is to be able to reach out at long-range distances. Unfortunately, at distances greater than 100 yards (and for some of the nearly blind among us much less) our eyes begin to fail when it comes to being able to make out the fine details of a target, such as where precisely a round is hitting—particularly on a black background target. While the first military issued M16s came with front and rear sights only, it wasn't long before soldiers were figuring out ways to put optics atop them. Fortunately for today's shooter, there is no shortage of options, though depending on the route you decide to go, you can expect to spend nearly as much on the glass as you do on the rifle itself.

Both dedicated tactical optics manufacturers, such as Meprolight, Trijicon, Nightforce, Aimpoint, EOTech, and others, as well as traditional optics makers, think companies like Bushnell, Nikon, Burris, Meopta and Zeiss, are all making a variety of optics tailored specifically for modern sporting rifles whether the purpose be purely tactical, competition, home defense or hunting. Small package fixed range optics in the ballpark of 3x and similarly compact variables in the 1-4x range are available just as high-powered varmint offerings with variable magnifications from 6-24x and large 50mm objectives can be had. For most shooters looking to hunt or shoot competitively, some level of optics will be important. But use care when selecting scopes with large bells, especially housing the ocular lens, as they can obstruct a shooter's ability to grip and pull the charging handle. Depending on your scope, you may have to replace your charging handle to include an oversized or extended charging handle

⌃ The view through a red dot sight.

latch in order to properly lock the bolt back prior to battery.

For those shooting enthusiasts simply looking to build a gun as close to military functionality as possible, as well as those with home defense as a focus, red dot or holographic sights, such as those made by Meprolight, EOTech, Aimpoint or TruGlo may well be the way to go. I've used Aimpoints on both ARs and a standard turkey shotgun and love the rapid target acquisition and reticle choices and illumination levels they offer no matter what they are mounted on. My Meprolight Mepro Tru-Dot RDS red dot (meprolight. com) was both affordable ($399) and ideal for CQB drills mounted atop an AR and for true bargain hunters, TruGlo red dots (truglo.com), such as the Tru-Brite Dual Color Multi Reticle at only $123 is hard to beat. Because red dot sights work on target no matter what angle you view the reticle or red dot from, they are more forgiving than a magnifying scope and also provide a much better field of view. A danger for a lot of scope users, whether in a tense defensive situation or

a hunting one, is they tend to close one eye to focus through the darkened scope. This creates a kind of tunnel vision where action or events at the periphery of your sight are lost. With a red dot, that is not the case. Even if you do close one eye to aim (which you shouldn't), the tube of a scope isn't there to obscure the view of what's going on outside of where you are focusing your aim. This can be critical in a defensive situation.

More scope makers such as Trijicon, Aimpoint, and TruGlo are making optics that deliver both—magnification and lit reticles—to provide improved visual clarity and supremely quick target acquisition. That was Castle's choice when he began researching the type of optic he wanted for his Bushmaster when he went with the Leupold.

"I'm not much of an iron sight shooter and I looked at all of the red dots on the market at the time, but in the end, I went with the Leupold Mark 1V CQT, a mil spec scope that delivers both magnification and an illuminated reticle," Castle says.

Lasers are also a popular option, though to some insiders, their appeal probably has as much to do with the Hollywood "cool" factor as they do real-world applications. That being said, most combat operators usually have one mounted on their rifles. A quality laser can aim out to 300 or 400 yards in broad daylight and even farther at night. A good one will also give the user the option between a constant beam and a pulse mode, with the latter making it quicker and easier to lock on to where the gun is aiming when sighting at longer distances. Most lasers aim with red or green beams, but former operator Jones offers a word of caution to anyone in a combat, law enforcement or defensive situation who is using one locked on constant.

"That laser goes both ways and an opposing shooter can track that laser back to the shooter holding it," he says. Most lasers typically work best from a side or bottom rail, leaving a clear sight plane along the top rail for iron sights or optics.

In fact, whether you opt for a scope or a red dot, for complete functional utility, it is vital to maintain some type of iron sights or alternate aiming system should an optic fail or become disabled.

"There is a saying one is none, two is one" when it comes to sights, Jones says, meaning for a soldier,

⌃ Flip-up sights (these made by FAB Defense) are an essential option for soldiers in combat as they work as back-up sights should their primary optic become damaged.

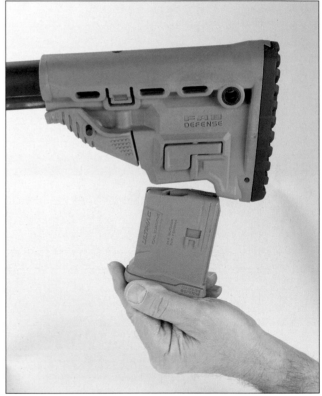

⌃ The GL-Mag from FAB Defense features an additional magazine for rapid reloads.

should a scope or laser get hit by a bullet or shrapnel, a BUIS (Back Up Iron Sight) is critical to still being in the game. But this concern extends beyond combat, which many readers of this book hopefully will never see. Even in quick competitive scenarios, such as when shooting 3Gun, or even on hunts, optics can fog or get knocked off zero, batteries can go dead on red dots and in high-glare situations, sometimes even be hard to see.

"Flip up sights are good if something should happen to your optics. You can rip the scope off and still be in the fight," says one soldier I met. Most soldiers will use a top-mounted short or mid-range optic with a side-mounted laser. Flip up front and rear iron sights are a great addition and will always work in a crunch. I've mounted FAB Defense FRBS Folding Back Up Sights on my Yankee Hill Machine (YHM) Spectre XL, which work great as primary open sights or when co-mounted with a red dot or variable optic.

During filming of *Gallery of Guns* television, of which I was a part of for three years along with show hosts Bo Keister and Anne-Marie Rhodes, we frequently pulled several modern sporting rifles straight from the box and began shooting them with iron sights. Most of the guns took no more than four or five windage and elevation adjustments before we were busting small bottles of juice and soda out at 100 yards. With a rear ghost ring aperture and front single iron blade, most shooters can be driving tacks quicker than they will be able to dial in an optic. Most shooters interviewed prefer both flip-down front and rear sights, though rail risers and high- or forward-mounted optics can still clear the visual obstruction fixed iron sights might otherwise prevent. For such uses, a buttstock that offers comb or cheekpiecce adjustment can be important in order to maintain a reliable cheek weld when shooting. FAB Defense's GL Shock buttstock boasts a thick recoil pad for negligible recoil (when shooting 5.56) and an adjustable cheekpiece and installs in seconds on a buffer tube designed for collapsible stocks. One version even very smartly holds a spare 10-round mag that inserts in the bottom of it.

LIGHTS

For most AR owners, a tactical light is a vital accessory, particularly if it will become a go-to gun when home defense comes into play. While tactical lights on semi-auto pistols have been in vogue for some time and certainly have their application, when using a long gun for home defense or tactical purposes—where both hands are required to maintain control of the firearm leaving no other way to practically hold a light—a side-mounted white light becomes an absolute necessity. Particularly when you factor in that the overwhelming majority of defensive uses of firearms occur at night when most crimes are also committed under the cloak of darkness.

While there are a variety of players in the weapon-mounted tactical light field these days, FAB Defense,

⌃ Lights can be a key accessory for an AR used for low-light shooting or for defensive purposes, since most threatening situations around the home will take place after dark.

Streamlight, L3 Warrior Systems, and Inforce are a few top options that come to mind, SureFire was one of the first—and remains one of the most visible—today. Surprisingly, they didn't start out as a light company, but rather as the Laser Products Corp., making a gun-mounted laser aiming system—something that isn't even in their product line anymore despite the fact that they also make much more than just lights, the one product line for which they are known best. That was back in 1984.

"In the first Terminator movie, that is our laser that Arnold Schwarzenegger is using when he is going around killing everybody," said Ron Canfield, the former public relations manager at SureFire. The first dedicated weapon light the company developed didn't come along until 1986. It was called the SureFire light. Over time, people came to know the company as SureFire more so than the Laser Products Corp. and in 2001, the company officially changed their name. Today, they make a wide range of suppressors, muzzle brakes, flash hiders, lights, even rails and sights, but the lights remain their "bread and butter," said Canfield. And for good reason, they are necessary to properly see at night.

In case you've been on a deserted island for the last fifteen to twenty years, LED lights are definitely the way to go over incandescent bulbs, both for the even, bright light they provide and their durability in the face of jolts and drops. The circuit boards used with LEDs reduce the chance for an electronic disconnect in the case of extreme shocking forces, such as can occur during recoil. Like other gun parts, lights can also be made from aluminum bodies or polymers, and while the latter might have broader tolerances and can withstand a lot of punishment, they are also more affected by temperature variations. Of course, unless you're operating in the Arctic or in the Iraqi desert, that may not be such a huge concern.

Go with a light that has a remount switch and pressure pad in addition to a tail cap thumb activator. Depending on the gas block design or rail system, a tail cap switch may be difficult to reach when needed, particularly in a lights-on, lights-off scenario where you want to avoid telegraphing your position by casting light until you are ready to acquire your target. By having a switch that can be mounted on a front vertical grip or down the side of a rail along your upper receiver, you can more readily access the light only when you need to.

STOCKS

The first ARs to be accepted by the military as the M16 featured fixed stocks similar to those on a traditional rifle though with a straighter stock design to allow better absorption of recoil and multiple shot management, as well as the placement of a buffer tube to return the bolt carrier assembly forward after it is slammed open by the gases from a fired round. Collapsible and folding stocks have been around since World War II and were even used on some early CAR-15 submachine gun versions based off the M16 as early as the late 1960s. However, according to *Black Rifle II: The M16 Into the 21st Century* by Christopher R. Bartocci, the U.S. Government met with Colt to develop and purchase a newly designed carbine that would accommodate the newly adopted M855 5.56x45mm NATO round in 1984. The next year, a contract was signed to procure 40 XM4 (later simply M4) carbines for testing in 1986, one of the specifications of which was "the carbine shall have a collapsible/sliding stock." A shorter barrel of 14½ inches was also specified. It wasn't until 1994, when the M4 was officially adopted that collapsible stocks became part of the standard issue carbine. Indeed, there are pluses and minuses to both designs and in fact, even among collapsible stocks there are a number of variations available that render a whole new level of functionality to modern stock design.

As for the benefits of fixed stocks, they offer a better cheek weld for precision or long-distance shooting. In addition to their length, they are also more rigid, which again, aids aim and ultimately accuracy. Standard, six-position collapsible stocks sacrifice some cheek weld due to their more compressed comb, but it is better for carrying in cramped vehicles or through thick brush, which can hang on it and hinder the user. It also packs more easily, requiring less space, and can be readily adjusted to fit multiple shooters taking turns target shooting with the gun.

Take your wife, a girlfriend or kids shooting with a fixed-stock rifle or shotgun and how many times have you watched the smaller shooters struggle to maintain

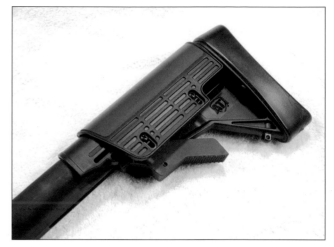

⌃ A six-position adjustable stock makes customizing length of pull for the gunowner a quick proposition.

a proper stance because the length of pull was too long for them? Typically, their backs will sway back as they struggle to center the weight, which leads to poor aim and quite possibly more pain from recoil. With a collapsible stock, you simply adjust the length to fit the shooter and let them go.

Some stock designs even fold forward, providing an even more compact overall package for storing, while others offer multi-plane adjustments that allow you to adjust comb height and cast in addition to length of pull, all of which will allow a shooter to fit the gun perfectly to their size and stance for rapid target acquisition and more accurate aiming.

"I don't believe in a fixed stock . . . a fixed stock forces you to compromise on fit," says ATI co-owner John Chvala. He points out to those who argue that a collapsible stock feels loose, that it is supposed to be a little loose.

"The traditional view of a stock is that it is rigid and doesn't move, but the purpose for a six-position stock is you want it to move and adjust easily. If it didn't move some, it would bind and adjusting it would be difficult," he says. His company's AR-15 Strikeforce Package with an aluminum civilian buffer tube features a six-position collapsible buttstock with a fully adjustable cheek rest and a comfortable nonslip, removable buttpad for reduced felt recoil. The cheek rest has a soft, rubberized exterior for improved comfort and weld and is adjustable not with dials like some stocks, but with four screws.

"I don't want guys in the field screwing with it," Chvala laughs. "I want them to set it where it needs to be and leave it and never touch it again."

MUZZLE ATTACHMENTS

With the sunsetting of the Clinton Assault Weapons Ban, muzzlebrakes no longer had to be welded onto the barrel, making them easier to swap out and customize. Today's shooter has a number of options available to them in the form of not just muzzlebrakes, but flash hiders and complete suppressors as well. It's important to know the differences and functions of each.

"Muzzlebrakes are the most effective way to eliminate the rise or recoil of a rifle," says Canfield. "You can get as much as a 60 percent reduction in recoil from a quality muzzlebrake." They move the recoil laterally front to back so a shooter firing multiple rounds can recover and get back on aim more quickly, but in their most basic sense, do nothing to limit flash and make the gun louder in a range setting where spotters or other shooters may be standing back and to either side of the primary shooter.

A flash hider or flash suppressor is designed to eliminate flash so an enemy can't spot where shots are coming from, but depending on their design, can also reduce recoil as well. Sound suppressors meanwhile offer the benefits of eliminating flash, dust signatures when a shooter is prone, and sound. They can also reduce recoil like a muzzlebrake, though

not all models are designed to do so. SureFire began to witness a notable surge in suppressor sales when this book was first published in 2011 and since then, the market has only grown and grown with more companies stepping in offer options for shooters. Suppressors are legal to own in 41 states, four more than permitted them in 2011. In 38 of those states, at least some hunting is even permitted with a suppressor. (See sidebar in this chapter, "9 Steps to Buying a Suppressor.")

Suppressors are also called silencers—though they don't completely silence the sound of a shot, they merely reduce it significantly. Not so long ago, most folks in the know would look at you like you called a mag a clip when you called a suppressor a silencer. But with companies like SilencerCo and the not-related Silencer Shop going balls out on promoting their products and helping educate more consumers, the word "silencer," as Darren Jones of SilencerCo told me during a long-range shooting event, is not a dirty word or even incorrect. While suppressors/silencers have been a little slower to gain a huge following in this country, largely due to the legalities and costs involved courtesy of laws in place since the 1920s, in Europe, it is considered almost rude to shoot without one. Their benefits are numerous. First, you can shoot without waking up or disturbing nearby neighbors. They reduce noise pollution. Some kids will also be more comfortable shooting a suppressed rifle because the noisy blast of shoot-

⌃ Flash hiders come in a variety of configurations.

⌃ Suppressors are legal for shooting in nearly every state and legal for hunting in most states as well. They make shooting much more enjoyable due to low noise and less recoil.

ing, which can frighten new shooters, is almost eliminated. Suppressed rifles tend to shoot better than unsuppressed rifles as well. Hearing protection isn't the concern it is when shooting unsuppressed firearms as well.

MAGAZINES

Magazines can affect the performance and cycling of an AR as much as the ammo and the gun itself. In fact, as noted earlier in this book, it is just as important to keep mags clean and working as it is to break down and clean the rifle. Standard magazines are designed to hold as many as five, 10, 20, or 30 rounds. Higher capacity magazines that hold 40, 60 and even 100 rounds, although seen as a little gimmicky, can bring a whole new dimension to high-volume shooting. Certainly where 100-round drum magazine designs are concerned, most shooters interviewed simply don't trust them.

"They're great when they work, but they do have a tendency to jam," says one soldier. "I'm not going to bet my life on something like that." He explains that he'll just stick to his tried and proven 30-round magazines.

Most magazines are made of either aluminum or polymer, but in the case of E-Lander magazines,

they are made of rugged steel for extended performance and life. Aluminum is the standard, however, but it can dent where polymer doesn't. Steel, while lightweight, is more resistant to denting than aluminum. As for polymer, it is actually stronger than aluminum as well, doesn't corrode, is easier to clean and provides more consistent operation. It can also be more expensive. The longtime popular PMAG by Magpul has a sight window that allows you to see how many rounds remain in the magazine and also comes with a dust cover where the rounds feed in order to keep them protected from grime when not in use.

Before you become too enamored with high-capacity mags, consider what type of shooting you'll be doing. When shooting prone, a 10- or 20-round mag is better than a 30-round because you can reduce your profile by keeping closer to the ground. Oh, and when an aluminum magazine becomes dented or any magazine quits working properly, smash it, throw it away and get a new one.

"It is pointless to keep a poorly working magazine around when there are so many quality magazines available on the market," says Kurt Dewort, a retired naval armorer at Dam Neck, Virginia, and current gunsmith at Chesapeake Pawn and Gun. "It is one of the easiest things to replace on a rifle that has a long list of features that are easy to replace."

⌃ This 100-round drum magazine is fun to shoot, but is also regarded as a little gimmicky by some serious shooters. When loaded, it adds significant weight to your firearm.

⌃ Mags come in a variety of materials including lightweight steel and durable polymer.

BIPODS

⌃ A bipod that attaches quickly to the rail via a Picatinny attachment is a great option for steadying your aim when taking shots at distance.

If you plan to do much prone shooting (maybe even bench shooting without bags) or varminting—or really any hunting—over wide, open country, a bipod may be as important as the light is to the AR owner concerned about home defense. Few shooters can hold a gun steady enough to deliver competition-level accuracy without the benefit of some sort of rest. A small folding bipod with telescoping legs attaches easily to a bottom rail and packs neatly out of place when not in use. However, it is there for quick use when needed.

It can make the difference between a hit or a miss, or when hunting big game, even worse, a wounded animal. For a uniquely functional tactical product that combines a vertical grip with a bipod, check out Grip Pods Systems Grip Pod, which looks like a grip with feet, but with the push of a button, deploys two spring loaded, polymer coated stainless steel legs and functions as a short, but steady bipod. When you don't need it, the legs slide and lock right back into place inside the grip. They even make a model that allows the attachment of a small rail for attaching a light. Similarly, FAB Defense makes a Tactical Vertical Foregrip with Integrated Adjustable Bipod Gen2, which operates with the single push of a button to morph from a simple vertical grip into a steady rest for your rifle.

⌃ The FAB Defense T-Pod G2 is a forward vertical grip that instantly transforms into an aim-stabilizing bipod.

Tactical Sling How-To

The sling is the piece of kit most taken for granted, and any rifleman or hunter who has ever forgotten to pack a sling (been there, done that) can attest to its importance. It performs two tasks for the user. The most common task, and probably the least important, it provides a manner in which to carry the rifle. If you had to carry the rifle by hand, 7 to 8 pounds isn't much at first, but after a long day of carry, it can leave your arms hurting. It can also free up a hand or two for other tasks, while keeping the rifle on your body. More importantly, it provides stability while shooting. It's becoming a bit of a lost art, but tighten the sling on your arm for leverage, and your rifle becomes nearly as steady as if you're resting it on a solid object. This is why long distances shooters, while laying in prone positions, roll into their slings.

Sling Mounts: First Things First

There are two primary styles of mounting points for slings. The first type is a slot or swivel for feeding web belt-style slings through. Traditionally on an AR these were located at the buttstock toe and under the gas block. Now most makers of carbine stocks form slots along the top of the buttstock, just under the gas block. Aftermarket swivel mounting points can also be added to the front inside rail. The second type is a quick release style that is either a ring for attaching a hook-type clip onto, or a push-button Quick Detach (QD) mount.

Quick release mounts are bought aftermarket, and are usually positioned towards the rear of the receiver. The most common ones are designed as a replacement to the stock lower receiver end plate, and are configured with some sort of mounting point to attach the sling, such as a QD hole, or a ring to clip the sling. Mounting points can attach to the top rail, just forward of the charging handle. Some buttstocks come with quick release mounts built in for two-point slings.

The One-Point Sling

A one-point sling relies upon some form of quick detach mechanism such as a Quick Detach (QD) mount, or a hook clip. It's generally something that locks into place—since there's only one point connecting the rifleman to the AR, it must be very secure. One-point slings are excellent for riflemen who frequently set their rifles down, such as people that get into and out of a vehicle or ATV, or a hunter in a deer stand. It allows you to keep the sling on, and just un-clip the rifle from the sling to take it off.

Another benefit to one-point slings is the ability to switch shoulders and shoot weak-side. This is important for rifleman in combat, especially in urban environments, where the need to shoot around walls and other objects often requires weak-side shooting. This is also beneficial to hunters, while shooting from a tree stand or blind with windows. When deer approach from the strong-side, from the rear, it's often impossible to position your body to give yourself a shot with the strong-side. The one-point sling allows for the mounting of the rifle in your weak-side shoulder for a better shot. One-point slings have a pull-tab

⌃ Single-point sling.

for rapid, on-the-fly length adjustments for making that shoulder switch.

Also, the one-point sling allows for secure hands-free carry. It forms a large loop that you stick your head and one arm through, and is worn diagonal across your upper torso like a bandoleer. The sling cannot slide off the user, even if the rifle is grabbed and pulled, so it frees up both hands for use. The benefit to military personnel is obvious, but it's also huge for hunters. Coyote hunters, for example, could have hands full with callers, decoys, etc., and not have to worry about carrying the rifle—yet it's held at patrol ready the whole time. Many one-point slings on the market can also be configured as a two-point sling.

The downside to the one-point sling is that it doesn't offer good muzzle control during hands free carry. While the user is walking, the rifle muzzle will often start swinging back and forth if the rifle isn't held. Another issue is that it's muzzle-down carry only, and if in a situation where muzzle-down is not the best option—in deep snow, for example—it doesn't allow you to rotate the sling so that the rifle is muzzle up.

Examples of one-point slings are the Magpul MS3 Multi-Mission Sling, the FAB Defense Tactical Single-Point Bungee Sling, the Vikings Tactic Bungee Sling and the Limbsaver SW Tactical Sling.

Two-Point Sling

The traditional two-point sling is the oldest type of sling. It attaches at the toe of the buttstock and at a swivel approximately two-thirds up the barrel from the breech. Tactical two-point slings mount at essentially the same locations—at the gas block, or just behind it on the forward grip rail, and on the buttstock, using swivels or slots, or with QD mounts. Increasingly two-point slings are being mounted towards the rear of the receiver instead of the buttstock, like one-point slings, especially with slings that can be configured as either one-point or two-point.

Tactical two-point slings are slightly different and have a pull-tab for fast length adjustments.

⌃ Vicker's Combat Application Swing.

Some two-point slings can be let out enough in length to allow weak-side shooting. It does not offer secure hands-free carry, however, which can be a big drawback. The two-point sling allows for better control of the rifle—particularly the muzzle—during hands-free carry.

An excellent two-point sling is from Blue Force Gear, the Vicker's Combat Applications Sling.

The Three-Point Sling

Three-point slings are typically more like a harness, and are not quick release. Whereas one- and two-point slings take a simple click or two to attach, three-point slings have a more involved installation and will often require you to pull out the instructions the first time you install one. Once installed, a three-point sling is usually not removed, mostly because it's a bit of a hassle to put them on. Three-point slings free the rifleman's hands for other tasks, and during hands-free carry the rifle is held in a more stable position than other styles of slings.

One downside to the three-point slings is that there's a lot more sling to snag on things. It has a section that runs the length of the rifle, connecting the rear mount to the front mount, in addition to the section that goes around the user, much like a triangle (which is why it is called a *three-point* sling). Another downside is it gets in the way while performing rifle maintenance. Not a deal breaker, but something to be aware of. Great examples of the three point sling are the Blackhawk Universal Swift Sling, and the Mamba from Spec.-Ops.

Shoulder Sling

The shoulder sling is a relatively new addition to slings, and started out serving the purpose of a lanyard, but has evolved into a simple sling. It's just a straight web sling of approximately 20 inches long—one end attaches to the very rear of the weapon and the other end attaches to the rifleman's vest or rig. It's then adjusted in length so that the rifle hangs straight down around 9 inches off the shoulder. It allows for weak-side shouldering and most have a quick-release buckle. It's great for troops getting in and out of vehicles frequently. It does not allow for a very steady platform as do the other sling types. This isn't really an option for hunters or target shooters, since it requires a combat vest or rig to attach to. The Spec.-Ops Wolf-Hook and Blackhawk Tactical Releasable S.T.R.I.K.E. sling are examples of the Shoulder Sling.

ⵌ Shoulder sling.

There are plenty of slings on the market that will suit your needs, it's just a matter of choosing a style that does everything you need it to do. I tend to be a pretty simple, easy to please user, and often choose simple over complex. So for me the one-point sling is perfect for all of my needs, though I've used and own all types.—*Robb Manning*

9 Steps to Buying a Suppressor

Silencer Shop, an Austin, Texas, suppressor retailer, who does much of their work online, has revolutionized the way many American gunowners have learned about the suppressor buying process and actually go about purchasing their silencers. SilencerCo (again, not affiliated with Silencer Shop though the retailer does sell their products) has been a leader in not only engineering and marketing silencers to a new breed of gunowning consumer, but has also been an industry leader in educating consumers as to the steps and benefits of suppressor ownership. Much of the information in this section has been provided by them.

1. First, make sure your state allows private citizens to own and purchase silencers.
2. Next, decide which type of suppressor works best for your needs. They are available for centerfire rifles and handguns, rimfires and with SilencerCo's Salvo 12, even shotguns. With threaded barrels, ARs are ready-made for suppressors.
3. Find a Class 3 dealer either locally or online, such as Silencer Shop, and choose the suppressor you wish to buy. Because it can take awhile for the paperwork to go through, buyers may need to pay a deposit or even the full amount up front.
4. Once you have an assigned product serial number from the silencer you are buying, the dealer will then give you two BATFE Form 4s (5320.4) [Application for Tax Paid Transfer and Registration of Firearm] with the serial number

and various details of the product entered in the appropriate section. If you are making this purchase as an individual, you will fill in both copies of the Form 4 as well as a BATFE Form 5330.20 Certification of Compliance (certification of US citizenship) with your personal information. If you are making this purchase through an NFA Trust or LLC, fill in the name and address of your Trust or LLC; a Form 5330.20 will not be required.

5. At this point, if you are purchasing the silencer as an individual, you will need your local Chief Law Enforcement Officer (CLEO) to sign your Form 4. Most often, this is your local Sheriff, Chief of Police, or deputy/officer appointed by the CLEO to sign on their behalf. While at the police station, have two copies of finger print cards made—this will be needed when you mail in your Form 4.

6. If you are purchasing the silencer through your Trust, you will not need the signature of your local Chief Law Enforcement Officer or fingerprint cards.

7. Finally, send in the following items to the BATFE according to whether you a purchasing the silencer as an individual or through a Trust/LLC. As an individual, send a check or money order in the amount of $200 to the Bureau of Alcohol, Firearms and Explosives; both copies of the completed Form 4s, two passport photos; and the completed form 5330.20. If submitting under a trust or LLC, send a check or money order in the amount of $200 to the Bureau of Alcohol, Firearms and Explosives; both copies of the completed Form 4s, and a copy of your trust or LLC's articles of incorporation. For information on NFA Trusts and whether setting one up is the course for you, visit http: /www. silencershop.com/how-to-buy-a-silencer.

8. Then you simply need to wait for the paperwork to clear. At the time of this book's writing, it was taking between a month to five months depending on which process you are using to buy the silencer through.

9. Once the paperwork clears and you are approved, the BATFE will affix a stamp to one of the two Form 4 copies and return it to your dealer from whom you purchased the silencer. Then, simply pay for your silencer if monies are still owed and take possession of your new toy.

OUTFITTING YOUR RIG

7. The Sporting AR

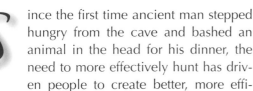ince the first time ancient man stepped hungry from the cave and bashed an animal in the head for his dinner, the need to more effectively hunt has driven people to create better, more efficient ways to fill the larder, and in more recent times, populate the trophy room. It is likely no coincidence that many of the most common artifacts discovered from our country's earliest inhabitants remain arrowheads and sharpened rocks used to scrape meat from animal hides. The lives of man and beast were intertwined in a way only a portion of our society can relate to today, and hunting, throughout most of mankind's history, perhaps all of man's history, has been a central activity. It still is despite the effort of many in our world to marginalize its role in wildlife management, the overall health of many species and the outstanding recreational benefits it provides. Hunting's importance is borne out by some of the earliest dated cave paintings in the famous Lascaux caves of southwestern France. Those paintings date back as far as 20,000 years ago, and many depict numerous large animals such as bison being chased down by groups of hunters. It is also reflected in events as recent as the late 1800s when Native Americans' lives continued to revolve around hunting for subsistence, and game meat helped sustain our young country's continued Western expansion. It was the strain unregulated subsistence hunting put on our nation's game populations that spurred sportsmen of the day, American President Theodore Roosevelt chief among them, to push for regulations in every state that would establish laws to limit when, how and how much game could be taken. The movement established the North American model of wildlife conservation that remains a model for the entire world today.

Hunting has always been a part of our history. But today, with the majority of the population living in developed areas and obtaining their food from stores instead of directly from the farm and field, there is more of a disconnect with the natural world. As a partial result, a number of modern hunting critics and even some purists among the sporting ranks question how much technology is necessary for hunters to carry with them in the field. But given our history, it is only a natural evolution of man to devise better ways to succeed against nature's creatures. This continued development is what has always ensured that we will be successful. After all, our minds are the one aspect that gives us the edge to triumph over beasts, most of which possess physical abilities—speed, strength, hearing, smelling and seeing—and innate instincts that would trump man's otherwise feeble efforts at every step. Few men who have ever lived would be able to run down a whitetail, sneak up on a turkey or overpower a bear or lion. It takes cunning, and ultimately, tools.

So we use the one ability we have that surpasses theirs. We use our brains. And with them we devise better ways to find game, track it down, get close enough to it and kill it. It could certainly be argued that today's battle-tested AR is the culmination of so many eons of evolutionary development in weaponry. It is certainly no surprise that it is finding its way into more and more hunters' hands.

With what is now a generation of American soldiers recently cycled out of Iraq and Afghanistan and as comfortable on the end of a tactical rifle, if not more so, than many traditional sporting arms, it should be no surprise that the popularity of ARs has migrated beyond an audience of target shooters and home safety practitioners and into hunting camps and lodges around the country. It has been a natural progression throughout American history that what is used and proven in war, nearly always makes its way into the fields and forests back home.

This trend heralds back to our country's earliest days when Revolutionary War soldiers, many remaining as

⌃ From hogs to predators, the .223 is an ideal option.

an at-ready militia prepared to marshal against any return threat of invading European or frontier forces, returned home to use their muskets to fill the larder with all manner of readily available game in what was still a very young, wild and undeveloped country. The lever-action Spencer rifles and Henry Repeating rifles developed about the time of the Civil War in response to the poor performing first ever lever-action, the Volcanic rifle, saw action in battles where front-end loaders still received the majority of service. The Spencer and Henry designs ultimately gave birth to such lever actions as the "Gun That Won the West," the famed Winchester Model 73, and the Sharps Model 1874. These latter creations both employed newer centerfire .44-caliber cartridges rather than the rimfire loads of their predecessors. Production of these guns during westward expansion and put in service by cavalry forces of the time made them a recognized presence and readily available commodity.

The lever action's popularity eventually gave way to the more versatile and accurate bolt-action, which had it's beginnings in the battle-tested rifle design of Paul Mauser, and saw extensive service as the U.S. military's standard service rifle in the form of the M1903 Springfield. That bolt-action design remains the central system on which most traditional sporting arms are still built.

With thousands of M16-toting soldiers returning from the Vietnam War in the late 1960s and 1970s, interest in modern tactical rifles was born.

In fact, Norfolk, Va., gun shop owner Robert Marcus notes that interest in tactical rifles, and more specifically the AR, really began about 1968.

"We are a Navy town with plenty of Army and Marines. There has always been an interest in tactical rifles here," he says. The fact that a number of these men in uniform enjoy hunting only enhances the opportunity for the rifles to pull double duty.

But it wasn't until the post-9/11 actions of our military in both Afghanistan and Iraq that interest began to peak. That, and as mentioned earlier in this book, the gun public's concern over a gun-grabbing administration in the White House backed by the once Democratically-controlled Congress and ever-present anti-gun media. As a result, tactical rifle makers found themselves at the center of a perfect consumer storm. Gunowners couldn't get enough of these guns—partially out of familiarity and interest, partially out of

⩘ Predator hunters were among the first sportsmen to embrace the AR platform for their pursuits.

concern that their availability could disappear—and manufacturers struggled to keep up with demand. Many backorders stretched as long as six or more months before they could be filled.

Adding to the fury of demand was the fact that ARs began to find a ready audience among the nation's estimated 13.7 million hunters.

ARs in Camp

While misperceptions about tactical rifles remain among the sporting public, and even some division remains among sportsmen in camp, opinions have changed rapidly in recent years.

One 2011 study commissioned by the National Shooting Sports Foundation found that just over 18 percent of all gunowners now own an AR-style rifle. Of those, nearly 20 percent say they use them for hunting. That was a sizable number just five years ago given the relatively recent arrival of ARs on the hunting scene and some of the biases that remained and still persist against the AR by traditionalists. Of course, nobody will ever accuse hunters—at least not most of them—for being on the forefront of cutting edge change. Admittedly, most of us hunt out of a respect for the traditions and simple pleasures the outdoors offers. But as younger hunters raised in a technologically saturated society take to the woods and start to produce their own income, the AR promises to be as continuing a presence in hunting camp as it does in the capable hands of our military forces. Indeed, even in the last five years since the first edition of this

⌃ With coyotes pushing into every corner of the country, ARs, with their light handling characteristics, long-range performance and plentiful ammunition options, make them the ideal predator-hunting rifles.

book hit store shelves, it has been meeting the needs of the hunting public—placing camo finishes on rifles and broadening caliber offerings of the platform—that have driven much of the recent innovation seen among tactical rifles.

In a 2010 survey by the NSSF, 94 percent of those surveyed said they approve of the use of semi-auto AR-platform rifles for target shooting. That number dropped to a 75 percent approval rating when asked if they thought those same guns should be used for hunting. Perhaps more telling at the time of where the field of sporting ARs was likely to go could be found in the responses where approximately 20 percent of those surveyed said they intended to purchase a modern sporting rifle within the next twelve months. In fact, when the NSSF performed a similar survey in 2013, they found among gunowners who own only one tactical, or modern sporting rifle (MSR), 49 percent bought them in 2012 or 2013. Of those MSR owners who own more than one gun, 92 percent frequently target shoot, 50 percent use them to hunt with and 19 percent use them in competition.

PREDATOR PERFORMANCE

With their ability to deliver tack driving performance, cycle rapid follow-up shots, cool quickly and shoot heavier bullets in a .223-sized caliber, thanks to the higher barrel twist rates most ARs have over more traditional arms of the same caliber, it is no surprise that ARs first found a home in the hunting world among predator and varmint hunters. The fact that much of that type of shooting and hunting revolves so keenly

around ballistic performance and fine tuning of a particular firearm to work in concert with optics, rests and the shooter's own abilities also played a significant role in the varminters embracing of tactical rifles.

Whether a shooter is perched in the bed of a pick-up truck and settled on a bench overlooking a troublesome prairie dog town or hidden among the brush working coyotes to the gun, the end game for the predator shooter is to be able to fire a lot of shots. Predators and varmints are not bound within bag limits like much larger and even some smaller game. That means a guy also has to be able to afford to shoot.

Before ARs became all the rage and demand soared for the guns, .223 ammo was relatively inexpensive when compared to some of the more specialized cartridges. This also enhanced the rifle's popularity. However, when AR demand soared, ammo costs for the rifle rose with it as the rounds became scarce. Don't forget that our military was also embroiled in battles on two fronts at this same time, requiring a significant demand for much of the same materials and production facilities that produced ammunition for the civilian market. Fortunately, for today's tactical hunter, ammo makers have been able to secure raw materials and ramp up production so that .223/5.56 ammunition is once again easily obtainable and available at a reasonable cost.

Few hunters are so specialized that they don't hunt other types of game. While the growth in predator hunting and interest in tactical rifles seemed to have moved in lock step with one another, arguably making predator hunting the fastest growing type of hunting today, its number of adherents is still far dwarfed by those who pursue the king of all game animals—the white-tailed deer. Despite all of the specialty firearms designed for particular niches of hunting, until a gun can deliver reliable knockdown power on deer (or bigger) sized game, it will likely remain just that, a niche product line without the consumer support to really generate the type of growth larger companies can remain viable on.

As the superheated AR market of 2012 and early 2013 cooled slightly, manufacturers sought to keep sales buoyed and what soon followed was a noticeable trend among tactical rifle makers to include hunting-centered features on their guns. These emphasized features included the installation of more comfortable handguards minus all of the unnecessary rails, a broader range of camouflage finishes, no sights and just a single top-mounted receiver rail for the inevitable optic and most notably, more big-game worthy chamberings beyond the otherwise diminu-

tive .223/5.56. While the ubiquitous .308 had always been a part of the AR mix—predating the smaller 5.56 chambering the military ultimately adopted—since AR-creator Eugene Stoner created the AR-10 in .308 first, deer-sized chamberings were otherwise limited.

Check any shooting website message board or review enough tactical gun magazines and you will find those writers and sportsman who advocate the .223 as a dependable caliber for deer-sized game, but most hunters feel the cartridge leaves little room for error. It is not a great caliber for breaking through heavy shoulders or other bones, which cause the light round to fragment and ultimately, wound if not delivered accurately into the heart and lungs. Even a lung shot can fail to deliver the penetration and transfer of hydrostatic shock essential to depressurizing a deer's circulatory system and spreading rapidly terminal damage. The .223 caliber is even illegal to use for deer hunting in some areas.

At least the .308 has long been one of the more popular cartridges among deer hunters and one of the most effective. It is a proven performer and readily available in nearly any gun shop you walk into. Ammo choices are abundant with bullet offerings ranging from 125- to 180-grains. The .308 also delivers excellent down-range performance, shooting flat out to 300-plus yards—and even farther for those capable enough.

Additional big game-suitable calibers that found their way into AR configurations early included the .450 Bushmaster, from Alexander Arms the .50 Beowulf and 6.5 Grendl, the .458 SOCOM and the 6.8 SPC, this last one gaining some modicum of popularity until the 300

Larger-caliber ARs, such as the AR-10 and its variants, are ideal for deer hunting or pursuing other large game. (Top left) the author with his first AR-taken whitetail, (lower left) a Texas cull buck taken with an AR, (lower right) writer Brad Fitzpatrick takes aim with an AR chambered in .308.

BLK (AAC Blackout) stole some of its thunder. For those who fall in either camp of whether the 6.8 SPC or the 300 BLK is better for deer, I will simply allow you to argue on. For his part, co-author Robb Manning prefers the former, so much so that he claimed it to be "my favorite AR cartridge" in an article he wrote for Deer & Deer Hunting magazine. Today, the list of calibers available in AR configurations run the gamut from the .17 Rem. and .22 LR to the .30 Remington AR (developed expressly for hunting), the .260 Rem., 7mm-08 Rem., the .338 Federal and more.

With the number of recreational shooters (including many self-defense adherents) far outnumbering our nation's hunters (some estimates put the number as high as 40 million shooters compared to nearly 14 million hunters), it's doubtful that hunting will ever exercise supreme influence over the AR market. But with nearly 14 million potential customers, customers who are among some of the most dedicated to their sport as any enthusiast can be and support their activities by freely spending a lot of money to participate, America's hunters are one segment that will continue to exert some influence over future AR rifle and accessory offerings, particularly as more hunters embrace the platform.

The Remington Effect

Remington has long been one of the most recognized brands among the hunting and shooting public. Even those who don't hunt or shoot recognize the Remington name for what it is, much as the iconic Winchester or Browning names are. In fact, Remington bills itself as "America's Oldest Gunmaker," having produced guns since founder Eliphalet Remington purportedly built his first flintlock in Ilion Gulch, New York, in 1816.

The company has a history of recognizing trends among the hunting community early and delivering products that will meet the growing demand. One of the best selling rifles, the Model 700 introduced in 1962, and best selling shotguns, the Model 1100, introduced a year later, both come quickly to mind. Remington was also among the first companies to develop a specialized turkey

gun for the legions of sportsmen joining the turkey hunting ranks in the early 1990s. They have now done the same for those sportsmen curious about modern rifles.

In January 2008, Remington introduced their first sporting rifle built on the AR platform. It was called the R-15 VTR (for Varmint Tactical Rifle) and it was originally available in none other than .223, as well as the .204 Ruger. It was a sporterized version of the ubiquitous tactical AR and came in a camo finish, but with all the tack-driving features of contemporary tactical performers. It should have. The gun was technically built by Remington's sister company, Bushmaster, which had, with less fanfare, been making ARs suitable to hunters' needs for some years.

The VTR's .680-inch OD barrel was made from Chromoly steel and then free-floated inside the machined-aluminum fore-end tube. A recessed hunting crown protected the muzzle from in-the-field use. Performance was enhanced by six longitudinal flutes in front of the gas block that not only reduced the overall weight of the gun to under 8 pounds or 7 pounds depending on the configuration, but also added rigidity to the barrel while allowing for more rapid cooling in frequent fire situations such as popping prairie dogs or ground squirrels. The aluminum-forged upper and lower also helped minimize the R-15s weight. The main Predator version came with a 22-inch barrel and fixed stock, while both carbine configurations, one with a fixed stock, one that was collapsible, both had 18-inch barrels. All of the versions came with a 5-round clip, but could accommodate standard AR aftermarket accessories.

I got a sneak peak of the new gun while on a turkey hunt in the Black Hills of South Dakota that year and to say it created more buzz among those in camp than the actual turkey hunting would be an understatement. A talked about day of prairie dog shooting never materialized, but we put the gun through its paces nevertheless on plastic jugs of water and empty cans behind the hotel where we were staying. It was, quite literally, a blast. Everybody asked the Remington rep how soon we could get one of our own to test back home. Having been a guest of numerous industry camps for the past 17 years, it was without a doubt, the most excitement I had seen a single gun generate among those in attendance.

Remington was quick to follow on the buzz of the R-15 VTR with a big game version, based off the AR-10, called the R-25. The R-25 was a beefier tactical rifle designed to cycle three popular short action cartridges for deer hunting: the .243; the 7mm-08 Rem; and the .308 Win. It was an express move to bring more deer hunters into the AR fold.

"ARs are becoming embedded in hunters' minds now, but that interest has still been limited by the availability of calibers," said a Remington representative at the time. "We're changing that."

The R-25 tipped the scales at nearly two pounds more than the smaller R-15, which helps dampen some of the increased recoil inherent in the more powerful rounds. In a single year, by virtue of being Remington, the company legitimized the AR as a bona fide hunting rifle and the general sporting public responded with enthusiasm. In 2009, Remington took steps to expand the applications of their lighter and AR-15 compatible R-15, by not only introducing three new specialized configurations geared toward the varmint and predator audience, but also to big game hunters.

That year, Remington introduced the .30 Remington AR, a cartridge capable of delivering ballistic performance similar to the .308, but from the more compact platform of the R-15. The game had changed for hunters interested in tactical firearms and it seemed anything was possible with the amazingly configurable—and durable—rifles.

"I honestly think a lot of guys initially like the AR because it's so cool looking," says Mark Olis, editor of the digital magazine *AR Guns & Hunting*. "But the rifle's proven ability to offer quick, accurate follow-up shots has maintained its popularity." *AR Guns & Hunting* produced its first issue in the fall of 2009, at the height of the initial tactical rifle craze. Olis says it is that ability for a hunter to stay on target while delivering quick, accurate follow-up shots when necessary, as well as the expansion of the guns into many popular big game rounds that makes the AR "the ideal option" for the modern hunter.

"The rifles' ability to be customized to the hunter's needs also makes it a deadly choice," Olis says. "A guy can buy an AR-15 in .223, then spend a few hundred additional bucks down the road and buy an upper in say, .30 AR, and he now has a coyote hunting rig as well as a whitetail hunting rifle. There isn't another gun on the market that offers such versatility."

While there were plenty of varminters and even rising ranks of hog hunters who had embraced the AR, Remington's visible foray into the market seemed to signal an ok of sorts to other mainstream gun makers and perhaps more importantly, made some sportsmen who had otherwise shunned the guns originally, stop and take notice.

It wasn't long before many companies were quick to produce models or alter their marketing approach in order to appeal to the growing number of hunters, including Remington's sister companies, Bushmaster and DPMS Panther Arms. Today, some of the more popular manufacturers of hunting ARs, besides Remington and its related companies, include such hunt-focused tactical rifle builders as Rock River Arms, Stag Arms and Windham Weaponry. In 2011, Mossberg also stepped squarely into the black-gun realm offering a pair of AR models, one specifically for a tactical-minded audience and the other for hunters.

—*Doug Howlett*

A Gun for the Young?

With the AR-15's low recoil and ability to easily adjust the length of pull, it can certainly be argued that the AR-15 makes a great gun for young shooters. In his May 2011 column in *Petersen's Hunting*, famed hunter and outdoor television host, Michael Waddell, recalls the first time he took his son, Mason, hunting with one.

"We hunted hogs over a couple of days and killed a couple on camera. It was Mason's first chance to hunt with an (AR-type rifle) and watching him hunt with it made me realize what a great gun this can be for kids or other smaller shooters," Waddell wrote. "There was little recoil and with the collapsible stock, I could adjust the length of pull perfectly for him and then turn right around and adjust it for my arms and use the same gun."

Naturally, given the semi-auto's nature of returning to battery upon each shot, special care needs to be taken to ensure that young shooters are always conscious of standard gun safety practices and return the gun to safe upon completing firing.

There's also no denying the "cool" factor these guns possess, and for young shooters raised on video games and familiar with the appearance and use of the guns in games and in movies, it is a natural draw to want to shoot the real things. ARs have that "extreme" feel that appeals to today's younger generations and as more of them flow into the shooting sports via the use of modern sporting rifles, it is likely these guns will only become more and more commonplace on ranges and in hunt camps across America.

"To younger people involved in shooting, modern sporting rifles are a more attractive style of firearm. They have grown up with them in video games and military games so this is certainly what they are more familiar with," says Bryan Tucker, owner of Davidson's Inc., one of the nation's largest firearms retailers. "Youth are into extreme sports and the AR has more of a sex appeal to that market."

Steve Sanetti, president of the NSSF, agrees, offering this bold prediction.

"They will become the dominant face of what the American sporting rifle comes to look like," he says.

—Doug Howlett

8. AR Rifles: Ultimate Home Defense

o on any message board or jump into a discussion with your buddies about what makes the best home defense gun the next time you're at the range and you're sure to hear a number of opinions. Shotguns—most often pump actions or semi-autos—are a top choice of many practitioners due to the spread of pellets making precise aiming a little less of a concern under duress, as well as a perceived lack of pass through on walls. For others, particularly concealed carry permit holders, the portability and familiarity of the handgun they carry is the way to go even in the home. It is, after all, the gun you carry and the one you should be most comfortable and practiced shooting. Certainly in a stressful situation, even in the home, falling back on the tools that deliver the most muscle-memory response and are more in line with natural instincts is the way to go.

But as AR-style rifles have become more popular with recreational shooters and collectors, it's important to note that this most versatile of tactical weapons also makes for an efficient and dependable firearm to use in home defense situations as well. Here are 10 great reasons ARs make a great choice.

1. More Velocity

Rifle rounds by their nature, because of more velocity, can deliver more energy and knockdown necessary to stop an attacker. Winchester's 60-grain Defender .223 rounds leave the muzzle at 2,750 fps. That compares to the same ammo line's popular 9mm +P rounds, which have a muzzle velocity of 1,095 or the big bore .45 Auto, which has a velocity that is 1/3 that of the AR at 882 fps.

2. Quick Stopping

While shotgun loads are often preferred for the perceived lack of pass throughon walls where other people may be in a home or even outside at other nearby homes, the lightweight .223 round is made to expand and dissipate energy rapidly for both maximum energy transfer into a target and for reduced pass through concerns.

3. Light Recoiling

Shotguns, with heavier recoil, may not be the best option for small-framed shooters such as women, who are less likely to practice getting familiar with their firearm because it isn't as enjoyable to shoot. Conversely, the .223 round delivers little recoil, tamed even more

⌃ The light recoil of .223/5.56-chambered AR rifles make them a perfect choice for smaller-stature shooters such as women.

ULTIMATE HOME DEFENSE

by the semi-auto action of the AR rifle and today's high-tech recoil pads and recoil reducing designs. Too frequently, misguided husbands looking to provide their wives with a means to protect themselves in the home if necessary, buy an inexpensive, yet pellet-packable 12-ga. pump-action shotgun. Bud, you can bet that gun will see much more dust collection than it will ever see range time, meaning should a time come that the firearm is needed in a defensive situation, the user will likely not have enough time behind the gun to be as prepared as they could've been.

4. Maneuverable and Versatile

With an adjustable stock, the AR can be instantly fitted to any shooter for the perfect length of pull. It can also be kept shortened for maximum maneuverability in tight spaces or when moving along hallways and around corners.

5. Easy Sighting

The longer sighting plain offered by a rifle allows for easier, and likely more accurate aiming than a handgun, by less experienced shooters in a stressful situation. Handguns are notoriously more difficult for new shooters to fire accurately.

6. Room for Accessories

A bright, white light for improved night vision and/or red dot or laser sighting systems can be easily attached to the rails of an AR, keeping hands free and the mind focused on one thing, using the rifle to ensure the safety of the person holding it.

7. Abundant Ammo

When it comes to rifles chambered in the common 5.56/.223 Rem., ammo is plentiful and can be found in virtually any store that sells firearms and ammunition. It can (and should) be purchased in bulk, which reduces the per round cost to virtual pennies and provides the shooter with plenty of loads with which to practice. There's even defensive-dedicated ammunition made by top-shelf companies such as Winchester Ammunition.

While long-distance accuracy is of limited concern to most citizens who find themselves confronted with a threat—studies show most defensive shootings occur at ranges of less than 15 feet—the popularity of AR-style rifles in recent times has made it the go-to option for protecting the home. For those defense-conscious AR owners, Winchester's Defender line of ammunition offers both a 60-grain and 77-grain .223 offering, as well as 120-grain loads in .308 and 7.62x39mm.

So what makes this Defender ammunition work so well for rifles? It's the bullet. It utilizes Split Core Technology, which means the bullet is formed from two lead cores. A traditional lead core at the front of the bullet is designed for rapid expansion, while a bonded core at the base aids in penetrating to a depth between 12 to 15 inches while expending all the bullet's massive energy. The design makes over-penetration a limited concern, and accuracy assured at any reasonable distance required. These are all critical features of any .223 round being considered for home defense.

8. Practice is Fun, Meaning Folks Will Practice More

Show me a gun that isn't all that comfortable to shoot—I'm thinking along the lines of the .458 Casull or .500 S&W—and I'll show you a gun that doesn't

⌃ Part of the fun of ARs is the ability to engage in high-volume target shooting. Save that brass though, as reloading your own ammunition can help you cut costs over always buying manufactured loads.

get shot too often (not to mention the per round cost!) But take a gun like the AR that is comfortable and easy to shoot, and gunowners will be eager to practice on targets, which breeds muscle memory and familiarity, which will build confidence and accuracy when the gun is needed for self-defense.

9. More Visually Intimidating

It's purely psychological, but the sight of a physically larger tactical rifle compared to a compact handgun can be enough to induce more fear in an attacker and send him fleeing before a shot ever has to be fired.

10. Serious Protection

Should the shit truly hit the fan and civilization, due to natural disasters, economic or governmental collapse or other catastrophic events, totally go medieval, that little handgun in your belt won't be worth much. But a hi-cap AR that is maneuverable and easy to use in close quarters, holds at least 30 rounds per magazine (mags that can instantly be switched out if need be) and can immediately transition to long-range accurate use whether to scare off marauding hordes or drop some dinner in its tracks, this is the ultimate versatile survival tool. We're talking a zombie-apocalypse-type scenario here, which thankfully will probably never happen. But don't you feel just a tad better lying in your bed, knowing that should your quaint neighborhood be transformed into a Middle Eastern battle zone overnight, at least you are suitably armed?

Fighting Fundamentals

Owning an AR—or any firearm for that matter with self-defense in mind—is just the first step toward being prepared for an emergency. The second, and perhaps biggest part is practicing and practicing some more, and training so that you are actually prepared should a situation arise. While everyone hopes the only gunfight they'll ever be in is on the Xbox, if you own a firearm for self-defense, you have to be prepared for the real thing, no matter how remote.

Tiger McKee is one of the nation's foremost tactical firearms trainers. A student and friend of the late Col. Jeff Cooper, who revolutionized combat training with small arms, particularly handguns, and was the founder of the famed Gunsite Academy in Arizona, McKee

himself has been an instructor at Gunsite and is currently the director of Shootrite Firearms Academy (shootrite.org) in Alabama. McKee is author of *The Book of Two Guns*, which emphasizes tactical use of handguns and the AR rifle. He is also a regular contributor to the daily online *Tactical Wire*, as well as *Gun Digest* and other shooting magazines and websites.

McKee offers the following advice and considerations to keep in mind when it comes to taking defensive actions with a firearm, be it handgun or a tactical rifle . . . or any firearm for that matter:

Defeating a dangerous threat—fighting—is problem solving at high speed. You're presented a problem. Normally, you have a short amount of time to come up with a solution and apply the actions necessary to defeat the threat(s). The exact details are unpredictable; each encounter is unique. But, we do know these fundamental skills will determine the outcome of the fight: movement, communication, the use of cover, possibly shooting and definitely the ability to think. Let's look at each of these areas and determine what are the critical steps of surviving a gun fight.

The Importance of Movement

In almost all violent confrontations your number-one priority is movement. If possible you move before the actual "confrontation" begins. You move to create distance from the threat or escape to a safer location. Moving to cover provides you with protection. It may be necessary to move in order to obtain a clear angle of fire on the threat without endangering bystanders. Another advantage of moving is that it puts your opponent(s) in a reactive mode. A threat armed with a knife charges you. You start stepping to the right. Now he must evaluate, make decisions in response to your actions and react. Forcing the threat to react to you is always a good principle to apply. Moving is an important, fundamental skill.

Programming movement into our threat response is difficult. Once we decide to fight, our natural instinct—which is programmed for fighting with our hands, feet, teeth, clubs and impact weapons or knives we use as claws—is to root to the ground. The beauty of firearms is that we can be moving and still hit the threat.

ULTIMATE HOME DEFENSE

⌃ From a tactical defensive standpoint, shoot around corners rather than over barriers. It exposes less of your body.

Communication is Key

Yes, communication is an essential fighting skill. You communicate with the threat, issuing verbal commands, telling them what to do. "Drop the weapon." "Lay on the ground." "Get back, I feel threatened." There are literally millions of documented examples when the mere presence of a firearm and strong verbal commands were all it took to diffuse a situation. In situations where you're with family or friends, through communication you check on their status, tell them what to do or where to go. There are bystanders without a clue. You have to step up, directing them toward an exit or safe area.

Communication is mandatory to coordinate your actions with armed partners or teammates. I use the acronym I.C.E. (Inform. Confirm. Execute.) for communication. I *inform* my partner I want to move left.

"Moving left!" I'm asking for permission to move. My partner *confirms* my intent by repeating the command, "Move left!" This is communication, an exchange of information back and forth between the two of us. Once I receive confirmation, I *execute* my action, announcing, "Moving!" There is also nonverbal communication, for example body language, paying attention to cues the threat may be exhibiting, or using hand signals to communicate with a partner.

Communication is an essential element to fighting and requires practice. If you don't work on it, you'll get lockjaw under stress. You can always choose not to communicate; some situations may not demand it or it may be imperative given the situation that you remain hidden and silent, but without practice it's really difficult to remember *to* communicate when needed.

Use Cover

Cover provides protection between the threat and their weapons. The attacker has a knife. Putting a car between you and the threat reduces the effectiveness of that weapon. That's a pretty simple concept. Using cover for protection against a firearm is more subjective.

An object that provides protection against handgun rounds may not hold up against high-velocity rifle rounds. Among rifle calibers there is a significant difference in penetration. A round of 5.56mm ball ammunition penetrates about 1.5 inches of concrete. A .30-06 armor piercing round penetrates five times that. Even a handgun round can punch a hole through a standard concrete block with three to four shots. Most objects in our environments are bullet resistant as opposed to bullet proof. When out and about you should always be paying attention to what the people around you are doing, looking for possible trouble. But you should also be taking note of where cover is located. In your own home or whenever staying somewhere other than home, you should note and consider ways to exit danger, and it may not just be a door. Think windows, hatches to hidden areas such as an attack, etc. Note the features of any environment to determine where cover exists and what it is made of. What will make the best cover from a threat, particularly a threat with a firearm. At the first sign of trouble you're moving to cover.

There are a few principles to apply when using cover. For example, creating distance between you and cover is a good idea. This distance greatly reduces the danger of being injured by fragmentation and debris created by any incoming rounds hitting your cover. Distance can create a larger area of protection created by your cover object, opening up your field of view so you can see more of what's going on around you. Whenever possible, work around the side of cover, exposing less of your body than if you were working over the top of cover. To properly use cover requires plenty of practice.

Shoot If Necessary

There are two ways to stop an attacker. One, you change their mind about what they thought they were going to do. You move to cover while issuing verbal commands and drawing your pistol or pulling out another firearm. (Pull an AR on a home invader and the mere sight of it will likely send him running.) The threat decides it's not worth it, breaking off the attack. The other option is to use your firearm to inflict the physical damage necessary to stop the attacker.

The key is you need to be able to shoot while moving, communicating, using cover or maybe from an unusual position, on your back from the ground. For example, you can move smoothly and shoot accurately, or you can move quickly and not shoot, at least not accurately. Each situation will determine the best solution. It may be a lot better to move quickly, get behind cover for protection, and then, if necessary, put hits on the threat. Or, the situation may require you to shoot while moving at a moving target. Shots to the chest don't stop the threat. Where do you hit him next? The pelvic girdle is a good choice. Again, this is a trained, learned response.

We drill this into students at my school, Shootrite Firearms Academy, on the range; make three or four shots to the chest and then hit the pelvic girdle if the subject is still moving. The threat could be drugged out, not sufficiently hit or wearing a bulletproof vest. Shots to the pelvic girdle can shatter where the legs join it at the hips and break them down, stopping their advance immediately. Remember, in real life it rarely plays out like we think it should or as we see it play out on television. You have to constantly be evaluating what you're doing, and what you're going to do next.

Critical Thinking

Violent confrontations—attacks—are sudden, dynamic and unpredictable. As the target of such an attack, most times, your mind will have to switch at an instant, from trying to remember what your wife asked you to get at the store, thinking about what needs to be done at work, enjoying a casual moment with the kids or a friend in front of your TV, to suddenly being forced to defend yourself from harm and even possibly fighting for your survival. Remember, high-speed problem solving. When and where will your fight take place? Answer that and you could avoid it completely, or prepare to face your opponents with overwhelming force. We don't know how

⌃ AR rifles provide the perfect balance between the easy sighting of a long gun and the maneuverability of a light gun.

getting the weapon back into the fight without delay. There's no time to think about how to reload. It just has to happen. Ditto for clearing malfunctions if they occur, and they will, moving, using cover and shooting accurately. These skills must be practiced until they can be performed at a subconscious level. Functioning at the subconscious level frees the conscious mind to think about the fight.

After the threat is down you still have to mentally stay plugged in. One threat is down. There may be others. You still want to get to a safer place or move whomever you're with toward a safe exit. The fight isn't over until everything is locked down, secured and there's no chance of anything else occurring. Then you're facing a completely new set of problems to solve.

Make a Strategy

Start the fight with plan A, but when it doesn't go like you think, have plan B and C ready. Plan X is for the unexpected. No two fights are the same, so remain flexible and adapt as the fight unfolds. Fighting is part science, like the geometry involved in using cover, and part art.

Sometimes something completely unorthodox is exactly the right solution. To be truly prepared you must train, practice and learn to apply the fundamentals on demand. It's great to read about it and become better informed, but until your response is ingrained in your nature, it's only untested theory that will likely fail you should you ever face a true dangerous encounter. Don't leave your survival to chance.

McKee has helped countless law enforcement officials, military operators and civilians master the art of self-defense with a firearm. It's key to remember as a civilian, however, that you lack the legal obligation to engage with an armed threat in a public area or even your home. Even self-defense expert Rob Pincus, who owns I.C.E. Training (icetraining.us) and is the developer of the Combat Focus Shooting Program, suggests whether a concealed-carry practitioner in a public place or someone relaxing in your home, the first and safest course of action, particularly if with family members, is to get them and you away from the threat and to a safe area. Only if forced to save yourself or another innocent from imminent harm, or if there is no other

many threats will be involved. Statistics say there will be more than one; they'll be at close range and moving. Over 70 percent of fights occur in low-light environments.

What will we do to win? Whatever it takes.

If you're not thinking about solving the problem, then all you're doing is reacting to what's being done to you. Reacting means you're always behind, a really difficult place from which to win a fight. In order to focus on your problem, the fundamentals—moving, communicating, using cover and shooting—have to be applied at a subconscious level. These skills are the result of training, where you are introduced to the techniques, practice and learning through repetition.

Some situations you could run into during a gunfight: your weapon runs empty. You reload efficiently, course of action left but to defend, should you engage the threat. But when you do, have the training to back you up, and do it without hesitation and with a clear conscience. After all, your life is at stake, and nothing else matters but protecting it at such a time.

In a CNN.com article on the increasing popularity of CRASE (Civilian Response to Active Shooter Events) courses around the country, they shared the response of a course instructor at a Georgia training when asked by a concealed-carry permit holding attendee what his responsibilities were as a gunowner caught in such a situation.

The instructor, a SWAT commander, replied, "Law enforcement officers seldom tell you to grab a gun, but do it here. If they're (an active shooter) bringing violence to you, they don't matter."

Low-Light Gunfights

More than 70 percent of violent confrontations occur in low-light environments. This means you need to be able to move, communicate, use cover, shoot, manipulate the weapon and think about solving the problem in the dark, probably using a flashlight. Yet, the majority of our training and practice occurs in the daylight. Therefore, it's important to learn to work with handheld lights.

Weapon-mounted lights may fail, usually when you need them most, and a handheld light offers more versatility. You'll probably need several lighting techniques to solve one problem. If checking out a potential threat in or around your property at night, and toting an AR that doesn't have a mounted light on a front rail, lay the gun across your forearm keeping the light in your forward hand so you can scan an area with the rifle ready. Or, if the light is slim enough, simply press it against the handguard and point the light and rifle simultaneously. For working around the right side of cover, or a corner to the left, the light should be on the right side of your weapon. When using the left side of cover, or clearing a right-hand corner, the light is on the left side of the weapon.

Switching sides with the light provides maximum penetration of the light into the environment, and reduces the amount of reflection back onto you. Modifying the old FBI technique by holding the light off to one side or the other allows you to scan the environment while keeping your weapon indexed on the last known threat or area of concern.

Use the light as little as possible, such as using ambient light to search until you locate a possible threat, then you illuminate them to identify and if necessary engage. Remember, however, you may have to use the light as much as necessary when it's too dark to see anything. Better too much light than stepping into an ambush because you couldn't see the threat. Remember, too, even with a weapon mounted light, utilize a handheld light as much as possible. This allows you to scan an area without pointing your firearm everywhere you are scanning. Remember, that bump in the night may just be a loved one who awoke to grab a glass of water or your teenaged kid straggling in after curfew. But if it isn't, be ready to quickly take the necessary action to engage if needed.

—*Tiger McKee*

ULTIMATE HOME DEFENSE

9. What the Future Holds

So what does the future hold for the AR platform and those fans of this popular rifle? From where we sit now, it looks like a very bright, and I will stress, continued, future indeed. Bear in mind this is a rifle that nearly missed ever being accepted by the military for use and one that when originally ordered, was meant as a stopgap measure and intended as a one-time buy until something else could be developed. Had it missed the opportunity to become the famed M16 through adoption by the military, odds are many of us would've never heard of an AR. And if they did still exist, they would likely do so under another moniker and in a very niche realm of shooting.

Following the original publication of *The Shooter's Bible Guide to AR-15s* in 2011, sales of ARs mellowed slightly from their earlier Obama-election surge, only to see further surges in sales and popularity following in late 2012 and through 2013. As more gun enthusiasts became AR owners, baseline model AR sales slowed . . . not as much as some industry insiders feared, but they definitely leveled off to more normal demand.

What did stay hot was sales of higher-end ARs—think JP Enterprises, Les Baer, Colt Competition or Wilson Combat—after all, for the guys lucky enough to score any AR model during the sales craze, now it wasn't about just owning one, it was about owning one that stood above the rest of the pack.

The other big sales driver during this period and continuing on at the writing of this book has been the sale of accessories that go on or work in conjunction with the rifles. After all, that is just another way guys have taken the rifles they could get their hands on just a few years ago, and rather than buying an entirely new gun, customized their own rigs to make them unique and specific to their tastes and performance demands. At a recent gathering of friends at C2 Shooting Center (c2shootingcenter-va.com), I saw all manner of mainline AR models from companies like Bushmaster,

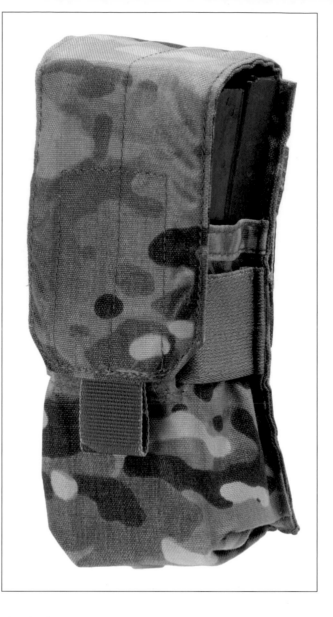

The sale of accessories for existing ARs continues to drive the overall market. Pictured are a (clockwise from bottom right) fiber optic front sight from TruGlo, the AR-15 Micro Tool from Real Avid, and a camouflage mag pouch by Eagle Industries.

DPMS, SIG and others, tricked out with a bevy of accessories such as laser sights, vertical grips with integrated bipods, some super high-dollar optics, both red dot and variable magnification, and a dizzying assortment of grips, rails and more. In fact, among my group, 20-plus men strong as part of an annual gathering at C2 (one of the best outdoor ranges in the Mid-Atlantic; if you are ever in the Virginia Beach area, you need to check the place out) most brought AR rifles. Perhaps even more interesting is the group spanned the economic and professional spectrum with everyone from restaurant owners, judges and business owners, to construction workers, former soldiers and bartenders. Behind the firing line, though, it didn't matter; everyone there loves to shoot and shares a deep appreciation for firearms . . . and in listening to some of the discussions in the rented bus on the way to range, many share an abiding interest and appreciation for gun performance.

The observation made by the NSSF's Steve Sanetti back in 2011 that AR rifles "will become the dominant face of what the American sporting rifle comes to look like" is standing up to that prediction. In fact, there's every indication that ARs are following the same trend that bolt-action rifles did following the first and second World Wars, where GIs returned home and chose to use the rifles they were most familiar with upon hitting the woods and fields for hunting. With more and more of our military population returning home to the woods and ranges where they call home, the AR-style rifle is now just as at home.

As noted in Chapter 9, cementing still-growing interest among hunters has been a tactic pursued by companies such as Daniel Defense, Rock River Arms, Mossberg, Remington and DPMS among other manufacturers as they seek to incorporate hunt-friendly (and hunt-legal) features on guns, such as larger calibers for bigger game, camouflaged patterns, smoother front rails that allow for some customization but don't have all the attachment points for accessories not needed for hunting and even smaller magazines, such as five-round magazines, required by law for deer hunting in a number of states.

Certainly, some of the effort in incorporating big-game friendly chamberings has been to find a way to deliver more knockdown performance and run larger calibers without adding all the bulk common to an AR-10, which can often run 3 to 4 pounds heavier than the average AR-15, as well as simply be physically larger in size. The AR-10 in .308 has always been around (it predates the AR-15 and was actually the blueprint for its smaller cousin) and certainly put in use by hunters seeking a tactical rifle for deer, but less weight without sacrificing downrange ballistics is something every hunter will appreciate. That is especially true when humping a rifle and gear over hill and dale all day in search of game.

A GUN FOR ALL SHOOTERS

But smaller isn't always better notes one early adopter of tactical rifles for sporing purposes. Retired long-distance competition shooter John Murphy, although he embraced the civilian benefits of the AR early for the purpose of competing many years ago, still likes to shoot his AR-10 despite past shoulder surgeries. He says it is the best platform available on which to shoot .308 loads.

"The gas operation of the semi-auto design takes a lot of recoil out of shooting a .308. A shooter can get back on target much more quickly than if they were shooting a bolt action," Murphy says. "I love the thing. I couldn't shoot prone with a bolt action like I can with the AR because I would be taking the full recoil through my shoulders and upper body." Although Murphy discovered ARs before any gunsmith in his rural Virginia county even knew how to work on one, many older shooters like him will find the low-recoiling AR to their liking as they seek out guns that won't beat them up.

With more sportsmen, like the rest of our society, living active lives much longer, this could prove to be another factor that keeps the AR leaping off sporting firearm dealers shelves.

With our military involved in military operations in Iraq and Afghanistan for pretty most of this century and a media focus on our military heroes, especially the role special forces have played and continue to play wherever trouble arises in the world, news coverage has translated into some incredible marketing for today's tactical rifle. The cool factor is undeniable and to younger and newer shooters, it's the modern gun they are more visually familiar with, even if some of

⌃ After gunowners buy their first AR, many become quick fans of the platform and look to buy additional ones for their personal collections.

that exposure has been via video games such as the Call of Duty franchise. ATI's John Chvala believes this is translating into more sales and will continue to turn into more sales for the foreseeable future.

"Young people have used them in the video games they play so they can relate to it better than an older sportsman," he says in an observation shared by Davidson's/Gallery of Guns owner Bryan Tucker and many others in the industry.

It's a gun that can grow with a young shooter as well, since uppers, barrels, stocks, fore-ends and other features of the gun can be swapped out as the shooter's tastes, abilities and even size all change.

"You can keep changing your gun into an entirely new one as your situation dictates or your budget allows. You don't have to go out and buy a completely new gun or go through the hassles of the paperwork that comes with buying a new gun. What other firearm

allows you to do all that?" asks Chvala. "There aren't any."

Just look at the way the sport of 3Gun has grown in recent years with more people taking part in local and regional competitions. Incorporating the timed transition between shooting shotguns, semi-auto pistols and ARs at various targets, the action is fast-paced and exciting to watch. It's even more exciting to participate in. At the higher levels of competition, sponsored competitors rock enough logos and color to resemble NASCAR drivers and it shouldn't be any surprise that their tricked-out firearms—particularly ARs—have followed suit.

Flashy finishes and colors that appeal to the young, females, and just people who like everything they own to sport a little style can now be had on a wide range of handguards, barrels, uppers, lowers, grips and even the entire rifle. Everything from Cerakoted or textured

⌃ ARs are as comfortable on the farm as they are on the competitive range. Millions of shooters today enjoy shooting them.

⌃ 3Gun competition is one of the leading competitive shooting disciplines driving interest in AR-15 rifles.

finishes; patterns like Muddy Girl, Toxic and custom color designs; and notched or machined artistry etched in the metal are just some of what is available to the shooter who desires a truly unique looking gun. Unique-ARs (unique-ars.com) offers virtual one-of-a-kind handguard designs that truly transform a functional AR into a functional work of art. Similarly Kaiser US Shooting Products creates rifles and accessories with custom anodized colors and polymers uppers and lowers. Shooters can even get laser engraved mags, receivers and other parts through companies like LEO Armory (leoarmory.com), while companies like Robar can apply any number of finishes to a new or existing gun. Today and for many years to come, I would

expect the limits of creativity applied to how a firearm looks will be limited only by the imagination of the gunowner . . . and of course, his or her checkbook!

But it isn't just looks, that are being impacted by today's competitive shooters, so are refinements in the AR's performance. Smooth, crisp triggers, oversized grips and charging handles, better sighting systems, improved barrels . . . all are making this rifle design, first intended for high-volume, center of mass combat shooting into a precision, long-range, fast-action performer that can rival any bolt-action or long-gun design available today.

A GREAT TIME TO BUY

If our predictions are correct, the threat of a Hillary Clinton presidency will fuel another surge in sales to rival those not seen since 2009 and 2013. Be that as it may, if you are interested in buying, upgrading, or adding more rifles to your collection, there is no time like the present.

⌃ There is no time like the present to buy your next AR, particularly with concerns of anti-gun politicians taking office every time there is an election.

As NSSF President Steve Sanetti said when interviewed for the first edition of this book, "We are at a golden period for firearm ownership in this country today and we expect it to continue for some time to come." That golden age continues, and should for some time. Too many people own and understand the merits of the AR to allow it to be relegated to outlaw status by anti-gun politicians. But as history has proven time and again, we should never take anything for granted. Every gun owner should be a member of the NRA (www.nra.org) or even industry groups such as the NSSF (www.nssf.org), which has a number of membership levels depending on a person's involve-

ment in the shooting sports. NRA has an excellent grassroots network that will help keep you abreast of local issues that might affect your rights.

Stay informed, stay involved and let your opinions be heard by legislators, and most of all, get your gun and introduce recreational shooting to a friend. The more people understand this great firearm and share in your love of shooting, the easier it will become to defend it from those who would restrict our rights. The AR is, after all, a gun that was designed to protect our freedom; and it has done so valiantly for more than sixty years. The least we can do is stand up to protect it, and in so doing, ourselves, in return.

APPENDIX I—AR MANUFACTURERS

2 Vets Arms
www.2vetsarms.com

556 Tactical LLC
www.556tactical.com

A
Accurate Armory
www.accuratearmory.com

Adams Arms
www.adamsarms.net

Adcor Defense
www.adcordefense.com

Aero Precision
www.Aeroprecisionusa.com

Alexander Arms
www.Alexanderarms.com

Alex Pro Firearms
www.apfarmory.com

American Spirit Arms
www.americanspiritarms.com

American Tactical Imports
www.americantactical.us

American Firearms Manufacturing
www.afmco.com

Anderson Manufacturing
www.andersonrifles.com

AR57 Center
www.57center.com

Ares Arms
www.aresarms.com

Ares Defense
www.aresdefense.com

Arsenal Democracy
www.arsenaldemocracy.com

ArmaLite
www.armalite.com

Armscor
www.armscor.com

Arms Tech Ltd
www.armstechltd.com

Astra Arms
www.astra-arms.ch

AXTS Weapons
www.axtsweapons.com

B
Barnes Precision
www.usamade-ar15parts.com

Barrett
www.barrett.net

Battle Born
www.battlebornusa.com

Battle Rifle Company
www.battleriflecompany.com

Bazooka Brothers
www.bazookabrothers.com

BCI Defense
www.bcidefense.com

Black Heart International
www.bhigear.com

Black Rain Ordnance
www.blackrainordnance.com

Black Dawn Armory
www.blackdawnguns.com

Bradley Arms
www.bradleyarms.com

Bravo Company USA
www.bravocompanyusa.com

Bushmaster
www.bushmaster.com

C
Chattahoochee Gun Works
www.c-gw.com

Christensen Arms
www.christensenarms.com

Christian Armory Works
www.christianarmoryworks.com

CMMG
www.cmmginc.com

Colt Competition Rifles
www.coltcompetitionrifle.com

Colt Firearms
www.colt.com

Compass Lake Engineering
www.compasslake.com

D
Daniel Defense
www.deztacticalarms.com

Del-Ton
www.del-ton.com

DEZ Tactical
www.deztacticalarms.com

Diamondback Firearms
www.diamondbackfirearms.com

Double Star
www.star15.com

DPMS
www.dpmsinc.com

Dragon Fire Armory
www.dragonfirearmory.com

Dreadnaught Industries
www.dreadnaught-industries.com

DSA Arms
www.dsarms.com

E
Edward Arms
www.edwardarms.com

Erathr3
www.erathr3.com

F
Firebird Precision
www.firebirdprecision.com

Fulton Armory
www.fulton-armory.com

FNH USA ***Now FN America****
www.fnamerica.com

Franklin Armory
www.franklinarmory.com

G
GAR Arms
www.gar-arms.com

H
Hatcher Gun Company
www.hatchergun.com

Head Down Products
www.hdfirearms.com

Hera Arms
www.hera-arms.com

High Standard Firearms
www.highstandard.com

HM Defense
www.hmdefense.com

Heckler & Koch
www.hk-usa.com

Hogan Guns
www.hoganguns.com

Huldra Arms
www.huldraarms.com

I
Integrity Arms
www.customar15.net

Invincible Arms
www.invinciblearms.com

Iron Ridge Guns
www.ironridgeguns.com

J
JARD, Inc.
www.jardinc.com

Jesse James Firearms
www.jjfu.com

JP Rifles
www.jprifles.com

K
Kaufmann Tactical Firearms
www.kt-firearms.com

KE Arms
www.kearms.com

Knights Armament
www.knightarmco.com

L
Lancer Systems
www.lancer-systems.com

Larue Tactical
www.larue.com

Les Baer
www.lesbaer.com

Lewis Machine and Tool
www.lewismachine.net

LWRC
www.lwrci.com

M
MGI Military
www.mgi-military.com

MHT Defense
www.mhtdefense.com

Midwest Industries
www.midwestindustriesinc.com

MMC Armory
www.mmcarmory.com

Mohawk Armory
www.mohawkarmory.com

Mossberg
www.mossberg.com

N
NEMO Arms
www.nemoarms.com

Noveske Rifleworks
www.noveske.com

O
Olympic Arms
www.olyarms.com

P
Palmetto State Defense
www.palmettostatedefense.com

Patriot Ordnance Factory (POF)
www.pof-usa.com

PEC Armory
www.pecarmory.com

Personal Defense Warehouse
www.pdwarehouse.com

Precision Firearms
www.precisionfirearms.com

Precision Reflex
www.precisionreflex.com

Primary Weapons Systems
www.primaryweapons.com

Q
Quality Arms
www.qualityarmsidaho.com

Quentin Defense
www.quentindefense.com

R
Radical Firearms
ww.radicalfirearms.com

Ranger Proof
www.rangerproof.com

Rebel Arms
www.rebelarms.com

Red X Arms
www.shop.redxarms.com

Remington Arms
www.remington.com

R Guns
www.rguns.net

RIP Tactical
www.rip-tactical.com

RND Manufacturing
www.rndrifles.com

Rock River Arms
www.rockriverarms.com

Ruger
www.ruger.com

S
Savannah River Armory
www.savannahriverarmory.com

Schmeisser Germany
www.schmeisser-germany.de

Seekins Precision
www.seekinsprecision.com

SLR15 Rifles
www.slr15rifles.com

Sharps Rifle Company
www.srcarms.com

SI Defense
www.si-defense.com

Signature Manufacturing
www.signaturemanufactures.com

Sig Sauer
www.sigsauer.com

Sionics Weapon Systems
www.sionicsweaponsystems.com

Smith & Wesson
www.smith-wesson.com

Specialized Dynamics
www.specializeddynamics.com

Specialized Tactical Systems
www.specializedtactical.com

Spikes Tactical
www.spikestactical.com

Stag Arms
www.stagarms.com

Sterling Arsenal
www.sterlingarsenal.com

Stubborn Mule Outdoor Supply
www.smosarms.com

Surplus Ammo and Arms
www.surplusammo.com

Superior Arms
www.superiorarms.com

S.W.O.R.D. International
www.sword-int.com

T
Tactical Arms Manufacturer
www.tacticalarmsmfr.com

Tactical Firearms Solutions
www.tfsarms.com

Teppo Jutsu
www.teppojutsu.com

Texas Black Rifle Company
www.tbrci.com
Texas Custom Guns

www.texascustomguns.net

Thor Global Defense
www.thorgdg.com

TNW Firearms
www.tnwfirearms.com

TR Enabling
www.tr-enabling.com

Trident Arms
www.tridentarms.us

U
USA Tactical Firearms
www.usatf.us

V
Valkyrie Armament
www.beltfedar.com

Vltor Weapon Systems
www.vltor.com

Vidalia Police Supply
www.kavodcustom.com

W
War Sport Industries
www.warsport-us.net

Wilson Combat
www.wilsoncombat.com

Windham Weaponry
www.windhamweaponry.com

X
Xtreme Machining
www.xtrememachining.biz

Y
Yankee Hill Machine
www.yhm.net

APPENDIX II—AMMUNITION MANUFACTURERS

Aguila
2014 Airport Road
Conroe, Texas 77301
888-452-4019
www.aguilaammo.com

Black Hills Ammunition
P.O. Box 3090
Rapid City, SD 57709
605-348-5150
www.black-hills.com

CCI Ammunition
2299 Snake River Avenue
Lewiston, ID 83501
208-746-2351
www.cci-ammunition.com

Cor-Bon/Glaser
Div. Of Dakota Ammo Inc.
1311 Industry Rd.
P.O. Box 369
Sturgis, SD 57785-9123
605-347-4544
www.corbon.com

Extreme Shock USA
182 Camp Jacob Road
Clintwood, VA 24228
276-926-6772
www.extremeshockusa.net

Federal Premium Ammunition
900 Ehlen Drive
Anoka, MN 55303
763-323-2300
763-323-2506 (f)
www.federalpremium.com

Hornady Manufacturing Co.
3625 Old Potash Hwy
PO Box 1848
Grand Island, NE 68802
800-338-3220
www.hornady.com

International Cartridge Corporation
2273 Route 310
Reynoldsville, PA 15851
814-938-6820
www.iccammo.com

Lapua
123 Winchester Drive
Sedalia, MO 65301
660-826-3232
www.lapua.com

Nosler
107 Southwest Columbia
P.O. Box 671
Bend, OR 97709
541-382-3921
www.nosler.com

One Shot, Inc.
6871 Main Street
Newtown, OH 45244
513-272-6764
www.oneshotmunitions.com

PMC
Suite 140-428
Conroe, TX 77304
281-703-8146
www.pmcammo.com

RWS
5402 East Diana Street
Tampa , FL 33610
813-626-0077
www.ruag-usa.com

Remington
870 Remington Drive
P.O. Box 700
Madison, NC 27025
336-548-8572
www.remington.com

Silver State Armory
12913 US Highway 12
P.O. Box 962
Packwood, WA 98361
360-200-6160
www.ssarmory.com

Ten-X Ammunition
8722 Lanyard Court
Rancho Cucamonga, CA 91730
909-946-8369
www.tenxammo.com

Ultramax Ammunition
2112 Elk Vale Road
Rapid City, SD 57701
605-342-4141
www.ultramaxammunition.com

Winchester Ammunition
427 N. Shamrock St.
East Alton, IL 62024
618-258-2000
www.winchester.com

Wolf Performance Ammunition
P.O. box 757
Placentia, CA 92871
714-632-9653
www.wolfammo.com

APPENDIX III—OPTICS AND SIGHTS MANUFACTURERS

Aimpoint
14103 Mariah Court
Chantilly, VA 20151
703-263-9795
www.aimpoint.com

Armament Technology Incorporated
3045 Robie Street, Suite 113
Halifax, CA B3K 4P6
902-454-6384
www.armament.com

BSA Optics
3911 Southwest 47th Avenue, Suite 914
Fort Lauderdale, FL 33314
954-581-5822
www.bsaoptics.com

Barska Optics
1721 Wright Avenue
La Verne, CA 91750
909-445-8168
www.barska.com

Burris
331 East 8th Street
Greeley, CO 80631
970-356-1670
www.burrisoptics.com

Bushnell
9200 Cody St
Overland Park, KS 66214-1734
913-752-3400
www.bushnell.com

Counter Sniper Military Optical Gunsight Corp.
2231 West Sunset
Springfield, MO 65807
417-883-9444
www.CounterSniperOptics.com

EoTech
1201 E. Ellsworth
Ann Arbor, Michigan 48108
734-741-8868
www.eotech-inc.com

Firefield
2421 Callender Road - Suite 123
Mansfield, TX 76063-5090
817-225-0310
www.fire-field.com

Kelbly's
7222 Dalton Fox Lake Road
North Lawrence, OH 44666
330-683-4674
www.kelbly.com

Kruger Optical
251 West Barclay Drive
P.O. Box 532
Sisters, OR 97759
541-549-0770
www.krugeroptical.com

Leupold
14400 NW Greenbrier Parkway
Beaverton, OR 97006
800-538-7653
www.leupold.com

Lucid
235 Fairway Drive
Riverton, WY 82501
307-840-2160
www.mylucidgear.com

Meopta
50 Davids Drive
Hauppauge, NY 11788
631-436-5900
www.meoptasportsoptics.com

Meprolight
107 Allen Blvd
Farmingdale, NY 11735
www.meprolight.com

Minox
P.O. Box 123
Merdien, NH 03770
866-469-3080
www.minox.com

New Century NcSTAR
18031 Cortney Court
City of Industry, CA 91748
626-575-1518
www.ncstar.com

Nightforce
336 Hazen Lane
Orofino, ID 83544
208-476-9814
www.NightforceOptics.com

Nikon
1300 Walt Whitman Road
Melville, NY 11747
631-547-4200
www.nikonhunting.com

Pentax
600 12th Street, Suite 300
Golden, CO 80401
303-799-8000
www.pentaxsportoptics.com

Shepherd Enterprises
P.O. Box 189
Waterloo, NE 68069
402-779-2424
www.shepherdscopes.com

Sightmark
2421 Callender Road, Suite 123
Mansfield, TX 76063
817-225-0310
www.sightmark.com

Sightron
100 Jeffrey Way, Suite A
Youngsville, NC 27596
919-562-3000
www.sightron.com

Simmons
9200 Cody Street
Overland Park, KS 66214
913-752-3400
www.simmonsoptics.com

Trijicon
49385 Shafer Avenue
P O Box 930059
Wixom, MI 48393-0059
248-960-7700
www.trijicon.com

TRUGLO
710 Presidential Drive
Richardson, TX 75081
972-774-0300
www.truglo.com

U.S. Optics
150 Arovista Circle
Brea, CA 92821
714-582-1956
www.usoptics.com

Valdada Optics
P.O. Box 270095
Littleton, CO 80127
303-979-4578
www.valdada.com

Vortex Optics
2120 W Greenview Dr Ste 4
Middleton, WI 53562-2547
608-664-9856
www.vortexoptics.com

Weaver Optics
N5549 County Trunk Z
Onalaska, WI 54650
800-635-7656
www.weaveroptics.com

Zeiss
13005 North Kingston Avenue
Chester, VA 23836
800-441-3005
www.zeiss.com/sports

APPENDIX III

APPENDIX IV—AR ACCESSORIES AND SUPPLIERS

Adams Arms
612 Florida Ave.
Palm Harbor, FL 34683
877-461-2572
www.adamsarms.net

Advanced Technology International (ATI)
2733 West Carmen Avenue
Milwaukee, WI 53209
414-464-4870
www.atigunstocks.com

Artisan Defense
2476 Nimmo Parkway #115/545
Virginia Beach, VA 23456
www.artisandefense.com

AR15.com
P.O. Box 464
Honeoye Falls, NY 14472
www.ar15.com

Blackhawk
6160 Commander Parkway
Norfolk, VA 23502
757-436-3101/3318
www.blackhawk.com

Brownells
200 South Front Street
Montezuma, IA 50171
641-623-5401
www.brownells.com

Chip Mccormick
105 Sky King Dr.
Spicewood, TX 78669
800-328-2447 (orders)
830-798-2863 (customer service)
www.cmcmags.com

Command Arms Accessories EMA Tactical
1208 Branagan Drive
Tullytown, PA 19007
215-949-9944
www.ematactical.com

Continental Machine Tool Company
533 John Downey Dr.
New Britain, CT 06051
860-223-2896
www.continentalmachinetool.com

Crimson Trace
9780 SW Freeman Drive
Wilsonville, OR 97070
503-783-5333
www.crimsontrace.com

Desert Tactical Arms
P.O. Box 65816
Salt Lake City, UT 84165
801-975-7272
www.deserttacticalarms.com

Elite Defense
3045 Broad Street, Suite B
Dexter, MI 48130
734-424-9955
www.elitedefense.com

Essential Arms Co.
P.O. Box 121
Krotz Springs, LA 70750
337-945-0185
www.essentialarms.com

Falcon Industries
P.O. Box 1459
Moriarty, NM 87035
505-281-3783
www.ergogrips.net

Fidelis Arms
14818 SW Chicadee Rd
Crooked River Ranch, OR 97760
541-848-8335
www.fidelisarms.com

Hogue
550 Linne Road
Paso Robles, CA 93447
805-239-1440
www.getgrip.com

H-S Precision
1301 Turbine Drive
Rapid City, SD 57703
605-341-3006
www.hsprecision.com

LaRue Tactical
850 County Rd. 177
Leander, TX USA 78641
512-259-1585
www.LaRuetactical.com

LRB Arms
96 Cherry Ln.
Floral Park, NY 11001
516-327-9061
www.lrbarms.com

M&A Parts Inc.
1298 Ensell Rd.
Lake Zurich, IL 60047
847-550-8246
www.mapartsinc.com

Magpul
P.O. BOX 17697
Boulder, CO 80308
303-828-3460
www.magpul.com

The Mako Group
107 Allen Blvd
Farmingdale, NY 11735
http://www.themakogroup.com

Mega Machine Shop
5323 Joppa St. S.W.
Tumwater, WA 98512
360-357-5372
www.megamachineshop.com

Mesa Tactical
1760 Monrovia Avenue, Suite B1
Costa Mesa, CA 92627
949-642-3337
www.mesatactical.com

Midway USA
5875 West Van Horn Tavern Rd.
Columbia, MO 65203
800-243-3220
www.midwayusa.com

Model 1 Sales
P.O. Box 569
Whitewright, TX 75291
903-546-2087
www.model1sales.com

MTM Case-Gard
P.O. Box 13117
Dayton, OH 45413
937-890-7461
www.mtmcase-gard.com

NoDak Spud
7683 Washington Ave. S.
Edina, MN 55439
952-942-1909
www.nodakspud.com

Otis Technology
6987 Laura Street
Lyons Falls, NY 13368
315-348-4300
www.otistec.com

Plano
431 East South Street
Plano, IL 60545
630-552-3111
www.planomolding.com

ProMag Industries
10654 South Garfield Avenue
South Gate, CA 90280
562-861-9554
www.promagindustries.com

Reset RIPR
49 Strathearn Pl.
Simi Valley, CA 93065
805-584-4900
www.RIPRrail.com

Roggio Arsenal
822 Shannon Dr.
Fayetteville, NC 28303
910-864-4137
www.roggioarsenalusa.com

SureFire
18300 Mount Baldy Circle
Fountain Valley, CA 92708

714-545-9444
www.surefire.com

Taccfour Systems
3061 Brickhouse Court Suite # 104
Virginia Beach VA 23452-6860
(757) 803-8880
www.taccfour.com

Tactical Innovations
345 Sunrise Rd.
Bonners Ferry, ID 83805
208-267-1585
www.tacticalinc.com

Tactical Solutions
2181 Commerce Avenue
Boise, ID 83705
208-333-9901
www.tacticalsol.com

Tango Down
4720 North La Cholla Boulevard, Suite 180
Tucson, AZ 85705
520-888-3376
www.tangodown.com

TAPCO
P.O. Box 2408
Kennesaw, GA 30156
770-425-1280
www.tapco.com

Umbrella Corporation
545 S Birdneck RD STE 202B
Virginia Beach, VA 2345123451
www.ucwrg.com

Viridian
5929 Baker Road, Suite 440
Minnetonka, MN 55345
800-990-9390
www.viridiangreenlaser.com

Vltor Weapon Systems
3735 North Romero Road
Tucson, AZ 85705
520-408-1944
www.vltor.com

Warne Manufacturing
9500 SW Tualatin Rd.
Tualatin, OR 97062
800-683-5590
www.warnescopemounts.com

White Oak Armament
101 S. Perry St.
Carlock, IL 61725
309-376-2288
www.whiteoakarmament.com

ACKNOWLEDGMENTS

We'd like to thank the following people and groups for their incredible insight, sharing of resources, effort, and support in bringing this project together:

Patrick "Buzz" Hayes, David Maccar, Cory Routh (ruthlessoutdooradventures.com), and Chris Castle for their contributions of photography and material for this book.

Kurt Derwort, a former Naval armorer and current gunsmith at Chesapeake Gun & Pawn. His sharing of technical gun knowledge and time, as well as his friendship on the range and in the field, is beyond value.

Mark Keefe, editor of *American Rifleman*, as well as John Zent and the rest of the staff in the NRA Publications Division. During the first stab at this book, they selflessly made their historical and other research materials available in compiling information needed for this book, the benefits of which continue to echo through the pages of this second edition.

Sammy Reese, editor at FNG Publications, who on that long-ago Remington hunt in Texas, selflessly shared his time to introduce me to the AR platform.

Mike Schoby, Eric Poole, the late James Guthrie, and a number of other editors and writers at *Outdoor Sportsman Group* who have amassed an unparalleled knowledge of firearms, their history and their function, and have always been happy to share that insight.

Nino Bosaz and Jay Langston, formerly with Harris Publications, for their keen insights on the business and the sharing of resources and contacts.

My publisher and editor, Jay Cassell and Jason Katzman, for their eternal patience and support in production of this book.

Additional thanks go to John Murphy, JJ Reich, Jason Gilbertson, Mark Schindel and the entire Mako Group, John Snow, Gerry Bethge, Kim Cahalan, Mark Sidelinger, Evan McNamara, the crew at *Gun Digest* and *Modern Shooter* magazines (Jim Schlender, Jamie Wilkinson, James Card, and Dane Royer) and the countless industry and PR folks who supplied information for this guide.

Doug Howlett
Virginia Beach, Va.
March 2016

I would like to first and foremost thank my Savior, Jesus Christ; through you all things are possible.

Doug Howlett, for the honor of co-authoring this book, and for all the articles you sent my way when you were editor of *Gun Digest* magazine.

I'd also like to thank my beautiful (and patient) wife, Ty, for putting up with me and my gun problem.

Robb Manning
Southeast Wisconsin
March 2016